Honest Numbers and Democracy

Social Policy Analysis in the White House, Congress, and the Federal Agencies

WALTER WILLIAMS

D1418066

GEORGETOWN UNIVERSITY PRESS / WASHINGTON, D.C.

ALBRIGHT COLLEGE LIBRARY

Georgetown University Press, Washington, D.C.
© 1998 by Georgetown University Press. All rights reserved.
Printed in the United States of America

10 9 8 7 6 5 4 3 2 1   1998

THIS VOLUME IS PRINTED ON ACID-FREE OFFSET BOOK PAPER

Library of Congress Cataloging-in-Publication Data

Williams, Walter.
    Honest numbers and democracy : social policy analysis in the White
House, Congress, and federal agencies / Walter Williams.
        p.   cm.
    Includes index.
    1. Social indicators—United States. 2. United States—Social
conditions—1945—Statistics. 3. United States—Statistical
services—Methodology. 4. United States—Social policy—Decision
making.   I. Title.
HN60.W55   1998
306'.0973—DC21
    ISBN 0-87840-670-0 (cloth)   97-37972
    ISBN 0-87840-684-0 (paper)

Honest Numbers and Democracy

306.0973
W728h
1998

262240

This book is for my first grandchildren
Charles Keenan Williams and Peter Courtland Williams
with love

Contents

Preface

Honest, credible numbers are an essential ingredient of deliberative governance in a democratic America. Over 175 years ago, James Madison wrote: "A popular Government, without popular information, or the means of acquiring it, is but a Prologue to a Farce or a Tragedy."[1] Faulty numbers beget bad public choices. This historical critique of social policy analysis over the last three plus decades explores both extended efforts to develop honest, credible policy information and analyses and the rise of the "hired gun" policy analysts ready to massage the numbers to tell their political masters what they want to hear. As one "present at the creation" of the first federal social policy analysis office, I believe honest numbers and *honest analysts* are now more central to reasoned public policy making and to American democracy itself than at any time in the postwar era.

The term "honest numbers" describes policy data produced by competent researchers and analysts who use sound technical methods without the application of political spin to fit partisan needs. "Honest numbers" became the mantra of congressional Republicans in the 1995 budget battle where they tagged Congressional Budget Office (CBO) budget estimates and economic projections as honest and cast the White House figures as dishonest, or to temper the charge, unsound, to imply partisan bias and likely technical flaws. Congress' charge was wrong in that the White House numbers were as sound as those of CBO. Despite this, the White House effort was not viewed as honest and that leads us to the second key dimension of policy information and analysis—"credibility." This concept requires that information and analysis not only be adjudged as sound but that a reasonable foundation exists to support the assessment. Credibility needs to be distinguished from "believability" where unsound information may be accepted as true. A striking example of the latter is Pierre Salinger, relying on unverified claims, declaring publicly that TWA Flight 800 had been shot down by "friendly fire." The Salinger case, where the respected journalist and former John F. Kennedy aide relied on an absolute Internet fabrication, underscores a basic theme of this history—that the electronic age can overwhelm the capacity for validation of policy information and ideas through data overload and distortion in the marketplace.

America, in the last handful of years before the end of the twentieth century, has developed an amazing technical capacity to bring mountains of data instantly to politicians, civil servants, and the public and to facilitate interactive electronic deliberations among them. But a number of vexing questions underlie this technical bonanza, particularly whether those who use information—be they elected officials, government bureaucrats, advocacy groups, or the public—have the will or the wits to use it wisely. In the current plethora of statistics and analyses, bad data may either drive out the good à la Gresham's Law or at least neutralize the superior information. Despite all the high-powered state-of-the-art techniques and the abundance of information experts, does the system produce the policy information and analyses most needed for responsible public deliberation and policy making? At basic issue is whether more and more policy information, analysis, and analysts enhance public decision making or overwhelm the democratic process with numbers and arguments of questionable validity that are beyond the capacity of both the governors and the governed to interpret.

I intended originally in writing the book to offer the first historical critique of over three decades of federal social policy analysis. Having served in the first social policy analysis unit, this effort could not claim the mantle of disinterested objectivity. Nor was the book meant to be an exhaustive account exploring the minutia buried in presidential libraries, but instead would rely heavily on my earlier work, first on the federal agencies and then on the presidency. In this highly selective historical account, I sought to portray the direction over time of federal social policy analyses and research and thereby provide a base for considering the future.

Moreover, I did not expect to offer detailed prescriptions in that I had set out numerous recommendations and dire warnings in my 1990 book *Mismanaging America: The Rise of the Anti-Analytic Presidency* that ended with the Reagan years.[2] There my final cry was a Cassandra warning of the dangers arising from eight years of President Ronald Reagan's outright war on policy analysis and numbers that severely reduced analytic capability and large-scale policy research including field experiments and evaluations. In the ensuing period running to the end of President Bill Clinton's first term, however, the honest numbers problem grew worse even though Clinton himself was the ultimate "policy wonk" president. The overriding issue became credibility as distrust in the federal government and in that government's policy information and analysis intensified. In *Mismanaging America* my recommendations on policy analysis focused mainly on the organization and staffing of the executive branch. The current work's prescriptions speak to the needed direction of the policy analysis profession and to the role and functions of federal social policy analysis offices amid rampant distrust and the thrust toward the devolution of federally funded social programs to the states that could make the national government a mere checkwriter. Whither federal policy analysis and research at the millennium? That is the question.

The period since the Reagan administration first brought George Bush, who was not anti-analytic but uninterested in domestic policy analysis, and then a president of phenomenal analytic skills who loved nothing better than to dive into the White House analytic process. Yet, by the end of Bill Clinton's first term, the credibility of federal government numbers was declining and their soundness called increasingly into question. To be sure, neither President Bill Clinton nor Speaker of the House Newt Gingrich invented sleaze, but their actions piled on top of Lyndon Johnson's Vietnam, Richard Nixon's Watergate, and Ronald Reagan's Savings and Loan and Iran-contra scandals made the notion of federal government credibility almost an oxymoron. The most recent threats came in part from highly questionable, if not dishonest, acts such as the Clinton White House providing personal access to Democratic Party contributors for $250,000 or more, and Speaker Gingrich mixing political and charitable funds to support his clearly political lectures to sell a Republican majority. There also were specific efforts to hide or distort information including Clinton's failed try at suppressing the Department of Health and Human Services' analysis that the Republican welfare legislation Clinton was embracing increased child poverty by a million kids and the Department of Defense's coverup of the numbers of Gulf War troops exposed to Iraqi chemical weapons. Such behavior taints even the most solid federal data including the underlying economic statistics on Gross Domestic Product, inflation, and unemployment. By 1996 nearly half of the respondents to a *Washington Post* survey said a "big reason" why the nation's underlying economic statistics were inaccurate was "because the federal government deliberately manipulates the numbers to mislead the public about how the economy is really doing."[3]

In the early days of social policy analysis, those of us who staffed the new policy offices were far too confident of the power of our available tools and unrealistically sought an exalted role of "objective scientist" above the fray, marvelously producing numbers that spoke for themselves. Soon thereafter, policy analysts found that their products had to be sold hard in the bureaucratic/political arena of the agencies and the Executive Office of the President (EOP). Status and clout had to be won with bureaucratic skills. But today certain of the writers on policy analysis go much too far in casting it as mainly argumentative with the analyst as little more than a hired gun ready to find "proof" for either side in the policy battle. In the same vein,

some students of the presidency now argue for "responsive competence" where advisers think only of the president's predilections. Neutral competence be damned. The validity of the numbers receives short
shrift as pure responsiveness, not analytic competence or integrity,
drives advisers' thinking. What stands out across the three plus decades
of social policy analysis is that both policy analysts' and researchers'
recommitment to sound methods, used without political spin, and
federal support of long-term policy research, including evaluations and
field experiments, have become increasingly critical if honest, credible
information and analysis are to underpin policy making.

There is a paradox. If state-of-the-art policy research could actually produce definitive studies, shoddy and slanted work could easily
be shot down. That is, such unchallengeable data would overwhelm
dishonest or distorted information; and policy experts, whatever their
political orientation, could use the demonstrably superior information
for their analyses. Although the availability of such data does not
mean that experts would necessarily agree in interpreting the policy
implications of the data, at least they could start from a common base
of definitive information that would withstand any challenge to its
underlying validity. This is not the case today, and the very fallibility
of the best tools and techniques—data on complex policy issues may
be sound but are never definite—makes integrity and nonpartisanship
more, not less, needed. The hubris and naiveté of the early social agency
analysts notwithstanding, they did seek sound data and adhered to
high analytic standards. Today, there are enough examples of analytic
integrity and competence and nonpartisanship in organizations such
as the Congressional Budget Office and the RAND Corporation to
indicate its value and the pressing need for it to support policy
decisions.

The current volume is the last of a triad of books on institutional
policy analysis that began with the publication in 1971 of *Social Policy
Research and Analysis*.[4] That book, which treated the origins of social
policy analysis in its formative Johnson administration years, drew on
my experience during that period as a policy analyst at the Office of
Economic Opportunity (OEO) that had established the first social policy
analysis staff. After the book came out, other policy analysts and researchers remarked on its underlying pessimism—I must confess, to
my consternation. But they were right. Pessimism had been submerged
for me in pride of accomplishment in helping foster social policy analysis. Gloom did dominate as I spelled out the technical and institutional
difficulties in developing sound, relevant, timely information and analysis to support policy making.

Mismanaging America came two decades later, and in that period
my focus had shifted from the federal agencies to presidential policy

analysis as power moved to the White House. In the 1980s, after studying the Reagan administration, I coined the term "anti-analytic presidency." The federal social policy analysis effort declined in this period
despite the rising number of competent policy analysts and the increasing organizational and technical capacity in the public policy research
industry to carry out high quality (state-of-the-art) social policy studies.
With the anti-analytic presidency in full flower, *Mismanaging America*
reeked of even greater gloom than two decades earlier as I observed
both a flight from serious analytic efforts and an American political
environment that made analytic techniques look increasingly puny
and suspect.

After inertia in the Bush administration left the residue of the
anti-analytic presidency in place, Bill Clinton emerged as *the* analytic
president with high intellect, in-depth policy knowledge, open-
mindedness, a belief in hard numbers, and a rational framework for
thinking about policy. Although I will be critical of Clinton for his
lack of organizational understanding, castigating him for undisciplined
rationality and for a near parody of the multiple advocacy process, he
did resurrect an analytic orientation in the White House not seen since
the 1970s. However, the Clinton administration did not launch a new
social policy research revolution aimed at providing the basic policy
information needed to materially improve federal policy making.

The current study that becomes the final part of my policy analysis
triad draws heavily on extensive off-the-record interviews with political
executives, career civil servants, elected officials, and Washington-
based journalists. A number of the key people were interviewed several
times over a number of years and their responses provided invaluable
comparative judgments. I have found that conducting off-the-record
interviews is far more revealing than engaging in those that allow
attribution. The obvious drawbacks are that the interviews are not
available to other scholars, and readers must rely on my general descriptions of the unnamed interviewees. As to its scope, this historical
critique does not consider specific policies. Instead, it focuses on what
the period under study can tell us about (1) the existing capacity of
the policy analysis and research structure to provide the level of sound
social policy information and interpretation needed to underpin more
effective policy making and (2) the likelihood that an extensive effort
will be undertaken to do so. The last book of the triad continues to
reflect both my belief in the value of social policy analysis and research
and my pessimism about its development and use. As to the former,
the basic theme is that, despite the inherent limitations of the available
policy analysis and research techniques and practices, supply is not
the problem. Policy research competence, far higher than in the early
days of policy analysis, is available to carry out credible studies

including the large-scale evaluations and field experiments that can inform future policy making. Moreover, the accumulated organizational knowledge about policy analysis and research in the federal government offers a strong base for building a viable institutional structure. The overriding questions are about demand. Will the political masters of the federal policy analysts have the competence and the will to support the development and use of sound policy information and analysis in their policy making and to fund needed policy research?

My experience and perspective on policy analysis and power needs spelling out. During the four years I served as a staff member and finally as chief of the Research and Plans Division of the Office of Economic Opportunity's Office of Research, Plans, Programs and Evaluation (RPP&E), I had one of the best ringside seats in the second half of the 1960s to observe the interplay of social policy analysis and power and the effort to develop social policy research. The OEO analytic office quickly emerged as a major power within the agency policy process and became a central actor in shaping social policy analysis and research as we know it. First, RPP&E dominated the OEO policy planning effort, and later its second head, Robert Levine, ranked as the agency director's closest policy adviser. Second, facing a shortage of information on the circumstances and behavior of the poor, RPP&E supported major survey research projects that included a two-year picture of the poor (the Survey of Economic Opportunity) and, more importantly, a University of Michigan survey of poor and near poor families that is still in operation. Third, RPP&E generally fostered poverty research and more specifically provided the funds to start the University of Wisconsin Institute for Research on Poverty that became the nation's top research organization on poverty issues. Fourth, RPP&E funded the first major social program evaluation and the initial large-scale field experiment to investigate a new social policy idea in a field setting.

After leaving OEO to go to the University of Washington's Graduate School of Public Affairs (GSPA), I continued my interest in the analytic organizations in the federal government, moving beyond the agencies to look very briefly at Congress and then in depth at the EOP and the White House. A related but new concern needs brief discussion. In 1995 I became codirector with GSPA dean Margaret Gordon of the school's Trust in Government project. This effort has brought me to a closer look at the interaction of institutional policy analysis and the electronic republic where expert policy information and analysis are far more widely available and must be considered in terms of the public's perception of its validity in the broader environment of often rampant distrust in the institutions of governance. As I look over the last three plus decades, I am impressed with improvements in the technical power to perform policy studies and encouraged by policy analysis units such as the Congressional Research Service (CRS) that have relentlessly sought credibility in their high-quality reports. But what stands out, particularly during the period I have concentrated on the presidency, is the overt misuse of information and analysis, the hiding of potentially relevant data, the ignoring of available information that could modify one's ideological tenets, and the failure to invest in the development of badly needed policy-relevant data for the future through large-scale policy research.

The policy analysis dilemma is that valid policy information and sound analyses have never been either more essential for reasoned policy deliberations or harder to develop as a polarized, dispirited nation considers a social policy transformation potentially more pervasive than that of the War on Poverty period. A central purpose of this history is to aid in thinking through both how to use the potential of social policy analysis and how to lessen its misuse. As one of those present at the beginning, I feel a special responsibility in this task. Yet I increasingly fear that my call for more honest, credible policy numbers can be likened to Don Quixote's quest for "The Impossible Dream" in the Broadway musical, *The Man of LaMancha*. In the three decades of writing the triad of books, I have become increasingly pessimistic about federal policy analysis and the analytic profession and look with rising alarm at the increasing harshness and dishonesty of the American political system that has inundated policy analysis and so threatens American democracy itself. I do not want to overstate the importance of public policy analysts and researchers and their organizations, but I am haunted by a question easy to state, yet hard to answer: How can American democracy survive without honest numbers and analyses to inform the choices of citizens and policymakers? I would go a step beyond Madison's great insight to hold that the American government without popular (read honest) information, or the means or the political will to acquire it, is the prologue to a tragedy. And this tragedy is well under way as the nation approaches the millennium.

NOTES

1. Gaillard Hunt (ed.), *The Writings of James Madison*, G.P. Putnam's Sons, 1910, vol. 9, p. 103.

2. Walter Williams, *Mismanaging America, The Rise of the Anti-Analytic Presidency*, University Press of Kansas, 1990.

3. *Washington Post*, October 13, 1996.

4. Walter Williams, *Social Policy Research and Analysis: The Experience in the Federal Social Agencies*, Elsevier, 1971.

Acknowledgments

I am most indebted to a number of unnamed interviewees, especially those who allowed me to interview them at length on several occasions since 1980 for this book and *Mismanaging America* published in 1990. A number of individuals provided comments on one or more of the chapters: Leigh Anderson, Worth Bateman, James Blum, Lynn Daft, Patrick Dobel, Stuart Eizenstat, Erwin Hargrove, Harry Havens, Ben Heineman, David Kershaw, Robert Levine, Peter May, Roy Meyers, Robert Reischauer, William Robinson, Peter Szanton, Harold Watts, John Wilson, and Sue Woolsey. Since my research on some chapters goes back to the 1970s, the earliest being the work on the New Jersey negative income tax experiment, there have been a number of funding sources: the Ford Foundation, the Stuart Foundation, the German Marshall Fund, the National Science Foundation, and the Graduate School of Public Affairs, University of Washington. I thank particularly the Ford Foundation and the Stuart Foundation whose funding over the last two years supported my expanding the work to broader issues concerning the impact on policy analysis of the electronic revolution and information overload and the rampant public distrust of federal data. However, I have sole responsibility for the final product. As one of that vanishing breed who still write both the first draft and subsequent corrections in pencil with a left-handing scrawl, I give special thanks to Karen McLaughlin for typing and retyping the book and on numerous occasions pointing out sentences that did not make sense. Finally, I am indebted to my wife Jacqueline (Jackie) Block Williams, an historian, who supported my entire effort and also helped me gain a needed historical perspective in an area where I had been both a participant and a researcher.

The book is dedicated to Charlie and Peter Williams born December 14, 1996. They are Jackie's and my first grandchildren who were so wanted and are so cherished by Jackie and me. For Charlie's and Peter's sake, I hope my gloomy predictions of what will happen to American democracy do not come to pass.

1 | Introduction

On an early December day in the fierce 1995 budget fight, the six o'clock television news showed a grim-faced Senate Budget Committee chairman Peter Domenici castigating the latest Clinton budget (his third) and Office of Management and Budget director Alice Rivlin doggedly defending it. The two protagonists—certified policy wonks— battled over two different sets of economic and budget forecasts by the Congressional Budget Office, and the Clinton White House team led by Rivlin's OMB. The CBO projections had become more credible than those of the White House during the time Rivlin had headed the CBO. As the CBO's first director, Rivlin's courageous leadership had been critical in establishing an analytic unit noted for its high competence and integrity where nonpartisanship reigned and its numbers were deemed "the best in town." Rivlin now sat on the other side of the table as Domenici extolled the CBO forecast and bashed the Clinton administration numbers with the White House forecast attacked as highly political in sharp contrast to the CBO's "honest numbers." Despite the fact that both sets of projections were soundly done, a few months later Rivlin's nomination as Federal Reserve Board vice chairman barely passed the Senate, 57 to 41, because of that body's concern about questionable budget negotiation tactics used by the Clinton administration. Her rise as a virtuous congressional policy analyst and fall in reputation as a White House policy expert symbolize the changes over the years covered in this history. But Rivlin's fortunes notwithstanding, policy analysis institutions and individual policy analysts stood at the center of the crucial 1995 budget debate. The power of the numbers and of the analytic institutions generating them shone forth for all to see. How we got to this point is a story that needs telling.

POLICY ANALYSIS AND POWER

Institutional policy analysis burst on the scene in 1961 when Secretary of Defense Robert McNamara, President John Kennedy's most powerful cabinet member, created an analytic office under his chief budget officer, Charles Hitch, who at RAND had helped develop the basic concepts of policy analysis. Hitch brought in a new breed of policy experts whose information and analysis aided McNamara in his efforts both to influence President Johnson and to control the entrenched military services below him. The clear power winners were McNamara, Hitch, and the policy experts. In 1965 with the success of the DOD operation in mind, the Bureau of the Budget (now Office of Management and Budget) issued a directive to major departments and agencies to establish "adequate" central analytic units that would report to the department or agency head or his deputy. I need to note that the Office of Economic Opportunity (OEO) analytic office actually started in 1964, but it did not begin full operations until mid-1965, a few months before the BOB directive. Hence, I have chosen to use 1965 as the starting date for my historical critique of federal social policy analysis.

Larry Lynn, one of the policy shop hands at DOD in the Hitch era and later an assistant secretary who headed two domestic policy analysis units, is correct in arguing that what distinguished these new institutions was not using science to undergird policy making but "the self-conscious incorporation of policy analysis and policy analysts as a matter of principle into the central direction of large, complex government organizations. . . . Henceforth the result of bureaucratic politics would reflect the influence of these policy analysts—the influence both of their ideas and of their access to power."[1] From the beginning, power stood as central to the development of institutional policy analysis.

The social policy analysis offices started with high hope that the powerful tools of science could produce honest, credible data that would underpin policy consensus and the establishment of effective new programs in Lyndon Johnson's War on Poverty. The ensuing analytic revolution over the last three plus decades made the analytic offices and top policy advisers major players in the Washington power structure, changed dramatically how governments think about policy, and spawned a vast public policy research industry. That period yielded much useful information to guide social policy. Competent policy analysis and research organizations within and outside of the federal government earned well-deserved reputations for the credibility of their studies. But the excessively high expectations of 1965 were not fulfilled. Social policy research has not produced, nor is it likely in the future to yield, data that cannot be challenged legitimately on technical or theoretical grounds. Nor have the lofty dreams of the early policy analysts been fulfilled. Their research did not find means of improving policy outcomes dramatically—say a doubling of wages after training or striking growth in reading skills. Moreover, at the top of the executive branch, the quest for bureaucratic power often drove policy analysis; and information became a weapon to be hidden or distorted to the detriment of sound policy making.

Even though the new social policy analysis offices sought power just as did other units in the agencies, the new players could be distinguished from their bureaucratic rivals. The analytic offices brought a new way of thinking about policy based on economics, statistics, and operations research and a kit of tools, drawn mainly from economics, that other players lacked. Moreover, they made skepticism their weapon in the power equation, asking whether or not operating programs worked or policy proposals stood up to rigorous analytic scrutiny. The new analysts combined research methods with bureaucratic politics because, however sophisticated the techniques appeared to be on paper, the policy analysts' data and analyses alone could not dominate their agency rivals. The latter had weapons ranging from hierarchical status to programmatic numbers and anecdotes with which to do battle in the power game. If policy analysts wanted to be central actors in the agency policy-making process, they had no choice but to play the institutional power game.

I wrote in 1971 based on the Johnson administration policy analysis experience in the federal social agencies: "The analyst is neither pure politician nor pure scientist. He probably should have at his fingertips both *The Prince* and a text on principles of experimental design, and use both of them."[2] Thus, analytic power has two separable dimensions—technical and institutional. The former derives solely from the intrinsic weight of the numbers. In the ultimate case, at least in theory, data alone would provide overwhelming evidence. There is, so to speak, the smoking gun, the claim that allowed analysts to cloak themselves as objective scientists, a much desired goal in the early days of policy analysis. Seldom, if ever, is totally overpowering technical evidence to be found. Still, the greater the validity of the evidence, the more its relevance and timeliness, the higher the likelihood of strong technical power influence. Institutional power depends on the organizational clout of the analytic office so that the analyst's power, like that of the other institutional players, flows from bureaucratic status and skills. That the early analytic offices reported to the top of the agency clearly raised their chance of influencing major agency decisions with their analyses. Access to the top decision makers still remains a major factor for the exercise of analytic influence. It helps to be well-placed and it helps to be competent too. The greatest social agency analytic power over time, as we will see, came from the combination of high institutional status; strong bureaucratic skills; sound, relevant, timely information; and the technical competence to use such information.

The analysts' quest for power in social agencies helped expand the public policy research effort. Expert information—the policy analysts' main weapon—was in extremely short supply so the early social policy analytic offices linked themselves to outside policy research organizations.[3] The rising demand brought an increase of both available policy information and the organizations that produced it. The new information raised the influence of both the agency analytic units and the public policy research organizations. The agency central analytic offices flourished. The success of the agency central analytic units begat other units. In the agencies, the operating programs sought analytic capacity to counter the influence of the central analytic units. The power game also brought analytic staffs to the White House and Congress. As to the former, President Richard Nixon created in the Executive Office of the President (EOP) a Domestic Council that had a staff much like the analytic staff of the National Security Council. Congress, in an effort to regain power lost to the Nixon White House, began its own analytic revolution by strengthening its analytic capacity in committee staffs and particularly in congressional support agencies such as the Congressional Research Service (CRS) in the Library of Congress and the CBO. The effort succeeded. Congress has become a major player with the capacity to joust with the executive branch on expert informa- tion and analysis.

In the current political climate, sound policy information and reasoned analysis have never been so badly needed to guide policy or so difficult to produce in a time of major redirection in social policy, including the rapid devolution of federal programs to the states and the 1996 welfare bill to "end public welfare as we know it." As noted, I came in to government service at the start of the federal social policy analysis offices in 1965; therefore, I underscore that my argument does not proclaim a time in the past when we giants did it right compared to the current pedestrian policy analysts. Today, there are far more competent policy analysts inside and outside of the federal government than in 1965, and they have available superior methods, vastly more knowledge and experience, and the wondrous electronic tools that can so enhance policy analysis and research through their power to manipulate data. What policy analysts also have today is a much tougher bureaucratic and political environment that makes it increas- ingly difficult both to develop honest numbers and to maintain high professional standards with analysts not bending their results to fit political demands. Be clear, the problems, as compared to 1965, flow from a level of institutional and political pressures far beyond those in my day, not from current technical incapacity or personal lack of competence and integrity.

THE NUMBERS MANDARINS

When I came to the Office of Economic Opportunity in the mid-1960s, the most respected numbers mandarins were the Bureau of the Budget career staff. This elite cadre practiced "neutral competence"—a term both elements of which were central to a well-served presidency. BOB staff prided themselves on the quality of their work in trying to provide the president with the best numbers and analyses that could be developed. Most critically, the numbers were not to be manipulated to produce answers desired by the budgeteers themselves or their masters. "Neutral," however, meant nonpartisan, not apolitical. BOB staff people did not avoid relevant political factors in their analyses; however, the product served up would not be slanted to fit a president's predilections. Speaking truth to power—telling it like it is—that was the ticket. Efforts at accuracy did not ensure that either the numbers or the analyses would be valid because there was then and still is no fail-proof set of technical tools and techniques. Still, the BOB mandarins gave it their best shot. Competence and integrity marked the effort.

The new social agency policy analysts who arrived in Washington in the early, heady days of Lyndon Johnson's Great Society, saw themselves as central actors leading the search to find highly effective means of combating poverty and other problems blocking minorities and disadvantaged whites from entering mainstream America. The archetypal analysts came to government armed with an economics Ph.D., had worked in a think tank or a university, and saw themselves as markedly different from the BOB mandarins. Although the former knew far less about specific programs and relevant political issues, they had a lot more research horsepower and saw research as a powerful means of developing needed information for policy making. In the 1960s the differences seemed huge; in retrospect, however, the similarities are more important. First, both the policy analysts and the budgeters believed in the value of sound information in policy making and considered developing it and using it in analyses as central tasks. Despite such purity of thought, corners were cut and some shading practiced; however, sound numbers and reasoned analyses based on high standards for using information were central to both the analysts and the BOB career staff. Second, and related, both valued competence and adhered to strong professional norms concerning how information could be developed and employed. BOB had an admirable reputation for inculcating high standards the staff should strive for. No one has stated the budget office code better than Paul O'Neill, who himself gained a justified reputation for probity in several budget staff positions both in BOB and its successor the Office of Management and Budget. In a 1988 talk, he told OMB staff that their "guiding light for this motivation" must be "a standard which says . . . in every decision the President has to make, he has from you . . . the best and clearest exposition of the facts and arguments on every side of the issue that it is possible for a human mind to muster."[4]

The code of the policy analysts came from the halls of academe and corridors of prestigious think tanks such as RAND and Brookings. If anything, these standards were even stricter than those guiding the BOB mandarins. The early policy analysts sought sound data without political spin that policy advocates could take as the starting point for discussion—the facts each side would accept before deliberating on their meaning. Both the new staffs in the central analytic offices and the BOB careerists accepted the institutional commitment to a code of conduct which demanded that practitioners strive for "the best and clearest exposition of the facts and arguments on every side of the issue that it is possible for a human mind to muster."

Another critical aspect of analytic professionalism was the need for an orderly process to support both the vetting of data and analysis for ongoing policy deliberations and to search over time for needed policy research information to guide future policy making. Given a policy-making environment that featured multiple advocacy, where policy proponents tried to sell their proposals or shoot down those of other advocates, the orderly process needed to have strong incentives that drove the policy advocates to do their homework and offer up written policy analyses subject to hard scrutiny by opposing advocates. Open verbal debate among advocates became most useful when informed by earlier sound analytic work that set the stage. In sum, competence and integrity gained from an orderly policy process that involved well-prepared advocates who had the necessary facts and arguments.

No message from this history of social policy analysis comes across more strongly than the continuing need for high analytic competence and a strong institutional and personal commitment, both to integrity in data development and use and to an orderly process that vets information and analysis and encourages the search over time for sound information. The social agency analytic offices met such demands in varying degrees to the end of the Carter presidency. The EOP analytic efforts tended to be more short run in focus, but professional standards still had saliency. Ronald Reagan's anti-analytic presidency brought in a totally different orientation toward data and professional norms. In the Reagan and Bush years, pure responsiveness dominated executive branch domestic policy analysis, producing what leaders wanted to hear. Agency analytic units declined in size, status, and competence. Distortion and the hiding of information became standard practice in the White House, as OMB career staff, although still adhering to analytic norms, were pushed further and further from the top where the key policy decisions were made.

SOUND POLICY INFORMATION AND ANALYSIS

At the start of social policy analysis, the new numbers mandarins in the agency central analytic offices were wont to claim that a little analysis is better than none. In their hubris, they ignored the dangers of using shaky data or of speculating far beyond even sound information. The early analysts were true believers, certain of the efficacy of their enterprise. In his 1968 Gaither Lecture, Brookings economist Charles Schultze, shortly after he stepped down as Lyndon Johnson's BOB director, argued: "Decision making is done by advocacy and bargaining. . . . Analysts at the Bureau of the Budget can and should play the role of efficiency advocates. . . . They are, in effect, 'partisan efficiency advocates'—the champions of analysis and efficiency."[5] The numbers mandarins should be partisans, advocates, champions pressing the benefits of their information and analysis. Today one can still make the case for this belief and remain, as I do, an advocate for using policy information and analysis.

At the same time, those who still champion analysis should be sobered by the messages of the thirty plus years of social policy analysis and be clear that responsible advocacy demands warnings as to dangers and difficulties. As to the former, information can be employed unwisely or dishonestly; analysis can be wrongheaded or devious. No one has made the point better than Elliot Richardson did two decades ago: "In a sense, all abuses of Watergate have been abuses of information: its theft, distortion, fabrication, misuse, misrepresentation, concealment, and suppression."[6] This historical critique will make uncomfortably clear that Watergate did not end the seven sins Richardson enumerated; and, indeed, the rise of a more ideologically based politics that marks the years since Watergate has brought new information atrocities in such cases as Iran-contra and S&L scandals. Misuse is but one of several potential problems that include the failures to develop sound information and to carry out solid analyses or to have this "good" information and analysis ignored by policymakers, nongovernmental policy advocates, and the public.

Those of us who argue for the development and use of sound information and analysis must confront how daunting are the necessary conditions for these to flourish. The first requirement is for top political leaders who recognize the importance of such policy information and analysis in policy making and support its continuing development and use despite significant bureaucratic and political barriers. The second need is for intelligent, principled heads of analytic units committed to an orderly process that allows the needed time to vet current information and analyses and that facilitates the search for needed new policy information over time. The third demand is for an adequate number of skilled policy analysts committed to high institutional norms in the development and use of policy information and analysis. Fourth is a ready supply of public policy research organizations capable of executing and utilizing state-of-the-art policy research, evaluation, and experimentation. The final requirement is a supportive external political environment for the validation and employment of policy information and analysis in public policy making. By the end of the Johnson administration, the play of all these factors, except the political climate, was well-recognized, but the intervening decades have brought both differing circumstances and a broader appreciation of their implications. The first four factors need to be considered only briefly in the remainder of this section, while the external political climate warrants more lengthy discussion in the next one.

Top political leaders who appreciate the value of sound policy information and analysis, grant high status to analytic units, and provide for a sufficient number of policy analysts to meet their demands have been central to effective policy analysis from the early days and remain just as important today. The experience over the last three decades underscores both (1) the increasingly high levels of competence required for political leaders and their top policy advisers, who are not necessarily professional policy analysts, to cope with policy information and analysis, and (2) the rising demands for slanted information and analysis to support the top policymakers' policy positions. The latter in turn will reduce the likelihood of top political leaders granting high status to strong analytic units, appointing heads of analytic units with sufficient competence and integrity to develop sound information and analysis, or providing sufficient positions for adequate staffing.

The competence and integrity of analytic leaders and their deep understanding of orderly process continue to be basic for an effective analytic effort. Orderly process needs to be stressed even more today than in the earlier period as politics has grown more frenetic. Short-term thinking and instant analysis have come to dominate, particularly in the White House. A clear victim of these heightened political pressures are long-term efforts to develop needed new data through policy research, evaluation, and field experimentation. An orderly policy process in an agency would involve undertaking analyses based on available information to support upcoming policy choices in, say, the yearly budget process.

That yearly process should uncover the information needed but not available and generate research to seek the missing information for coming budget processes over time. My definition of policy analysis in *Social Policy Research and Analysis* included as a basic function the development of needed, but missing, policy information to support future policy making. The book's overriding concern was how to obtain an adequate flow of sound, timely data from a then underdeveloped policy research sector. The New Jersey negative income tax experiment and the Westinghouse Head Start evaluation, developed in the Johnson years by OEO, were examples of where the federal policy analysis and research effort needed to go. Such projects flourished in the Nixon presidency with extensive expansion of negative income tax projects and major experiments involving policy areas such as health care and housing allowances. The latter two experiments carried out by the RAND Corporation involved thousands of experiment participants and a number of outstanding researchers, extended over a decade, cost tens of millions of dollars, poured forth a mountain of programmatic information and book-length policy analyses, and still can provide useful policy insights.[7]

POLICY ANALYSIS AND THE CHANGING POLICY ENVIRONMENT

Policy analysis in government sprang forth at a time when the United States was about to experience immense changes that transformed the political environment. Social policy analysis started just as Americans reached the cusp of their belief in the nation itself and in the power of government to solve problems. The United States in 1965 dominated the world as the economic hegemon underpinned by a scientific community held in highest regard because of its great contributions in peace and war. An optimistic America still trusted its government and believed that Lyndon Johnson's War on Poverty could make significant progress toward eliminating poverty. None of those who came confidently, as I did, to OEO and the first domestic policy analysis office imagined the chaotic events that came so quickly. As I wrote:

> Standing on the battle-scarred ground of the War on Poverty in 1971, it is easy to see the naiveté and innocence of the time scarcely half a decade ago. The situation was to change so quickly, and so dramatically. Vietnam was to end any hope for large funds. Riots, militancy, and the rise of separation made the earlier idea of harmony seem quaint. Those with established power did not yield easily either to moral suasion or to more forceful means. Real power is still a well-guarded commodity.[8]

Over a quarter century after this statement, America remains the richest of nations, but rivals have moved much closer; the federal government has come to be seen as the problem, not the solution; science, like most other institutions, no longer stands unquestioned; and the high optimism of the mid-1960s has faded to be replaced by far less faith in the nation and rising cynicism and mistrust. A joint *Washington Post*/Kaiser Family Foundation/Harvard University national survey late in 1995 showed (1) personal trust ("Would you say most people can be trusted or that you can't be too careful in dealing with people?") fell from 54 to 35 percent from 1964 to 1995, and (2) public trust in the federal government ("How much of the time do you trust the government in Washington to do the right thing?") dropped more precipitously from 76 to 25 percent.[9] It was hardly a political climate that supported the search for sound policy information by the federal government or made findings by the Washington agencies credible.

A major factor in the rising mistrust of the federal government has been the failure of its programs to live up to the early, unrealistically high expectations. As noted earlier, the new policy analysts coming to the War on Poverty joined others in Washington who believed they could create effective new social programs that would produce dramatic improvements for participants. That did not happen. As two RAND researchers, Robert Reville and Jacob Alex Klerman, wrote in a 1996 review of research on the effectiveness of federal job training programs:

> Since federal involvement in job training began in the early 1960s, great expectations have been attached to job training as a policy that can reduce poverty and unemployment at minimal cost to the government. It has been a policy that has failed to reach its anticipated potential. . . . [T]he modest, short-term job training programs offered by the federal government are largely ineffective.[10]

The agency policy analysis offices have had a major role in determining this failure through the development and/or funding of systematic assessments of the effectiveness of current and proposed policies. Agency analytic offices funded (1) evaluations that showed new programs such as Head Start and most of the manpower training efforts at best yielded small gains, and (2) experiments that indicated policy ideas, too, were far less effective than had been hoped. The agency-funded evaluations and experiments often were of high quality so that the message itself was credible. Unfortunately, it told much about the limited effectiveness of the many federal attempts to help persons in need through a wide array of programs but offered few insights into means of doing materially better.

The hard truth delivered by policy research that no one could figure out how to provide highly effective programs for poor persons further undermined belief in the federal government. This bitter message of failure has pushed numerous politicians and policy analysts toward recommending the shift of social programs to state and local governments with few if any federal strings attached. Major changes are well under way as the federal devolution moves rapidly, driven both by legislation such as the 1996 welfare changes and administrative edict. Based on the shaky assumption that the subnational governments' policies will be more effective than federal ones, the expected big savings are extracted up front to facilitate budget reductions. As the long-time student of American federalism, Richard Nathan, has written:

> Since the 1994 election, this "Devolution Revolution" for American feder-
> alism has entered an accelerated phase. . . . [T]he federal government is
> not simply loosening the regulatory apron strings. . . . Not only is federal
> spending being cut, but it is no longer the *modus operandi* of Washington
> to discover problems and provide money to solve them. The federal
> money machine is turned off. This is not just a fiscal event; it shifts the
> social policy agenda to others—mainly to state governments.[11]

Another critical transformation that impinges on policy analysis and research is the heightened technical capacity to develop, analyze, and transmit information to the public. The expert policy data, which in the early days of policy analysis had mainly been restricted to the closed environment of the institutional policy process, have now become part of the highly visible world of instantaneous, interactive electronics. These changes, which have so increased electronic capabilities, yield instant information and access for more and more citizens and have made the relatively closed policy world of the mid-1960s much more transparent (e.g., President George Bush and the public both watching the Gulf War on CNN). The downside of these changes is that the technical capacity to provide information instantly has far outrun people's capability to interpret policy-relevant information. The mark of the information transformation has been overload and deep doubt about data and the interpretation of them. In *The Electronic Republic* Lawrence Grossman, former head of PBS and of NBC News, spelled out the information dilemma facing policymakers and the public:

> Since information has become "society's main transforming re-
> source," the public's ability to receive, absorb, and understand informa-
> tion no longer can be left to happenstance.
>   No military general would willingly send his army into battle
> untrained and ill-prepared, no matter how well-equipped. Yet today,
> the American public is going into political battle armed with increasingly
> sophisticated tools of electronic decision making but without the informa-
> tion, political organization, education, or preparation to use these tools
> wisely. . . . Without a conscious and deliberate effort to inform public
> judgment. . . the new interactive telecommunication technologies. . . are
> more likely to undermine the democratic process than enhance it.[12]

In sharp contrast to the earlier, more closed, data-scarce milieu, the policy domain today is overburdened with both information and policy entrepreneurs who compete relentlessly to be heard. Misleading manipulation to make the data support an ideological position has become an integral part of many a policy entrepreneur's game. The new technologies can be a blessing or a curse, used to inform or confuse in the battles for the minds of policymakers and the public.

The final critical change is in the structure of the executive branch itself, with the White House becoming far more centralized and politicized since 1965. Power has shifted from the executive agencies to the Executive Office of the President while EOP career policy analysts have been pushed lower and lower in the White House policy-making process. In the Johnson administration below the politically appointed BOB director, power resided with a career deputy director and career staff. The handful of politically appointed assistant directors had minor roles. BOB division chiefs were the top executive branch mandarins with the clout to strike fear at the top of the agencies. By the 1990s several layers of political appointees occupied all of the top Office of Management and Budget positions. Over the years OMB, which had replaced BOB during the Nixon administration, granted less and less authority over agency budgets to agency heads and their numbers mandarins. The changes in the balance of power between the president and the agencies has gone so far that John Hart writes of a fourth branch, labeled the "presidential branch."[13] (The media would, in this splitting of the executive branch, become the fifth branch.) This new fourth branch disturbs and frustrates the relationships among the president, the remainder of the executive branch, and the Congress and reduces a president's dependence on the agencies for information and analysis. As we shall see, this dramatic power shift dominates the practice of executive branch policy analysis in affecting both the kinds of analysis and research undertaken and the norms of acceptable conduct by analytic staffs.

KEY DEFINITIONS

Several definitions are needed for the remainder of this book. The first group of definitions focuses on the meaning of policy analysis and various forms of policy research. *Policy analysis* is a means of (1) treating available information, including research results, to develop a sound statistical and analytic base for public policy making, and (2) determining unavailable information needed to guide future analytic and research efforts. That is, policy analysis has the two main functions of illuminating upcoming decisions by public officials and of specifying needed analytic and research activities to support policy analysis efforts over time. *Policy research* involves efforts using scientific methods to investigate policy issues and includes evaluations and experiments. *Evaluations* seek to measure the degree to which programs are helping persons or organizations receiving program benefits and services. *Experiments* assess the impact of new policy ideas in a setting corresponding, at least in part, to actual program operating conditions. Besides evaluations and experiments, policy research can address a variety of topics including the seriousness of public policy issues such as homelessness, drug abuse, loss of revenue from federal tax loopholes, and urban sprawl.[14]

It is useful to think about an agency analytic and research effort over time. A policy analysis might find needed but missing information about the nature and dimensions of a policy issue, such as when is the best time to intervene in early childhood education for poor children. Then, a funded research project addressing the issue might show that Head Start reaches poor children too late, and the best time to help is in the first year of life. Based on the research results, an experiment might try several intervention approaches for very early childhood learning in an actual field setting to provide information on the effectiveness of different approaches and the organizational demands made by projects in a real-world environment. The experimental results could provide policy information that had been needed but had not been available in an earlier policy-making process and help policymakers decide on a new program. If a new very early childhood program were to be launched, an evaluation could assess various efficiency and effectiveness aspects and provide policy information that would illuminate another policy-making process. In turn, this later analytic effort could indicate missing information on very early childhood intervention efforts that would generate a new policy research effort.

The next group of definitions—centralization and politicization, neutral and responsive competence, multiple advocacy, and policy generalists—addresses a number of complex questions, including who are the president's main policy advisers and what is the degree of control the White House exerts over the agencies? To avoid making the definitions unduly complex, the Executive Office of the President will include all persons with policy concerns in the presidential branch except for the president and his inner circle of top political and policy advisers. Hence White House, White House staff, and EOP often will be used interchangeably. Further, the cabinet secretaries as a group are treated as different from the inner circle, although some cabinet secretaries may occasionally be in the inner circle or have greater freedom than other cabinet secretary colleagues. *Centralization* generally refers to the division of power over major decisions, both in making them and advising on them, as distributed among the president and his inner circle, EOP staff, and the cabinet secretaries. Greater centralization can involve a shift of power to either the president's top people and the rest of the EOP staff away from cabinet members and their agencies, or to the top White House advisers away from both the EOP and the cabinet secretaries. *Politicization* indicates the relative power of political appointees and career civil servants in making or advising on major presidential decisions with greater politicization, meaning more relative power in the hands of political appointees.

John Burke, after considering a number of treatments of *neutral and responsive competence*, argued that the two stand at the opposite end of the spectrum from each other and wrote of neutral competence: "[I]t is uncommitted (although not opposed) to the president's ideological program; it is continuous in that it transcends a particular presidency, having 'institutional memory' about both policy substance and procedure and drawing upon professional expertise, not just political loyalty and acumen."[15] The general assumption is that responsive competence is exhibited by political loyalists and neutral competence by career civil servants even though the former may have both professional expertise and institutional memory (e.g., an ex-civil servant with a political appointment or an in-and-outer). At the same time, responsive competence can become responsiveness driven only by individual loyalty to a leader, not by any concern for technical standards. Burke, in his critique of the competence issue, points out that "taken together, centralization and politicization form . . . a strategy of 'responsive competence.'"[16]

Roger Porter has contrasted *multiple advocacy* with centralized management, which places primary responsibility for policy formulation on an inner circle aided by EOP staff, and has defined multiple advocacy as involving an open, inclusive system "designed to expose the President to competing arguments and viewpoints made by advocates themselves rather than . . . filtered through a staff to the president."[17] It needs noting that because Porter focused exclusively on presidential decision making, he cast the definition for a president, but the multiple advocacy process also applies to other final decision makers such as agency heads. In a well-ordered multiple advocacy process, competing views should be deliberated by the advocates collectively before a final decision maker to foster exchange and argument. On major presidential policy issues, the process at the top would include cabinet secretaries, not just EOP staff. In a multiple advocacy process over time, advocates would use their staffs to produce policy papers in support of their positions; such papers would be circulated among advocates and the final decision maker for scrutiny; and competing policy ideas would be argued by advocates before the top policymaker, such as the president or an agency head. A multiple advocacy process establishes an institutional means for challenging weak analysis, questioning the validity of information, and supplying missing data.

If a multiple advocacy process is to work, it needs to be well-managed and orderly. First, the top decision maker must not interject himself or herself into the process so early as to bias it with his or her views—be a "magistrate"—and wait for reasoned analyses by advocates. Second, a day-to-day manager needs to maintain the fairness of process—be an "honest broker" and keep that process orderly and on schedule. Third, a well-structured process must be in place to give order to needed information gathering, the preparation of written analyses, the reading of the analyses by the advocates and the final decision maker, and the final deliberations. Needless to say, decision-making demands often do not allow the time for the full process to play out, but a well-established procedural structure can facilitate decision making even as shortcuts are taken. Beyond management and order, the process depends for its efficacy on the communication skills of advocates, the quality of the available data and analysis, and the knowledge and analytic competence of the participants.

Policy generalists are the inner circle members the president picks to provide him with policy advice. The members of this highly select group likely will not be professional policy analysts and may not be competent users of analytic products. The key point is that whatever their technical competence, the policy generalists are the critical White House staff actors determining the extent that a president is linked to the executive branch analytic process. In the extreme case, policy making at the top will involve the president and a small number of policy generalists who make little or no use of available analytic capacity.

Finally, definitions are needed concerning the quality of policy information, research studies, and analyses. *Definitive information* describes data that cannot be legitimately challenged on theoretical or technical dimensions. In the case of complex social issues, such information is almost certain not to exist. The definition has been set out to contrast it with *sound or honest information and analyses* where accepted technical procedures have been applied both appropriately and without political bias. An analysis or research effort that does not have a partisan spin in being tailored to the predilections of particular policymakers will be labeled as *nonpartisan*. Generally, the term "objective" will not be used because it connotes a pure scientist, the policy analyst or researcher having no personal or political values, figuratively arriving from Mars with no biases of any kind to speak truth to power. Although nonpartisan and objective are often used by others as synonyms, as will be the case in a later chapter on the congressional support agencies, nonpartisan for me carries less baggage than the Olympian concept of objectivity.

In thinking about policy numbers, a key distinction is between an estimate of a specific piece of data for a past time period, such as the first quarter 1997 Gross Domestic Product, and projections of that same information for the future, such as GDP for the next five years. As to the former, the early GDP estimate for a just past quarter made by the Department of Commerce's Bureau of Economic Analysis (BEA) may be subject to large errors, for example, because it is based on partial data. BEA will refine the estimate over time and increase the accuracy even though the number remains subject to sampling errors and so on. But finding out what happened in the past for various economic variables is far easier and much less prone to errors than projections of future results. However sophisticated their projection models, economists, like the rest of us, have only a highly fallible crystal ball.

Federal budget deficit projections offer a case in point with spring 1997 providing a striking example of how far off these projections can be. At that time, the president and Congress had before them what loomed as hard political choices, including a couple of dreaded choices affecting the aged. Just at the last moment, based on a booming economy that yielded a lower-than-anticipated budget deficit, the Congressional Budget Office projected that $225 billion dollars more would be available over the next five years than the CBO had projected previously. A five-year total of $225 billion can easily come about in a six trillion dollars a year economy with relatively small changes in projected growth rates. And GDP growth for the first quarter 1997 had come in at an unexpectedly high 5.6 percent rate. Although CBO itself did not "fudge" the numbers, the forecast was a hurried guess made over a brief period, not an extended formal analysis.

Former CBO director Robert Reischauer has made the key point that, even in the most careful projections, the one thing forecasters should accept is that "what you predict won't come to pass."[18] He could have added, *often by a large amount.* Not long before the new CBO projections in spring 1997 of lower five-year deficits, the agency had published *An Analysis of the President's Budgetary Proposals for Fiscal Year 1998* that underscores this last point.[19] The document indicated both the CBO and the Clinton administration deficit projections made each year from March 1993 through April 1996 for fiscal year 1996. The actual fiscal year 1996 budget deficit came to $107 billion, but both CBO and the administration in 1993 had projected a fiscal year 1996 deficit of nearly $300 billion with one projection missing by $172 billion and the other by $183 billion. Misses for this one year, it may be noted, are amounts within shouting distance of the five-year projection of a $225 billion reduction. In 1996, six months before the end of the 1996 fiscal year, the two projections were off $37 billion and $44 billion.

That is, the CBO and administration projections for just six months into the future were in the neighborhood of $45 billion, the yearly deficit reduction projection that "produced" $225 billion for the president and the Congress. The unpredictability (uncertainty) problem involved in projections is not one that will go away however wondrous the technical improvements.

The hard truth is that the social sciences, including economics, are not strong in predicting the results involving the interaction of variables within a complex system. While social scientists often look with envy at the predictive power of the hard sciences, great uncertainty resides there too:

> It is a tribute to the power and precision of science that it was able to predict so far in advance that on April 1, Comet Hale-Bopp would make its closest rendezvous with the Sun. But what science could not reliably say was whether, in any particular part of the country, clouds would . . . block the view—a cosmic April Fool's joke.
>
> Some of the grandest phenomena, like the coursing of comets around the Sun, are marvelously predictable. But some of the most mundane, like weather, are so convoluted that they continue to elude the most diligent forecasters. They are what scientists call complex systems.[20]

As we will see, what so intensifies the uncertainty problem in policy making is that politicians like to ignore it and act as if the $225 billion, for example, is not a rough guess but an exact amount.

LOOKING AHEAD

Executive branch policy analysis will receive most of the attention in this book for five main reasons. First, it has the longest history and better illustrates central issues concerning power and policy analysis and the institutional difficulties of developing and using honest numbers and sound analysis in the policy-making process. Second, the public policy research industry has already been treated extensively in several books and need not be considered in depth but rather can be dealt with in the next chapter. Third, although congressional policy analysis has received insufficient treatment, what has happened and its import for our purposes can be captured in a chapter on the congressional support agencies. Fourth, the executive branch has the strongest institutional base for shaping the policy analysis and research effort. No single individual in Congress has nearly so much institutional power to change policy analysis and research over time as the president and his political delegatees who appoint all of the top decision makers and policy analysts in the executive branch. Moreover, the executive branch historically has been the main federal buyer of the products of public policy research organizations, and this domination has been particularly strong in the area of major long-term studies. The final reason has a normative cast to it. I believe the executive branch policy research and analysis has gone badly wrong and that the central figure has been the president. In particular, with much of the federal social policy effort being devolved to the states as America undertakes a major social policy redirection, there is limited demand by the federal government and subnational governments for the large-scale evaluation studies and experiments that can address basic questions about implementing and managing the social policy effort at all levels of government. Here strong presidential leadership is critical in demanding the needed rigorous large-scale research to underpin future policy deliberations.

A few more remarks are needed on how this book proceeds. The main focus is on social, and to some extent domestic, policy as opposed to economic or national security policy; however, the latter two are not completely excluded. In two cases, policy analysis in the national security area from John Kennedy through Richard Nixon and Gerald Ford's Economic Policy Board, the impact on social policy analysis is too important to ignore. Further, trying to separate domestic and economic policy in a small number of cases would have limited our understanding of the policy process efforts being studied. The Bush administration offers a clear case where the chief of staff and OMB director dominated both domestic and economic policy making.

With much of the book centering on the staff and structural aspects of presidential policy analysis, a president's style, competence, and predilections, and in some cases those of key advisers such as David Stockman, cannot be ignored in asking both how and how well policy analysis operated in a particular administration. The assessments of the analytic capabilities of presidents and their top advisers are central in the study; however, efforts to critique an individual president's overall performance are usually avoided. I will argue, for instance, that President Bush had less analytic competence (mainly because of disinterest) than any of the presidents considered in this book except Reagan, but I will not go the next step to ask whether his presidency failed overall. Based on the restricted nature of the study, such an assessment should not be made because such factors as a president's political skills, integrity, courage, judgment, and the challenges he faces clearly are more important to success or failure than policy analysis practices. Further, policy analysis is both a means that can be used for good or evil and is quite fallible so that its use hardly ensures beneficial results even if well-used. To recognize that policy analysis is only one of several factors in presidential effectiveness in no way conflicts with the key premise of the book—that honest num-

bers and sound analysis are important to how well a president performs. This last comment leads to one more point about presidents. I
will discuss presidential courage and integrity in that whether or not
a president will follow the dictates of sound policy analyses does
depend in part on the president's willingness to take the numbers and
run in a risky political environment. At issue is the question of whether
the available means—policy analyses—actually will be used by the
president.

As to organization, this chapter and the next one both delve into
the history of federal government policy analysis and the concomitant
development of the public policy research industry and provide a
framework and definitions to undergird the remainder of the book.
The seven chapters after that focus primarily on the historical critique
of social policy analysis in the executive and legislative branches over
the last three plus decades. The first six cover the executive branch
and trace the shift from the executive agencies as the focal point of
policy analysis to the president and his top staff as the central focus in
the executive branch policy-making process; the final historical chapter
turns to Congress and its support agencies.

The chapter after that casts the issue of honest numbers and
honest analysts in the larger context of the harsh political setting and
of the emerging electronics era. The latter offers the promise of wider
and faster information dissemination to policymakers and the public of
relevant policy data and interpretation as well as information overload
where unbelievable amounts of hard-to-validate policy data can overwhelm the government analytic process. The current political environment makes reasoned policy making increasingly difficult. The central
point for institutional policy analysis in the federal government is that
it is caught up in the hostile political environment where ideology and
fierce partisan politics can drive out sound analysis. The problem, as
this history will underscore, is particularly bad in the White House.
My main objective is to discuss how deeply institutional policy analysis
is caught up in the current turmoil of American politics and how much
the development and use of sound policy information and analyses
are jeopardized by the larger problems.

The final chapter draws on the framework and history to look at
the future of federal government social policy analysis by considering
two key questions that need brief elaboration. The first one concerns
the role and functions of policy analysts. Here is the bedrock question
of professional standards. The issue has already been considered briefly
in the previous section where the concepts of neutral versus responsive
competence were juxtaposed. Much of the recent writing that makes
the policy analyst a political partisan is wrongheaded in terms of what
policymakers need and will do lasting harm to the policy research and

analysis enterprise. I will argue both that honest numbers and honest analysts are essential if trust in government is to be restored and that the required behavior fits well with the historic role and professional standards of policy analysts and researchers within the federal government and outside of it. The second question focuses on the future role of the federal policy analysis units in the emerging environment of devolving social programs to the states. Placing greater responsibility for service delivery programs with subnational governments is an idea whose time has come. At the same time, shared governance will continue, both because federal dollars will still be involved so there must be accountability to Congress and the president and because national interests still exist that need to be reconciled with state and local interests.

In my 1980 book *Government by Agency*, the main recommendation advised federal agencies to consider adopting "an agency management strategy that has improving local commitment and capacity [to deliver social services] as a central objective."[21] In this new world of devolution, the recommendation, expanded to include the state governments, makes as much structural sense and more political sense than it did nearly two decades ago. Unlike the period covered in the 1980 book, the federal agencies will not now be nearly so active as partners in managing the federally funded programs and well might take a stronger role as advisers on capacity building and program improvement. Needless to say, Congress must be willing. But if it is, policy analysis offices could have as a central function the search for tested means of doing a better job of delivering state and local services.

To date, states generally have done a poor job of rigorous research design in innovative programs such as those started under the federal welfare program waivers, and the federal agencies have not been much help. As University of Wisconsin-Madison economist Michael Wiseman wrote in a 1996 book review of *The Politics of Welfare Reform*: "The oft-cited notion that states are playing the role of 'laboratories'. . . in welfare reform receives little support. . . . The experiments are uncoordinated and ill-designed, no one seems to be keeping notes, and there is no peer and little federal pressure for serious and timely review of program contents or results."[22] Even if states on their own take rigorous assessments seriously, the federal agency analytic offices need to have a role in multi-state studies to determine valid results that can be generalized across states and communities. I will recommend a new federal policy analysis unit effort that funds well-designed, carefully implemented experiments and evaluations to provide solid information for state and local policy making.

Although I will maintain that federal social agency policy analysis in its golden decade of funding large-scale evaluations and experiments shows what can be done, Richard Darman, the former director of the Office of Management and Budget, is broadly right in his argument in the *New York Times Magazine* article entitled "Riverboat Gambling with Government":

> There is, quite simply, too little reliable empirical evidence to suggest that any. . . [new domestic] program would work. It is this missing evidence that America should recognize as a national scandal. . . .
>
> The problem is that we know little more now than in the '60s about how, on a large scale, to achieve . . . shared objectives. And the reason is a continuing surrender to ignorance. Major public-policy initiatives are routinely advanced, but rarely do we organize to evaluate what works. We [the public] thus allow politicians to mislead us. Then we act as helpless victims.[23]

Darman praised the earlier evaluations and experiments of the golden years and to some extent understated what has been learned, but in an overall sense, he is right. The overriding point, basic to this history, is the scandal of failing to do the needed rigorous evaluations and experiments. It is the scandal that has helped fuel the rise of ideological politics.

This historical critique of social policy analysis since the establishment of the Office of Economic Opportunity central analytic office in 1965 sweeps selectively over much terrain. To aid in the trip, let me set out key points that will be made, separating them as to whether they are historical statements or recommendations:

Historical Statements

1. Federal agency social policy analysis reached its peak in its first decade, not because of the competence of the policy analysts as compared to later ones, but because of the earlier analysts' high status in the agency hierarchies, the available resources to fund policy research including large-scale evaluations and field experiments, and a political environment that supported high professional standards and extensive efforts to develop sound information and analysis to guide policy making.
2. The Executive Office of the President gained power vis à vis the social agencies beginning in the Nixon administration and reached nearly total dominance in the Reagan years and beyond.
3. Executive branch social policy analysis in an increasingly harsh political environment has witnessed power moving mainly to the president and his close advisers, a decline in the

role of EOP civil servants in top policy making, an increasing emphasis on responsive competence, a lowering of professional standards, and little support for long-term, large-scale policy research.

4. Over the thirty-plus-year period, there have been such material increases in the number of competent policy analysts and capable public policy research organizations that supply has ceased to be a serious problem in federal social policy analysis.

5. The electronics revolution offers both the promise of improved data development and use in the policy-making process and the potential peril of information overload and increasing difficulties in validating a plethora of policy information and analysis, so much of which is highly partisan and does not incorporate high research and analytic standards.

6. Reduced federal government funding for the development of social and economic data by its own statistical units is undercutting the soundness of the basic information needed for government, business, and public policy making.

7. Rising political partisanship now threatens the major nonpartisan, nongovernment public policy research institutions that have historically developed honest numbers and analyses to support government and public policy deliberations.

8. Honest, credible information, sound social policy analyses, and well-funded, carefully planned and executed social policy research, particularly large-scale evaluations and field experiments, have never been so difficult to develop than in today's political climate of limited executive branch demand and rising public distrust and cynicism about the federal government and its numbers.

9. In the 1970s, Congress began establishing greater policy analysis capability in the congressional support agencies and now has strong analytic units whose competent staffs engage in a large number of nonpartisan efforts to inform congressional decision making.

Recommendations

10. Social policy analysts and researchers should recommit to neutral competence and high professional standards embracing nonpartisan studies that employ state-of-the-art techniques without political spin and reject responsive competence which seeks to provide policymakers the answers they want, whatever the underlying evidence indicates.

11. Social policy analysts and researchers also ought to make clear to potential users the fallibility of even the best techniques and the inherently limited capacity to project into the future when the critical variables interact in complex systems.

12. In this period of devolution of federal programs by Washington to subnational governments, the federal social agencies should have a major role in (a) providing technical assistance aimed at building the capacity of subnational governments to implement and manage programs funded in whole or in part by the federal government, and (b) developing the information needed to support both a strong technical assistance effort and sound analyses to guide government decision making on these social programs.

13. Federal policymakers in both the executive branch and Congress should acquire a better understanding of the usefulness and the limits of honest information, sound analysis, and well-designed, well-executed policy research and have the political will to support the development of such work and use the results in policy making.

The historical critique mainly delves into the bureaucratic politics of social policy research and analysis. This means that methodology and competence issues, both in the federal government and the public policy research organizations, generally will be embedded in the bureaucratic and political discussions and not treated separately. The reason is that I believe the current methodological techniques and the supply of competent social policy analysts and researchers are adequate to perform the high-quality policy analysis and the longer term, large-scale policy research, evaluation, and field experimentation needed to guide a possible social policy transformation that could be played out over the coming decades. Moreover, in the broader issue of policy information overload, technology and the technical competence to use it are not the main problems. At basic question are the bureaucratic and political steps demanded to make the beast facilitate, rather than overwhelm, the policy process.

The main missing ingredients in the case of the federal government are the political will and analytic integrity to develop and use sound policy information and analysis in the executive branch and a level of bureaucratic mastery not seen in recent years in the White House and the agencies. Further, the question of the credibility of expert policy information and analysis is now entangled in the crisis of trust in government itself and more broadly in the public's rising distrust of other institutions such as the media. Sound data and analyses may hold little or no credibility for those who doubt whatever

ALBRIGHT COLLEGE LIBRARY   62240

government does or believe only other true believers. Nonpartisan competence in the world of information overload and mounting distrust may be weak armor against ideology and ignorance. If many of the public have lost faith in the main institutions of society, will information from these institutions, including government and media, be credible? It is an issue this historical critique of social policy analysis must not avoid. But in confronting it, I warn readers that my concluding pessimism about the development and use of honest numbers and analysis is greater even than the pessimism expressed in my two earlier books on policy analysis as noted in the Preface to this volume. This historical critique supports my growing gloom about the policy analysis profession and the sound practice of policy analysis and research in the federal government and ultimately the viability of American democracy without honest, credible numbers and analyses.

NOTES

1. Lawrence E. Lynn Jr., "Policy Analysis in the Bureaucracy: How New? How Effective?", *Journal of Policy Analysis and Management,* Summer 1989, pp. 374–375.

2. Walter Williams, *Social Policy Research and Analysis: The Experience in the Federal Social Agencies,* Elsevier, 1971, p. 170.

3. Ibid., pp. 58–66.

4. Paul H. O'Neill, a presentation to Office of Management and Budget staff, The Center for Excellence in Government, Washington, D.C., September 6, 1988, p. 2.

5. Charles L. Schultze, *The Politics and Economics of Public Spending,* Brookings, 1968, pp. 95–96.

6. Elliott Richardson, *The Creative Balance,* Holt, Rinehart & Winston, 1976, p. 105.

7. Joseph P. Newhouse and the Insurance Experiment Group, *Free for All? Lessons from the RAND Health Insurance Experiment,* Harvard University Press, 1993; Ira S. Lowry (ed.), *Experimenting with Housing Allowances: Findings of a Ten-Year Study of Housing Assistance for Low Income Families, with Implications for National Housing Policy,* Oelgeschlager, Gunn & Hain, 1983.

8. Williams, *Social Policy Research and Analysis,* p. 3.

9. *Washington Post,* January 21, 1996.

10. Robert T. Reville and Jacob Alex Klerman, "Job Training: The Impact on California of Further Consolidation and Devolution," in James Hosek and Robert Levine (eds.), *The New Fiscal Federalism and the Social Safety Net: A View From California,* RAND, 1996, pp. 127 and 138.

11. Richard P. Nathan, "The 'Devolution Revolution': An Overview," in Michael J. Malbin (ed.) *American Federalism Today,* Rockefeller Institute Bulletin, 1996, pp. 5 and 12.

12. Lawrence K. Grossman, *The Electronic Republic: Reshaping Democracy in the Information Age*, Viking, 1995, pp. 31–32. Grossman took the quoted words "society's main transforming resource" from Walter B. Wriston, *The Twilight of Sovereignty*, Charles Scribner's Sons, 1992, p. 8.

13. John Hart, *The Presidential Branch*, Pergamon, 1987.

14. These definitions draw on Williams, *Social Policy Research and Analysis*, pp. 12–13.

15. John P. Burke, *The Institutional Presidency*, Johns Hopkins University Press, 1992, p. 185. Examples of treatments of neutral and responsive competence include Hugh Heclo, "OMB and the Presidency: The Problem of 'Neutral Competence'," *Public Interest*, Winter 1975, pp. 80–98; and Terry M. Moe, "The Politicized Presidency," in John E. Chubb and Paul E. Peterson (eds.), *The New Direction in American Politics*, Brookings, 1985, pp. 235–271.

16. Burke, *The Institutional Presidency*, p. 181.

17. Roger B. Porter, *Presidential Decision Making: The Economic Policy Board*, Cambridge University Press, 1980, p. 241.

18. *New York Times*, May 3, 1997.

19. Congressional Budget Office, *An Analysis of the President's Budgetary Proposals for Fiscal Year 1998*, March 1997. All data in the remainder of the paragraph are from Table B–1, p. 60.

20. *New York Times*, May 6, 1997.

21. Walter Williams, *Government by Agency: Lessons from the Social Program Grants-in-Aid Experience*, Academic Press, 1980, p. 261.

22. Michael E. Wiseman, Book Review, *Journal of Policy Analysis and Management*, Spring 1996, pp. 286–287. The book reviewed is Donald F. Norris and Lyke Thompson (eds.), *The Politics of Welfare Reform*, Sage, 1995.

23. Richard Darman, "Riverboat Gambling with Government," *New York Times Magazine*, December 1, 1996, pp. 116–117.

2 | The Marketplace for Expert Information and Analysis

The federal policy analysis and research effort has been and is driven by four main factors: federal government demand for expert policy information and analysis; the size, competence, and direction of the public policy research industry; the underlying institutional structure for information development, validation, use, and transmission; and the political environment. The latter cuts across the first three factors and sets the stage for how each evolves. For example, political factors such as the press for greater openness in policy making, the decline of the public's trust in the federal government, and the rise of ideology that makes for increasing numbers of true believers have had profound impacts on one or more of the other variables. The treatment in Chapter 1 of the political environment and in this chapter of executive branch demand for policy analysis and research, the public policy research industry, and the underlying information structure provide a broad frame of reference for the upcoming historical account.

This chapter is cast in terms of a marketplace of policy ideas and more specifically of the marketplace for expert policy information and analysis that fuels social policy. In the federal marketplace for information and analysis, demand is dominated by the government and the supply flows mainly from the public policy research industry composed of over 1,200 free-standing think tanks and university policy-oriented organizations. Federal demand for social policy analysis and research comes from the president and his inner circle of top White House advisers, the "institutional presidency" which embraces the rest of the Executive Office of the President, the executive agencies, and the Congress. A president's inner circle may include an analytic office head, as was the case with Office of Management and Budget director Richard Darman in the Bush years, but well may not. The remainder of executive branch demand for expert policy information, analysis, and research is generated in the main by policy analysis and research units in the EOP and the executive agencies where the agencies' top policy analysts may be far below the inner circle. These many agency analytic offices, however, historically have made the everyday decisions about policy research and analysis. Congress demands a great deal of extensive analysis, mainly from its support agencies. Congress, however, has funded little policy research directly although it historically has mandated agency research studies. The supply of expert policy information and analysis comes from a diverse group of research organizations that can execute state-of-the-art policy studies to illuminate policy making. Here is the underlying external capacity that government policy analysis offices, if they so desire, can draw on both to build staff competence and to undertake domestic policy studies. The underlying information structure at any one time reflects the interaction of technical, political, and bureaucratic forces. The available technology—the existing state-of-the-art capacity—sets the potential limits or outer boundaries for the information structure. The actual boundaries up to the technical limits, however, are established by such forces as the public's demand for information availability, the prevailing political concerns for secrecy, and the mores of the institutions that develop and use information.

EXECUTIVE BRANCH POLICY ANALYSIS AND RESEARCH

While Congress does get into the act, the executive branch has been the main buyer of policy research. Among the three components of executive branch demand for policy analysis and research, the big change has been the dominance of the EOP over the agencies. Still at issue, however, is relative power balance between the president and his top aides and the institutional presidency. Although the case will be made that the president and his inner circle are the more powerful, it is the interaction among the key actors that is most important for understanding executive branch demand for policy analysis and research. The argument for a president's prominence, as compared to the remainder of the executive branch, in determining federal policy analysis and the agenda of the policy analysis and research industry rests on two main points. First, as touched on earlier, is the president's constitutional power of appointment where he chooses the top staff members in the White House and EOP and the heads of the cabinet agencies and other major departments and hand picks more and more subcabinet members. President Reagan offers the most striking case in vetting all subcabinet members for adherence to Reagan objectives and then choosing a number of them whose first loyalty flowed to the president, not their direct bosses, the cabinet members. Bill Clinton and Hillary Rodham Clinton also dipped down into the subcabinet with race and gender diversity a driving force in contrast to Reagan's ideological criterion. Second, increasing EOP centralization and politicization have raised the importance of EOP staff relative to agency political executives and made the president's inner circle more and more powerful in the policy analysis equation. All EOP policy units except OMB are primarily, or exclusively, political appointees. Thus, the Office of Policy Development, which was the new title in the Reagan administration for President Jimmy Carter's Domestic Policy Staff, fired everybody in the latter group down through four of the eight secretaries. Moreover, the members of the DPS felt free, as political appointees, to take their files with them so institutional memory approached zero. Even in OMB, which has several hundred professional staff members who stay on at changes of government, increasing numbers of political executives have been placed at the top with career staff pushed further and further down in the chain of command. Clearly, the institutional presidency has gained greatly vis à vis the executive agencies. But is the president master of his own house or does the institutional presidency dominate him?

The Man Versus the Institutional Structure

What drives the presidential policy marketplace? On the one side is the president's personality, ideology, governance style, and political and policy competence. On the other side are powerful institutional factors arising from the growth and bureaucratization of the EOP. Joseph Pika, in discussing the question of the man versus the office in presidential policy making, distinguished between "personalists" who see the EOP as a mere extension of the president who is the master of his own house and "institutionalists" who "regard the presidency as a collectivity of specialized staffs manned by aides with expert skills whose goals may diverge from those of the president."[1] Pika then made the key point that both the personalists and the institutionalists have made contributions to the understanding of presidential policy making, "but have tended to avoid the central analytic task: examining the effects of both the man (management style) and the office (organizational matrix)."[2]

The nature of the interaction between the president and the White House structure and the search for a linking factor between the chief executive and his institutions are central to this book. A key question is what policy information and analysis a president needs for sound policy making. In addressing this question, Roger Porter, who served in senior domestic policy positions in both the Reagan and Bush presidencies, wrote in 1980 based on his experience in the Ford administration: "Presumably all presidents want reliable information and careful analysis, all necessary but not extraneous data, information and advice in an understandable form, a full range of realistic alternatives, and clearly identified trade-offs—advantages and disadvantages—between various policy alternatives."[3] As presidents have sought greater political control, Porter's presumption becomes increasingly questionable, and we need to ask why a president seeks policy inputs. It is the basic question of knowledge for what purpose. Is the president's eye mainly on political standing, getting legislation through Congress, and reelection; or, is it on policy direction? Domestic policy often forces the president to choose between reelection and good policy. University of Minnesota professor Paul Light has argued that reelection comes first: "If good policy follows, that is a bonus."[4] The potential conflict between political control and policy direction is an inherent tension in the presidency so that the real issue is one of balance between politics and policy.

The balance problem manifests itself most clearly in John Hart's "presidential branch," discussed in Chapter 1, that now stands alone, pitted against both the "executive agency branch" and the Congress. More and more power has been pulled to the presidential branch away from the agencies either by increasing the power of White House staff at the expense of the agency heads or by both increasing White House staff power and putting presidential loyalists with stronger ties to the president rather than the secretaries in key subcabinet positions. The latter control strategy has been labeled the "administrative presidency."[5] Nixon tried unsuccessfully to initiate an administrative presidency after his reelection. Reagan succeeded by reaching further down in the agencies with his subcabinet appointments than any president in history. The concept of the administrative presidency, as originally developed, postulated that the strong loyalties to the president would be determined in a president's first term with his loyalists put into key subcabinet positions after having demonstrated such commitment, most likely in a White House staff job. President Reagan rewrote this part of the theory at the outset of his first term by using a White House screening process that vetted potential subcabinet members for loyalty to Reagan. As Light told Hedrick Smith in one of his interviews for *The Power Game*: " 'They appointed people [to cabinet departments] who would cut their boss's throat to please the president. They are an entirely different breed of appointee than in the Carter, Nixon, Ford administrations. They are ideologically committed. There is no allegiance to the department, but to the Oval Office or the conservative cause.' "[6]

The dramatic presidential shift toward politics away from policy alters the kind of staff persons presidents want for advisers, and concomitantly the type, quantity, and quality of policy information, analysis, and advice demanded. As Terry Moe argued:

> Whatever his particular policy objectives, whatever his personality and style, the modern president is driven by . . . formidable expectations

to seek control over the structures and processes of government. In view of his limited constitutional powers and the sheer complexity of modern government, the president clearly needs the kind of information, expertise, and coordinating capacity that only a large organizational apparatus can provide. Yet the precise kind of institutional presidency he needs is determined by the kind of expectations that drive him. *He is not interested in efficiency or effectiveness or coordination per se, and does not give preeminence to the "neutral competence" these properties may seem to require.* He is a politician fundamentally concerned with the dynamics of political leadership and thus with political support and opposition, political strategy, and political tradeoffs. What he wants is an institutional system responsive to his needs as a political leader. He values organizational competence, to be sure, but what he seeks is "responsive competence," not neutral competence.[7]

The president's fixation on control over the structure and process of government characterizes the modern presidency. But wanting control does not indicate why it is sought. Control for what purpose and knowledge for what purpose are central, interrelated questions that cut to the heart of the issue of presidential objectives. Moe's answer is that a president "is not interested in efficiency or effectiveness or coordination per se." But Moe's three qualities are the essence of policy. The degree of efficiency and coordination signal how well policies or programs are being implemented and managed; effectiveness indicates the extent to which policies or programs are bringing intended substantive benefits (e.g., better education, health, or income support) to program participants.

Critical to the question of the degree of presidential control is how he views the executive agencies and his cabinet secretaries. If the secretaries are seen as enemies of the presidential branch and as likely to "go native" and favor the career civil servants over the president, the pressing need is for tight presidential control over the agencies that grants little or no discretion. In contrast, the president may understand that (1) public bureaucracies, like all large-scale organizations including those in the private sector, are prone to bureaucratic pathologies and need to be well-managed, (2) presidents formulate policies but agencies implement and manage them, so that (3) agencies are central, indispensable actors in presidential policy performance. Presidential control becomes a question of balance between presidential and agency staff because effective agency implementation and management require a significant amount of agency autonomy and flexibility. There are critical trade-offs between essential presidential control and essential agency power to act that demand a careful blending of power.

The milieu of electoral policies pushes toward a short-run perspective. The search is for policy ideas that will move quickly through

Congress or win public favor. Focusing on policy outcomes generally forces a longer time frame where competent staff and sound structure support the development of reliable information and analysis for policy formulation and implementation. The key question is how the presidential policy process affects both the development of a wide range of policy alternatives and the deliberation over these alternatives among the major policy proponents. The answer depends on the interaction between the individual president and his institutional structure.

The President's Mind

Important for our purposes is the wide range of various presidents' beliefs about the efficacy of sound, timely, relevant policy data and analysis in policy making. Nowhere is the difference more striking than in the case of Richard Nixon and Ronald Reagan. In the Nixon years, domestic policy analysis in the executive branch, as discussed, reached its high point, while Reagan took a dramatically different route:

> [P]olicymaking at the top of the Reagan White House operated with a few people using a most limited amount of information and analysis. The value of policy information and analysis was seen mainly as fuel feeding quick efforts to put out [political] fires. The two "conservative, anti-government, anti-bureaucracy" presidents arrived at diametrically opposite answers on the usefulness of policy analysis, making it clear that policy analysis is an available means to serve any political persuasion. Where it cannot compete is where ideology completely rules out facts that threaten its basic tenets.[8]

How dramatically a particular president can change executive branch policy analysis and research is limited by his persuasive powers, but the direction of the change rests upon that president's predilections (ideology, style, and personality) and policy competence.

The baggage a president carries into office is so crucial because there is no breathing period to learn on the job and on-the-job training can be costly—e.g., John Kennedy's Bay of Pigs fiasco or Clinton's task force of six hundred plus policy wonks set up under Hillary Clinton and Ira Magaziner to brainstorm health reform. Actually, the president-elect's predilections and competence become critical during the transition period when he makes the choices that will shape his administration by picking his top aides and cabinet members. Then January 20 likely will trigger the Rooseveltian hundred-days syndrome which demands an immediate all-out effort by an activist president lest an open policy window close. Alexander George lists as important in a president's baggage, his cognitive beliefs such as ideology and world view, political tactics and strategies, and a "sense of personal efficacy."[9]

Paul Light underscores a president's skills and experience in observing that "expertise is the most important resource that varies directly with the individual president."[10] A president's underlying skills and knowledge help determine both the intensity of his demand for policy information, analysis, and advice and the quality of the inputs he seeks. Deep presidential knowledge, or lack of it, about the value of information and analysis and about the often stringent organizational requirements for developing high-quality policy inputs will be a pivotal factor, not only in shaping presidential demand, but in how the supply function for policy ideas is structured and staffed.

An individual president's policy competence is a driving force determining his key appointments to the top White House and executive agency policy-making positions and in his structuring and staffing of the EOP policy-making processes. The authority that the president grants his inner circle policy advisers and their competence are major factors in determining both the quality of policy information and analysis and the extent to which these reach the president and fuel the policy debate. Further, presidential authority given by a president to his top White House staff appointees and his EOP structure establishes the relationship between that staff and the agency political executives, including the degree to which cabinet members are involved in key decisions about their agencies and have reasonable autonomy in managing their organizations. The agency political executives in turn will shape how their agencies treat information and analysis in their policy-making processes.

Strong policy competence does not mean a president will stress longer run institutional needs. However, policy ignorance makes the overemphasis on politics and the short run a near certainty. Three related points need making about a president's expertise and EOP structure and staffing. First, sound structure and process and competent staff are necessary components of effective presidential policy making but not sufficient to produce it. A strong White House policy-making process will not substitute for a president's policy incompetence. Mere structure and staffing are not enough. Second, political mastery comes first. A president must have the leadership skills to mobilize broad support for his policies. Without such mastery, it does not matter how well the president measures up on policy competence. With only such skills, a president is more technician than politician and cannot exert effective political leadership. Third, political mastery alone is not sufficient as the Reagan case made so clear. Also needed is policy competence, which has three components—strategic thinking capability, analytic skills, and organizational mastery. The broad vision of where a president wants to take the nation is fundamental to any presidency. Strategic thinking, however, goes beyond a broad vision to setting realistic objectives that reflect the concrete dimensions of the path of change. An effective president needs to have a probing mind capable of grasping complex policy ideas. No matter how much staff help a president has, his own critical analysis or lack of it will underpin his policy making. A president should demand a wide range of advice and be capable of assessing it. At the same time, a president's superior analytic skills can be destructive if he tries to be his own chief policy analyst as we will see in President Clinton's case.

Organizational mastery (competence) refers to both a president's understanding of how large-scale organizations work and his capacity to exercise influence over vast organizations in the executive branch. I have argued: "[O]rganizational mastery has been the pivotal missing ingredient in the presidencies since Eisenhower."[11] Burke, in discussing recent presidents, observed that their management practices—a similar concept to organizational mastery—are "likely to be critical in establishing an effective staff system and, ultimately, an effective presidency" and are "products of deliberate choice and less intimately connected to individual personality than the term [management] 'style' seems to convey."[12] This experience and knowledge about large-scale public institutions will be important to effective presidential governance whatever a president's personality characteristics, such as cognitive style, or his broad management model, such as formalistic or collegial.[13] A president's knowledge and experience set the standards for the quality of policy information, analysis, and advice and the level of policy sophistication in the vetting of these inputs. Each president's errors of commission, such as appointing incompetent top policy advisers or weak cabinet members, and omission, such as not demanding sound information and analysis, reverberate through the entire executive branch and shape its policy making. *Organizational mastery in the portfolio of policy skills stands as the critical link between a president's persona and the institutional presidency—between the man and his office.*

THE SUPPLY OF EXPERT POLICY ANALYSIS AND RESEARCH

Outside the federal government are a potpourri of organizations that package and market policy ideas; undertake information development, research studies, and policy analyses from which policy ideas are crafted; or do both. In his 1995 book on the public policy research industry, James McGann wrote of estimates of 1,200 to 1,400 of these institutions, which he labeled as "public policy research institutes or think tanks," and then restricted his own analysis to the 112 major institutions that are nonprofit, nongovernmental, nonuniversity affiliated, and generally are the dominant organizations in the industry.[14] Also fighting to be heard in the marketplace of policy ideas, mainly as packagers and marketers, will be hundreds of advocacy and lobbying groups representing industry and numerous causes. Getting their policy ideas out may range from published reports to private contacts with White House personnel or members of Congress and their staffs.

Within McGann's one hundred plus major public policy research institutes are a top handful (a much smaller subset of the 112 institutions), such as RAND, Brookings, and the American Enterprise Institute, that are distinguished by four factors: First, they have high quality standards like those in the university research community, and many members of their staffs are interchangeable with university faculty. Second, although there may be a well-known political bias (Brookings, somewhat left of center; AEI, a similar position on the right), these institutions bill themselves as nonpartisan, something that organizations such as the sharply right-of-center Heritage Foundation would not claim. These organizations' research results generally have high credibility with other analysts and researchers, although their interpretation of the findings may be discounted to some extent because of their political bias. Third, unlike the great bulk of university researchers, members of the top public policy research organizations spend most, if not all, of their time working on policy issues. Fourth, and relatedly, members of these prestigious organizations move back and forth between government and these organizations.

Political purity is not like pregnancy with its dichotomous dimension but rather has various shades. University policy researchers—even those unlike the author who have worked neither in a government policy office nor at a think tank—hardly stand above politics. The critical point is that policy researchers generally, and most especially in the social sciences, have become more ideological. The early public policy research organizations inside and outside the government saw their staffs as scientists operating within the boundaries of accepted research practices in studying policy issues. But as James Allen Smith wrote in 1991:

> Over the past fifteen years, marketing and promotion have done more to change the think tanks' definition of their role (and the public's perception of them) than have any other phenomenon. The metaphors of science and disinterested research that informed the creation and development of the first think tanks, naive as they sometimes were, have now given way to the [also naive] metaphor of the market and its corollaries of promotion, advocacy, and intellectual combat.[15]

While the industry still has research-oriented institutions that base their standards on the precepts of the university and try to maintain a nonpartisan image, the growth has occurred in the advocacy think tanks that promote their strong ideological perspective with a vengeance in the marketplace for policy ideas.

The best example of the two types are the Brookings Institution that can trace its origins to 1916 (the Brookings name was not used until 1927) and the Heritage Foundation established in 1973 to package and promote conservative ideas aggressively.[16] Alice Rivlin noted that books are Brookings' dominant product and "the Brookings research staff is much more like a graduate school faculty without a formal teaching program than like a bureaucracy."[17] Brookings not only has disciplinary scholars interchangeable with academics but people who have both solid research credentials and top-level public service, including the economist Charles Schultze who served as the Bureau of the Budget (now OMB) director in the Johnson administration and as chairman of the Council of Economic Advisers under President Jimmy Carter. Heritage is strikingly different as McGann observed: "My visit to Heritage revealed it is run much like a newspaper; weekly editorial meetings are held to set production schedules, identify hot issues and develop market strategies and policy angles. The dominant culture is clearly a corporate/journalistic one."[18] The typical staff member, who is youngish and without a Ph.D., writes easy-to-read issue briefs that can fit neatly in a crowded briefcase of a Congress member or executive branch political executive. Smith underscored that "Heritage is the salesman and promoter of ideas par excellence" and quotes its head, Edwin Feulner, Jr., as observing that his organization is " 'a secondhand dealer of ideas.' "[19] The foundation's innovative marketing effort, however, has been so successful in promoting their strong ideological views that even the research-oriented institutions that have nonpartisanship as a main objective have become active sellers of their products, albeit without the degree of partisan spin Heritage has employed.

If we consider these nongovernment entities including universities as a group, two aspects are critical. First, the organizations' main activity is producing policy information, research, and analysis. Politicians come and go; ideas gain, lose currency, and die (perhaps to be reborn); these nongovernmental entities continue to produce the raw materials for policy ideas year after year. Second, and closely related, the large number of persons in these organizations working on policy means that there is a ready supply of qualified people to staff and, if desired, expand the policy analysis effort within the federal government. *The key point is that the necessary human resources and institutional base for policy research and analysis have been available for a number of years so that the amount and type of policy work can be changed relatively quickly and the executive branch policy effort can be restaffed and/or expanded when a new president takes office.*

The rapid growth in the public policy research industry over the last thirty plus years has brought far more sound information and analysis that can illuminate the policy process. Even though the ideological bias has risen and the marketplace for policy ideas does at times seem like a political battlefield, Smith is broadly correct when he asserts that the market metaphor does not "portray the think tank in its most typical roles—operating discreetly to define the middle ground and providing an environment in which the knowledge of experts can be channeled to serve political ends. The sheer number of policy analysts and experts and their shared academic assumptions tend to narrow the terrain on which policies are contested."[20] The qualifications to that statement, however, are large. First, the policy debate fueled by the strong ideological bent of some of the think tanks has veered from the middle ground amid the partisan claims. Second, the credibility of the public policy research industry overall has suffered from the low quality of some think tanks' arguments or by misuse of information and analysis by opponents in the policy debate. Third, the partisan nature of the policy debate with the accompanying demand for instant information and analysis has been one factor driving out the long-term social research in such areas as health, education, and housing that potentially could concentrate debate sharply by indicating specifically how people behave and how incentives work. Gone are big research projects as exemplified by the RAND Corporation's health insurance experiment which Barbara Williams and Malcolm Palmatier labeled as that organization's "flagship" study and argued: "Rarely have government-funded domestic studies offered such long-term, adequately funded, 'hands-off' conditions for policy research. A 15-year, $100 million effort, it enrolled over 2,700 families at various sites . . . to observe the effects of various methods of financing health care on the use of health care and on personal health."[21] The absence in recent years of such costly, long-term experiments has severely limited the amount of policy information that can aid in major policy redirection.

In a roundtable "The Evolution of Policy Analysis and Evaluation" at the 1995 Association of Public Policy Analysis and Management annual meeting, David Lyon, now president of the Public Policy Institute of California and for many years an executive at RAND, offered some conflicting and disturbing remarks on where the policy research and analysis industry is today and what can be expected in the future. Lyon first observed that standards today are higher than ever, better work is being produced than earlier, and think tanks are a "growth industry." In response to a plaintive question from a young Ph.D. student in the audience asking exactly where this growth was, Lyon said that the new jobs were not necessarily for Ph.D.s interested in extensive research but rather for people to write pithy, ideologically slanted briefs to sell a partisan position. Also in speaking of growth, Lyon underscored how demand-responsive and aggressive the industry is in searching for new customers. The decline in federal demand for domestic policy research and analysis has been replaced by projects for state and local governments and business. My off-the-record interviews with public policy research institute personnel further illuminated the federal funding decline. Much of the current federal agency funding is for short-run, narrow projects—looking say at "little tweaks" in Medicare, not major issues requiring multiyear research. That is, federal domestic policy research dollars mainly buy studies on a tightly defined issue, which can be performed quickly, and eschew longer term efforts involving extensive external analysis of major questions.

By far the most disturbing issue raised by Lyon and my interviewees concerns the trend toward more and more ideological work by the industry. Lyon said "plain research" is seen as boring by clients who want answers that fit their biases and want them quickly. Lyon went on to claim that the greatest liability for the most prestigious think tanks is nonpartisanship. Interviewees from the policy research industry believe that the RANDs and Brookings of the world may be in trouble if they stress nonpartisan studies that do not promise rapid answers or results likely to fit the funders' predilections. These Cassandra-like warnings of danger may not come to pass, at least for the top nonpartisan organizations, but the threat of less and less nonpartisan work clearly can be seen. A counterargument is that nonpartisanship is a vestige of the earlier naive view of the objective scientist and that a multiple advocacy approach backed up by sound studies is the only sensible path in the harsh ideological climate of today. Much depends on whether standards remain high and ideology does not drive out sound studies and thereby undercut the capacity of the policy research industry over time.

The greatest threat is that rigorous studies of major social policy problems will dry up in the federal government without the devolution to the states of social programs bringing major new demand at the subnational level. Even if such demand materializes, and that is a huge if, uncoordinated studies across the states are likely to be more costly than an effort led by a single entity (e.g., the federal government or a consortium of states) and yield less useful data because of the lack of comparability. That is, public policy research industry growth and continuing high standards—surely questionable in the current political climate—do not ensure the development of sound social policy data needed to formulate and implement policy.

This history of social policy analysis and research sweeps from a period of almost no supply to the current environment of well over a thousand public policy research institutes. As to the earlier time, those who came to the Office of Economic Opportunity in 1965 were confronted by the supply shortage with almost no think tanks doing social policy research—defense drove the fledgling industry. OEO started and supported its own think tank, the Institute for Research on Poverty at the University of Wisconsin, funded the first domestic policy research at RAND, and developed both the first social policy experiment and the initial large-scale evaluation of a social program. Today, the industry is large and has a goodly number of institutes featuring high competence and a commitment to nonpartisan policy research where policy-relevant research is carried out using sound methods without political spin.

Currently, the major problem is not supply but demand both from the federal government and other governments and from a number of private organizations. The federal government has become less and less of an actor especially in the support of large-scale projects seeking new policy approaches (e.g., major experiments such as those in income maintenance and health) and evaluating the effectiveness of existing social programs. Devolution has shifted much more social program responsibility to the states but whether they will engage in major policy research including evaluations and experiments is unclear. On the nongovernment demand side, partisanship often rules and the desire is for answers that fit with the ideological position. The quest is not for sound policy data but for political ammunition. In this environment questionable information and slanted analyses may drive out high-quality work. Whether competition in the marketplace for policy ideas will vet the flawed studies and cast out the bad is far from clear. The task of looking to the future will concern us in later chapters. What we do know now is that the public policy research industry has grown dramatically in capacity and competence as has ideological fervor that devalues nonpartisan research competence. It could be a lethal mix tending to diminish both the number of nonpartisan public policy research institutes and the general credibility of think tank research and analysis.

INFORMATION AVAILABILITY AND VALIDITY

This section continues the discussion of supply and demand factors by delving into broader areas concerning the underlying quality of information, its availability as determined by the political and bureaucratic structure's philosophy on openness and secrecy, the demand for policy information by political elites and the public, and their competence to interpret it. All of the elements in some degree are affected by the growing complexity as policy information and the analyses based on it have increasingly become the domain of highly trained experts employing technically sophisticated methodologies and following complex institutional processes. The quality issue speaks to how and by whom policy information and analysis will be developed and validated. Whether the underlying data are sound is a fundamental question at the heart of policy analysis. All of the available methods are fallible because of the technical limitations of state-of-the-art tools and are subject to improper manipulation aimed at producing policy and/or political justification. Thus, a partisan political actor might tell the information expert, "I know the answer I want, now make the numbers support it." The critical professional issue is whether that analyst will have the commitment and the courage to employ existing research tenets and to follow accepted standards, even when the results conflict with the expert's own goals or those of the policy specialist's political masters.

Government efforts to keep critical information secret is an ever-present problem in the American political system. Also of concern are whether political elites and the public want sound, relevant, timely policy information and analyses (consumer demand) and whether these elites and citizens, using such information and analyses, will be able to evaluate its quality and interpret it reasonably (the competence dimension). In contrast to the case of quality, the concern is not with the available methodologies per se, but rather the level of demand by potential consumers, the willingness of those who have policy-relevant information to share it, and the competence of the various potential consumers to interpret policy information and analyses. The next two sections consider these various aspects of expert information.

The final section of this chapter looks at these issues in the context of personal computers, the Internet, and the other electronic means that have propelled us into the age of information overload. What we will see is that the new instantaneous, interactive communications devices, with their power to immediately transmit policy information to a vast number of people, raise serious problems for policy analysts, political elites, and the public. For example, information overload complicates the validation problem and raises the level of competence needed by the consumers of policy information and analysis. Data can be distorted in the marketplace for policy ideas by true believers, sent instantly into the fray, and difficult to refute because the increased electronic capacity to transmit dishonest numbers can make the time-consuming process of validation a losing game. Does the World Wide Web make more likely a battle of policy ideas based on unvalidated data that can be manipulated again and again and discharged instantly in a fiercely ideological battle where no holds are barred? Such issues go far beyond the technical and organizational aspects of the development and use of expert policy information and analysis to the issue of

American democracy itself as expert policy information and analysis reach greater and greater numbers of the public and in their pervasiveness become increasingly critical input that can enlighten or mislead their consumers.

Availability

This section treats generally the issue of the availability of government information, with much of the discussion drawing on works dating back to the 1950s and then considers *Secrecy*, the 1997 Report of the Commission on Protecting and Reducing Government Secrecy chaired by Senator Daniel Moynihan of New York.[22] The clear message of these works that essentially span the postwar era is that secrecy has flourished and continues to do so in the federal government. The Moynihan Commission Report concentrated on secrecy in the national security area, but it is equally relevant for the domestic arena. In its summary, the commission wrote: "Secrecy is a form of government regulation. Excessive secrecy has significant consequences for the national interest when, as a result, policymakers are not fully informed, government is not held accountable for its actions, and the public cannot engage in informed debate."[23]

Secrecy and openness are ever present issues, integral to democracy. Edward Shils, in his 1956 book, *The Torment of Secrecy*, defined secrecy as "the compulsory withholding of information, reinforced by the prospect of sanctions for disclosure."[24] Writing in 1961 in his seminal treatment of publicity and secrecy, Francis Rourke observed:

> [I]nsofar as secrecy in government seriously impedes the free flow of communications among citizens, it constitutes a real threat to the informed public discussion that is at the core of democracy. Where this occurs, it is not at all certain that a community should not choose, from the point of view of its own value system, to tolerate some measure of insecurity in order to gain access to information it needs in order to exercise influence over decisions on vital matters of public policy. This choice takes on increased rationality today from the fact that the net of secrecy has been thrown around so wide a span of scientific and technical data, far broader in scope than was the case in the day when nations had only to conceal a few matters of a purely military nature. A situation has been created in modern democracy in which governmental decisions affecting entire populations are made by a few individuals operating on the basis of information with which they, and they alone, are familiar.[25]

These words that foreshadowed Vietnam, Watergate, and Iran-contra are even more relevant today. Americans now find themselves trying to cope with the age-old problems of the governance of a democracy made more difficult by our society's size, diversity, and complexity. And few things complicate the equation of governance more than the pervasiveness of expert information within the complex bureaucratic structure of American government. Recent events make clear that our society badly needs a reasonable balance between openness and secrecy in trying to validate the information on which to base governmental decisions.

Openness may be defined as the right of citizens, including their nongovernmental organizations, to scrutinize what the government does and to interact with their elected representatives and other government officials in making the key decisions that affect their lives. A most fundamental concept of democracy, openness, can be viewed as an end in itself to be striven for even though its increase may bring abuses as well as benefits. Openness also can be seen as a means of improving the information and ideas available for decisions. Even if Americans were less distrusting of the motives of politicians and civil servants, a closed system would be dangerous because wrong information might go unchallenged or important data and different points of view might not be considered. Yet secrecy—or, to use a less loaded term, confidentiality—too has its place when it either protects against the disclosure of information that may harm individuals or groups or fosters a governmental setting in which people can carry out their legitimate functions in an orderly, timely, flexible manner. Few would deny that at times it will be useful, not just to those who govern but to society itself, to have a degree of shielding from public scrutiny of both information and advice. However, within large-scale bureaucratic institutions, the tendency is toward secrecy with it often becoming an end rather than only a means. Modern society must ever strive to keep the channels of access open. At issue are the degree of public access to policy-making information, the form of the institutional arrangements that will facilitate the public scrutiny of analytic information and advice, the nature of the role of public "validators," and the extent to which scrutiny can be carried out prior to the use of expert policy information in the decision-making process. Can a workable openness be found that is compatible both with democratic principles and with a legitimate degree of secrecy in the current complexity and contentiousness of American society?

A strong argument can be made for some shielding of information from public scrutiny or from other governmental entities (e.g., executive privilege vis à vis Congress). To simplify matters, let us confine this question to the kinds of information, ideas, and advice that do not involve national security or law enforcement issues or pose a threat to the privacy of individuals or organizations outside of the government (e.g., business secrets). Also excluded from discussion are individual privacy issues arising from the collection of information either through ongoing governmental processes (e.g., tax returns) or from surveys. The strongest argument for confidentiality in the case of the remaining kinds of information is that the threat of disclosure may stifle a willingness to develop unpopular points, to dissent, to argue for change, to speak one's mind—generally to be able to press one's ideas without fear that the words will be used later in a public attack. As Harold Wilensky has observed: "If men at the top feel vulnerable to attack for advice tentatively offered in private, they will keep quiet or avoid the strong expression of opinion; good intelligence will be lost. Passionate debate behind closed doors is as much a requirement of informed policy as the 'right to know.' "[26]

The case for confidentiality has its greatest force in the early stages of the decision process where public scrutiny may stifle creative thinking and speculative discussion. One issue is whether or not a policy analysis staff can investigate controversial or unpopular ideas and make recommendations concerning them without having to worry constantly that premature public exposure will embarrass or threaten the analysts or their organization. Indeed, there is the difficult question of whether some levels of advisory staff and their internal communications should be shielded completely from public scrutiny, including congressional investigation. Government conducted in a fishbowl setting well may exacerbate the negative bureaucratic tendencies to which public organizations are so susceptible. As the author has observed: "One important facet of public accountability is a studied appearance of extraordinary prudence in the sense of being purer than Caesar's wife. ... *Administrative purity may become a public manager's greatest concern.*"[27] A blind commitment to openness may focus many bureaucrats and even entire organizations almost exclusively upon safety rather than upon the substance of issues. They may—and often do— collect massive amounts of information to protect themselves, asking not whether it facilitates decision making but whether it may be useful in a later investigation.

Large-scale government cannot operate on the New England town meeting format. It is often difficult to see how decision-relevant information and analysis can be put before the public or its representatives in a reasonable time sequence in light of the very real time pressures of fiscal-year decision making and the desires of decision makers for flexibility. In spite of the formal organizational flow charts indicating highly structured and ordered decision-making procedures in the federal government, the process is often chaotic and likely to remain so. Last-minute changes, hurried conferences, and searches for information and so on can make public scrutiny at key points extremely difficult. However, if logistics and the dynamics of operations were the only barriers to disclosure, they could be overcome or at least mitigated materially, particularly with the new electronic techniques that enhance information availability and interactive processes. However, as Max Weber pointed out long ago in his classic discussions of bureaucracy, secrecy is a fundamental characteristic of administrative organizations in their search for power and image. A government or a business protects its secrets from those who might use those secrets to damage it. Also, secrecy can serve to provide greater orderliness and efficiency. Secrecy, then, has a firm basis in terms of organizational rationality.

Other reasons for secrecy within bureaucracy are reasonable from the point of view of the individual, but far more self-serving. The last thing that people want is to make available information or to allow outsiders to dig it out if that information shows errors, brings into question current policies, or in any way provides a basis for challenging action or authority. Further, the dangers of disclosure for the individual civil servant generally are much greater than those for classifying information as secret. Overt punishment—firing, censure, even jail sentences—has been meted out for leaks, not overclassification. The British have the Official Secrets Act; the United States is less specific, but law and custom still make it safer to suppress than to disclose. The push for bureaucratic secrecy goes deeper still. As Rourke has written: "[I]t is in the nature of bureaucracy to transform procedures into purposes [and] . . . an obsession with secrecy is but a single manifestation of this general tendency."[28] Secrecy becomes pathology, a culture of secrecy. Career bureaucrats are not the only ones who thrive on secrecy. So do the White House and Congress. President George Bush was paranoid about leaks; and, if anything, Clinton may have reached a higher plane yet. Those who deal in inside information find it is to their advantage for that information to be hidden from others. Other things being equal, the more closely held the information, the greater its value. Even more insidious is the tendency of elected officials to try to keep information from career staff. Recent presidents and White House staffs have looked upon career bureaucrats as the enemy; and, in frustration, the careerists may take on that role with leaks that drive the White House to even greater frenzy. Secrecy serves lots of people.

The Moynihan Commission is only the second statutory inquiry into secrecy in the past eight decades, with the earlier one being in 1955. The management, and more likely the mismanagement, of information has been an area of great concern in the mid-1990s. President Clinton issued Executive Order 12958 in 1995 with the objective of "seeking to bring the system for classifying, safeguarding, and declassifying national security information into line with our vision of American democracy in the post-Cold War world."[29] The Moynihan

Commission Report found that in most agencies "declassification under the Order. . . is occurring slowly."[30] The Electronic Freedom of Information Amendments of 1996 is the latest effort to increase agency responsiveness under the Freedom of Information Act. Relatedly, Congress in 1996 also passed the Information Technology Management Reform Act that established agency chief information officers with the job of "making proper decisions on information technology acquisitions" in recognition that the efforts by federal agencies to upgrade their information capacity through state-of-the-art electronic fixes have too often been disastrous, costly failures.[31] Graeme Browning, in the 1 March 1997 issue of the *National Journal,* reported that the Internal Revenue Service (IRS) had invested almost ten years and over $3 billion "on a computer modernization program that's fizzled. The story of how the agency's ambitious plans went so expensively awry isn't for the fiscally faint of heart."[32] Browning listed as culprits "turf wars, bureaucratic snafus and congressional micromanagement" but notes that those familiar with the working of IRS single out its "culture of secrecy and its tradition of stubborn self-reliance."[33]

The Moynihan Commission was seriously concerned about the pervasiveness of secrecy. First, they pinpointed one of the best markers of poor performance: the lack of reasonable oversight. The Commission found that ". . . oversight of agency implementation of declassification policies and practices barely exists."[34] The failure to monitor is the failure to see whether or not new policies and existing programs are being carried out as desired. Strong oversight over time is critical if materially greater openness for executive branch information and analysis is to be achieved. Historically, as noted, the pervasive cult of secrecy has brought heavy sanctions on persons who improperly declassified or leaked information but has excused overclassification. Call it bureaucratic pathology, call it the culture of secrecy, no real improvements will come without both committed, competent, hard-nosed monitoring to ferret out and punish specific acts of overclassification and a concerted, high-level effort to institutionalize a policy of reasonable bureaucratic openness.

The Moynihan Commission highlighted an even deeper flaw. The cold war mentality still prevails with its fetish for secrecy that tries to hide needed information at the expense of sound analysis:

> Which brings us to the present. The central fact is that we live today in an Information Age. Open sources give us the vast majority of what we need to know in order to make intelligent decisions. Sound *analysis,* far more than secrecy, is the key to our security. Meaning decisions made by people after debate and argument, in which both assumptions and conclusions are scrutinized with great care. Decisions made

by those who understand how to exploit the wealth and diversity of publicly available information, who no longer simply assume that clandestine collection, i.e., "stealing secrets," equates with greater intelligence. . . .

The Soviet Union is gone. But the secrecy system that grew in the United States in the long travail of the 20th century challenge to the Western democracies, culminating in the Cold War, is still in place as if nothing has changed. The system is massive, pervasive, evasive. Bureaucracies perpetuate themselves; regulations accumulate and become even more invasive.[35]

The secrecy problem continues in much the same outmoded form in domestic policy making where the secrecy that hides needed information is undercutting sound policy analysis. To paraphrase the Moynihan Commission: Sound analysis, far more than secrecy, is the key to more effective domestic policy making. The issue is not that a choice must be made between total secrecy and total openness but that the balance between the two must reflect the realities of the information age.

Validation

Several institutional processes used by individuals and groups (including the amorphous group termed "the public") for verifying information or ideas or for determining that a decision is legitimate need considering. Verification has to do with the accuracy of data and the soundness (internal logic, external reasonableness) of analysis and of ideas. "That's a well-thought-through piece of work" captures the soundness notion. Legitimacy stresses process. Has the decision reached followed the letter and the spirit of the law? A fair trial indicates the essence of legitimacy. As we will see, verification and legitimacy get tangled together. Be the issue that of verification, legitimacy, or both, we will refer to the process as that of validation. Two critical elements will be stressed in looking at specific validation processes: (1) the framework for submitting findings and claims to scrutiny and challenge and (2) the degree of access by parties at interest prior to the making of decision. In looking at validation processes, I start with the scientific model for two reasons. First, rightly or wrongly, it is the model to which people often look when thinking about a rigorous process of checking and challenging data and interpretations. Second, and relatedly, information experts generally have had research backgrounds and think in terms of this process.

The scientific disciplines have a well-established validation process utilizing scrutiny and competition. Generally speaking, the results of a research project will be made available publicly to be analyzed and challenged by a researcher's peers. In the ideal case, the study will provide sufficient detail about data and the design and procedures used to obtain it so that other researchers *independently* may replicate the results by rerunning the experiment or reworking the data analysis if the accuracy of the information itself is not subject to challenge as may be the case with widely available secondary data. Under such circumstances, the integrity of the original researcher and his or her organization in a meaningful sense may be of little consequence because the validating process makes it unnecessary to take anything on faith or reputation. Ideas and interpretations can run a similar course. First, if the data base contains "unvalidated" information, it will be subjected to the procedures discussed above. Second, interpretations and ideas presented will be scrutinized for internal (logical) consistency and for external consistency in terms of other information and theory. If the new notion challenges or conflicts with existing ones, it may be subjected to strong attacks by proponents of the established ideas. If a new thesis survives all of these tests, it becomes the accepted doctrine or at least one of several accepted ones. After that, other scholars may challenge the thesis with new evidence or reinterpretations of existing evidence, or use it as a base for developing testable hypotheses that may support, invalidate, or alter it markedly. This paragraph has presented an idealized version of how science progresses. The intent is not to suggest that the practitioners in the scientific disciplines do not err both through commission, such as letting shoddy ideas slip through, and omission, such as ignoring important problems. Nor are scientists simply objective searchers for truth who would never take unwarranted shortcuts, stoop to advocacy, or falsely accuse their rivals. At the same time, the scientific process over time has proved to be a viable means of validating information and ideas within the academic disciplines.

A number of problems arise in using this mechanism in the complex and often hurried bureaucratic process of governmental decision making. First, the scientific community's validating structure is so well-established, so smoothly functioning, that we hardly realize its complexities and the difficulties of using the process for activities, including policy research and analysis, that may be outside the mainstream of scholarly pursuits. The existing scientific communications network made up of scholarly publications, disciplinary societies, and other formal and informal means of exchanging and assessing data and ideas may be difficult to use if policy information and interpretations are in the wrong form, say in an internal document or in an outside consultant's report. This may be true especially if the document blends information with bureaucratic and political factors so that scientists may be uncomfortable with or incapable of making meaningful judgments about the information used. Second, and even more debilitating, is the fact that the scientific process can be tedious and time-consuming. Determining the validity of a new theory may take a number of years, and science may be quite willing to wait—to forego action until sufficient results are in to make a relatively strong case for the new theory. For long periods of time, there may be no verdict so that competing interpretations will be allowed to stand. In a number of domestic policy areas, we simply may not have the available evidence to rule out alternative theories, and such competing theories may indicate diametrically different policies. Government decision making may not permit such time delay or lack of resolution.

The phrase "formal adversary process" denotes an established legal framework such as the judicial system or the administrative hearing mechanism of government agencies. The process is designed explicitly to enable individuals or groups to settle disputed issues in such a way that at the end of the process they and others will view the decision as legitimate. The essence of the ideal process is that evidence (information and interpretation) is presented and directly challenged by advocates. These advocates, who are clearly designated as such (e.g., lawyers for plaintiff and defendant), must argue within the constraints of a detailed set of rules concerning admissibility and procedures. The argument will be before relatively impartial observers who are charged either with enforcing the rules of evidence and procedure, rendering a decision on the merits of the case as presented by the advocates, or both. The challenge mechanism and the capacity to resolve diverse issues with reasonable speed, including those that blend scientific, social, and bureaucratic/political issues, make the adversary process an appealing validation mechanism for treating disputes over information and interpretations. But it has obvious flaws. As Wilensky has observed:

> The deficiencies of adversary procedure are obvious. A circus atmosphere may develop as attorneys become preoccupied with press releases rather than legal briefs, with courtroom histrionics rather than reasoned argument ("When you can't win a case, jaw it"). . . . But these limitations, not inevitable, are offset by the overriding advantages of partisan advocacy, including the opportunity to test the credibility of witnesses through cross-examination. In or out of court, the adversary process is the best way to assure that assertions are exposed to systematic scrutiny by men with countervailing interests who are motivated to press hard. . . .
>
> [A]lthough adversary proceedings do not involve critical experimental tests, they resemble science in their systematic regulation of the clash of views, and they have the additional advantage of sensitivity to political interests, greater availability to non-expert officials and judges, and speed.[36]

Wilensky's point about the resemblance between scientific procedures and the adversary process has been made by a number of people. Wilensky himself has argued that the claim to neutrality or objectivity of science is often overplayed and that many scientific advances have come about through the resolution of conflicting scientific models presented by unabashed advocates.[37] Science often does have many of the features of the formal adversary process, but the advocacy model is not a perfect substitute for the scientific validation process. It is critical to keep in mind that the formal adversary process is an extremely demanding one with a number of key elements. To the extent that key elements are omitted or compromised, the adversary process may not be a useful validation mechanism. These elements include the impartiality of the judgment process, the underlying strength and usefulness of rules of evidence and the capacity to enforce them, the competency of the advocates, and the quality and sufficiency of the evidence.

Far more important for vetting policy information and analysis are less formal approaches exemplified by Alexander George's multiple advocacy model spelled out in 1972 and elaborated on by Professor George and others.[38] The starting point for a viable multiple advocacy process is the relative impartiality—at least the basic skepticism—of the final decision maker vis à vis competing claimants. He or she, in effect, must act as a magistrate. This role does not demand that a final decision maker strike an Olympian pose standing above the fray as a disinterested party; however, he or she cannot have a closed mind and be unwilling to listen with a reasonable degree of openness to various inside advisers and outside advocates. An adversary model is a charade if decision makers are unwilling to pay any attention to the arguments of the advocates.

By stimulating competition among advocates, top decision makers can gain greater control over information. The various power players below top decision makers often "work" to shut them off from important information. Competition among advocates, to the extent it can ferret out information, serves decision makers in their search for power. Competition, rivalry, and advocacy are all there to be used by the decision maker. The fundamental argument is that it is in the self-interest of a principal decision maker to place subordinates in competition so as to gain from the interplay of their self-interests. Bureaucracy often tries to minimize competition, to have tables of organization and clear functional lines that emphasize cooperation. But the organizational neatness that makes for order in the life of the bureaucrat can render the organization complacent or arrogant toward criticism and questioning. Too much cooperation *within* can be deadening. The threat of scrutiny and challenge should be there, both from within and without.

George's multiple advocacy model, which stresses the need for continuing decision-maker leadership, a reasonable power balance among advocates, and enough time to deliberate, still has much merit and provides a solid foundation for further discussion about managing an advocacy process to vet policy information and analysis in a public decision-making process. A reasonable balance of power among advisers has the purpose of providing a better flow of information to the decision makers with the expectation that it will enhance their knowledge and hence their power. In organizational terms, the distribution of resources among advocates should be controlled (regulated, bounded) so that the potential for a fair fight continues over time. Moreover, the notion of a balance of power among partisan advocates is a dynamic one. Although advocates' institutional status and functions on an organization chart may indicate a reasonable power balance, the most important ingredients, such as competence and bargaining skills, are not reflected in the organizational structure. Further, a relatively balanced setting may deteriorate over time. A decision maker interested in a fair fight may have to take active—often unpleasant, if not heroic—steps to curb the power of a staff adviser or a line operator so as to restore what is always likely to be a delicate balance. In short, the power balance must be managed over time, off the organization chart, and this may take a great deal of doing.

Power balance alone is not the only consideration in an area such as policy analysis. Also critical are the absolute levels of technical resources and analytic capability, the rules of evidence, and the incentive structure governing information development and use. There are no absolutes. What constitutes acceptable or unacceptable behavior in treating information will be a matter of judgment with a number of gradations. For example, tampering with raw data can end a career in science; pushing evidence too far or omitting contradictory evidence from another study may only chip away slightly at a person's reputation unless the violation is flagrant. In controversies over policy issues where one finds conflicting evidence and theory, strongly committed advocates, who are unlikely to be fair or balanced, often operate with ideological blinders. Such behavior, however, may not be a major problem if the criteria for information acceptability, professional standards, and rigorous procedures can make inaccuracy, selectivity, and the failure to search widely costly to analysts in terms of their credibility and influence. For the advocacy model to work, the professional and organizational reputation of the analyst must be put in jeopardy for sloppy or unprincipled performance.

Although the discussion thus far has stressed structural and process issues, the most crucial factors are individual qualities including analytic and bureaucratic competence, the commitment to professional standards and the courage to follow them, and the willingness or capacity of a decision maker to tolerate the conflict and ambiguity. Even when the right kind of decision maker emerges, the nature of the desired process remains difficult to specify in precise terms. Needed is a controlled tension that moves an organization beyond the deadening effect of forced bureaucratic consensus, yet constrains advocates' behavior sufficiently through institutional and professional standards to keep the power of the advocates in bounds. With detailed prescriptions about structure and function, some precision can be added. But the fact remains that no organization chart or rules—basically static concepts—will capture the required leadership behavior or the dynamics of how people should interact in an organization. No structural prescriptions are certain to work and none cannot be subverted. That is an uncomfortable bureaucratic fact of life.

THE EMERGING ELECTRONIC REPUBLIC AND INSTITUTIONAL POLICY ANALYSIS

The world of executive branch institutional policy analysis has been invaded by the electronic world via the presidency and today's hyperpolitics. Robert Denton, writing in 1988, labeled the Reagan years as the "primetime presidency," claimed that governing for Reagan meant "controlling the videos in the evening news," and went even further to pronounce television as "the primary tool and battleground for governing the nation."[39] Although Denton went too far in his argument about television's role in presidential governance, who today can doubt the impact of electronic communications where both talk radio and the Internet have gained increasing importance in the political environment since Denton wrote. Paul Light used the Reagan experience to explore another problem, what he labels as "short-term-itis."[40] The interaction of political forces and the Reagan distaste for policy analysis, as Light emphasized, had a devastating impact on the executive branch analytic structure:

> [T]he incentives and constraints that Presidents now face are overwhelmingly directed to short-term goals. They are increasingly pols and pols only. . . . Reagan's year of greatest legislative achievement, 1981, was built almost entirely on short-term policy proposals designed to pay off quickly, whether politically or economically. . . .
>
> [The] disinvestment in the government's policy planning capacity may be one of the most important long-term consequences of the Reagan Presidency. . . . As Stockman learned, it may take as much analysis and planning to dismantle a program as it does to create one. . . .
>
> If it was a place in history that Reagan wanted, he earned it through a legacy of continuing deficits and what Walter Williams calls the anti-

analytic Presidency. In winning his war against the traditional sources of ideas, Reagan may have ensured that his successors will have little choice but to go short-term, too.[41]

In discussing the highly analytic Clinton, a veteran of thirty years experience with federal analytic offices and think tanks told me that Clinton had limited interest in extended policy research, such as social experiments, because his perspective was so short-term. Whether presidential predilection or the play of politics or a complex interaction of the two drove Clinton is not something this author or even the president himself can answer definitively. However, it is clear that the pressure for instant action—Light's short-term-itis—dominates the current political system and may have shaped how the first "boomer" president thought about politics in his formative years.

Before turning to the history of earlier federal policy analysis offices and their efforts to develop sound policy information, efforts that indicate what needs to be done currently to improve executive branch policy analysis and research, two points need making. First, a president is not helpless before the press of hyperpolitics and can still make dramatic improvements in the executive analytic process. Second, and relatedly, the emerging electronic capacity is a means that can be used either to improve the flow of sound policy information and analysis in the executive branch or to generate and transmit misleading information and analysis to the public. The first point can be addressed quickly; however, the potential and the peril of the electronic era needs more elaboration. As to point one, the need is for a president who can and will exert the "organizational mastery [that] has been the pivotal missing ingredient in the presidencies since Eisenhower."[42] Required of a president are both organizational competence and a continuing commitment to establish an orderly policy-making process that values in-depth analysis and the development of needed policy information over time. Today's hyperpolitics, with its pressures toward short-term-itis and instant information to feed the electronic media, is hardly conducive to orderly process. Still, I will argue that much about what needs to be done to improve the executive branch analytic process is now known; that political forces do not rule out the implementation of such changes; that the president is the person who must lead the change; and that getting the right leader is the most difficult task, not technical ones.

The new electronic technologies can help the policy information and analysis effort succeed, or destroy it. The loss, if that is the case, will do damage not only to the federal policy-making process but to the basic structure of American democracy. The new electronic technologies afford those who develop expert policy information and analysis a set of tools that can enhance the collection and manipulation of that information and make its transmission to the policy research community, political elites and their institutions, and the voting public far quicker and cheaper than anytime in the past. This technology not only exists today but is likely to improve by leaps and bounds, if recent history is any guide, so as to support wider and wider public participation in policy making. Visions of an increasingly large, committed, and active public with the technical capacity to interact with policymakers at all levels of government jump to mind. The promise is American democracy restored in a well-functioning free marketplace of policy ideas fueled by honest numbers and honest analysis. But whether this desirable state comes to pass depends on two questions that embody the factors of quality, supply, and demand: Will relevant, sound, timely policy information and analysis be produced and made available to potential consumers? Will consumers be willing and able to cope with the plethora of information that ranges from the best that can be produced by state-of-the-art techniques properly used to information distorted to propagandize the public?

The fundamental issue is whether the powerful new information technologies will be used to foster or to thwart American democracy. The latter may be more likely. In *The Electronic Republic: Reshaping Democracy in the Information Age*, Lawrence Grossman, who has been president of both PBS and NBC News, has argued:

> The economics of political information—solid, responsible, and meaningful information about significant issues in contrast to gossip, sensationalism, personal scandal, and the like—do not encourage its widespread distribution in the telecommunications marketplace. The commercial potential of major documentaries, serious discussions, public affairs forums, and analytical pieces about important issues is severely limited, especially if the issues involved are intensely controversial.[43]

The term "political information" is used broadly by Grossman to include important information on politics and policy. As to the latter, a critical component is "solid, responsive, and meaningful [policy] information about significant issues." Grossman's scarce political information is the holy grail of policy analysis. As I wrote in 1971: "The degree of policy relevance of information . . . depends on how pertinent the question is, how sound the work behind it, and how timely it is."[44]

What has changed in the last quarter century is not the need for sound, relevant, timely policy information but the degree to which the new technologies force together the two different worlds of government policy analysis and research and of the Electronic Republic. The former still clings, as much as it can, to limited access, particularly in the early stages of information development and analysis. The latter is the extreme of open, unregulated exchange where the rule of no rules makes validation extremely difficult. The coming together of these two vastly different environments means that scholars concerned primarily with one of the worlds run the risk, in ignoring the other one, of distorting their findings. The two worlds have another critical overlap from the book's perspective. The validation requirements that demand high professional standards, skills, and integrity and a sound institutional structure and process still hold and so does the need for consumer competence. Put differently, technical wizardry does not wipe out these demands and well may make the development and use of sound expert information harder rather than easier. The interactive speed of the electronic devices can be employed to circulate policy information and analysis for vetting far more rapidly and widely; but, on the deleterious consequences side, this capacity can overwhelm the validation system with questionable policy information and analysis. The new techniques may expand openness yet threaten needed confidentiality in early deliberations. One does not need to be a Luddite to recognize that the electronic devices are means, not ends, to use for good or evil and that improvements generally are oversold as to their strengths with weaknesses either played down or unsuspected. As we move to the less visible world of policy research and analysis, the same problems and difficulties occur again and again and are relevant to the future. Sadly, no technological fix can produce sound, timely, relevant data at the press of a button.

NOTES

1. Joseph A. Pika, "Management Style and the Organizational Matrix: Studying White House Operations," *Administration and Society*, vol. 20 no. 1 (May 1988), pp. 4–5.

2. Ibid., p. 5.

3. Roger B. Porter, *Presidential Decision Making: The Economic Policy Board*, Cambridge University Press, 1980, p. 230.

4. Paul C. Light, *The President's Agenda: Domestic Policy Choice from Kennedy to Reagan*, Johns Hopkins University Press, Revised Edition, 1991, p. 221.

5. Richard P. Nathan, *The Plot That Failed: Nixon and the Administrative Presidency*, Wiley, 1975.

6. Quoted in Hedrick Smith, *The Power Game: How Washington Works*, Random House, 1988, p. 302–303.

7. Terry M. Moe, "The Politicized Presidency," in John E. Chubb and Paul E. Peterson (eds.), *The New Direction in American Politics*, Brookings, 1985, p. 239, emphasis added.

8. Walter Williams, *Mismanaging America: The Rise of the Anti-Analytic Presidency*, University Press of Kansas, 1990, p. 83.

9. Alexander L. George, *Presidential Decisionmaking in Foreign Policy: The Effective Use of Information and Advice*, Westview Press, 1980, p. 5.

10. Light, *The President's Agenda*, p. 231.

11. Williams, *Mismanaging America*, p. 119.

12. John P. Burke, *The Institutional Presidency*, Johns Hopkins University Press, 1992, pp. 116 and 190.

13. George, *Presidential Decisionmaking in Foreign Policy*, p. 139.

14. James G. McGann, *The Competition for Dollars, Scholars, and Influence in the Public Policy Research Industry*, University Press of America, 1995, pp. 3–4.

15. James Allen Smith, *The Idea Brokers: Think Tanks and the Rise of the Policy Elite*, Free Press, 1991, p. 194.

16. McGann, *The Competition for Dollars, Scholars, and Influence in the Public Policy Research Industry*, pp. 46–53.

17. Alice M. Rivlin, "Policy Analysis at The Brookings Institution," in Carol H. Weiss (ed.), *Organizations for Policy Analysis: Helping Government Think*, Sage, 1991, p. 22.

18. McGann, *The Competition for Dollars, Scholars, and Influence in the Public Policy Research Industry*, p. 130.

19. Smith, *The Idea Brokers*, pp. 200–201.

20. Ibid., p. 213.

21. Barbara R. Williams and Malcolm A. Palmatier, "The RAND Corporation," in Weiss (ed.), *Organizations for Policy Analysis*, p. 57.

22. *Secrecy*, Report of the Commission on Protecting and Reducing Government Secrecy, Senate Document 105–2 Pursuant to Public Law 236, 103rd Congress, U.S. Government Printing Office, 1997.

23. Ibid., p. xxi.

24. Edward A. Shils, *The Torment of Secrecy*, Free Press, 1956, p. 26.

25. Francis E. Rourke, *Secrecy and Publicity*, Johns Hopkins University Press, 1961, pp. 226–227.

26. Harold L. Wilensky, *Organizational Intelligence: Knowledge and Policy in Government and Industry*, Basic Books, 1967, p. 138.

27. Walter Williams, *Social Policy Research and Analysis: The Experience in the Federal Social Agencies*, Elsevier, 1971, p. 135, emphasis in the original.

28. Rourke, *Secrecy and Publicity*, p. 22.

29. Quoted in *Secrecy*, p. 55.

30. Ibid., p. 56.

31. Ibid., p. 107.

32. Graeme Browning, "Crashing Computers," *National Journal*, March 1, 1997, p. 414.

33. Ibid., p. 415.

34. *Secrecy*, p. 66.

35. Ibid., pp. A75–A77, italics in the original.

36. Wilensky, *Organizational Intelligence*, pp. 152–153.

37. Ibid., p. 153.

38. Alexander L. George, "The Case for Multiple Advocacy in Making Foreign Policy," *American Political Science Review*, September 1972, pp. 751–785.

39. Robert E. Denton Jr., *The Primetime Presidency of Ronald Reagan: The Era of the Television Presidency*, Praeger, 1988, pp. xii, 71, and 91.

40. Light, *The President's Agenda*, pp. 250–276.

41. Ibid., pp. 236, 263, and 276.

42. Williams, *Mismanaging America*, p. 119.

43. Lawrence K. Grossman, *The Electronic Republic: Reshaping Democracy in the Information Age*, Viking, 1995, p. 182–183.

44. Williams, *Social Policy Research and Analysis*, p. 57.

3 | The Golden Age of Executive Branch Policy Analysis

The years 1965–76 stand as the golden era of executive branch—and particularly agency—social policy analysis where social agency central analytic staffs sprang up and reached their apex. A reviewer of this book chided me on labeling a past period, particularly one in which I was involved, a golden age. So I need to be clear what I mean when claiming the first years of social policy analysis were the best ones. There is a one sentence short answer that paraphrases Bill Clinton's advisers' refrain that "it's the economy, stupid," pointing out that "it's politics, stupid." The argument most certainly is not that the policy analysts of yore were a superior breed. What the earlier analysts and their offices had going for them was a political environment marked by general optimism, the belief that research could solve policy problems, and political leaders willing to pay for large-scale studies. Nor had the White House moved to the point where agency analytic offices had lost both status and the resources to support extensive policy research, including evaluations and experiments. In contrast, the current political environment features ideological fervor, a power centralization in the White House, a constant budget-cutting mentality, and a distaste for poverty outlays. This combination has brought a dark period for social policy analysis and research, despite the numerous competent policy analysts and the sophisticated technology of today.

To investigate how and why policy analysis in its greatest era developed as it did, the five arresting figures who set the tone for the period need to be considered. It was a time dominated by two towering leaders—Lyndon Johnson and Richard Nixon—who blended extraordinary capabilities with darker sides that shaped (or misshaped) their policy-making processes. At the top of the list of supporting actors in the policy analysis story are John Kennedy, Robert McNamara, and Henry Kissinger. Gerald Ford, the one ordinary person, at least by the standards of the five names mentioned above, deserves a credit too because he sought to bring back the Eisenhower approach to policy making. The latter, while not on stage, casts a long shadow because of his organizational mastery, although his great institutional expertise was not recognized at the time, and this turned out to be a critical factor in the development of executive branch policy analysis.

This chapter focuses on the key players and on the model analytic office in the golden age of the executive branch social policy analysis. Also discussed is national security policy analysis under Presidents John Kennedy and Richard Nixon, two cases essential to understanding the social policy analysis efforts. The upcoming section looks at the five main actors and Dwight Eisenhower. The Eisenhower discussion lays out my views on organizational mastery and presidential governance and their relationship to the development and use of policy information and analysis. As indicated in Chapter 1, this historical critique is primarily about executive branch policy analysis, not about how individual presidents or their political appointees handled specific policies or performed overall. However, the book does make assessments of traits, such as secrecy, commitment to objectives, and courage, as will be clear as we proceed. After looking at the key actors, the chapter turns to the history's longest consideration of national security policy analysis because that effort in the early years impinged heavily on social policy analysis both in the agencies and the presidency. For example, the Office of Economic Opportunity (OEO) central analysis staff was modeled on Secretary McNamara's Department of Defense analytic effort and President Nixon's Domestic Council and its policy staff drew heavily on the National Security Council experience. The subsequent sections focus on executive agency and presidential social policy analysis, with the brief exception of President Ford's Economic Policy Board, which offers an excellent example of multiple advocacy in action. Social policy analysis reached its heights of power and accomplishment in the OEO and in the Department of Health, Education and Welfare (HEW) (now the Department of Health and Human Services) in the Johnson, Nixon, and Carter administrations. The model analytic office began in OEO and went to HEW at OEO's demise. The fullest social policy analysis effort came in the Nixon years with the decline beginning under Carter. This chapter treats this agency experience, and the next chapter extends this portrait by focusing in-depth on the first of the federal social policy experiments—the OEO New Jersey negative income tax study.

THE MAIN ACTORS PLUS IKE

A brief discussion on effective presidential governance provides a prelude for considering the dominant actors in policy analysis for the period 1961–76. To do so, the notion of the anti-bureaucratic, anti-government presidency needs defining. The label "anti-bureaucratic, anti-government presidency" describes an administration where the chief executive attacks both the government itself and its permanent staffs and distrusts the cabinet secretaries and the agency subcabinets because they may try to represent the interests of the agency rather than those of the president. Government bashing by a president may be restricted to his winning campaign but can continue in office. President Reagan is the champion in railing against government for eight years, never really viewing himself and his top aides as part of it. Bill Clinton too has continued to castigate "big government" during his presidency. The anti-bureaucratic president fears civil servants will undermine his presidency and also may worry that his agency political executives either cannot withstand the careerists' efforts to turn them from full presidential loyalty or else have their own agendas.

Effective presidential governance demands realism about government itself, civil servants, and political appointees. As to the former, the president would understand that the federal government can be a problem, a solution or, more likely, both mixed together. The term "bureaucratic pathology" is hardly an empty theoretical construct. Civil servants can operate only to fulfill organizational and/or personal goals in defiance of a president, his political executives, or both. Political executives too may play their own games at the expense of the president and perhaps their agencies. Presidents can fight such behavior both through wise appointments and personal leadership, and further demand high organizational competence from political appointees. The requirements for a reasonable shot at effective presidential governance can now be set out in a long paragraph quoted from my *Mismanaging America* that followed policy analysis through the Reagan presidency, noting that the subsequent two presidencies reinforce the argument:

> Sound EOP analytic structure and strong agencies are highly interrelated in terms of effective presidential governance and ultimately of desirable societal outcomes. On the one hand, the White House needs to develop a strong analytic structure that supports both policy formulation and the monitoring of the implementation of presidential policies. On the other hand, the actual implementation must be carried out by the agencies. Implementation can be monitored within the EOP analytic structure but not executed from it. To weaken agencies in order to gain political control strikes at the heart of the organizational capacity needed for strong presidential governance. Sound information and analysis are not intrinsically valuable but they acquire value through use in decision-making and management—that is, in the policymaking process. *Sound policy analysis without underlying organizational capacity and competence to implement formulated policies is of limited value, except to indicate the basic organizational deficiencies that block effective policies.* The anti-bureaucratic, anti-government presidents did not appreciate this organizational truth and thereby diminished the value of sound information and analysis by

undercutting agency capacity to manage implementation and operations. This is why the Eisenhower presidency is so critical. The big difference between Eisenhower and the anti-bureaucratic, anti-government presidents is organizational competence. Eisenhower was the master of large-scale organizational processes, of obtaining well-critiqued, well-thought-through policy alternatives, and of choosing cabinet and staff based on their particular skills and their blend of skills. Later presidents often lacked in-depth experience with large-scale public organizations. They did not understand the intricate processes of these large institutions and had little appreciation of fitting the person with the specialized demands of the job, a debilitating flaw. Presidential organizational mastery had been the missing link in the presidential policy equation. Its absence has contributed materially to both inept presidential governance and deleterious policy outcomes.[1]

Two final points need making before turning to the main actors. The first is to emphasize again the pivotal role of the president in shaping the development and use of policy analysis in the executive branch. A newly elected president's predilections, competence, and key personnel decisions are the main *new* factors determining whether the executive branch will be structured and staffed so that sound policy information and analysis will be developed and can be well-used in the White House and the executive agencies in policy formulation, implementation, and management. Such a statement in no way denies the importance of existing competence levels. However, any president at his inauguration inherits an institutional legacy of agency and EOP structures, procedures, and career staffs that provides a starting base, which generally will not be markedly different from the one inherited by his predecessor. Thus, the president himself is the potentially volatile factor in the mix. Second, organizational mastery can be employed for laudable or reprehensible purposes. High organizational competence in leaders does not speak to whether they are courageous or high-principled or open-minded or decisive. To claim Eisenhower is *the* organizational president of the modern presidency is not to argue he is that era's greatest president. But the lack of organizational competence can thwart the president possessed of the loftiest goals and the stoutest heart. If nothing else, this historical journey bespeaks the validity of these two points.

John Kennedy's presidency began the Washington invasion by policy analysts when Secretary Robert McNamara established an analytic operation in the Department of Defense. (Kennedy will be discussed again at some length in Chapter 7 on the Clinton administration because the two men are so alike in being highly intelligent, extremely rational, open-minded, and oriented toward verbal exchanges in their policy deliberations while at the same time lacking organizational competence and spurning a well-ordered White House policy-making process.) This combination of high analytic skills and orientation and organizational incompetence that marked President Kennedy was to have a profound effect on policy analysis. Of Robert McNamara who created the first analytic unit staffed by the new breed of policy information experts, Richard Reeves wrote: "He was, above all, a rationalist, like his boss the President."[2] This analytically oriented secretary became the dominant adviser in the national security area to the highly analytic president, and the DOD analytic operation played a major role in underpinning McNamara's advice through the flow of its policy information and analysis.

President Kennedy's organizational inexperience and the then current flawed assessment of Eisenhower as trapped in a stultifying policy-making process led Kennedy to spurn immediately as policy advisers most of his cabinet secretaries and their career civil servants and to centralize control in the White House. The great irony is that Dwight Eisenhower, who had commanded the Allied forces in Europe in World War II and had vast organizational knowledge and highly honed skills, had been viewed incorrectly in 1960 as a dolt dominated by staff, while John Kennedy, who had commanded a small boat in World War II and had the most limited organizational experience and competence, had been hailed in 1960 as a president who could create a modern organizational presidency. Fred Greenstein, whose book is revealingly entitled *The Hidden-Hand Presidency: Eisenhower as Leader*, portrayed the real Eisenhower:

> Eisenhower's capacity to think organizationally—to conceive policy problems in terms of the formal and informal group processes through which they could best be clarified and implemented—is of course far less transferable than the specific instruments and arrangements he employed. . . . Eisenhower was far more concerned than either of them [Kennedy and Franklin Roosevelt] to build into his routines the requirements that policies be exposed to "multiple advocacy." . . . Eisenhower's keenness as an organizer of advice he received was rooted in his makeup and experience. . . . [H]is formal procedures . . . [supported the] rigorous staff work and systematic institutional back-up for policymaking [that are] persistently lacking in modern presidencies, as is the teamwork that is an informal offshoot of this procedure.[3]

Eisenhower stands out as the organizational genius of the modern presidency, the master of formal and informal processes. Multiple advocacy produced a flow of sound policy information and analysis. Although he did not start the policy analysis offices per se, he understood the value of sound analysis and, most of all, the organizational requirements for using it effectively. The portrayal of his successors will not show such organizational mastery.

Although Kennedy was not anti-government, only anti-bureaucratic, he started the attack on the cabinet, not just as principal presidential advisers, but as the chief executive officers (CEOs) of their agencies. The change did not mean that no powerful secretary could be a key presidential adviser and master of his or her department with McNamara as clear example. But the Republican McNamara had demanded and received "the right of final approval of all appointments in his department," and through his skills won a remarkable autonomy over DOD as secretary.[4] Kennedy's secretary of state, Dean Rusk, certainly had no such autonomy, and that limiting status for secretaries became increasingly likely over time.

Based on the perceived success of the DOD analytic office, President Lyndon Johnson had the Bureau of the Budget draw on that experience to develop an October 1965 directive establishing central analytic offices in federal departments and agencies. In August of that year, the president had spoken in glowing terms of the power of policy analysis:

> This morning I have just concluded a breakfast meeting with the Cabinet and the heads of Federal agencies and I am asking each of them to immediately begin to introduce a very new and very revolutionary system of planning and programming and budgeting throughout the vast Federal government, so that through the tools of modern management the full promise of a finer life can be brought to each American at the lowest possible cost.
>
> Under this new system each Cabinet and agency head will set up a very special staff of experts who, using the most modern methods of program analysis, will define the goals of their department for the coming year. And once these goals are established this system will permit us to find the most effective and the least costly alternative to achieving American goals.
>
> This program is designed to achieve three major objectives; it will help us find new ways to do jobs faster, to do jobs better, and to do jobs less expensively. It will insure a much sounder judgment through more accurate information, pinpointing those things that we ought to do more, spotlighting those things that we ought to do less. It will make our decisionmaking process as up-to-date, I think as our space-exploring programs.[5]

The analytic revolution had made the next big step in going from DOD to the executive agencies. But just as with the War on Poverty, the analytic revolution emerged with such unrealistically high expectations that reasonable achievements appeared as failures.

The man who launched policy analysis across the executive branch remains a baffling, bigger-than-life figure who brought massive changes—both good and bad—to America. What can we say of Lyndon Johnson? One of his close advisers, Harry McPherson, remarked: "Outside of being the smartest man I've ever known, he had twenty-five or thirty years of profound and far-reaching political connections in Washington, which even the smartest president, maybe in just sheer IQ points, Jimmy Carter, did not have."[6] Certainly no modern president combined Johnson's brains, political savvy, policy knowledge, and congressional experience, nor had his legislative mastery. On the executive side, however, he lacked strong managerial skills. Johnson's head of the National Aeronautics and Space Administration, James E. Webb, argued Johnson did not understand administration.[7]

The most arresting Johnson characteristic is his brute force: "[Johnson's] brightness, stamina, determination, toughness, meanness, and constant hard work kept him on top of the government. By bullying, intimidating, and wearing people down with brute force, Johnson got his way where others would fail."[8] He would sweep aside barriers that would block other leaders. After remarking that Johnson "was not, regrettably, one who would win lasting renown for central elements in his character or personality," Vaughn Davis Bornet speculated: "It would be a nice test of wisdom to say how far some of the less admirable traits were essential to the extent of achievement."[9] Having observed for a number of years former British prime minister Margaret Thatcher, who had the Johnson style in practically every dimension but physical size, aggressiveness, and crudeness, strike fear in civil servants, members of Parliament, and her ministers alike, it seems clear the brute force traits explain many of the achievements, and also the failures.[10]

At the same time, I agree fully with Bornet's underscoring of Johnson's deep commitment to high objectives and his overall evaluation:

> An unremitting ardor to improve the nation and the world remain the most praiseworthy single thing about the Johnson team and its famous leader. John F. Kennedy once said of Lyndon B. Johnson, "He really cares about this nation as I want a president to care. . . ."
>
> In final assessment, during the years 1963 to 1969 the executive branch of the United States government developed, in the hands of this leader and his associates, into a dynamic administrative unit never likely to be equaled. It prodded history into new directions. The presidency of Lyndon B. Johnson will inevitably be remembered—and ought to be—. . . , especially, for the many worthwhile changes it embedded deeply in legislation, in the lives of millions, and in American society.[11]

Cynics might argue that President Johnson's domestic policy efforts were no more than opportunism, a cashing in on the Kennedy assassination to show his legislative prowess and to feed his bigger-than-life ambitions. Even if readers agree with Bornet and the author that President Johnson truly cared, caring is not enough. Wise choices must be made and sound policy information and analysis and organizational mastery can guide in their development and management. But lack of courage and commitment to worthwhile objectives can put political safety ahead of making badly needed policy changes, however sound the policy analysis and however high the level of organizational competence.

Joan Hoff in *Nixon Reconsidered* cited an unpublished poll in which Richard Nixon had been rated the most imperial president, with Lyndon Johnson not far behind, and the two men deserved to be linked together.[12] Like his predecessor, President Nixon stands out as a president of extraordinary capabilities with high intelligence; in-depth policy knowledge and experience, particularly in foreign affairs; a keen analytic mind, much more orderly and more oriented toward hard data and strong analysis than Johnson; political savvy; and courage. Edwin Harper, who served as a special assistant to President Nixon and as an OMB deputy director under President Reagan, called Nixon "a man with a perfect résumé to become president—military officer, congressman, senator, vice president for eight years."[13] But on his dark side, President Nixon combined a passion for secrecy and intrigue, an excessive suspicion of others' motives, and an obsession for control. This volatile mix of traits led Hoff to rate him the best and worst of modern presidents.[14] It is a ranking that can be questioned, but one that captures the extreme variation in the impact of this conflicted man. His main challenger for both best and worst, of course, would be Lyndon Johnson.

Too often Richard Nixon's darker side drove his actions. In terms of policy analysis, as will be discussed shortly, Nixon's negative traits misshaped his foreign policy decision-making process, despite his wide experience in and deep knowledge of foreign affairs and his well-honed analytic skills in that area. The darker side ultimately led to Watergate, which drove President Nixon from office, and still blinds people to his accomplishments. The point that needs underscoring, beyond the usefulness of looking at the record before Watergate, is that Richard Nixon's good and bad traits became indelibly bound together. Tom Wicker, who wrote a 1991 biography of President Nixon, caught this aspect of him in a later article:

> It's easy to say, and it often is said, that had Nixon come clean about Watergate in the beginning, when he had no direct responsibility, the affair would quickly have blown over and he would have survived. That may be true but it ignores the fact that the man Richard Nixon was by 1972 *couldn't come clean.* . . .

> [W]ith his view of life as battle and crisis as challenge, his determination to prove his worth, particularly to himself, his consequent inability to "give up" and his reluctance to show weakness, as well as his conviction that through "personal gut performance" any height could be scaled . . . it would have been impossible for Nixon to do anything but fight back, stand fast, "stonewall" his enemies.
>
> So he did—and the indelible marks Richard Nixon left on American history are Watergate and his resignation from the presidency before he could be impeached. . . . And looking back at Watergate, many Americans can't see beyond it the achievements of a president who often responded to the pressures of his time with knowledge and skill and sometimes even with courage—qualities the American people apparently don't find in most of their leaders today.[15]

Moreover, just as Bornet suggested in the case of President Johnson, we need to ponder "how far some of the less admirable traits were essential to the extent of achievement."[16] It is a question that will be prominent again in the discussion of Bill Clinton who, too, exhibited brilliance, sharp political skills, deep policy knowledge, and extraordinary analytic skills along with striking flaws.

Robert McNamara and Henry Kissinger, who respectively came to rank as one of the most powerful secretaries and one of the most influential presidential aides in the modern presidency, became central actors in the development and use of policy analysis in the period 1961–76. Both possessed high intelligence and a strong analytic orientation but otherwise could hardly be more different. Secretary of Defense McNamara, Harvard Business School graduate and former president of the Ford Motor Company, had a number of the characteristics of the early policy analysts who came to the new central analytic offices. He believed so strongly in data that he could let the numbers drive out softer evidence. For example, in 1963 the secretary of defense accepted "hard" evidence that the government of South Vietnam (GVN) had control of most of the country's hamlets despite on-the-spot newspaper reports to the contrary. Richard Reeves quoted a 1963 McNamara memorandum for the record saying, " 'It is abundantly clear that the statistics received over the past year or more from the GVN officials and reported by the US mission on which we gauged the trend of the war were grossly in error,' " and then himself observed: "For McNamara, if there were no numbers—'Where is your data. Don't give me your poetry'— there was no way to make rational decisions."[17]

Two characteristics of the early policy analysts, at least in the social agencies, marked McNamara too. First, most of the former knew little about their substantive policy areas at the outset, but were confident that their analytic skills and rational framework would allow them to master the new topics quickly. Second, as analysts began to get on top of policy areas, overconfidence often blinded them to what they did not know until a gap in knowledge exploded on them. Reeves wrote of the Bay of Pigs that Secretary McNamara "[believed] that the debacle was his fault, that he was just an automobile company executive who knew nothing about his job."[18]

My comments should not be construed to imply McNamara's incompetence as they derive at least in part to make a sharp contrast with Kissinger. Indeed, McNamara stands out as just the type of decision maker policy analysts would want—bright, rational, data-driven, open to strong analytic argument, and powerful. Bornet observed that President Kennedy "thought of building up McNamara as a 1968 presidential candidate for he thought more highly of him than of anyone else in the cabinet."[19] McNamara stood out as perhaps "the best and the brightest" of the highly intelligent group who played so big a role in the Kennedy administration. Further, McNamara's overall reorganization of DOD made a major contribution to more effective structure. And nowhere is that more clear, as will be discussed, than in the area of policy analysis.

Henry Kissinger differed from Robert McNamara in a number of respects. First, Kissinger is a classic case of the academic for hire who will provide policy ideas and advice for different rising political stars. Before Nixon, Kissinger served Nelson Rockefeller. Second, Kissinger had an established reputation in foreign affairs as a leading light who combined the work of the academy with policy and politics. Third, Kissinger operated more as a grand theorist/strategist than as the rational policy analyst although, like McNamara, he sought good information. Fourth, in sharp contrast to McNamara, Kissinger had not headed a large, complex bureaucracy or worked in such a setting for an extended period. Fifth, Kissinger, a master of political intrigue, was far more Machiavellian than McNamara. This last quality is particularly important because, as Hoff has argued, "instead of compensating for each other's weaknesses and enhancing strengths, Nixon and Kissinger shared their worst characteristics."[20] Former British cabinet minister and Nixon biographer, Jonathan Aitken, cast the Nixon-Kissinger relationship in more complex terms: "The two men shared a child-like enthusiasm for springing surprises; a conspirator's love of secrecy; a guerrilla's contempt for the regular forces of the bureaucracy; and a manipulator's enjoyment of power politics. These traits gave them the guile and cunning they needed to carry out the tortuous diplomatic manoeuvres of their negotiations with Vietnam, the Soviet Union and China."[21] At the same time both the president and his national security adviser also demanded sound information to which they would apply their in-depth knowledge of foreign policy, their sharp analytic skills, and their grand strategic visions. The result, when the hard analytic approach and the secrecy and intrigue were blended, was a system of real strengths and critical weaknesses that demonstrate strikingly the practice of policy analysis at the top.

NATIONAL SECURITY POLICY MAKING—KENNEDY AND NIXON

Both Presidents Kennedy and Nixon considered foreign policy their principal area of competence and concern. Each gave it highest priority from the outset of their administrations and wanted control over the flow of information and the early formulation of policy. Both used their national security advisers and strong, analytically oriented National Security Council staffs to enhance their power. The sharpest contrasts arose in part from differing personalities—not just those of the two presidents but of the other key actors in the White House and the cabinet—and in part from differing circumstances. Kennedy had to grope his way in a relatively unexplored situation while Nixon could use the Kennedy and Johnson experience as a base for his quick, concerted effort toward highly centralized control of foreign policy by the president using White House policy analysis staff as an integral element.

The Kennedy Administration

In 1961 McNamara asked his comptroller, Charles Hitch, who had been the head of the RAND Corporation's Economics Division and one of the leaders at RAND in formulating the basic concepts underlying policy analysis, to establish the Systems Analysis unit. That shop started as part of the assistant secretary-level comptroller office but was upgraded in 1965 to assistant secretary status. Alain Enthoven, its head during the remainder of the Johnson administration, became like Hitch, a major adviser to McNamara. The first of the self-consciously developed analytic offices—pure bred out of RAND—it had tremendous influence on McNamara and provided support to him in his role as the strong man of the Kennedy and Johnson cabinets.

During his tenure at Defense, McNamara also used extensively the Office of International Security Affairs (ISA), sometimes referred to as the "little State Department," as another source for analysis.[22] ISA, which had been established in 1953 to help coordinate DOD's participation in the foreign policy area, provided analysis and advice to McNamara under a number of assistant secretaries: Paul Nitze, William Bundy, John McNaughton, and Paul Warnke. With a staff of more than 200 professionals, ISA also had a number of staff operations duties, but it devoted a goodly amount of staff time to foreign policy analysis similar to that being performed by the White House National

Security Council staff. No agency head appears to have made more use of policy analysis than McNamara.

McGeorge Bundy's NSC staff was not dominated by the RAND policy analysis approach that gave a particular cast to the DOD Systems Analysis office. Yet, like such analytic offices, NSC had a critical mass (albeit small, the professionals numbered about ten) of analytically oriented individuals. The staff acted as Kennedy's eyes and ears into the departments concerned with foreign policy and aggressively sought to insure the flow of policy ideas and information to the president. The Bundy staff, however, does not appear to have been organized to take control of foreign policy with Bundy as a super secretary à la Kissinger. Indeed, McNamara, with his own institutional analytic strength, not only kept the Bundy staff out of DOD's primary domain but became involved in foreign policy issues himself. State, on the other hand, often became angry with perceived White House interference by the Bundy staff, but this seems to have occurred mainly because of Secretary of State Dean Rusk's perceived failure to perform as seen by Kennedy. As I.M. Destler concluded: "It is not necessary to assume that Kennedy secretly planned the central White House staff role which finally evolved. The other explanation is more plausible: State did not provide him what he wanted, while Bundy and Co. were both *able and willing* to do so in its stead."[23] Be that as it may, the Bundy staff became the first analytic office that stood between the president and a cabinet member.

The Nixon Administration

The Nixon administration made a quantum leap in terms of the NSC staff by increasing dramatically its size, scope, and power. Staff size rose from twenty-eight professionals in February 1969 to fifty-two in April 1972.[24] But it is breadth of responsibility and degree of power and control that made the Nixon-Kissinger operation so different from the Kennedy-Bundy effort. Joan Hoff captured the stunning centralization of power:

> Shortly after Nixon and Kissinger joined forces, they began "to create the first full White House-dominant system for the management of foreign policy." That Nixon intended the White House to function as State Department cannot be doubted, and during his first year in office the "White House-centered organization model of foreign-policy making" became the "most centralized and highly structured model yet employed by any president." In the first months of his administration, when former Republican national chairman Leonard Hall visited Nixon in the White House and asked the president how he was getting along with the State

Department, Nixon pointed in the direction of the Oval Office and said: "There's the State Department. . . ."

I. M. Destler observed that Nixon's and Kissinger's "'two-man' system for conducting our foreign policy 'blurred' the once-emphasized distinction between 'policy' and 'operations.'" Moreover, he noted that Nixon and Kissinger assumed at the time that they "could dominate the operational decisions that count." And, for better and sometimes worse, they did. Ultimately, even this "system of closed policy-making is limited by the limits of Presidential power at home." What Destler did not point out was that Nixon and Kissinger also intended to bypass the NSC whenever they did not need bureaucratic support to carry out policy.[25]

The NSC staff in the Nixon administration became the first planned effort at the presidential level to develop a professional staff of sufficient size, experience, and analytic competence to rival the strong agency analytic offices established in the 1960s. Clearly, this staff smoothed the path to greater centralization because of its ability to gather and use large amounts of agency information and analysis in its own analyses. The NSC staff, however, was not intended simply as a competing source of analytic power with the agency staffs. Nixon wanted much more. As Alexander George has observed: "One of the major objectives of Nixon's reorganization of the NSC was to curb, if not altogether eliminate, the play of 'bureaucratic politics' in the making of foreign policy within the executive branch."[26] George, whose 1972 article remains the definitive conceptualization of multiple advocacy, argued for a number of controlled centers of analytic competence in the policy process, thereby fitting well with the notion of multiple analytic offices. He claimed that the Nixon centralization went too far in wiping out both bureaucratic politics and analytic capability within the executive branch.

President Nixon wanted both to be his own secretary of state, as reflected in the appointment as secretary of his long-time friend and colleague William Rogers who had limited foreign policy experience, and to have agency information and options to flow up to him through the NSC staff. But George argued that neither Nixon nor Kissinger, at the outset, saw that their new structure would move toward such a high degree of centralization, in part because of the complex dynamics of the process:

> If we grant that the present system curbs some dysfunctional fea-
> tures of "bureaucratic politics," we are still left with the question of the
> cost and limitations of so centralized a system. To be sure, interested
> personnel in the departments, agencies, and subunits are by no means
> excluded from participating in the present policy-making process. In
> fact, in some respects, via their membership in the various NSC-centered

committees, many departmental personnel are involved more systematically and more closely at least in preparatory stages of policy making
than was the case under previous administrations. At the same time,
however, the roles of leading departmental officials have been subtly
redefined and delimited; indeed, cabinet officials and other senior officials *have been seriously weakened in their roles as policy advocates and advisers.*
While this may not have been intended by Nixon and Kissinger, it is
nonetheless a consequence of the way in which they have restructured
the system. In the course of developing and evaluating policy options,
the intricate machinery of the NSC coopts foreign policy specialists and
analytical resources in the departments. As a result, when department
heads and senior officials finally do have an opportunity at top-level
NSC meetings with the President to express their views on alternative
options, as indeed the present system permits and encourages, they may
not be in a position to offer well-considered *departmental* points of view
backed by solid independent analysis. In this weakening of independent
analytically-oriented staffs at department levels, even senior departmental officials are placed at a disadvantage in performing as advisers to
the president in the final stages of decision making.[27]

Whatever Nixon and Kissinger had planned, the system grew
increasingly more centralized and department analytic capability dwindled. The latter happened for three reasons. First, Secretary of Defense
Melvin Laird gutted policy analysis at DOD by weakening both ISA
and the Systems Analysis office. In the former case, Laird brought in
as assistant secretary G. Warren Nutter and with him a number of
individuals whom Joseph Kraft characterized as "a corps of right-wing
clowns."[28] Then, Laird ceased to pay much attention to the Systems
Analysis office (again showing how much analytic influence is a product of a personal relationship between a decision maker and an analyst)
in his wider move to reduce or eliminate the capacity of independent
civilian staffs to do battle with the military over priorities. Second,
tight centralization, to use George's words, "nicely suited to Nixon's
preference for solo decisions made in private."[29] This approach ultimately cut out the National Security Council staff itself and as Destler
noted, "by contrast with the Bundy era, [Kissinger was] the only NSC
staff member with significant Presidential access."[30] Third, the process
also narrowed in terms of access to Kissinger. Not only did the super
staff at NSC lose access to the president, they more and more came to
be cut off from Kissinger which could be explained in part by the fact
that the president commanded so much of Kissinger's time. At the
same time, the secrecy perfectly suited Kissinger himself who like
Nixon tended to operate with limited counsel and to show little regard
for the ideas of subordinates. Destler contrasted Kissinger's style with
that of Bundy and suggested that the difference might be explained

in part by their academic experiences. Bundy had been primarily an academic administrator, rather than a scholar, whose forte was getting cooperation from and contributions by independent scholars. Kissinger in contrast stands out as an independent academic thinker with a reputation for his toughness in fighting in the marketplace of ideas.[31] Writing two decades later, Hoff probably comes closer to the explanation when she observed that Kissinger's " 'advanced megalomania' remains legendary."[32] As subsequent chapters will testify, Hoff and others had the advantage of seeing the likes of David Stockman and John Sununu as challengers to Kissinger in the "advanced megalomania" league.

The Kissinger style brought a rapid exit from the original NSC staff of twenty-eight that had been so strong. Ten of the twenty-eight shown on a February 1969 listing had departed by that September, and only nine remained after roughly two years. Although the Kissinger staff lost many of its stars, it kept growing in size as it employed people with lesser reputations, some of whom were on loan from other agencies. The NSC staff certainly did not collapse and continued to provide a flow of information and analysis that supported White House control over the foreign policy departments and yielded an empirical base for Kissinger's tremendous influence. From the perspective of the president and his senior analyst, presidential national security policy analysis in the Nixon years became a smashing success in gaining control and influence over foreign policy. Given the Nixon and Kissinger styles, one may feel they would have gained control without policy analysis and relatedly too much has been made of the importance of policy analysis. At the same time, the evidence indicates both men wanted information and analysis (albeit on *their* terms) and used it. As always, the decision makers' desires and behavior predominated; policy analysis in this case, however, became a critical facilitating factor.

Viewed in a broader context, it can be argued that the deleterious consequences of the tight centralization outweighed the gains. First, the Nixon foreign policy system reduced the competition of ideas. At least after the Bay of Pigs, Kennedy sought the opinions of a number of analysts, some of whom were on the White House staff and others from the agencies, particularly DOD. What the Nixon White House lacked was not a flow of good information and useful analytic documents but rather a challenge mechanism from multiple, credible sources so that information and analysis could be improved by subjecting it to scrutiny by those with differing views. This demand for hard data and reasoned analysis needs emphasizing because the secrecy at the top in the Reagan and Bush years would keep out the information and analysis as well as people who could challenge ideas during deliberations. Second, the Nixon foreign policy system suffered span-of-control problems. Nixon and Kissinger miscalculated how much effort would be required to put into operations the top-level decisions they were making with monopolistic power. Destler captured the problem in this long statement:

> These gaps would not necessarily arise if the foreign affairs govern-
> ment problem was solely, or even mainly, that of making what Nixon
> has termed "rational and deliberate" Presidential choices, and if these
> could rather easily shape actions on "operational issues." In that case,
> service to the President's need for options would be equal to bringing
> what Kissinger has called "coherence and design" to the bureaucracy.
> Management of the system would be a relatively routine matter, and
> the costs of weakness outside the White House acceptable. Put otherwise,
> if decisions on "first order," "policy" issues really can predetermine
> "second order," "operational" matters, then the system would handle
> best what is most important. Apparently Nixon and Kissinger believed
> this when they entered office, and the scarcity of foreign affairs crises
> in 1969 may have strengthened such a conviction.
>
> But Kissinger's heavy involvement in operational matters suggests
> the opposite. It corroborates, rather, one of the basic insights of the
> bureaucratic politics view: the inherent limits of any effort to have general
> decisions or guidelines control actions taken and commitments made
> day-to-day at the "working level." For power is inevitably dispersed
> through the foreign affairs government because officials at various levels
> have bargaining advantages, created in part by the sheer limits on the
> time and attention of those at the top. Schemes to centralize power can,
> if wisely developed, strengthen the influence of those at the top, and
> this has certainly happened under Nixon and Kissinger. But much policy
> will still be made at lower levels. Unless, therefore, a system seeks to
> develop centers of strength at several hierarchical levels and to make
> them responsive to top-level influence and priorities by the sharing of
> authority, communication, and confidence with them, power will not
> all rise to the top but simply become even more diffused throughout
> the government.[33]

Nixon's and Kissinger's foreign policy system, much like Johnson's social agenda, ran afoul of implementation problems. Nixon won the game of foreign policy making at the highest levels at the expense of the departments which made it more difficult for them to carry out the president's directives as they tried to put decisions in place.

The Nixon-Kissinger relationship remains the extreme example of the extended interaction of a president and an inner circle policy analyst. Several summary points need making. First, policy information and analysis drove the president's national security policy-making process. Second, both key actors possessed strong analytic and policy competence. Although Kissinger could hardly be described as the prototypical Ph.D. economist policy analyst so prevalent in this book, he clearly brought to his position high intelligence, sharp analytic capabilities, deep substantive knowledge, and an orientation toward sound data and analysis. Indeed, he assembled the first White House analytic shop that drew on the RAND policy analysis model, which had underpinned the DOD analytic unit started in 1961 and the domestic agency policy staffs, discussed in the following section, that began in the mid-1960s. Finally, personality and style defined the Nixon-Kissinger interaction and ultimately undermined it. Betty Glad and Michael Link caught the deterioration of the two men's relationship:

> By the early 1970s, however, the president's relationship with Kissinger had deteriorated considerably. Nixon saw the foreign policy arena as his forté, and Kissinger as the instrument for accomplishment in that area. Kissinger had started out by deferring to the president in their interactions, and working for his policies behind the scenes. But as Kissinger became a major public figure in his own right, the president (with some justification) became suspicious that the national security adviser was using his press conferences to build himself up at the expense of the president. Sometimes Kissinger seemed to be posing as the reasonable statesman checking Nixon, "the mad bomber." Kissinger's egocentric November 1972 interview with an Italian journalist, in which he suggested he was the "lone ranger" of foreign policymaking, was especially galling.[34]

In the next section, when President Nixon's overall policy-making process and the Domestic Council staff are discussed, the president's style of operation looks similar to that in foreign policy but without adviser megalomania.

NIXON'S DOMESTIC POLICY NSC

The discussion of the Domestic Council and its staff component headed by John Ehrlichman requires a consideration of the three organizational demands that drove the White House policy-making process and were so clearly illustrated in the Nixon-Kissinger dynamics in the national security area. Above all, Nixon wanted extremely tight control by gatekeepers who fiercely protected the president. Betty Glad and Michael Link observed of chief of staff Harry Robins "Bob" Haldeman: "As the chief gatekeeper, Haldeman strictly carried out Nixon's wishes to see only a small number of people. . . . Haldeman let himself be the target of resentment for those people Nixon did not want to see."[35] James Pfiffner has pointed out Haldeman's lack of tact in being "Nixon's S.O.B.", but no one has argued that Haldeman had any secret agenda or a need to aggrandize himself as did Kissinger.[36] Haldeman carried out his orders with every effort made to do what the president wanted. The second organizational requirement of no bureaucratic or personal infighting before the president can be seen as an elaboration of the first demand but one too important not to elevate to separate status. Glad and Link note that Haldeman "was the perfect person to handle some of the president's tougher tasks. . . . [because] staff conflicts did not bother him"; and he not only settled disputes such as battles between Secretary of State Rogers and Kissinger but helped Nixon avoid meetings where multiple advocacy might flair up.[37] Finally, Nixon wanted sound information and analysis.

To understand the differing dynamics in domestic, as opposed to national, security policy is to recognize Kissinger's special relationship with Nixon that provided a base for cutting out rivals and controlling the information flow. Nixon set up the Domestic Council to mirror the National Security Council and gave John Ehrlichman as head of its analytic staff an institutional position on paper much like Kissinger's. But Ehrlichman lacked Kissinger's desire to block rivals and the national security adviser's megalomaniacal drive to sell his own agenda. Glad and Link observed that "Ehrlichman would personally go through any report prepared by his staff to be sent to the president to make sure the briefing paper showed the president both sides of the picture," and Richard Nathan, a presidential scholar who had been a player in the Nixon White House, has written in retrospect that Ehrlichman "did a good job managing the domestic policy process."[38]

Chief of staff Haldeman, over a decade after the Nixon presidency, clearly set out his and Ehrlichman's operating philosophy as honest brokers:

> The president's function is to take all that information and make the decision on the basis of that. The whole effort that the White House staff person responsible for that area is making every minute of his working day is to ensure that the president is making the right decisions for the right reasons. That means getting the right information to him on all sides of an issue, along with the recommendations of those advisors from whom the president wants recommendations on that particular issue.[39]

To claim the chief gatekeeper and the domestic policy gatekeeper were excellent, honest brokers seeking to bring President Nixon sound analysis on all sides of an issue does not deny their culpability in Watergate as they "acquiesced in the abuse-of-power side."[40] Whether anyone could have remained powerful and overcome President Nixon's darker side is not a question that can be answered definitively or needs to be speculated on here in order to tell the story of the Domestic Council and its staff.

In a March 1970 Reorganization Message to Congress, President Nixon stated: "The Domestic Council will be primarily concerned with *what* we do; the Office of Management and Budget will be primarily concerned with *how* we do it and how *well* we do it." How the division of labor between the Domestic Council and OMB played out offers a useful picture of EOP dynamics in showing why the intent to downgrade OMB and remove it from major policy activities failed. In considering presidential domestic policy analysis in the Nixon years, the key questions are how well the Domestic Council worked, how viable the division of labor between the Council and OMB was, and how much the reorganization and later related changes altered OMB.

A Nixon administration Domestic Council staffer, Raymond Waldmann, called the last two years of President Nixon's first term the heyday of the Domestic Council and argued that the Domestic Council staff "succeeded to a degree never before attempted in gaining centralized political control over the Executive Branch for the President. . . . It kept information, analysis, and proposals flowing from the Oval Office and reactions, decisions, and presidential priorities flowing to the agencies."[41] It is an overstatement, to be sure, if the domestic level of control is compared with that of Kissinger. But like the NSC staff, the domestic unit, too, pushed aside its cabinet-level council. As political scientist Thomas Cronin noted: "[T]he Domestic Council staff at the White House became, at least under Nixon, a kind of operating center. . . . Some of the Domestic Council staff soon became more prominent in policy decisions than the members of the Council—the cabinet officials—whom they were supposed to assist."[42] The Domestic Council never really functioned as a policy-making body which may have been part of Nixon's strategy for centralized control. Still those who would propose a strong cabinet council supported by an analytic staff should recognize the dangers that the Domestic Council experience makes so vivid even when the head of the staff is an *honest* honest broker.

The Domestic Council staff in its heyday did not run over OMB as it did the Council. The question of pure power became central. The proposed split between the Domestic Council staff and OMB did not become fully implemented because of OMB director George Shultz. Allen Schick observed in 1970, early in the development of the Domestic Council: "Ehrlichman's Domestic Council has not grown to its predicted staff size and Shultz seems to be at least his co-equal in matters of presidential policymaking."[43] Further, the Domestic Council staff did not have OMB's established institutional channels to information. The problem went deeper as Hugh Heclo has observed:

> It was an ill-starred division of tasks [between the Domestic Council and OMB]. Thinking about what to do turned out to be difficult without

having the people around who could tell you how to do it. Since they had a great deal of the necessary experience and expertise, OMB staff were increasingly drafted into Domestic Council operations—and even directed by Council leaders not to inform OMB colleagues of their work (a secrecy which, predictably enough, was rarely pledged and even more rarely maintained). With the departure of John Ehrlichman as its head, the short-lived Domestic Council experiment faded, as did White House intervention in departmental line operations; and today it is no exaggeration to say that apart from a few specific issues and political brushfires, the Council has developed as a weak sister of OMB. Thus not only by design but also by inadvertence, the political importance of OMB grew along with the demise of the other principal actors.[44]

Even with OMB as a strong rival, the Domestic Council staff under Ehrlichman well might have grown more and more powerful if Watergate had not intruded as the case of the Carter Domestic Policy staff will show.

The politicization of OMB is crucial to an understanding of presidential policy analysis. That politicization of the central budget agency came about at first mainly because of Nixon's never ceasing effort to gain control over the permanent bureaucrats (be they in the agencies or on his own staff). The reorganization and subsequent changes placed a new layer of political appointees between the career staff and the OMB director and hence the president. A panel of the National Academy of Public Administration has observed: "The emergence of a powerful White House staff which has progressively assumed the role of speaking for the president has seriously diminished the responsibilities of the career, professional staff of OMB and its capacity to provide the kind of objective and expert counsel to the president which characterized earlier operations."[45] The problem, as Heclo saw it, was that OMB had stepped beyond the bounds of its competence, beyond the line that delimited its special professional skills. Heclo argued that a strong Domestic Council staff with the competence to do high-level policy analysis would make for a better budget office:

> By choosing this mixed strategy, one avoids the misleading question of whether OMB is too strong or too involved in policy. For the sake of the President's own influence within the executive, and the commonsense need to link spending with policy decisions, OMB needs to be involved in policy. For the President's and its own sake, OMB has gained too much political power and lost too much of the governmental authority that stems from neutral competence. This is a matter not of *how much* power but of *what kind* of power.[46]

The lesson to draw from this situation is that technicians—be they OMB staff or policy analysts—should operate as much as possible within the confines of their techniques, and do what they do best. There are boundaries which if exceeded (e.g., OMB moving too much into politics) threaten to diminish the usefulness of the technical function for the organization it is intended to serve, *and over time, if not necessarily to lessen the analyst's influence, to misshape the desired function.*

FORD, IKE, AND MULTIPLE ADVOCACY

Gerald Ford was decidedly ordinary and uncomplicated by presidential standards generally and certainly by comparison with his two predecessors. At the same time, he brought to the White House a balance and reasonability not found in the decade of Johnson and Nixon. Most of all, Ford's personality and predilections made him comfortable with a well-ordered policy-making process underpinned by multiple advocacy as it should be practiced. The Ford experience shows so strikingly that a president with extended congressional leadership experience— but without the level of the organizational mastery gained by Dwight Eisenhower during a career as a staff person and leader in large-scale, complex institutions like the federal agencies—could establish a sound policy process by drawing on the lessons left by that organizational genius himself. It was no small accomplishment in that none of the elected presidents since Ike had the understanding and the temperament to implement and maintain a sound policy-making process.

The Ford process employed a combination chief-of-staff and spokes-of-the-wheel structure. He was quite accessible to his key staff (the spokes) and did not see them as subordinate to his chief of staff, as Nixon had. Ford's first chief of staff Donald Rumsfeld and the cabinet secretary James Connor were responsible for establishing an orderly flow of documents *up and down* to support multiple advocacy. Ford's organizational structure evolved into "one of the more orderly and more open systems of those used by modern presidents."[47] Two reasons explain the success in terms of organizational structure and information flow. First, Rumsfeld and Connor were great admirers of the Eisenhower structure and process and established the key elements of it in the Ford White House. Second, Ford liked the system and had the *communication and analytic competencies* to use it well. Dick Cheney, his second chief of staff, pointed out that Ford would receive a decision memo, see it was not "staffed out," and say "Look, these guys aren't ready for the meeting yet. Scrub it. Don't let them in until they get their act together."[48] In short, the Ford White House organization followed both the structure and the dynamics of the Eisenhower process.

The Ford presidency also provides the best example of successful multiple advocacy à la Alexander George. The Economic Policy Board was established as the focal point for presidential economic policy when a serious economic crisis cut across the agencies. Roger Porter, a key EPB staff member, claimed that Ford also thought the EPB would be a device for reviving the cabinet's role as White House advisers and had Secretary of the Treasury William E. Simon as chair and most of the cabinet as members.[49] However, a five-member executive committee dominated the board and all except Simon were EOP staff—the heads of the Council of Economic Advisers, the Council on International Economic Policy, OMB, and L. William Seidman, who served as executive director of both the EPB and the executive committee. Here is strong evidence of how much economic policy responsibility had come to be centered in the EOP, not the agencies.

Porter maintained that the EPB did meet President Ford's needs for wide-ranging, well-staffed economic analysis and quoted one senior official who claimed that "[the EPB's] most important strength was that it provided a mechanism for reaching into various departments and finding staff expertise on issues," and another who said that "it was a model for interdepartmental communications, cooperation [and] resolution of issues."[50] The president himself and Seidman played the key roles in this successful case of multiple advocacy. President Ford wanted solid evidence and liked oral debate. The president would listen to different points of view *and* do his homework including reading a number of economic analyses. In addition, Ford would act as a judge during much of the argument by not revealing the way he leaned, and his neutrality became the key to open debate. Seidman had been a top assistant to Vice President Ford and was the rare case of a relatively modest assistant to the president. He let Secretary Simon act as point man on economic policy because the latter liked being the administration's spokesperson. Seidman also took easily to being the honest broker, seeing his management of the presidential policy process, not policy advocacy, as his main function. Seidman became "a surrogate for the executive in attempting to assure the quality of the search and analysis phases of policy making that precede final action. . . [and] to insure that the executive will have a number of well-considered, well-presented options to choose from."[51]

Multiple advocacy is a hard process to do well. First, only a particular presidential personality can handle it. A president's high intelligence, encyclopedic knowledge, and sharp analytic mind will not ensure that multiple advocacy will be his choice. Second, an honest, able broker is a rarity in the ego-driven White House. Third, multiple advocacy almost always involves time-consuming conflict, and, further, the best debater may not produce the wisest policy advice. Strong process management skills and a stress on written documents can help counter these problems. Finally, a multiple-advocacy process will be most difficult to implement at an administration's outset, when it is most needed, as the Reagan experience will illustrate. A president well may avoid openness if he seeks immediate control as did Reagan in 1981. Unlike Reagan, Ford did not have an agenda; but rather inherited an ongoing administration that had in place veteran policy adviser generalists. Still, the EPB is indeed impressive in its policy process dimensions.

THE DOMESTIC AGENCY ANALYTIC OFFICE IN FULLEST FLOWER

In this book an agency analytic office and two congressional support agencies—the Congressional Budget Office and the Congressional Research Service—will be singled out as exemplary analytic units. Alas, and it is an integral part of the story, no EOP unit during the period under consideration (1965 to the present) achieved such distinction. Great power, yes; outstanding competence and integrity, no. The congressional units themselves will be treated in Chapter 9, while Chapter 4 traces, during a critical multiyear period, the New Jersey negative income tax experiment developed by the Office of Economic Opportunity central analytic office. This extended account of the first social policy experiment explores the workings of an analytic office internally within the federal agency itself and externally in its relationship to Congress and to the policy research community. The current section on the exemplary agency analytic unit discusses the staff size question and three critical functions in central analytic offices—advice, policy planning and program examination, and research management—that are important in the rest of this book. The model domestic agency analytic office has an unusual history in that it flourished in two agencies—the Office of Economic Opportunity and the Department of Health, Education and Welfare (now the Department of Health and Human Services)—and can be labeled the OEO/HEW model. The Office of Research, Plans, Programs and Evaluation (RPP&E) was created by Lyndon Johnson's Economic Opportunity Act and was headed by an OEO assistant director (the equivalent of an assistant secretary in a noncabinet agency); renamed the Office of Planning, Research, and Evaluation (PR&E) in the Nixon administration and much expanded; and at OEO's demise, transferred to HEW's Office of the Assistant Secretary for Planning and Evaluation (OASPE) and further expanded.

Agency Analytic Offices and the Institutional Structure

The first two analytic offices at DOD and OEO began before the October 1965 Bureau of the Budget directive that established the Planning-Programming-Budgeting System (hereafter PPBS or PPB) in major federal departments and agencies. The main dimensions of PPBS were central analytic offices reporting directly to agency heads or their deputies, a formal program structure cast in outcome-oriented terms, and an explicit linking of the new system to the yearly budget cycle. The agency analytic offices came forth as the new kids on the block and immediately found it necessary to struggle for power with the established agency and EOP actors in the budget process. As I wrote:

> Although it sometimes seemed in the early, unsullied period of PPBS that, before Robert McNamara became Secretary of Defense, the government made all of its critical decisions on a Ouija board; such was not the case. Under the old system, the federal agencies submitted to the Bureau of the Budget a yearly budget request presenting in detail the funds required to operate their programs in the next fiscal year. In developing the budget, the key cast of characters consisted of the agency head and the major program operators, the agency budget office, and the Bureau of the Budget's program examiners. The latter . . . worked with various agency program people and the budget staff on a continuing basis to develop the budget, and were the key factors in the BOB decision structure.[52]

Despite all the rhetoric, the new policy planning system itself did not represent that dramatic a change in the underlying budget process. The main agency budget actors prior to PPBS had entrenched power, deep knowledge about programs and budgets, and extensive ties to other powerful persons and organizations in the agency and the EOP. The policy analyst's main rival as a staff adviser in an agency usually turned out to be the budget officer or comptroller because the final budget—both the dollar amounts and the written documentation—centered on the yearly agency resource bargaining process.

The two most successful analytic offices in the Johnson administration—Systems Analysis at DOD and RPP&E at OEO—both escaped the usual entrenched budget office problem. At DOD the chief budget officer, Charles Hitch, who, as discussed earlier, was an authority on policy planning and at RAND had helped in developing the basic concepts that underlay PPBS, created the systems analysis unit. That is, the man who dreamed up policy analysis had the budget function too. When Systems Analysis became a separate office in 1965, its power had been firmly established. A small budget office at OEO, which had been a unit in the Office of Administration, was moved to RPP&E early on, thereby enhancing RPP&E's status as the agency staff responsible for determining major budgetary issues. Placing the macro-level budget responsibility in RPP&E cut off the potential bureaucratic danger of a combination of the budget function with related activities in the Office of Administration that could have provided an institutional base for a strong comptroller in that office. At the same time, the Office of Administration retained the heavy workload involved in executing the micro-control functions such as administering travel requests and personnel ceilings. Policy analysis and macro-level budgeting were merged in RPP&E with the latter clearly subordinate to policy analysis.

If a clear superiority over the budgeter did not exist, the likelihood of a battle for influence could arise whatever the formal status on the organization chart. The case of HEW's able and influential comptroller during the Johnson administration exemplifies the strong budget person who knew how to use budget information for power. The comptroller's many years at the agency prior to PPBS had established wide influence within the agency and outside in HEW's various congressional committees. The agency's great diversity and multiple appropriations meant a huge logistical problem each year as the budget moved through the Congress. Much mundane effort was required to answer the often routine questions concerning the working details in a complex agency. This service function, however, involved extended interaction with individual members of Congress to ensure that their special problems within the scope of HEW were taken care of. Helping Congress gave HEW's comptroller an outside constituency and hence a power base in the Congress that enhanced the position of the agency budget officer in addressing major upcoming agency budgetary decisions.

In response to the BOB October 1965 directive creating PPBS governmentwide, HEW secretary John Gardner picked William Gorham to head the Office of the Assistant Secretary for Planning and Evaluation. Gardner granted Gorham both responsibility for executing agency policy analysis and what then seemed a reasonable cadre of competent staff. Never as influential with the secretary as some of his Republican successors or his counterparts at OEO, Gorham still had a base for exerting considerable influence with Gardner. However, OASPE did not dominate the budget office, and probably the reverse was closer to being the true situation during Gorham's tenure. The budget office, as will be seen, gained even more power at the expense of OASPE in the remainder of the Johnson administration.

The OEO/HEW Model Analytic Office

RPP&E, the first domestic policy office established in the federal government, started with two divisions—one responsible for planning and research; the other, for program examination—and added an evaluation division. Although RPP&E at its largest had fewer than fifty staff persons, it engaged extensively in the three critical functions of planning and program examination, advice, and research management.

RPP&E had agency responsibility both for program examination and for policy planning. The latter included working with other segments of the agency to develop a yearly policy plan and to defend that plan, once approved by the agency director, before the Bureau of the Budget (now Office of Management and Budget). The policy planning and program examination function produced a large flow of programmatic data and policy analyses, as well as voluminous agency planning documents. This output underscored the hard technical side of the analytic operation. Advice had a much more amorphous dimension. For the RPP&E director to be one of the, or even the principal adviser to the agency head, the main ingredient was trust. The OEO agency head needed first to believe the numbers and that required a chief analyst with competence and integrity. To become *the* principal policy adviser as did the second RPP&E director, Robert Levine, necessitated a further step to establish an extended confidential relationship in which information had to be treated with great discretion. "None of this will go out of the room" is the extreme case, but more generally such information would be used only on a need-to-know basis for trust to be maintained. Several of the OEO and HEW analytic unit leaders in the 1960s and 1970s gained this insider role where the top policy analyst had daily access to and the strong trust of the agency head. And this status became the central element of continuing bureaucratic power.

Research management can involve both developing research ideas and approaches and monitoring and fixing ongoing research. The chapter on the New Jersey negative income tax experiment will examine the various aspects of agency research management in great detail, but three related points need emphasizing. First, research management to be well-done will be labor intensive because keeping an external research team on schedule and on task requires close watching and may demand a goodly dollop of fixing by the agency staff person. Second, the policy analysis unit is not like the National Institutes of Health where the staff often carry out their own research projects. In specific cases, I have seen an agency research manager become more heavily involved in the research than monitoring and fixing, but that was the exception and still involved an outside grantee organization as the main actor. Finally, sound policy research management demands a high level of substantive area knowledge and research competence from the manager.

RPP&E, although large by the standards of the Johnson administration, could carry out all three functions adequately because OEO itself was a small agency. The Office of Planning, Research, and Evaluation (PR&E), as the OEO analytic unit was renamed in the Nixon administration, grew significantly larger because of a major increase in the research budget, with policy experiments expanding rapidly and added responsibilities, because its director was also a presidential assistant. The transfer of PR&E staff and research dollars to HEW as OEO was broken up in the Nixon administration made OASPE the premier domestic analytic unit of the 1970s. A look at changes in size over time is illuminating. OASPE and RPP&E began in the mid-1960s with professional staffs numbering twenty to thirty persons and at most doubled by the end of the Johnson administration. By the beginning of 1975, OASPE had roughly 150 professional staff positions filled by persons with a wide range of social science (still predominantly economics) and program examination skills including a number of specialists in experimentation and large-scale data management. One unit within OASPE, the Office of Planning Systems, had responsibilities for overall agency planning including integrating the work of other elements within OASPE and the department. This institutional effort established throughout the agency a level of control over critical information and analysis that put OASPE at the center of agency policy making. The Office of Planning Systems with its many functions resembled an analytic office within an analytic office. Its staff grew as large or larger than the staffs in the original policy analysis and research offices in HEW and OEO. In the Carter administration, OASPE rose to three hundred staff members and funded major experiments in income maintenance and health; however, the assistant secretaries did not attain the level of insider status held by some of the earlier OEO and HEW chief analysts. By 1990 OASPE had fallen to one hundred persons and did little in the area of large-scale policy research.

The issues of the number and of the composition and competence of the staff in OASPE need to be considered further. Needless to say, the existence of a large, competent staff by itself does not bring strong influence. However, in an agency as vast as HEW with its great complexity, staff size, and competence may be necessary prerequisites in order for the analyst to gain adequate control over information. Recall that the HEW comptroller's advantage over the central analyst in 1965 flowed partly from his office's command of detailed information. The beginning OASPE staff did not have much direct HEW experience with over 80 percent of the members coming from outside the department.[53] In his analysis of three federal agencies based on the Johnson administration and very early Nixon administration experience, Doh rated the analytic effort at Agriculture superior to that of HEW (the National Aeronautics and Space Administration was a poor third) in part because of the experienced analytic staff in Agriculture, all of whom came from within the department.[54] I held that the OASPE staff in the Johnson administration was too small and also lacked program-oriented people:

The sharpest distinction between OASPE and RPP&E was the latter's *program examination* staff, which had no counterpart in HEW's analytical office. The typical program examination staff member had a public administration and/or accounting (budgeting) background and extensive government experience (mainly in a *staff* as opposed to a line position), but generally lacked the formal training or the experience needed to perform or supervise extensive research studies. The good program examiner brings to a problem a sound analytical orientation without high-powered empirical techniques, in essence compensating for this lack of technical research capability, vis-à-vis the researcher, by having a greater understanding of the bureaucracy and its peculiarities.[55]

Program examination staff and policy analysts had complementary skills, especially where the former aided the policy analysts in understanding bureaucratic nuances.

OASPE chief analyst William Morrill, who had a program examiner background, brought in a number of program examiners and also developed a formal mechanism in the Office of Planning Systems to gain control of detailed agency information. Morrill and OASPE came to have great influence in HEW during the tenure of two secretaries. Part of the success must be attributed to Morrill's considerable bureaucratic and political skills matched by few other policy analysts. However, the large and able staff that provided the senior analyst with control over information and a response capacity to informational and advisory requests also had been important in making Morrill such an extremely formidable opponent in the HEW influence game. Finally, the developmental aspects of OASPE should not be overlooked. In a vast, complex agency such as HEW, gaining real control over information may demand both personnel with extended knowledge of the workings of the agency bureaucracy and an established system of information control—both of which may require time to put in place.

In the period 1965–76, the exemplary analytic staffs, first at OEO and then at HEW, established and maintained the greatest power achieved by agency units. The OEO/HEW staff in general gained high institutional positions, both on the organization chart and on a personal level with the agency head, from the combination of strong bureaucratic skills; high analytic integrity; the development of sound, relevant, timely information; the technical competence to use such information in producing policy analyses and in providing advice; and a chemistry between the agency head and the chief analyst. This special relationship is the critical intangible in the power equation that can develop even when the chief analyst is not technically competent or not exist when the analytic office head combines high competence and integrity.

The OEO/HEW model well-illustrates this key point. In the Johnson administration, OASPE was first headed by William Gorham who had a good relationship with HEW secretary John Gardner although not nearly as close as Levine had at OEO or Morrill at HEW. When Wilbur Cohen replaced Gardner and Alice Rivlin succeeded Gorham in 1968, the influence of the senior analyst with the secretary declined precipitously even though Rivlin later became an analytic superstar as director of the Congressional Budget Office and OMB, and Cohen himself had outstanding credentials. Just out of graduate school, Cohen had been involved in the development of the original social security legislation in the mid-1930s. Between that time and his appointment as secretary, he had two distinguished careers as an academic and as a civil servant and political appointee at HEW. It may have been his deep knowledge of the agency that led him to doubt his need for help from the relatively new analytic staff; it may have been his extremely strong ties to the agency's senior budget officer built up over a number of years; but whatever the reason, analytic influence dwindled to by far the lowest point in either the HEW or OEO settings during the golden era of agency policy analysis. President Richard Nixon's first HEW secretary Robert Finch, who had little understanding of policy analysis, appointed as OASPE chief analyst his close associate from California, Lewis Butler. Even though Butler had limited experience as a policy analyst, he and John Veneman, the undersecretary who also was from California, were Secretary Finch's two principal advisers. OASPE under Butler gained both additional staff and clear supremacy over the budget head in the pecking order. However, Butler's influence flowed far more from the past relationship with Finch than on the use of analysis, and policy analysis *qua* policy analysis fell into a somewhat suspended state at the agency during Finch's tenure. But let us not miss the point that Butler's influence remained high with the HEW secretary.

The steam completely went out of the analytic revolution at the start of the Reagan years. Executive agency domestic policy analysis and research thereafter suffered a marked decline from the golden years that started in 1965 and reached the high point during the Nixon years. Central agency analytic offices, where they still existed, were likely to be highly bureaucratized organizations plodding along, doing useful tasks, but no longer among the most powerful players in agency policy-making process. The policy research revolution, using that term broadly to include rigorous, large-scale experimentation and evaluation spawned by the War on Poverty, had run its course. The federal agencies no longer were the leaders in fostering major efforts to evaluate whether their policies were working or to experiment with new policy approaches in areas such as education, health, housing, and income maintenance. Nor had other organizations stepped in to take a strong leadership role in funding such efforts.

The Multiple Roles of the Agency Policy Analyst

In the upcoming chapters, much attention will be focused on the behavior of policy analysts. The sharpest contrasts will emerge between the congressional support agencies that serve 535 masters and have neutral or nonpartisan (the words are roughly interchangeable) competence as their operating norm and White House staffs that answer only to their president and his inner circle and have often exhibited some combination of extreme partisanship, limited competence, and minimal professional standards in their efforts to be responsive to their political bosses. In the golden years of executive agency policy analysis units, analysts' behavior fell in between the two extremes with them having a variety of roles that moved from nonpartisanship to strong advocacy. Both were appropriate, but the multiple roles threatened the claim of neutral competence, whereby the analyst, to use former OMB deputy director Paul O'Neill's ringing charge to OMB budgeteers, is seen as the provider of "the best and clearest exposition of the facts and arguments on every side of the issue."[56] To illustrate the differing roles and potential conflicts, I will rely on my experience as a staff economist and chief of RPP&E's Research and Plans (R&P) Division. As staff economist, I worked on income maintenance and then manpower policy, in both cases being responsible as a member of an analytic team to develop policy proposals for an overall War on Poverty plan. Our team had the most basic analytic function of developing and comparing program alternatives for top people in RPP&E, particularly our immediate superior the R&P Division chief and the RPP&E director (assistant director for RPP&E, the rough equivalent of an assistant secretary in a cabinet agency) whose task was to put together the overall plan for the agency director.

A team did not work in splendid isolation hatching a full-blown policy analysis but rather interacted most frequently with the R&P Division chief and with the RPP&E director. Nor should a team and its superiors be seen as only nonpartisan seekers of truth, but the analysis did not begin with preconceived answers and reasonable alternatives and a sound recommendation were sought. The team engaged in ex ante, not ex post, analysis. Doing rigorous analysis means being skeptical so that the ex ante effort might show how poorly a favored policy is working or that a hot new idea does not withstand scrutiny. Ex post analysis starts with a preconceived answer (recommendation) and works backwards to report only the evidence that supports that answer. The ex post case may show responsive competence with the

analyst exhibiting great skill in presenting a political leader's preconceived judgment. Still, the exercise is "ersatz" policy analysis.

Although RPP&E had a number of career civil servants whose
competence and knowledge I came to value highly, people from research organizations and universities dominated. The assistant director
for RPP&E, Joseph Kershaw, had been a long-time head of the RAND
economics department and R&P chief Robert Levine, the office's number two person, came directly from RAND. I joined the staff in mid-
1965 on a year's leave from a university economics department, stayed,
and eventually occupied a career position but did not expect to remain
in government. At the same time, the in-and-outers saw themselves
both as experienced professionals adhering to the research standards
of academe (RAND conceived itself as a university without students)
and as innovators developing the first domestic policy analysis office.
RPP&E's charge to develop an overall plan for Lyndon Johnson's War
on Poverty was taken most seriously as the expected base for policy
deliberations.

RPP&E wanted to have its plan accepted by OEO director Sargent
Shriver (a Kennedy by marriage and a hard charger with an idea a
minute), but Kershaw spent a lot of time trying to keep Shriver from
pushing too far. Given the agency mission of fighting poverty and
reducing the barriers blocking minorities (the disadvantaged), the OEO
plan developed by RPP&E offered a liberal agenda. But the RPP&E
staff considered itself charged with skepticism about program claims
and sought to keep the program offices such as the Community Action
Program (CAP) and Job Corps honest. The analysts did not see themselves as laboratory scientists above the fray and recognized the bureaucratic reality of having to sell their arguments within the agency.
Moreover, once the smoke had cleared from internal agency battles
and the OEO plan (really the RPP&E plan as modified) had become
OEO policy, RPP&E became advocates for that plan within the executive branch. Once I became chief of the R&P Division, my external
duties both within the agency and representing the agency expanded.
Particularly in the latter role, my involvement was usually with peers
from the agencies and the EOP, often with the BOB mandarins. Making
the case for OEO positions and/or protecting its turf (under threat
both as a new agency started in 1964 and as an organization outranked
by cabinet departments) became a continuing task. But here, too, professional standards set boundaries and maintaining analytic credibility
enhanced one's capacity to advocate effectively.

This does not mean that analysts never found themselves in a
position where the game had few rules. My best example comes from
the time I was still a staff economist working on manpower policy.
My initial input in helping to develop a new agency manpower pro-

posal did not deviate from RPP&E's or the agency's standard policy process. Based on the analysis, RPP&E recommended a new approach aimed at strengthening the weak CAP manpower effort by integrating local Community Action Agencies (CAAs) and Department of Labor Employment Service (ES) offices. Shriver accepted the new approach and the OEO proposal went to BOB where many an OEO idea had been rejected.

Then events took on a life of their own as Vietnam spending overwhelmed any new War on Poverty initiatives. In this particular case, BOB staff saw that unspent funds from OEO, the Department of Labor (DOL), and HEW were available to create a new, highly visible effort—the Concentrated Employment Program (CEP). Being well into the fiscal year, BOB also knew it had to move rapidly so as not to lose unspent funds and wanted to go well beyond the original fairly modest OEO plan. The budget office mandated that each of the three agencies send two representatives to work with BOB on a hurried schedule, figuratively locking us in the meeting room each day. In *Social Policy Research and Analysis* published in 1971, the development of CEP was set out in some detail; however, the more personal aspects that now follow were not presented.[57]

The OEO team had a CAP staffer and me; and for a number of reasons, including that I was the main author of the original plan, I had the senior role. DOL and HEW teams were led by deputy assistant secretaries so I (as well as the CAP staffer) was badly outranked on the official status chart. Moreover, this was not an analytic exercise as DOL aggressively sought to take over the program, reducing the local CAAs to a subordinate role relative to the ES personnel. Policies were being decided on the spot. When in doubt, the HEW and DOL team leaders rushed out to call their assistant secretary bosses who had clear lines to the agency secretaries. I finally called Levine to say I was making agency policy flying blind with no idea what Shriver and Bertrand Harding, the OEO deputy director, wanted. Being unable to talk to the two top OEO officials (I do not recall why), Levine said in effect "you're on your own, go for it."

My role no longer was that of agency advocate trying to uphold a clear agency position approved by the OEO director but OEO's chief negotiator without a well-specified charge. Now in truth, as the main designer of the originally proposed program, I knew far more about it than the top officials that included the director, the deputy director, and the CAP assistant director. Further, I did have advice from the CAP staff member on the OEO team and from Levine and knew my most basic task by far involved creating a CEP structure where the local CAAs either controlled the operation or were equal partners with DOL and HEW. The other agency teams contained program people, not policy analysts, and the setting differed dramatically from an inter-agency meeting of analysts. Moreover, once the Concentrated Employment Program was launched, I became involved in interagency implementation efforts and again had far more of an operating program role than an analytic one.

The CEP experience took me from a traditional inside-the-agency policy analyst role, to an analytic/advocacy one, and finally to being the chief agency advocate in the BOB meetings. The latter was exceptional for a policy analyst at my staff level but would be less so for higher analytic positions. The top policy analyst may move back and forth from being mainly an analyst to being an agency advocate in dealings with other executive agencies or EOP units. No simple rules cover all cases. But two things stand out. First, within the agency, the analyst hat should be the main one worn. Giving one's best judgment derived from available information and being clear about going beyond the available evidence both fit professional standards and sustained credibility. As head of the R&P Division that was made easy by Bertrand Harding, who had succeeded Shriver as OEO director and had been a career civil servant before becoming a political appointee. He valued good information and analysis and wanted a careful discussion that indicated when the analyst was speculating without much information to go on. Even in the case of Shriver who tended to rush to judgment more quickly, the RPP&E leadership tried hard to slow him down and would tell him at times what he wanted was unrealistic.

Second, absolute purity is not possible if the analyst also wants influence. The agency head may have a favorite program that is not safe to attack. Shriver thought Head Start to be OEO's most popular program (right) and a great success (wrong). And there was evidence, albeit shaky, that the big summer-only program had little impact. RPP&E, however, did not "waste" its resources on hard assessments of Head Start because Shriver was most unlikely to accept strong criticism and be furious if such an effort was considered by the analytic office. In the main, RPP&E followed the Head Start program as it did other programs for reporting purposes and discussed marginal adjustments while Shriver headed the agency. Under Harding, RPP&E's new evaluation division funded a major Head Start assessment, not because RPP&E had become more bold but because Harding supported evaluations. The other side of the coin was that OEO program staffs such as those in CAP and Job Corps both feared and distrusted a powerful central analytic office that could do them harm. The top staff in RPP&E, especially under Harding, had clout with the agency director and were not viewed by other units as the friendly policy analysts with no ax to grind. Being hard-nosed could be seen as RPP&E trying to gain more power and greater access to the director.

That Harding considered RPP&E director Levine as his top policy adviser and also relied heavily on other RPP&E staff hardly cheered the program advocates unless RPP&E was pressing the program's case.

Ambiguity marked the multiple roles of the agency analysts even in the golden era of analytic power at OEO and HEW. But in the main, the analytic units combined competence and high professional standards and these underpinned their credibility within and outside of the agency. The reputation for credible work became the analytic unit's most valuable intangible asset to be protected even when playing it straight temporarily reduced clout. If we look across all domestic agencies, there has been fluctuation with some offices gaining high analytic credibility and/or clout and others losing one or both. In the case of the OEO/HEW model, that "office" flourished from its start at OEO through the transfer of OEO staff and funds to HEW until the end of the Carter presidency. We need to look at what happened in the executive branch with the coming of the Reagan anti-analytic presidency and in Congress from the 1970s on before coming back to my argument for high analytic competence and professional standards—for neutral competence—all across the federal government.

NOTES

1. Walter Williams, *Mismanaging America: The Rise of the Anti-Analytic Presidency,* University Press of Kansas, 1990, pp. 108–109, italics in the original.

2. Richard Reeves, *President Kennedy: Profile of Power,* Simon & Schuster, 1993, p. 611.

3. Fred I. Greenstein, *The Hidden-Hand Presidency: Eisenhower as Leader,* Basic Books, 1982, pp. 245–247.

4. Reeves, *President Kennedy,* p. 25.

5. *New York Times,* August 25, 1965.

6. Quotes in Samuel Kernell and Samuel L. Popkin (eds.), *Chief of Staff: Twenty-Five Years of Managing the Presidency,* University of California Press, 1986, p. 81.

7. Vaughn Davis Bornet, *The Presidency of Lyndon B. Johnson,* University Press of Kansas, 1983, p. 350.

8. Williams, *Mismanaging America,* p. 115.

9. Bornet, *The Presidency of Lyndon B. Johnson,* p. 350.

10. For my critique of Prime Minister Thatcher's governance style, see Walter Williams, *Washington, Westminster and Whitehall,* Cambridge University Press, 1988, pp. 98–106.

11. Bornet, *The Presidency of Lyndon B. Johnson,* pp. 350–351.

12. Joan Hoff, *Nixon Reconsidered,* Basic Books, 1994, p. 342.

13. Edwin L. Harper, "Domestic Policy Making in the Nixon Administration: An Evolving Process," *Presidential Studies Quarterly,* Winter 1996, p. 41.

14. Hoff, *Nixon Reconsidered*, p. 9.

15. Tom Wicker, "Richard M. Nixon 1969–1974," *Presidential Studies Quarterly*, Winter 1996, p. 257, italics in the original. The biography is Tom Wicker, *One of Us: Richard Nixon and the American Dream*, Random House, 1991.

16. Bornet, *The Presidency of Lyndon B. Johnson*, p. 350.

17. Reeves, *President Kennedy*, pp. 610–611.

18. Ibid., p. 113.

19. Bornet, *The Presidency of Lyndon B. Johnson*, p. 27.

20. Hoff, *Nixon Reconsidered*, p. 150.

21. Jonathan Aitken, *Nixon: A Life*, Regency, 1993, p. 379.

22. For a brief description of ISA, see I. M. Destler, *Presidents, Bureaucrats, and Foreign Policy: The Politics of Organizational Reform*, Princeton University Press, pp. 228–230.

23. Ibid., p. 114, italics added.

24. Ibid., p. 126.

25. Hoff, *Nixon Reconsidered*, pp. 157–158.

26. Alexander L. George, "The Case for Multiple Advocacy in Making Foreign Policy," *American Political Science Review*, September 1972, p. 753.

27. Ibid., p. 754, italics in the original.

28. Quoted in Destler, *Presidents, Bureaucrats, and Foreign Policy*, p. 242.

29. George, "The Case For Multiple Advocacy in Making Foreign Policy," p. 755.

30. Destler, *Presidents, Bureaucrats, and Foreign Policy*, p. 125.

31. Ibid., p. 145.

32. Hoff, *Nixon Reconsidered*, p. 148.

33. Destler, *Presidents, Bureaucrats, and Foreign Policy*, p. 150–151.

34. Betty Glad and Michael W. Link, "President Nixon's Inner Circle of Advisers," *Presidential Studies Quarterly*, Winter 1996, pp. 25–26.

35. Ibid., pp. 15 and 21.

36. James P. Pfiffner, "The President's Chief of Staff: Lessons Learned," *Presidential Studies Quarterly*, Winter 1993, pp. 82–85.

37. Glad and Link, "President Nixon's Inner Circle of Advisers," p. 21.

38. Ibid., p. 22; and Richard P. Nathan, "A Retrospective on Richard Nixon's Domestic Policies," *Presidential Studies Quarterly*, Winter 1996, p. 155.

39. Quoted in Kernell and Popkin (eds.), *Chief of Staff*, p. 129.

40. Glad and Link, "President Nixon's Inner Circle of Advisers," p. 33.

41. Raymond J. Waldmann, "The Domestic Council: Innovation in Presidential Government," *Public Administration Review*, May/June 1976, p. 262.

42. Thomas E. Cronin, *The State of the Presidency*, Little, Brown, 1976, p. 127.

43. Allen Schick, "The Budget Bureau That Was: Thoughts of the Rise, Decline, and Future of a Presidential Agency," *Law and Contemporary Problems*, Summer 1970, p. 536.

44. Hugh Heclo, "OMB and the Presidency—The Problems of Neutral Competence," *The Public Interest*, Winter 1975, p. 89.

45. *Watergate: Its Implications for Responsible Government*, National Academy of Public Administration, March 1974, p. 43.

46. Heclo, "OMB and the Presidency," p. 98.

47. Patricia Dennis Witherspoon, *Within These Walls: A Study of Communication between Presidents and Their Senior Staffs*, Praeger, 1991, p. 156.

48. Ibid., p. 158.

49. Roger B. Porter, *Presidential Decision Making: The Economic Policy Board*, Cambridge University Press, 1980, p. 45.

50. Ibid., pp. 185–186.

51. Alexander L. George, *Presidential Decisionmaking in Foreign Policy: The Effective Use of Information and Advice*, Westview Press, 1980, p. 170.

52. Walter Williams, *Social Policy Research and Analysis: The Experience in the Federal Social Agencies*, Elsevier, 1970, pp. 19–20.

53. Joon Chien Doh, *The Planning-Programming-Budgeting System in Three Federal Agencies*, Praeger, 1971, p. 120.

54. Ibid., pp. 119–121.

55. Williams, *Social Policy Research and Analysis*, pp. 177–178, italics in the original.

56. Paul H. O'Neill, a presentation to Office of Management and Budget staff, The Center for Excellence in Government, Washington, D.C., September 6, 1988, p. 2.

57. Williams, *Social Policy Research and Analysis*, pp. 36–52.

4 | The Struggle for a Negative Income Tax: 1965–72

This chapter offers a case study of the attempt within the federal government during the period from 1965 to 1972 to enact a negative income tax. It is mainly an editing of a short 1972 monograph—*The Struggle for a Negative Income Tax*—that started with the emergence of the negative tax concept as a serious idea within the government in 1965, moved to the development of the New Jersey negative income tax experiment, and ended with the defeat of President Richard Nixon's Family Assistance Plan in the Senate Committee on Finance in mid-1970.[1] The chapter also draws on a 1975 *Journal of Human Resources* article entitled "The Continuing Struggle for a Negative Income Tax" where I considered President Nixon's second try at enacting a negative income tax plan (H.R. 1) that also ended in a defeat of the plan itself but saw the adoption of two programs with strong negative income tax dimensions—the Supplemental Security Income program and the 1971 amendments to the Food Stamp Act.[2] Seldom does one case portray so dramatically the interaction of policy analysis, policy research, and high politics. In particular, the various events of the period discussed illustrate:

1. The interrelationship of policy analysis and policy research, and the potential for close cooperation between analytic staffs and outside researchers;
2. The demanding nature of policy research, conceptually and methodologically, including the fact that policy demands may require path-breaking research;
3. Technical and procedural problems in large-scale field research that almost always render it vulnerable to criticism on legitimate methodological grounds;
4. Organizational difficulties involved in undertaking large-scale social policy field experiments;
5. Difficulties of meshing research findings with the time demands of the decision-making process;

6. The relationship of research results to other factors in the policy process, in particular the important but limited role of research results in policy making; and

7. The highly political nature of policy research when its actual or expected results are relevant to major social policy decisions and the potential consequences of a political milieu for social science researchers.

Three comments about the chapter's provenance are needed. First, I was a participant in certain of the activities considered, with my involvement dating from the earliest analysis of the negative income tax at the Office of Economic Opportunity. James Lyday and I were the staff members in the Research and Plans Division of the Office of Research, Plans, Programs and Evaluation (RPP&E) responsible for developing the negative income tax recommendations in OEO's first national anti-poverty plan submitted to the Bureau of the Budget in October 1965. In addition, I also served on a number of intergovernmental task forces on income maintenance. After these early efforts, I specialized in the manpower area and had almost no involvement with the negative tax until mid-1967. Specifically, I did not participate in the development of the MATHEMATICA proposal to OEO for a negative income tax experiment. However, when OEO director Sargent Shriver decided to include the OEO-funded Institute for Research on Poverty (IRP) at the University of Wisconsin in the experiment, I had the assignment of bringing the various parties to a signed agreement before June 30, 1967. In the fall of 1967, I became the chief of the OEO's Research and Plans Division, one of the three people in RPP&E with formal responsibilities for the conduct of the New Jersey experiment. The other two—Robert Levine who headed RPP&E and James Lyday who had continued as the income maintenance specialist in the division and was the liaison man with the project—were far more active than I. Lyday handled most of the regular interaction both with IRP and with MATHEMATICA. On major issues, Harold Watts, the director of both IRP and the project, contacted either Lyday or more likely Levine with whom he had a long working relationship stretching back to a period when both were at Yale, and I would become involved only at a crisis point that generally necessitated a face-to-face meeting with members of IRP, MATHEMATICA, and RPP&E.

Second, I did not keep a journal record of events. But I did retain (not in a systematic way, however) a large number of documents pertaining to income maintenance and subsequently obtained copies of several key documents that I did not have among my papers. Much of the discussion of the events leading to the development of the New Jersey income tax experiment is based upon unpublished documents in my possession. Further, Worth Bateman, David N. Kershaw, Robert A. Levine, Harold W. Watts, and John O. Wilson, all of whom were key actors in the events, made both written and oral comments on an earlier draft of the 1972 monograph responding to my request to pay particular attention to the accuracy of factual statements. Several of these individuals also provided extensive help when I sought to trace a point or to verify some aspect of history, particularly in preparing the section on the development of the Family Assistance Plan, an event which I had no involvement in and little information on prior to working on the paper.

Third, the first of the several large-scale field experiments that characterize the golden era of agency social policy analysis, the New Jersey negative income tax experiment, remains the best case study of such efforts and an excellent vehicle for expanding on the section of Chapter 3 that looked at the OEO/HEW model. The other social field experiments in areas such as health and housing have increased our knowledge of the special aspects of these areas but in the main addressed questions similar to the major ones considered in this chapter. The most basic issue in all the experiments is the extent to which governments can obtain information about the feasibility of new program ideas *before* decisions to launch large-scale programs are made. That is, can the government, at the time of decisions, have valid evidence drawn from field research that a proposed new program is likely to work better than an already existing program? It is a question important both to social science and to politics.

As a guide to the detailed discussion that follows, it is useful to summarize briefly the events that led up to the development of the New Jersey experiment, the experiment itself, and the factors that politicized it. The experiment came about after an unsuccessful attempt in the fall of 1965 to get President Johnson to support a negative income tax. Key members of the Executive Office of the President tried to interest the president in the negative tax as a means of reforming welfare. A number of factors, particularly the escalation of the war in Vietnam and the general unpopularity of the idea of making money payments to able-bodied men who it was alleged would quit work, doomed negative tax ideas at that time. Moreover, no then current empirical study had addressed the claim of a reduced labor response. To obtain such evidence, a group of OEO policy analysts and university researchers developed a seminal social experiment addressing behavioral questions of fundamental importance to economic theory. The OEO analysts believed that sound empirical evidence would give the negative tax a new hearing in the White House and the Congress. Yet no solid data from the New Jersey experiment had come forth when President Richard Nixon opted to support the Family Assistance Plan.

Quite the contrary, once the Family Assistance Plan became a serious legislative proposal, the New Jersey experiment researchers decided to move quickly to process preliminary data so the results could be available for congressional hearings. Once these preliminary data had been presented to the House Ways and Means Committee, a suspicious Congress ordered its investigative arm, the General Accounting Office, to look closely at the procedures used by the researchers in preparing the preliminary results. Thus, political needs that generated a project of great scientific importance also embroiled it in presidential and congressional politics.

EVENTS LEADING UP TO THE EXPERIMENT

Within the federal government, OEO took the lead in trying to initiate major income maintenance reforms. The various government money transfer programs making payments to the poor, such as social security and public welfare, were a major area of concern at OEO starting in the summer of 1965. Even the simplest analysis showed grave deficiencies in the federal government's income maintenance structure. In particular, the public welfare system, then the only national program designed to provide income support exclusively to the poor, covered only about one-fourth of all poor persons and discouraged work among those covered by reducing benefits dollar-for-dollar of additional earnings, which can be seen as a 100-percent tax rate. Moreover, this state-administered system had a welter of almost unintelligible regulations that resulted in arbitrary determinations of eligibility and widely varying payment levels among the states (some Southern states had payments of only a few dollars a month). Finally, critics of the welfare system argued that the intensive checking and rechecking of eligibility by case workers degraded and debilitated the recipients.

In light of these grave deficiencies, various scholars began investigating possible alternative income maintenance programs. One of the most appealing, the negative income tax, could provide coverage for all family units and persons below some specified income level (perhaps, the poverty line); determine eligibility by means of a simple income declaration, much like a federal income tax form; and encourage work more than public welfare through a less-than-100-percent tax rate. Although the basic concept of income transfers goes back to the Speenhamland System of 1795, the negative tax in approximately its present form is of much more recent origin. University of Chicago economic theorist and Nobelist Milton Friedman had proposed the negative income tax in lectures at Wabash College in 1956 and then discussed it in his 1962 book *Capitalism and Freedom*, but his proposal had no discernible impact on the government.[3] Christopher Green has pointed up that correspondence with Friedman and others indicates that the general idea of a negative tax was discussed informally in the 1940s including some conversations in the Division of Tax Research of the Treasury.[4]

RPP&E started a crash effort in the summer of 1965 to prepare a national anti-poverty plan covering major social policy areas including income maintenance. Robert A. Levine, the head of the Research and Plans Division and number two man in RPP&E under Joseph Kershaw, assigned James M. Lyday and me from that division to perform the analysis for the income maintenance area, and the OEO policy analysts sought help from outside scholars. The academic whose work on the negative tax had a major effect on government thinking was Robert Lampman, a well-regarded economist at the University of Wisconsin. Lampman became an early consultant to RPP&E and in August 1965 provided OEO with a paper entitled "Negative Rates Income Taxation" that addressed the form a negative tax might take, how it might be administered, and what it might cost. Drawing on this paper and discussion with Lampman and Green (then his graduate student), Lyday and Williams prepared "Transfer Payment Programs, " a paper that considered alternative changes in the major income maintenance programs including the possible adoption of a negative income tax. The paper presented (1) a negative income tax covering *all* individuals whose income was below the poverty line, referred to as a universal negative tax to distinguish it from other plans for specific groups such as families or the aged, and (2) another negative income tax providing payments only for families with children under age eighteen.

The 1965 Attempt to Secure Presidential Support for a Negative Tax

In October 1965 OEO presented to the Bureau of the Budget its first national anti-poverty plan including a universal negative income tax estimated to cost $4.7 billion in fiscal year 1967. During the same summer, the White House established a Task Force on Income Maintenance chaired by Gardner Ackley, chairman of the Council of Economic Advisers, with other members drawn primarily from the subcabinet ranks of the Departments of Health, Education and Welfare, Labor, and Treasury, as well as OEO (the author served on it), and the Bureau of the Budget. On September 20, 1965 Ackley transmitted the task force report to the White House with a covering memorandum addressed to Joseph A. Califano, the president's chief adviser on domestic policy issues. The Ackley report claimed a strong case could be made for a negative income tax and urged that a follow-up group develop a coordinated income maintenance program for the nation. In its next anti-poverty plan submission sent to the BOB in June 1966, OEO again recommended a negative tax and provided a much more detailed treatment developed by an RPP&E team of Lyday and Harold Watts, who soon left OEO to become the first director of the Institute for Research on Poverty. By that time OEO knew the president would not buy a negative tax but wanted to keep the idea alive.

In retrospect one can ask why President Johnson turned a deaf ear on a proposal similar in its basic mechanics to the one that President Nixon endorsed a few years later. A number of reasons come to mind. First, the negative tax lacked a well-placed, articulate, and tenacious advocate in the inner councils of the president, a crucial role that Daniel P. Moynihan assumed in the Nixon administration. Second, the costs of the war in Vietnam were moving to their peak point so that the White House had little interest in major and expensive new initiatives. Third, congressional and public opinion toward the negative tax was quite hostile. For example, once it became public knowledge that OEO had been looking into income maintenance questions including the negative tax, the agency began receiving angry letters calling the negative tax amoral and probably a communist or socialist plot. Individual congressmen were also critical, often in the same terms as the public. Fourth, the negative income tax had a powerful opponent, Wilbur Cohen, then the undersecretary of HEW, who favored a reform of the public welfare system. As noted, Cohen as a young man had been involved in the writing of the original social security legislation and over the years had been a prominent figure in its later development. Both the White House and the Congress saw Cohen as the government's foremost authority on income maintenance. He in effect held a veto in the executive branch over any new income maintenance plans much as Congressman Wilbur Mills did in the House of Representatives.

Finally, no sound research evidence existed that indicated how people would respond to a negative income tax. Social science theory gave some general hints about what might happen. First, one would expect that the higher the tax rate, the greater would be the decrease in work. For example, a tax rate of 90 percent would discourage more work than a disincentive rate of 10 percent. Theory also suggested that the higher the guarantee level, the more likely it was that people would decrease their work response. Given a 50-percent tax rate, a break-even income of $2,000 for a family with no pretax income provided only a guarantee of $1,000; a break-even income of $10,000 established a $5,000 income floor. But theory only indicated the direction of the work response. Neither theory nor any empirical information then available showed the precise dimensions of the labor-supply response to various tax rates and levels of break-even income.

Without such information, estimates of how much a negative income tax proposal would cost were at best rough ballpark figures.

"Cost" as used here has two dimensions. First, there would be the cost of a negative plan in direct federal outlays. What is the expected bill to the government if a particular type of plan were adopted? While technically such cost is a transfer of income from one group (taxpayers) to another group (recipients of allowances), the government needed to know the dollar amount for budget purposes. Beyond these "transfer" costs, the negative tax could bring a reduction in work efforts from recipients of payments and thereby decrease the level of production in the total system, i.e., decrease real Gross Domestic Product. Various cost estimates made at the time either assumed away the disincentive effects of a negative tax or made some very rough estimates of what these disincentive effects might turn out to be. Neither means of estimating the cost of the negative income tax produced estimates in which one could have great confidence.

Lack of knowledge about the level of work response also produced philosophical/political problems. Transfer payments to able-bodied men (note: this group, not welfare mothers, were the central issue in the 1960s) undercut cherished notions about the work ethic. Serious proponents of a negative income tax almost certainly would be confronted by the claim: "You mean you are going to give taxpayers' hard-earned money to some bums who will stop work and just collect their welfare checks?" No empirical information could support a strong rebuttal. It would be a complete misreading of history to claim that the missing information on the dimensions of the labor-supply response represented a crucial factor blocking adoption of the negative income tax. In fact, President Nixon accepted the argument for a negative tax before the availability of the information then being generated in the New Jersey experiment. At the same time, opponents of a negative income tax could score debating points effectively by arguing that the negative tax would encourage massive idleness. This factor did become important when the Family Assistance Plan entered the legislative process.

Development of the New Jersey Experiment Proposal

Work on income maintenance, including the New Jersey experiment, stands as one of the high points of policy analysis in the social agencies. That effort shows the potential both of analytic work in policy making in that policy analysis gave the negative income tax a hearing in the highest councils of government and of significant interaction among agency analysts and outside researchers in developing major policy research to support future decision making. The New Jersey experiment, which had been initiated because of a lack of evidence concerning the extent to which people would decrease work if they received various negative income tax allowances, became a major conceptual/meth- odological undertaking to probe the dimensions of the labor-supply response in a dynamic rather than a cross-sectional setting—a matter of great importance in economic theory. In order to address these basic questions, a distinguished team of academic researchers designed a seminal study. It is also important to note that the policy analysts in RPP&E, while interested in the same general questions as the social scientists, approached them from the perspective of what they believed to be a sensitive political question that hindered policy decisions. Unlike the experimental study team whose most fundamental interest focused on the scientific issue of socioeconomic behavior, RPP&E's primary motivation in funding the study was the political need to be able to counter the claim that able-bodied men would stop work and just collect welfare checks. Strong congruence between scientific and politi- cal needs marked the joint venture. Not only did science and politics need answers to the same basic questions, the RPP&E policy staff members and the outside scientists were in general agreement about the methodological and procedural approaches to be employed by the study team. Robert Levine, the head of RPP&E, clearly recognized this happy merger when he observed in an internal June 7, 1967 OEO memorandum arguing for the funding of the negative income tax exper- iment:

> The negative income tax is a national policy issue which has been the subject of considerable discussion and has received support from individ- uals representing the full range of the political spectrum. Still there are important questions remaining unanswered which no amount of discussion can settle; what is needed now is more hard data about the possible effects of this form of income maintenance. The most important question is the extent to which a negative income tax (or different forms of such a program) would lead to a reduction of the work effort of recipients of the negative tax payments. This is the primary question to which the project is addressed. . . . In addition to its specific contribution to examination of the possibility of a negative income tax, this project represents a landmark in increasing the sophistication of federal policy- making in general. The attempt will be not only, as in the past, to apply social science theory to national policymaking, but to go a step further by undertaking social science experimentation as a part of the develop- ment of more rational national policies. This will be an advance not only in the "science of government" but in the social sciences in general.

Policy analysts at OEO, as advocates for the negative income tax, were frustrated by their inability to get their ideas accepted by the key policy makers in the White House but struggled on. Over time, in his advocacy role, Lyday became a top government technician on the negative tax. Robert Levine, who had replaced Kershaw as RPP&E director, emerged as one of its foremost proponents within the subcabinet ranks. Negative income tax advocacy had other executive branch players beyond OEO. HEW's Robert Harris and Worth Bateman were extremely knowledgeable about the technical aspects of the negative tax; and their boss Alice Rivlin, assistant secretary for planning and evaluation, worked within the Johnson administration for a consideration of the negative tax at the higher levels of the government. Beyond this limited advocacy, mainly within the executive branch, a research project represented the only viable option open to the policy analysts in strengthening their case for the negative tax. They had neither the authority nor the skills to try to sell the Congress or the public on the negative tax. The policy analysts in OEO and HEW in the 1960s were neither public relations nor "Hill" staffers but rather academically oriented social scientists. They understood their one comparative advantage—going after hard evidence in support of the negative tax.

With the key political question in mind, the search began in RPP&E under the direction of Robinson Hollister, the head of the Research and Plans Division, who was joined by two members of the division, Lyday and Glen Cain (on a year's leave from the University of Wisconsin). Hollister and Cain were to play the principal roles within RPP&E in the intellectual development of the New Jersey experiment. Both men, who would be on the University of Wisconsin faculty within the half-year, were well-trained, quantitatively oriented economists, neither of whom had had a significant role in the earlier OEO analysis of the negative tax. Thus, the New Jersey negative income tax experiment was developed primarily by the two individuals in RPP&E who adhered most strongly to the values of academia and not by those persons still on the RPP&E staff who had earlier played important roles in developing and advocating the OEO negative income tax position—Levine, Lyday, and Williams.

In the search for a means of investigating the labor response rate to negative taxation, the team looked primarily to the academic community. A young graduate student, Heather Ross, then working with the staff of the United Planning Organization (the Washington, D. C., Community Action Agency) had been trying to develop a negative tax experiment for her dissertation at the Massachusetts Institute of Technology. In December 1966 she had prepared a first draft of a paper, "A Proposal for a Demonstration of New Techniques in Income Maintenance, " spelling out her methodological approach to a negative tax experiment. Guy Orcutt, then a member of the faculty at the University of Wisconsin and one of the nation's leading econometricians, offered a critique of the Ross paper entitled "Experimental Study of Negative Income Taxation" (rough draft, dated March 14, 1967) that supported many of the ideas in her paper, criticized segments of the methodological approach, and set out an alternative methodological strategy. Drawing on these two papers, MATHEMATICA, a Princeton-based, for-profit research organization, brought together a group, including Ross, to develop a negative income tax experiment proposal.

On May 6, Levine wrote a memo to OEO director Sargent Shriver to describe in fairly sketchy terms the ideas being worked on at MATHEMATICA and to alert him that a formal proposal would soon be forthcoming. Shriver wrote across the face of the memo, "I'm all for the experiment, but let's button down as many corners as possible in advance." The Levine memo, however, did not get the enthusiastic support of everyone in the agency. Desperate political trouble in Congress had forced OEO's legislative staff to work feverishly in trying to create goodwill in that legislative body. After seeing the Levine memo, George McCarthy, head of OEO's legislative staff, wrote to Shriver:

> The proposed negative income tax demonstration program would be political suicide at this particular time—regardless of the demonstration aspect which would be too sophisticated as the reason for funding—you and OEO would be charged with starting this highly controversial program without waiting for congressional discussions regarding the whole issue. If Levine is looking for a research and demonstration plan on how to "effectively kill legislation" or "mobilize the negative reactions of Congress to legislation"—this will do the job.

In a handwritten note at the bottom of McCarthy's memo, Shriver replied: "We have never waited for congressional discussions on Headstart, Upward Bound, Foster Grandparents, Legal Services, Neighborhood Health Centers, 'Success Insurance,' etc. This is just an experimental, pilot project involving only $1.3 million." In early June, MATHEMATICA submitted to RPP&E a proposal to investigate the possible effects of a negative income tax on the recipients' labor-supply response with a study sample to be drawn from the poor urban families with male heads and at least one child located in low income areas in two or three cities in New Jersey.

Three questions need posing. Why choose New Jersey as the site of the study? First, in a technical sense, it was desirable to work with a test population not receiving other transfer payments to keep the integrity of the tax rate structure fairly clean in the experiment. At that time the state of New Jersey did not have the Unemployed Parent (UP) segment of the Aid for Dependent Children program, UP being the only federal program paying transfer payments to able-bodied men. Second, the New Jersey government had been approached and had promised a high level of cooperation in the experiment. Finally,

MATHEMATICA had its home base in New Jersey. If that state offered no major barriers as compared to other states, small wonder MATHEMATICA opted for New Jersey.

The next question is, why did OEO, despite the real political dangers, fund the experiment? The simple answer is that no one else would do it. Ross had tried without success to interest HEW, the logical funding source as the operator of the nation's major income maintenance programs. In early 1967 RPP&E approached both HEW and the Ford Foundation asking that they support the emerging experiment. Neither was interested, so Sargent Shriver decided to gamble. He showed great courage in going forward with the grant, as well as a degree of recklessness, in the face of the serious threat of Congress punishing OEO. The agency did take some precautionary steps. First, Shriver himself coined the term "graduated work incentives" as a replacement for the unpopular "negative income tax." Second, he held back the press release on the grant for two months until Congress's Labor Day recess, although OEO administrative procedures mandated a speedy release. Finally, someone in OEO decided that the press release would be cast in the blandest terms and the assignment fell to me. The press release began: "The University of Wisconsin Institute for Research on Poverty will study the effects of graduated work incentive payments on the lives and habits of the poor with a $620,078 demonstration grant, the Office of Economic Opportunity announced today. It will be the first effort to study the impact of work incentive payments." The remainder of the press release described the grant in completely accurate terms, but offered no clue to the fact that OEO had funded a negative income tax experiment. Robert Walters observed in the November 1, 1967 issue of the now defunct Washington newspaper, the *Evening Star*: "That announcement was so cautiously worded that it attracted virtually no public attention at the time of the release." Beyond noting the praise for bureaucratic writing at its best (worst?), I would alert readers that the phrase "graduated work incentives" will shortly take a prominent place in the story.

Finally, how did IRP become involved in the study? When RPP&E presented the MATHEMATICA proposal to Shriver, he liked it. Yet possibilities of severe political criticism bothered him. Shriver proposed that the project be administered by the OEO-funded Institute for Research on Poverty, rather than directly through OEO. According to those who dealt with Shriver on the issue, his bringing in the IRP was motivated by a combination of (1) political fear that the project might hurt OEO in Congress, (2) an interest in seeing the project go forward, (3) a belief, based on his political fears, of the need to stress symbolically the research aspects of the project, and (4) a desire to get the most out of the IRP, for which he had held high hopes that had not been fulfilled.

It is not clear how heavily each of the four factors weighed in Shriver's mind, but two things are certain: politics played a big role, and Shriver had no particular scheme for working out the details with the University of Wisconsin. The task of negotiations fell to me. The climate could hardly have been worse. Very much in the minds of the University of Wisconsin officials were recent headline stories telling of the CIA's use of various organizations, including universities, as conduits for funding clandestine activities. The university took a hard line, demanding at a minimum a full partnership role in the research project, and even had doubts about any involvement in which funds passed through that university to support the MATHEMATICA portion of the project.

The RPP&E staff, though it questioned whether or not Shriver was right in his belief that IRP's involvement would reduce political pressures, saw the great advantages of including several IRP staff members experienced in the income maintenance area and pushed to work out the arrangements. The institute, as separate from the highest university officials, also recognized the research potential of the undertaking and began to describe in some detail a possible relationship between it and MATHEMATICA. An expanded proposal made IRP both the funding agent and a partner with MATHEMATICA in the research; Shriver accepted it; and the forced marriage somewhat fortuitously set (perhaps more accurately shoved) the Institute for Research on Poverty on a path toward becoming the most important academic institution in the United States concerned with poverty problems.

IMPLEMENTATION OF THE NEW JERSEY EXPERIMENT

OEO officials signed the New Jersey experiment proposal on June 30, 1967, the final day of the fiscal year. At the time of funding, the hastily put together team of MATHEMATICA and IRP had not determined how it would proceed in substantive terms or how the work between the two would be divided. Grafting IRP onto the experiment somewhat complicated the staff structure. Where previously there had been a first-rate MATHEMATICA team, including Albert Rees, one of the foremost labor economists in the United States, and William Baumol, a leading economic theorist, a second group of stars joined the venture— Harold Watts, the director of IRP, and Lampman. While the shotgun marriage may at times have been a rocky one with conflicts among talented researchers, it also produced a team of unquestioned excellence.

The bright illumination of hindsight shows clearly that both the OEO policy analysts and the study team at the inception of the project made two gross miscalculations, one technical and the other political. The project fell well behind schedule and stayed there—a most unfortunate circumstance in light of the great need in early 1970 for sound evaluative results in the deliberations over the Family Assistance Plan. First, the team underestimated the difficulty of actually getting an experiment into the field. Logistics became an almost overwhelming problem. While MATHEMATICA had been promised cooperation by the state of New Jersey, it had to work out a great number of legal details not only with the state but also with the Internal Revenue Service. Further, the team had to determine how negative tax payments should be made—by whom, how often, with how much checking, etc. These problems, which required the study team to resolve a number of legal and administrative issues, later provided a great deal of information on the procedural problems of constructing a negative tax system that proved useful in the design of the Family Assistance Plan.

Determining the appropriate sample population turned out to be equally difficult. The only available socioeconomic data on the New Jersey population came from the 1960 census. From this the study team could pinpoint the low income areas of cities but nothing about the levels of household income in 1967. The team found that it would be necessary to screen thousands of households in order to determine male-headed families whose income levels would make them eligible for the experiment. Neither MATHEMATICA nor IRP had the staff capability to undertake large-scale surveys. After an unhappy first try at screening with an outside survey team, MATHEMATICA decided that it had to build its own staff field capability.

It is hardly surprising that the study team underestimated the complexity of the logistical problems. First and foremost, they simply had no precedent upon which to base their estimates. The New Jersey project represented the first effort to mount a large-scale social policy experiment of this type. Further, the MATHEMATICA group consisted mainly of academic economists whose reputations came either from theoretical work or from research utilizing secondary data sources, not from studies involving primary data collection and certainly not from experimentation in the field. Not perceiving the complexity of experimentation in the field, the study team tended to concentrate on developing the needed economic concepts and to downgrade the other problems.

The political miscalculation is equally understandable. Given both the expenditure levels of the Vietnam war and the unpopularity of the negative income tax concept, the RPP&E analysts and the study team believed that negative tax legislation, if it was to come at all, would be many years away. This is not to say that those involved in the experiment failed to see its great importance, both in the political and the scientific arenas, or that they operated without a sense of urgency to get new evidence before decision makers. They could not foresee, however, that two and one-half years after the experiment had been funded, the president of the United States would be supporting a negative income tax and would be greatly in need of hard evidence showing how people responded to tax allowances.

MATHEMATICA's transmittal letter submitted to OEO prior to IRP's involvement stated: "We propose that the study last four years: one half year for planning and setup, three years of negative tax payments, and one half year for final analysis. The first analysis of intermediate results will be submitted between twelve and eighteen months after the start of the negative tax payments." Had the project stayed on schedule, a critical intermediate report would have been available in mid- or late 1969 in excellent time to mesh with the Family Assistance Plan. The negative tax project, however, fell behind schedule. In part, the slippage could not be avoided because of the unanticipated technical difficulties just described. In part, it came about because both the policy staff at OEO and the New Jersey team of social scientists saw themselves as much ahead of their time, engaged in an effort to develop rigorous scientific evidence that would revive meaningful debate on the negative income tax. Time, usually a key element in political considerations, had importance. Still, it was the factor most likely to give way.

This perception of political reality led all concerned to believe that research dollars for the experiment had to be relatively fixed, with no justification for extra spending so as to have results available for upcoming policy decisions. Also the social scientists at RPP&E and on the study team suspected that the initial audience for the results would be their peers and that only after the study had passed scientific inspection would it generate political interest. This pushed toward an emphasis on scientific quality, certainly a direction compatible with the rigorous standards of the senior members of the study team. Given this frame of reference that all major actors accepted, it is not very likely that the experiment could have progressed at a much more rapid pace. Second guessing at this time is hardly fruitful.

THE EXPERIMENT AND THE FAMILY ASSISTANCE PLAN

The question of why Richard Nixon accepted the negative tax proposal, finally labeled the Family Assistance Plan (FAP), while Lyndon Johnson did not is interesting in light of our concern with the relationship of research evidence to policy making. In an ex post facto critique, key factors leading to the already known outcome usually are easy to discover. Yet the central question—the place of policy analysis and research in the decision—cannot be answered with any precision. Several factors, however, seem important. First, when John Veneman, the newly appointed HEW undersecretary, put together a negative tax working staff, veteran analysts from the previous administration dominated it. The basic technical design of the proposal made to President Nixon was developed in part by two government experts, James Lyday and Worth Bateman (then deputy assistant secretary for planning and evaluation at HEW), both of whom had been key figures in the negative tax analysis during the Johnson administration. Second, no empirical evidence of the extent to which negative tax payments affected work response had yet come out either from the New Jersey experiment or any other research. Moreover, major gaps in knowledge existed that could have been addressed with available information. In particular, no one had developed an integrated income maintenance system combining a negative tax with other transfer programs such as public welfare and food stamps, a deficiency that emerged with grave consequences before the Senate Committee on Finance.

Third, the most obvious factor in the acceptance of the negative tax by President Nixon is that an administration at its start generally is looking for new initiatives to propose. One might argue that the negative tax did not meet the test of a new initiative, but it was in the sense that it had never received any kind of endorsement by President Johnson. Yet lots of new initiatives existed and many were far less costly than the several billion dollar price tag for a negative income tax. Fourth, despite the gaps in information and analysis, a far better case could be made for the negative tax in strong analytic terms than other potential major proposals. The earlier analyses of the negative tax and the existing capacity to do further analysis stood available at the right time. Fifth, the political and bureaucratic climate had changed significantly since the mid-1960s. Public welfare, which had been viewed as a major problem in the earlier period, stood out as an outright disaster area. An almost desperate search was going on for some means of stemming the rapidly rising welfare outlays, and HEW, the agency that managed the major income maintenance programs in the United States, endorsed the proposal while in the earlier period Wilbur Cohen had blocked it. Moreover, the notion of a negative tax had become much more acceptable to Congress and the public. And the New Jersey negative tax experiment seemingly had had a positive influence in this direction. At the time of the funding of the New Jersey experiment, OEO had good reason to fear a negative congressional reaction. However, the mood of the Congress had shifted at least to the extent that the experiment itself had become quite respectable because of its stress on determining systematically some of the key answers needed to make more intelligent decisions about income maintenance programs. In a congressional committee meeting attended by an assemblage of high-ranking OEO and HEW officials, Wisconsin Congressman Melvin Laird said:

I am very interested in the project which is being financed by the OEO through the Poverty Institute at the University of Wisconsin. I think we should watch the results of this project very carefully, because I see in the year 1975 a tremendous welfare bill as far as this country is concerned if we continue along the present program level. . . . Having served on the HEW Appropriations Committee ever since that committee was created, I have watched these growing costs and felt that our system was not accomplishing what it was devised to accomplish, and that is to help those people that are the most in need. So I think we have to watch this study very closely. I had felt that the Social Security Administration should really finance this study and that it should have been done in the Department of Health, Education, and Welfare. They were very slow in moving. So, I commend OEO for going forward with this study. I believe that this study is most important.[5]

Finally, and perhaps most important of all, the negative income tax had a champion in the White House itself. How Daniel P. Moynihan by tongue and pen convinced President Nixon of the wisdom of the Family Assistance Plan despite the strong opposition within the administration has been written about extensively and need not be repeated in any detail here.[6] What is worth underscoring is that the HEW policy analysis by the Johnson administration holdovers had a major impact in converting Moynihan to the negative income tax. Previously Moynihan had supported a children's allowance in part because he believed initially that President Nixon would oppose anything but the mildest changes in welfare. According to Evans and Novak, an HEW analytic document shifted Moynihan's opinion:

What changed Moynihan's outlook and persuaded him to raise his sights was the first meeting of the Welfare Subcommittee of the new Urban Affairs Council (with Nixon not present) late in January a few days after the inauguration. Robert Finch, then still the self-confident presidential confidant and leader of the progressive forces in the Nixon administration, presented a paper recommending revisions in the welfare law that he had inherited from the HEW bureaucracy. While avoiding the incendiary words "guaranteed annual income," that is precisely what it amounted to.[7]

The Decision to Use Preliminary Results from the New Jersey Experiment

The remainder of this historical account centers on a single document entitled "Preliminary Results of the New Jersey Graduated Work Incentive Experiment" issued by the Office of Economic Opportunity on February 18, 1970 where Shriver's title "graduated work incentives" had replaced that of the "negative income tax."[8] In the OEO report, the purpose of which was to influence legislative thinking, the agency made a case for the Family Assistance Plan based on preliminary results from the New Jersey experiment. These events—perhaps more clearly than any other single set of circumstances—crystallize both the potential importance of field research results for social policy making and the potential threat of such endeavors for social scientists.

As to these events, two comments are needed. First, if what transpired is to be fully appreciated, the importance and excitement of the situation needs to be perceived. We are not in the laboratory but in the center of a political fight. On one level, at stake is a landmark piece of legislation about which the New Jersey experiment social scientists as citizens feel very deeply; on another level, at risk are their reputations as scientists. Such a statement should not be construed as implying that members of the New Jersey study team necessarily supported the Nixon administration Family Assistance Plan with its strong work provisions and low guarantee levels. Some members of the team wanted a more expensive negative tax system without forced work requirements, e.g., Harold Watts recommended double the levels in FAP.[9] Still, pressures for an early release of preliminary data from the experiment were intense—particularly on Harold Watts, the director of the New Jersey experiment; David Kershaw, the chief of field operations for the New Jersey experiment; and John Wilson, the director of OEO's Office of Planning, Research and Evaluation (PR&E), and the senior policy analyst responsible at OEO for the New Jersey experiment. Despite some published reports to the contrary (discussed below), the pressures do not appear to have been direct and heavy-handed—e.g., the White House ordering Wilson to order the New Jersey team to provide preliminary data by a specific date. Second, my purpose here is not to judge the individuals involved in the events to be discussed in that the scientists were operating in completely uncharted terrain, the complex interface between social science and social policy as played out with no good precedents at the presidential-congressional level.

Following the Nixon administrative formulation of the Family Assistance Plan came the start of hearings on the legislation before the House Ways and Means Committee in January 1970. While precise tactics might have been at issue in getting any major welfare legislation through the House of Representatives at that time, the overriding concern had to be on winning the approval of Chairman Wilbur Mills and Wisconsin Congressman John Byrnes, the senior Republican on the committee. After that, the House almost certainly would follow along.

Prominent among the witnesses testifying before the Ways and Means Committee were Watts and Kershaw. Interestingly, OEO officials had not been invited. This set of events appears to have come about for two reasons. First, by early 1970 the New Jersey study team collectively had become the recognized authority on almost all aspects of the negative tax (except, of course, on the Nixon administration political views, but these would not have come from OEO). Second, Watts in particular had strong ties to the Ways and Means Committee through his fellow Wisconsinite and had arranged with Congressman Byrnes to help the committee in any way he could. So it came to pass that PR&E was aware of these relationships between the study team and the committee and believed them to be useful, but had no role at the time.

In their testimony before the Ways and Means Committee, Watts and Kershaw discussed the New Jersey experiment at length, pointing out how the previous experience offered an excellent guide for the legal and administrative development of the Family Assistance Plan. This in-depth field experience in a large-scale social experiment can provide valuable information both for the decision-making process and later for a full implementation effort if the decision is made to proceed. As we will see, President Bill Clinton's attempt to enact national health insurance suffered because of legitimate implementation questions that the Clinton health team could not answer satisfactorily concerning the complex organizational structure proposed to administer the plan. Here is one of those "what if" issues: Would the Clinton health team, with solid field data on implementation and management, have still proposed such a difficult administrative structure, or would the information have shown the proposed national health insurance structure would have been easier to administer than critics claimed?

Watts and Kershaw also observed that those close to the experiment had not detected in preliminary results any evidence of a significant decrease in the work response. But they offered no data to shed light on the critical work response rate—a most frustrating experience. If only they could have been able to see the need for all deliberate speed two and one-half years before. Now a bill before the Congress had won serious consideration in the Ways and Means Committee, and the study team that had labored so hard could not provide data showing the labor-supply response to negative taxation, the main variable that the New Jersey experiment had been designed to investigate. Shortly after his testimony, Watts wrote Chairman Wilbur Mills on January 30 on a number of issues and closed by indicating that the study team was working to extend and augment the early experimental results.

Upon his return to Princeton, Kershaw reexamined the status of the data then being generated in the experiment to see if it might not be possible to derive some relevant evidence. After looking at the available information, he decided that some very preliminary tables could be developed that would get at some of the points bothering the House Ways and Means Committee. Kershaw first telephoned and then observed in a January 28, 1970 letter to Lyday:

> It became clear at the hearings that there are five or ten questions which are central to the decision on FAP. . . . In the next week or ten days I can have some findings (primarily frequency distributions, before and after in a couple of cities) which will supply answers to these questions. We stressed the fact that families have a strong work ethic, that administrative costs will be relatively low, that the families actively seek better jobs,–etc., but I think these points would be more effectively reinforced if I wrote a letter to Byrnes with some additional concrete findings. He is most interested in the experiment and clearly very influential with Mills on this issue. Essentially, I would like permission to send him such a letter in the near future. Following my own testimony such a missive would be very natural.

John Wilson at OEO confronted another problem that also led toward the need for preliminary data. The staff of the Ways and Means Committee had prepared a "confidential committee print" dated January 20, 1970 and entitled "Issues Involved in Provisions of H.R. 14173 Relating to Family Assistance Payments for the Working Poor" that set out much of the conventional wisdom about negative taxation in stressing the potential for family breakup and the possible deleterious impact of work disincentives. Wilson wrote a draft memorandum trying to point out fallacies in the committee print and sent a copy to Moynihan, who replied in writing on January 29 that Wilson failed in his chosen task because hard evidence was unavailable on several key issues. Wilson went to see Moynihan, and the meeting got reported as follows in a *New York Times Magazine* article:

> "I sat down to write a report," Wilson recalls with a rueful grin, "and I took it to Pat Moynihan. Pat jumped all over me. He stomped around the room, waving his arms, that Irish temper of his flaring. 'Wilson,' he said, 'you mean to tell me that you've had a $5-million experiment running in New Jersey for almost two years now and you don't know what you've got?'
>
> "I tried to explain that you had to let the experiment run its course before you could evaluate your data. 'Wilson,' Pat snorted, 'the fact is that you haven't got any answers. Why don't you have answers? That's the trouble with you economists—you never have any facts until it is too late.'
>
> "He got me so mad that I said, 'Damn it, I'll get some answers.' "
>
> This confrontation took place on Thursday. Wilson returned to his office and, as he says, "stewed" about the decision he had to make all the rest of that day and most of Friday. The first sizable group of families

in the experiment had been getting aid for only about 15 months. Wilson doubted whether this was enough to show any positive trends; he was afraid that a premature compilation of data might jeopardize the whole experiment—but he decided, with the political pressures what they were, that he had to chance it. So on Friday afternoon he telephoned Dave Kershaw in Princeton and ordered him to collate all the information available on the first 509 test families in the Trenton area. The group included 364 families who had been receiving assistance and 145 in the control group.

Wilson's telephone call triggered a frenetic weekend for Dave Kershaw and MATHEMATICA. Forty Princeton students were called in to help the MATHEMATICA staff cull details from the files; the data were flown to Wisconsin to be run through computers; the results were taken to Wilson in Washington the following week, and a report was prepared for submission to President Nixon and his Cabinet.[10]

The quote above hinted that Moynihan—or, more generally, the White House—had a direct role in pressing for information and that Wilson ordered Kershaw to prepare the preliminary data. Neither allegation appears to be accurate. In a letter to the author dated July 23, 1971, Wilson observed: "[A]fter our initial meeting as reported in the *Times*, Pat left on vacation in New Mexico and was not even aware of our decision to examine preliminary data. Pat only served to raise in my mind the possibility of examining the data, a possibility that I had not thought about even with the suggestions being made by Watts and Kershaw." According to Wilson, no one at the White House pressed OEO for preliminary data, nor did Wilson order the New Jersey team to process the data. In later testimony before the Senate Committee on Finance, Wilson, on being asked about the *New York Times Magazine* article, observed:

> As I recall, the article was quoting me, and where they obtained the quotes I don't know. But it was quoting the process I was going through in making the initial decision whether to examine the data, and the decision was made jointly by Professor Watts and myself. After examining the data, I was convinced it was reliable.
>
> I requested the data from Professor Watts. I cannot demand the data from him. I made a request to Professor Watts. Is there anything in the experiment that would give us a lead on how much it would cost, from a cost point of view, for a New Jersey type program?[11]

Once the decision had been made that the experimental data would be processed, time became crucial. Under the circumstances, if it wanted the information to be of use in the emerging policy debate, the study team had no choice but to do the work as rapidly as possible. Whether the decision to prepare the early results was a wise one is a matter to be speculated upon later. What does seem clear at this point is that the decision had not been forced by the White House but rather represented a joint effort of OEO and the New Jersey study group.

The OEO Pamphlet: The Controversy and Its Implications

On February 18, 1970 OEO issued the paper entitled "Preliminary Results of the New Jersey Graduated Work Incentive Experiment" that drew on these results to make an extremely strong case for the Family Assistance Plan. The report observed in its "Conclusions" section:

> We believe that these preliminary data suggest that fears that a Family Assistance Plan could result in extreme, unusual, or unanticipated responses are unfounded.
> Furthermore, we believe these preliminary data from the New Jersey project indicate that a Family Assistance Plan is practical. The data suggests that:
> 1. There is no evidence that work effort declined among those receiving income support payments.[12]

The OEO report is an interesting document, best described as a political tract rather than a scholarly document, running only twenty-six pages with many of the pages having only a few sentences or presenting a brief table. While the report does point out that the results are preliminary, it offers the reader few additional caveats. Further, while the authors used such relatively weak terms as "suggest," the report made the best case possible, seeking to convince readers that the data strongly supported the Family Assistance Plan in showing no significant decrease in work effort. Congress then asked its investigative arm, the General Accounting Office (GAO), to consider the validity of the results produced in the OEO report. In June 1970 GAO issued a paper entitled "Preliminary Comments on the New Jersey Graduated Work Incentive Experiment" critical of OEO's claims: "We believe that it is premature to conclude generally that, 'There is no evidence that work effort declined among those receiving income payments.' The data reflected in the OEO report represents less than a year's activity. Moreover, on the basis of the material in the OEO report and other material to which we were given access, we do not believe the data has been subjected to sufficient analysis to support conclusions from it."[13]

Almost immediately OEO produced a five-page rebuttal, only slightly longer than its title, "The Office of Economic Opportunity's Reply to the United States General Accounting Office June, 1970 Report Entitled 'Preliminary Comments on the New Jersey Graduated Work Incentive Experiment.'"[14] The Institute for Research on Poverty then published a paper by Harold Watts entitled "Adjusted and Extended Preliminary Results from the Urban Graduated Work Incentive Experiment."[15] Both of the papers addressed and tried to answer many of the points raised by the GAO paper. The Watts paper also presented a much more extensive and careful analysis of the New Jersey data than had been done in the first OEO document.

It is not necessary to critique these several documents to observe that together they raise a number of questions which are important in the development and use of policy research:

1. Was the release of the preliminary data from the New Jersey negative income tax experiment premature?
2. Did OEO overstate its case in the February 18 document?
3. Did the social scientists from the New Jersey study team respond appropriately (in accordance with what set of professional standards?) either in terms of the processing of the preliminary data or of the publication of the OEO February 18 document?

The General Accounting Office claimed that the New Jersey findings were premature and Watts addressed this question at length in his paper:

> At that point [after OEO had requested the data] analysis of the first returns had not yet been planned, let alone carried out. Only a fraction of the eventual data base was available, and attempts to draw conclusions from such a slim base would have been premature—at least from the viewpoint of conventional scientific research.
>
> As soon as we began to consider how to respond to OEO (at the very end of January), it became clear that a special crash effort was required simply because the data and processing system being developed for "normal" use would have taken at least two months to produce the data instead of the two weeks we had. Consequently, quick decisions had to be made as to which variables would be of greatest interest and also from which of the available interview waves these variables could best be measured. . . . We encountered, in the process, minor errors of punching and coding; but simply had no time to trace them and correct them if we were to meet the deadline forced upon us. . . .
>
> In a number of very important respects the evidence from this preliminary and crude analysis of the earliest results is less than ideal. If there were other evidence, approaching the relevance of these data but having fewer problems, it would be highly questionable whether an attempt to interpret and use the New Jersey data currently available should be made. Such is not the case, however, and as a consequence (at risk of being premature) we have tried to be responsibly responsive to a pressing public need for information. That response is simple: No

evidence has been found in the urban experiment to support the belief that negative-tax-type income maintenance programs will produce large disincentives and consequent reductions in earnings.[16]

Clearly the data were released prematurely in that normal quality controls on processing were not used. Although GAO found a number of clerical errors in their investigation, Watts' careful analysis of data in his paper showed that the errors were minor ones and did not in any way invalidate the major finding that participants did not significantly reduce their work effort.

Even if the data could be labeled as premature in research terms, the question remained as to how policy makers should have responded. Their concern was not with the validity of existing theory but with whether the evidence then available offered the best indicator of how people would respond to a policy treatment. If it could be shown with a low probability of error that a negative tax did not reduce work response, policy makers might be justified in acting upon the information despite the fact that they did not fully understand it nor have a theory to explain it. The situation is analogous to that in medicine in which a physician may be justified in prescribing a medication shown to be effective under controlled test conditions even though medical researchers have not been able to determine to their satisfaction why it works. Here is a good example of the difference between the needs of the academic scientist for the explanation of the results and the policy analyst, who is also a researcher, seeking reasonable results speaking to the effectiveness of present or proposed policy.

In the case of the OEO publication, a fair question is whether the preliminary information should have been published at all; and, if the answer is that it should have been, whether it was wise to analyze the data hurriedly and present the information in a brief document with no backup material. The haste in processing the information set up the February report for criticism of the type that emerged from GAO, and also in a sense politicized those involved in giving the appearance of a crash effort to influence policy. Yet a detailed analysis of the type performed by Watts would have missed the struggle being fought in the Ways and Means Committee and, moreover, been likely to have received little attention by being long, scholarly, and lacking in the forcefulness of the February document.

In deciding whether OEO pushed the evidence too far, it is necessary to keep in mind that the February 18 pamphlet must be judged as a political, not a scholarly, document. Political documents, generally speaking, will make the best possible case for the position that is being advocated. If the documents are made public, the checks and balances of subjecting it to attack will exist. In the case at hand, however, any intelligent questioning of the OEO pamphlet required more data than were made available in that short document, and that put the social scientists involved in a difficult and complex position. It is well to recall that some members of the study team had not simply been working away in the laboratory but had suggested the possibility of preliminary analysis. Such an offer, however, did not necessarily indicate a willingness to generate a large body of preliminary data under a crash program as a basis for a widely circulated, controversial report. Yet, could they have reasonably refused the request for preliminary results or demanded a longer processing time? If the study team had been unhappy with the way OEO had interpreted the data in the February 18 report, should they—as the only social scientists with full knowledge of the details—have openly recorded a dissent to the claims made in the OEO report? Watts had been involved in the development of the February 18 document but seemingly did not see the final version. Although some members of the New Jersey team were displeased with the strong, unqualified way that the February 18 pamphlet stated its case, they did feel the results supported the main thesis that the negative tax allowances had not reduced work responses. The policy researchers faced two strong pulls. They had professional responsibilities to the funding agency to be responsive to its need for information within the time demands of the decision process, and they had responsibilities to their peers in the scientific community to inform them of the improper use or interpretation of preliminary information when the study team members are the only nongovernment scientists with access to enough information to make such a judgment.

THE NEXT ROUND: H.R. I

The OEO negative income tax proposal had a number of features, including universal coverage for all those below a specified income level, more humane (than welfare) income determination, and strong work incentives deriving from a relatively low tax rate (50 percent being a kind of magic upper number). The analysts, who were mainly economists, naturally wanted the whole package, not partial victories. Yet, as Vincent and Vee Burke point out in discussing the 1967 welfare amendments that contained a 67-percent tax rate: "So it happened that Congress enacted a negative income tax for welfare mothers while economists still debated the political feasibility of the negative income tax."[17] Politicians are no doubt more realistic than policy analyst economists; however, it surely is not unreasonable to think that the choice of a less than 100-percent tax rate was affected by the economists' work.

The Family Assistance Plan, once on the table, paved the way for the 1971 food stamp amendments and the new Supplemental Security

Income (SSI) program. Food, like welfare, was an immediate issue for the Nixon administration and a highly competitive one with the Democratic Congress in seeking expanded provisions. The 1971 amendments made most low income single and family households eligible for food stamps which were, in effect, a specialized form of money that could be used to buy food. The 1971 amendments provided "earmarked money" rather than "regular" money and required that able-bodied household members over the age of eighteen to register for employment, while the OEO negative tax only used the tax rate as an incentive. But here is a scheme that covers all households below specified income levels varying by family size, and had a less than 100-percent tax rate— surely an outcome foreshadowed by the earlier events.

It might be said that SSI arose from FAP, emerging after FAP's demise in the H.R. 1 package. The most fascinating thing about SSI is not that it is so radical, but that it received so little attention in Congress. The Burkes observed that "since it was couched in technical phrases that understated its impact, SSI received little scrutiny."[18] And Bowler cited the following statement by a legislative aide of Senator Abraham Ribicoff: " 'People were so concerned about Title IV (the family provisions) that no one paid any attention to [SSI]. If SSI had been on its own it never would have made it. Also, it passed because it looked like peanuts next to the family programs.' "[19]

The pieces of the jigsaw may fall into place too precisely in the brilliant precision of reconstruction; still strong evidence is available, dating from mid-1965, of the crucial role of policy analysis in the events that transpired. Clearly there were several incremental steps along the way, and the work of policy analysts was an important factor in that movement. But we must take care not to be too deterministic, especially about policy analysis. First, as Nixon administration insider Daniel Patrick Moynihan made clear, at the height of decision, politics reigned.[20] Second, even though policy analysis probably was the key factor keeping things going and so paved the way for the decisions that came, no one should think that the decisions were preordained. Nixon could well have sided with FAP's strongest opponent within the administration, Arthur Burns, then counselor to the president and a long-time adviser, against Moynihan who was below Burns in the pecking-order, a Democrat, and a relative newcomer to the Nixon inner circle. The point—and it is a key one—is not that available analysis *impelled* action (politics did), but that it facilitated that action.

The long struggle for a negative income tax is surely one of the finest hours of social policy analysis. Never before or since have policy analysts been so prominent for so long in a major social policy debate. Policy analysts emerged as heroes of the Burkes' tale and, to some extent, of Moynihan's account. But we need to recognize that policy analysts, even in the golden age, had a winning season at best, not by any means an undefeated one. Over the long period in question, policy analysis came up short more than once in the executive branch, and analytic weaknesses in Congress were a major factor in dooming FAP.

A question amenable to reasonable analytic treatment shot down FAP. The fatal blow came from Senator John Williams's destruction of Secretary Robert Finch in his testimony before the Senate Finance Committee. Senator Williams sandbagged Finch on the critical question of high marginal tax rates in that a family eligible for several cash and in-kind transfer programs could face combined marginal tax rates rising to 100 percent or more, so that working yielded less income than not working. It is important to note that policy analysts favoring the negative income tax had been forewarned of these disincentive problems during the struggles within the administration to get FAP accepted. In a meeting of executive branch officials, Martin Anderson, representing Arthur Burns, arrived "with charts pointing out the problems of including the working poor, of coordinating state supplementation with other programs and with the tax rate . . . [and became] the Senator Williams of the White House working group."[21] Yet, the clear warning did not move the administration to prepare for such arguments when the debate moved to the Congress.

How does one account for this particular failure of analysis? First, at the height of the early analysis on the negative tax (1965–66), program integration represented much less of a problem than it did in 1969. What stands as a far more important factor is that the policy analysts and others during the Johnson administration believed a negative income tax would be considered, if at all, well in the future and only after the results of the negative income tax experiment were in. Analyst/advocates in the Johnson administration had become tired and disheartened, marking time until the New Jersey experiment got further along. A study of marginal tax rates among various programs was the kind of hard and tedious exercise likely to have appeal only if policy decisions were perceived as near. If seen politically as distant, why do a laborious job that appeared to have neither a research nor a political payoff? In short, the analytic gap itself derived more from politics—or at least the analysts' perception of politics—than from technical limitations.

The fact remains that we simply do not know if an analysis of marginal tax rates had been available when FAP came before the Senate Finance Committee, whether it would have affected the committee's view. It well may be that the Senate Finance Committee intended to kill FAP one way or another. Yet Moynihan, in my opinion, made a strong case that the lack of discipline and the lack of analytic capability were important factors in defeating FAP:

The Senate Finance Committee had none of the institutionalized competence of Ways and Means to deal with an initiative as divisive on ideological grounds and complex in technical detail as Family Assistance. . . .

Had there been more general analytic competence on hand, it is not likely that the measure could have been so utterly misrepresented—which was recurrently the case—with near total impunity. Social policy has entered a stage in which the ambitiousness of government must be matched by analytic competence if the nation is to avoid a condition . . . in which the grandiosity of official pronouncement is equaled only by the absence of result.[22]

Senator Moynihan's comments lead to four final comments. First, the struggle over the negative income tax is the high-water mark of social agency policy analysis. The bottom did not fall out all at once, but the journey downhill has begun. Second, this golden age example, ending in the failed Nixon effort to enact a universal negative income tax, continues to best illuminate how an agency office might use social policy analysis and research over time in the policy-making process. Third, policy analysis had not yet come into its own in Congress. The Congressional Budget Office had not even been established and the Congressional Research Service had only recently moved toward strong analytic capability. We can only speculate as to whether a powerful congressional analytic capacity interacting with a strong executive branch analytic structure in the early 1970s would have made the difference between failure and success in the struggle for a negative income tax. Finally, before considering the exemplary cases of CBO and CRS, we need to take the long, mainly gloomy, historical path through presidential policy analysis from Carter through Clinton.

NOTES

1. Walter Williams, *The Struggle for a Negative Income Tax: A Case Study 1965–1970*, Public Policy Monograph No. 1, Institute of Governmental Research, University of Washington, 1972.

2. Walter Williams, "The Continuing Struggle for a Negative Income Tax: A Review Article," *Journal of Human Resources*, Fall 1975, pp. 427–444.

3. Milton Friedman, *Capitalism and Freedom*, University of Chicago Press, 1962.

4. Christopher Green, *Negative Taxes and the Poverty Problem*, Brookings, 1967, p. 57.

5. *Income Maintenance Programs*, Hearings Before the Subcommittee on Fiscal Policy, Joint Economic Committee, U.S. Congress, Volume 1: Proceedings, U.S. Government Printing Office, 1968.

6. Robert Evans Jr. and Robert D. Novak, *Nixon in the White House: The Frustration of Power*, Random House, 1971; Daniel P. Moynihan, *The Politics of a Guaranteed Income*, Random House, 1973; and Vincent J. Burke and Vee Burke, *Nixon's Good Deed*, Columbia University Press, 1974.

7. Evans and Novak, *Nixon in the White House*, p. 225.

8. *Preliminary Results of the New Jersey Graduated Work Incentive Experiment*, Office of Economic Opportunity, February 18, 1970.

9. *Family Assistance Act of 1970*, Hearings Before the Committee on Finance, U.S. Senate, Second Session, U.S. Government Printing Office, 1970, pp. 1621–1622.

10. F. J. Cook, "When You Just Give Money to the Poor," *New York Times Magazine*, May 3, 1970, p. 110.

11. *Family Assistance Act of 1970*, pp. 958–959.

12. *Preliminary Results of the New Jersey Graduated Work Incentive Experiment*, p. 3.

13. U.S. General Accounting Office, "Preliminary Comments on the New Jersey Graduated Work Incentive Experiment," prepared for the Senate Finance Committee, U.S. Senate, mimeographed, June 30, 1970, p. 16.

14. Office of Economic Opportunity, "The Office of Economic Opportunity's Reply to the United States General Accounting Office June, 1970 Report Entitled 'Preliminary Comments on the New Jersey Graduated Work Incentive Experiment,' " mineographed, no date.

15. Harold W. Watts, "Adjusted and Extended Preliminary Results from the Urban Graduated Work Incentive Experiment," Discussion Papers, Institute for Research on Poverty, June 10, 1990.

16. Ibid., pp. 8, 12, and 40.

17. Burke and Burke, *Nixon's Good Deed*, p. 26.

18. Ibid., p. 198.

19. Quoted in M. Kenneth Bowler, *The Nixon Guaranteed Income Proposal*, Ballinger, 1974, p. 5.

20. Moynihan, *The Politics of a Guaranteed Income.*

21. Bowler, *The Nixon Guaranteed Income Proposal*, p. 55.

22. Moynihan, *The Politics of a Guaranteed Income*, p. 454.

5 | Brains and Character Are Not Enough: Jimmy Carter and the DPS

While Chapter 7 presents an extended comparison of Bill Clinton with John Kennedy that provides greater insight into the decision-making styles of both men, this chapter provides a comparison of Bill Clinton and Jimmy Carter that goes far beyond them having been southern, small-state governors. What will be seen in both these chapters is that brains and, in the case of Carter, high moral character, do not necessarily produce an effective presidential policy-making process or sound domestic policies. The similarities between the two southerners are striking. Both possessed high intelligence, keen analytic minds, and a willingness—indeed a desire—to do the hard work needed to master policy issues. Neither had solid organizational skills, despite Carter's claim to such capability gained in reorganizing the Georgia government. Further, Carter and Clinton did not want a chief of staff at the start of their presidencies. The former did without initially, while Clinton picked a nonentity. In addition, both wanted to be their own chief analysts, but at the same time brought in able policy generalists to advise them and sought strong policy staffs to provide sound information and analysis in support of policy deliberations by the president and his top generalists. However, once in action, the two had dramatically different styles. Clinton liked open debate on the run; Carter preferred to work from policy papers and, much like Nixon, to read and contemplate. The best example of Carter in action is the Domestic Policy Staff (DPS) led by a brilliant, analytically oriented lawyer, Stuart Eizenstat. How Carter interacted with Eizenstat, how DPS operated, and how it related to other EOP units offers an excellent base for considering presidents, policy generalists, and policy analysts. Moreover, Stuart Eizenstat and his staff still offer the best extended example of an inner-circle member who dominated domestic policy and drew heavily on a powerful domestic policy unit that more than held its own with OMB.

As to this chapter's organization, the next section looks at the key concepts of policy peers and generalists who advise the president on major issues. After that, the chapter turns to the Carter presidency, focusing on the president's leadership capacity; his basic views on analysis, strategy, and White House organizational structure; his White House inner circle; and the president's external relationships. The next section looks at Eizenstat and the Domestic Policy Staff, considering a variety of leadership and organizational and staffing issues. That is followed by a discussion that takes a broader look at the domestic policy generalists within the Carter administration. The final section tries to sum up the perplexing presidency of a man of high ideals with the rare political courage to tell American citizens they were part of the problem.

THE TOP POLICY ADVISERS

In any of the broad policy areas, a president may choose to have a policy peer—i.e., a Henry Kissinger who is accorded roughly equal status by the president. Any president will have inner-circle advisers in foreign, domestic, and economic policy, but he may not accord any of them the status of peer. Two comments are needed about these special people labeled policy peers. First, there is much written about the fact that presidents do not treat any of their advisers as equals. It may be that it is the rare adviser who feels comfortable enough with a president to tell him that his idea is wrongheaded or even stupid and to argue face-to-face with the president when alone with him. Be that as it may, beyond Kissinger, John Foster Dulles had a peer relationship with President Dwight Eisenhower; Bert Lance occupied such a role with President Carter. We need to be clear that being a policy peer does not mean that there is ambiguity about the president being the "boss" in the sense of being the final decision maker. A presidential policy peer is not necessarily a surrogate president or an assistant president.[1] Second, presidents seem more likely to have political peers rather than policy peers. The former relationship may flower because politics, not issues, dominate the increasingly long presidential campaign. Of course, a major presidential candidate will have a policy issues coordinator (Eizenstat's position in the presidential campaign), but this role is more likely to be of lower status than that of the top political people.

The mark of professional policy generalists is that they draw on broad deductive or analytic frameworks believed to be sufficient to allow them to conceptualize or analyze a wide variety of problems. Their frameworks (e.g., law or economics) are seen by the generalists as sufficient "handles" for tracking a broad array of policy issues, even in areas where they have no special knowledge. The White House needs professional policy generalists who can go beyond the narrow microanalysis of the area specialist to integrate across policy areas. The most needed capability is that of policy/political synthesis which involves determining the quality of the underlying technical analyses of policy proposals coming to the president, the degree to which proposed policy meshes with the president's immediate and longer-run objectives, the impact on his political standing, and the potential for selling the proposal in Congress. Good analysis and advice generally demand the blending of technical, political, and program knowledge in order for the president to be well-informed about critical policy/political choices. Ben Heineman, Jr. has underscored the importance of integrating policy and politics: "Reconciling the tensions, even antagonisms, between the world of policy . . . and the world of politics . . . is, in my judgment, the supreme act of political leadership. EOP policy management is a crucial process for trying to make that marriage work."[2]

Heineman and Hessler, writing at the end of the Carter administration, make this key point about the difficulty of policy/political integration: *"The increasing professionalism of both the political advisers and the policy advisers has served to widen, not narrow, the gap in language and approach."*[3] Although some presidential units have a disproportionate number of inexperienced people whom the specialists may view as "amateurs," the critical problem is the distance between the political professional and the policy professional. Ideally, policy and political analysts, both highly professional in their specialties, would have what Heineman and Hessler label "double vision." The policy analysts would keep an eye out for political implications and vice versa. With such double vision, the two professionals would be comfortable coming together to develop a policy/political synthesis. Without such a setting the policy/political synthesizer looms as the critical link. The need is for the person who can work with both sides—that is, politics and policy—separately when necessary, to guide a process of synthesis that blends policy (technical, organizational, and programmatic) questions and political considerations.

THE CARTER DOMESTIC PRESIDENCY

Jimmy Carter, in the decade and a half since his presidency, has become an admirable ex-president—an activist trying to follow his high moral principles. Moreover, a number of scholars have judged him a much better president than did his contemporary critics and emphasized his role in seeking the public good. Erwin Hargrove subtitled his study, "Leadership and the Politics of the Public Good," seeing Carter as a skillful leader facing intractable problems.[4] Charles Jones entitled his book, *The Trusteeship Presidency*, observing that Carter "arrived in Washington prepared to teach that community some lessons about good government and doing the right thing," and closed his study with this judgment: "Jimmy Carter may never be rated a great president. Yet it will be difficult in the long run to sustain censure of a president motivated to do what is right."[5] After reviewing both the contemporary assessments of Carter and the more recent ones including those of Hargrove and Jones, Burton Kaufman rendered this judgment:

> I am persuaded, however, that the earlier critics of his administration were justified in giving the president mediocre marks—and largely for the reasons they cited. First, I am not convinced that the nation was as ungovernable as some of Carter's defenders contend. Second, I find that the people who have called for a fresh look at the Carter presidency have too easily passed over the elemental fact that, for better or worse, there is a political process in any system of representative government which no leader can simply ignore on the basis of being above the fray, especially one who, like Carter, lacks a political mandate from the voters. . . . Third, it is troubling that those people who comment favorably on Carter's concept of a "public trustee" ignore a real danger inherent in that concept—namely, that the trustee has a wisdom about the national welfare superior to the collective wisdom of the nation's elected representatives on Capitol Hill—and disregard the need for a person in the Oval Office to be attentive to the pluralistic nature of American society. Fourth, I find that while Carter viewed himself as a trustee of the public good, he never adequately articulated an overarching purpose and direction for his administration.
>
> Finally, and perhaps most important, I conclude that Carter failed to establish the base of public support and political legitimacy he needed in order to be successful in his role as a trustee president. Instead, the events of his four years in office projected an image to the American people of a hapless administration in disarray and of a presidency that was increasingly divided, lacking in leadership, ineffective in dealing with Congress, incapable of defending America's honor abroad, and uncertain about its purpose, priorities, and sense of direction. In my view, this contemporary image of the Carter presidency was, unfortunately, all too accurate and helped assure a mediocre, if not a failed, presidency.[6]

Although Carter deserves great praise for his good works since 1981, Kaufman, if a bit too harsh overall, is much closer to a realistic assessment than the revisionists, particularly in the case of domestic policy.

In the domestic sphere, Carter exhibited limited political and management skills with no idea of how to integrate politics and policy; he lacked a strategic vision and jumbled together many objectives without setting priorities; and he tried to be his own chief of staff, a step that led to a seriously flawed policy-making process. Lack of leadership doomed Carter's domestic presidency. One of my most astute interviewees, a critical observer in a high EOP position in the Carter administration, said that the "first, second, third, and fourth most important factors in understanding the failed Carter presidency was the vacuum at the top." Partly because of the Nixon experience and partly because of his own style (discussed shortly) Carter chose not to have a White House chief of staff until much too late. In 1979 Hamilton Jordan assumed that title. Before that time Jordan never seemed to want that role. If Carter was his own chief of staff before 1979, he failed at that task too.

Beyond the chief-of-staff position itself, Carter envisioned a generally weaker White House staff. As Haynes Johnson wrote: "His White House staff would be smaller, less rigidly structured and subservient to cabinet secretaries. All its members would be equal in rank."[7] Carter and his "non-chief of staff" did not manage the White House and did not create a process for resolving issues. What emerged so often was a civil war between White House factions. The clash involved organizations, not of personalities—in fact, the interviewee mentioned above said that some of the people personally got along reasonably well. And if a battle did not emerge, organizations went around playing their own games without much presidential leadership or help.

Strategy and Analysis

Carter had no strategy, no broad vision of the future with clear priorities as his objectives. Betty Glad, near the end of her long Carter biography, lamented: "[Carter] lacks, it seems, a well-thought-out conceptual framework to guide his concrete political choices. He immerses himself in the technical details of programs that interest him, testing various strategies and rhetorical appeals. Yet he fails to bring the components together in an integrated approach that would give him a sense of direction and set up priorities for his various programs."[8] William Leuchtenburg depicted Carter as "a technocrat with little awareness of history" and cited writers who characterized Carter as "Jimmy Hoover" (that is, the second disastrous engineer president) and "the country's first national city manager."[9] Johnson pointed out late in Carter's one term that " [Carter] still got up at five o'clock each morning, had a CIA briefing, and began going through papers that he continued to consume voraciously—at least three hundred and fifty pages every day."[10] Hargrove argued that he found "little evidence Carter got bogged down in details and failed to see the forest for the trees, a criticism outsiders sometimes leveled."[11] That is correct in the sense that details did not keep Carter from seeing the big picture, his mentality did. Joy for Carter was in the details.

The strategic problems of the Carter administration were captured by the following statement repeated by an interviewee who could not recall the source: "Secretary of Defense Harold Brown looks at the trees; the president himself looks at the leaves; national security adviser Zbigniew Brzezinski looks at the biosphere; and the forest goes unnoticed." In their study of welfare reform, Lynn and Whitman state:

> Carter seemed to encourage his advisers to focus on discrete, technical issues, rather than inspiring them to a noble calling. . . . In the hundreds of pages of memoranda and the records and recollections of discussions generated during the seven months of welfare-reform debate within the administration, there is scarcely a word about how welfare reform was related to the problems of the cities, federal-state relations, the economy, or equality of opportunity by race and sex. . . . This was a classic case of missing the forest for the trees. Only Carter could have been the chief forester; instead, he was just another lumberjack.[12]

Carter's first HEW secretary, Joseph Califano, wrote: "Carter was bent on mastering every detail. . . . [H]e was, as an HEW staffer remarked after one of my welfare reform briefings, the highest paid assistant secretary for planning that ever put a reform proposal together."[13] While Califano is hardly a neutral observer (more later), he wrote what interviewees kept telling me privately.

Brains were not the problem. An interviewee high in the administration, who himself was considered to be one of the brightest persons around Carter, admired Carter's exceptional intelligence and quickness in being able to grasp new, complex ideas rapidly and discuss them with surprising understanding. The interviewee thought Carter had a first-rate analytic mind and would put him up against any of the recent presidents for quickness and capacity to master complex issues. Indeed, Carter often looked very much like the classic policy analyst *qua* economist/operations researcher who seeks some pristine optimum solution without concern for political, institutional, or bureaucratic reality. In discussing Carter's political personality and style of leadership. Hargrove has observed:

1. He liked programs to be comprehensive attacks on problems rather than incremental steps.
2. He was hostile to interest groups or any form of particularism that might block comprehensive solutions.
3. He believed that there were "correct" answers to problems that rational people could find.[14]

These grand comprehensive attacks on problems should not be confused with vision. Comprehensiveness is on the "means," not the "ends," side. In reality, the grand solution is not broad but rather a kind of tunnel vision representing a stress on rationality, solvability, and the power of science combined with a disinterest in and lack of understanding of organizational processes and a distaste for politics. But then whoever said that an assistant secretary for policy analysis would make a good president? And in truth, Carter more often seemed like the extremely hard-working deputy assistant secretary who turned out great quantities of work, got his facts right, chased down the numbers no one else could find (because no one else loved number chasing nearly as much), but had to be guided because he really did not understand politics.

Like Nixon, Carter preferred to work through papers, not discussion. Here too is another manifestation of an analytic bent where written analyses are favored because that pins people down much more than verbal discussion. In the case of Nixon, beyond precision was his personal antipathy toward working with very many people. But this does not seem to be the causal factor for Carter.[15] Whatever the cause, the control over the paper flow in the Carter White House was extremely tight. All relevant actors were expected to send in their memos before they were forwarded to the president. There were exceptions at the very top. Elizabeth Bumiller wrote that Jordan, Jody Powell, Zbigniew Brzezinski, and Eizenstat would slip into Carter's office while the president was away and put one of their memos on the top of the pile of the president's "in" box.[16] For others, the process followed the standard procedures and had the positive effect of stopping end runs. However, it also cut off communication. Given Carter's brightness and inquisitiveness, a real loss occurred in that he certainly would have benefited from open discussions and could have contributed as a major participant himself.

Carter and Staff

Carter's staff difficulties started at the top with Jordan. The president's inner circle came to be a key part of his problems. Carter had a tendency to surround himself by inexperienced, young men who looked and sometimes acted like junior clerks, not senior inner-circle advisers. One critical event was shaping in this regard—the fall of OMB director Bert Lance. As Havemann wrote in mid-1977 before that fall: "[A]mong all of Carter's White House policy advisers, the one man who seems to wield influence greater than that of all the others is Bert Lance, whose role might accurately be described as confidential adviser to the President."[17] Haynes Johnson captured the importance of the Lance and

Carter relationship by comparing it to other peer relationships such as Harry Hopkins and Franklin Roosevelt, and Robert and John Kennedy, and then observing: "Carter and Lance were an extraordinary White House team. They were like the Corsican Twins; you could not cut one without wounding the other . . . Lance fed something in Carter, fulfilled a need. They joked together. They played tennis together. At times they prayed together."[18] President Jimmy Carter himself best depicted the importance of Bert Lance. The president recorded in his diary on February 18, 1977, less than a month into the new administration: *"Bert Lance is a key to the entire process of budgeting and reorganization, and has been tremendous in his job."*[19] Carter then went on to write:

> It is impossible to overestimate the damage inflicted on my administration by the charges leveled against Bert Lance. . . .
>
> It is difficult for me to explain how close Bert was to me or how much I depended on him. Even my closest friends in Georgia have never understood the extent of our relationship. Calm and mature, Bert also had an easy boyish way about him, and used his sense of humor effectively among all kinds of people. He had a vicious tennis serve, and played and talked a good game. Surprisingly agile for so big a man, he described himself often as having "the size of an elephant and the grace of a gazelle."[20]

Carter's own account revealed the depth of his feelings toward Lance and the president's dependence on Lance both as a friend and companion and as a policy adviser. *Lance was Carter's only real peer among the trusted Georgian inner circle.* The reader should not infer that Lance's leaving robbed Carter of his master strategist/analyst and that Lance might have given overall direction to the administration. The basic point is that Lance not only was approximately Carter's age but was treated differently from the other key Georgians who were in their early or mid-thirties. Lance operated as the administration's free-floating adviser, drawing on the OMB's analytic staff when needed but standing apart as the president's man, not the bureau's man. Lance may have been a Georgian but he was very different from Hamilton Jordan, Jody Powell, Frank Moore, Jack Watson, and Stuart Eizenstat. In the main, these Georgians were almost young enough to be President Carter's sons, and certainly his much younger brothers who had come to maturity with big brother as the ideal. In no way were they Carter's peers. President Carter wrote in his diary November 3, 1980 after Pat Caddell, his principal pollster, had told him that he was going to lose the 1980 election: *"On the way back to Plains, where I was going to meet Rosalynn and vote, Stu [Eizenstat] came up to my cabin to try to say something about it, and burst into tears. I put my arms around him to comfort him. It was hard for us to believe the dimensions of what Pat was telling us, but it later proved to be accurate."*[21]

After Lance left, it was "Carter & Sons" with all the connotations carried by a small family business. This was not a group of outsiders such as, say, James Baker and Max Friedersdorf in the Reagan administration, brought in because of special skills that the president's home-grown staff did not have. These were the "boys" coming into the business. I would underscore that my statement does not speak to the individuals' capabilities but rather to how they were perceived by the president himself. Harry McPherson, in discussing the father-son relationship between President Lyndon Johnson and Bill Moyers, observed that Moyers faced "the danger as he became his own man, he would risk Johnson's anger if he strayed from him."[22]

Another thing that stands out about the inner circle after Lance left is that none save Eizenstat were substance people. Over time they began to defer to Eizenstat on domestic program/policy questions. Their main judgments were political, made with little or no appreciation for or understanding of the interrelationships between policy and politics. Two qualifiers are needed. First, Vice President Walter Mondale had a key advisory role, but in none of my interviews does Mondale's name come up in the domestic policy arena. Second, some of the others in the inner circle did on occasion have a significant involvement in policy. Jordan, for example, had a major role in the Panama Canal neutrality treaty. Also, Jack Watson joined Eizenstat in welfare reform. Watson, to some extent, does not fit my characterization as well as, say, Jordan and Powell. However, as Eizenstat's role in domestic policy increased, Watson seemed to become less and less of a factor until he became chief of staff toward the end of the Carter presidency.

How important did staffing problems loom in this failed domestic presidency? There can be no definitive answer. The lack of presidential leadership and staff performance are so intertwined that it is hard to isolate the contribution of staff alone. We do know that staff strength cannot overcome the lack of leadership. A much stronger staff would not have saved the Carter presidency. Indeed, the Carter EOP had considerable staff strength and a number of outstanding people. Carter's failure to use his staff people better appears to have damaged his presidency. This last statement applies much more to the EOP analytic staffs than to the inner circle that itself became a big part of Carter's problems. How many critics felt about the inner circle was captured by Representative James Oberstar (D-Minn.) who told a *Congressional Quarterly* writer in discussing Stuart Eizenstat: "It's too bad there aren't more like him [at the White House]. He's nothing like the rest of them—Jody Powell, Hamilton Jordan—in Fortress Georgia."[23] At least in terms of public perception the negative opinion applied particularly to Jordan, who seldom returned phone calls and had a poor reputation with Congress during much of Carter's four years, and to Frank Moore whose Congressional Relations Office got off to a terrible start with Congress.[24] Here is one of the fundamental problems of the presidency: However capable the EOP staff may be on paper, the president and/ or his inner circle must be able to communicate with them—not just send word down for this or that piece of analysis but engage in fruitful two-way communication. Again, it is Eizenstat who emerges as an interesting figure because he was the only one in the inner circle who had the inclination (and probably the only one with the capacity) to make these critical linkages.

Carter as Manager

Organizational mastery was not President Carter's strong suit, to put it mildly. He came to office with the reputation for successfully reorganizing the Georgia government by reducing dramatically the number of state agencies. That he expected to do the same with the federal executive branch in and of itself might be sufficient evidence of the president's organizational ignorance. But we can go further starting at the top. Hargrove observed: "Carter was criticized for being a poor manager of relationships among his lieutenants. He did not have clear ideas about the division of labor between line and staff functions. . . . And he was thought to be ineffective in managing conflict among lieutenants."[25] Carter really was an engineer who did not stress people problems and believed that management mainly boiled down to getting the boxes right on the organization chart.

Nowhere is Carter's organizational ineptitude more clear and more damaging than in the management of his cabinet. To explore this deficiency, we need to look briefly at the notion of cabinet government that Carter sought at the outset of his presidency. To begin with, in the British parliamentary system, the one that American scholars historically look to as the model, cabinet government is centered on the collective responsibility of the entire cabinet and the prime minister. They are all collectively responsible for each government decision, a tricky concept itself and hardly relevant to the American presidency.[26] Moreover, British cabinet ministers, like the prime minister, are elected representatives, often with their own political power bases, and prime ministers themselves are at least in theory but the first among equals. Cabinet government, with ministers as principal advisers to the prime minister, has historically been central to the British parliamentary system. Even so, to quote an insightful student of British government,

Peter Hennessy, "cabinet government remains a putty-like concept," which a prime minister can use and misuse in a variety of ways as Margaret Thatcher's often dictatorial regime makes clear.[27]

Cabinet government, to which so many recent presidents have paid homage, is a stage beyond putty-like in its lack of clarity for the American political system. But the notion does have to do generally with either the cabinet as principal advisers to the president, as the managers of their agencies without White House staff standing between them and the president, or both. Carter embraced cabinet government by giving his secretaries appointive power for subcabinet positions. As I will argue later, the notion makes sound organizational sense if cabinet secretaries are to be effective managers, but requires that the president himself be a good manager. However, the idea of strong cabinet members has fallen out of favor, and Carter's performance had a lot to do with its rejection. Ronald Reagan, on the other hand, tightly centralized the White House by putting most of the power in the hands of a few top aides at the expense of the cabinet secretaries. The White House controlled the key subcabinet appointments and made the main criterion loyalty to the Reagan doctrine, sending this clear message to a cabinet member: "We don't trust you and my loyalists in the agency stand ready to catch you." The great appeal of White House centralization is political control. Democrats wring their hands over the loss of control by President Carter after he gave his cabinet the power to appoint their subcabinets. They point to the worst case: HEW secretary, Joseph Califano, who defied Carter.

The cause of Carter's troubles, however, was not his management approach but his inept management, which included both a poor selection of people and a failure to exert discipline over them. In the case of Califano, his public record as President Johnson's domestic policy chief made clear he would be a hard person to deal with. Carter's problems after appointing Califano flowed from the president not exerting a strong hand and letting Califano defy him for three years before firing the secretary. Richard Neustadt has made the same point arguing that Califano would have been "perfectly controllable. . . if the president had personally spelled out in no uncertain terms to Joe [Califano] what he would and wouldn't tolerate."[28]

Any management approach will fail in the hands of a weak manager. Eisenhower, the last elected president who fully understood how complex public organizations work, had the capacity to keep his cabinet members on course. Dillon Anderson, an Eisenhower special assistant, pointed out that the president "invited a lot of give-and-take" from cabinet representatives before making a decision, but after it was made, the department "damn well knew what it was and there'd be no fuzzing up as to what the president's decision had been."[29] If the department was subverting Eisenhower's decision, the secretary answered to the president. Clean lines of responsibility provide a base for discipline. Jimmy Carter either did not understand that fundamental management concept, did not know how to implement it with a strong cabinet member, or, more likely, both.

Carter and Broader Relationships

Carter campaigned as a Washington outsider—the man who owed nothing to party, Congress, or interest groups. He saw himself as his own man who was going to reform the federal government. Carter's campaign theme of the outsider was unfortunately all too true for the president and his trusted inner circle. Johnson quotes an unnamed "Washington operative" right after the election observing that " 'ignorance is as bad as arrogance.' "[30] Congress became an immediate problem in part from Frank Moore's early troubles in congressional relations but also because of Carter himself. House Speaker Tip O'Neill tried to explain to the Carter people that members of Congress had run ahead of Carter so that "the Democrats in Congress owed Carter nothing."[31] Carter had to make some effort himself. Johnson reported: "But the Carter people didn't seem to understand that. . . . [One congressional leader said]: There was a great reservoir just waiting to be tapped, dying to be tapped, and they never tapped it."[32] At the same time the Democrats in Congress were in the main an unruly lot. Glad noted: "In all fairness to Carter, it must be stated that Congress itself, though mainly Democratic, was composed of independent types determined not to be a rubber stamp for any administration."[33] It is unfair to Carter to imply that he failed at the easy job of mastering a Democratic Congress while Ronald Reagan conquered a partly Democratic Congress. In truth, given the mood of Congress in Reagan's first two hundred days, his task may have been far easier than Carter's. The fact remains, Carter often performed poorly with an unruly, fragmented, independent Democratic Congress that would have taken far more political skills to master than Carter had.

STUART EIZENSTAT AND THE DOMESTIC POLICY STAFF

A *National Journal* article written early in the Carter administration quoted one cabinet member's aide as saying that Eizenstat seemed to him to function as "a high-powered research assistant."[34] Over time, however, Eizenstat became the most important domestic policy adviser to President Carter—the only head of a domestic policy-oriented unit in the inner circle and the only member of that inner circle consistently looked to for advice and analysis on domestic policy substance.

Eizenstat and his rise are both intriguing and important for an appreciation of the dynamics of a policy office and the development of a policy
generalist. Eizenstat himself is an appealing figure—bright, hard-
working, fair-minded, and seemingly without the burning drive for
power which often almost oozes from a young White House insider.
I found no evidence whatsoever in my interviews that Eizenstat sought
power or tried to increase the responsibilities and size of the Domestic
Policy Staff as a means of gaining preeminence in domestic policy.
Indeed, one interviewee told me that Eizenstat never really understood
how much power he had and "at times seemed not to understand that
he had much power at all." Now, Eizenstat may have been the most
Machiavellian of individuals, harboring an exceedingly strong drive
for power which he was able to keep hidden from view. However, I
can only report that no writer or any interviewee even hinted at such
a drive in Eizenstat. I leave that question either to those with a psycho-
analytic bent or else to later historians who might find evidence in
now unavailable papers.

Whatever the case, Eizenstat did emerge as the only adviser to
dominate domestic policy individually—i.e., without a competitor—
since Joseph Califano in the Johnson years, recalling that Ehrlichman
who did have a great deal of influence had to share center stage with
OMB director George Shultz. There is another side to the Eizenstat
story, however. On-the-job-training at the top for the policy generalist
can be a costly endeavor. A member of the Carter administration subcabinet told me after reading an earlier version of this chapter: "You
are far too nice to Stu. He is a super person—of the highest quality.
But you should not judge Eizenstat by how he acted at the end of the
Carter administration. By that time, Stu was much more sophisticated,
but he had messed things up for two years getting to that point."

DPS Operations

DPS roughly doubled in size over time, finally numbering fifty-five to
sixty members of whom about half were professionals. The three top
people—all lawyers—were: Eizenstat, assistant to the president for
domestic affairs and policy; David Rubinstein, deputy assistant for
domestic affairs and policy; and Bert Carp, deputy director of the
domestic policy staff. There were ten associate directors in the following
areas: agriculture and rural development, economics, transportation
and labor, housing and urban development, government reorganization, human resources (health), human resources (employment), arts
and humanities, and civil rights and justice. Also, at least seventeen
assistant directors generally had subspecialties in the areas under the
associate directors and worked for these people. With so many titles

floating around, some claimed that DPS had all chiefs and no workers. But in truth the assistant directors and often the associate directors did their own work rather than supervising other professionals.

DPS over time took on more and more policy development responsibilities. The staff continued to work with the agencies, which generally performed the major analyses, and with their counterparts in OMB. One high DPS official stressed the good working relationships at lower levels with OMB and said that "OMB was involved at all stages." From its earliest days in the Carter administration, DPS produced a covering memorandum that went to the president summarizing the agency positions and offering DPS's own recommendations on domestic policy decisions. Over time DPS recommendations became more important. In the pecking order, DPS moved to the top. Further, on occasion DPS prepared a Presidential Review memorandum where DPS engaged in "policy entrepreneurship with the president as the ultimate client."[35]

Articles written in 1979 in the *Congressional Quarterly* and the *National Journal* offered glowing descriptions of DPS at the height of its influence.[36] The former observed: "Eizenstat's staff, handpicked by him, is perceived throughout the administration as being young, energetic, politically aware, highly intelligent and dedicated. It is also said to be short on experience."[37] A goodly number had congressional or executive branch experience. A high percentage of the professional staff were lawyers. The staff also has been criticized as lacking in-depth substantive knowledge, and being spread too thin. The strongest published criticism of the staff comes from Heineman and Hessler:

> DPS has consisted of forty to sixty people who specialized (though they were infrequently expert) in a variety of substantive areas. They attempted to manage great numbers of interagency issues and to maintain close liaison with all manner of constituencies. Too often, DPS has been a complicating factor throughout the government, and institutional rival of OMB in the routine business of government . . . and a powerful magnet for interest group pressures on the White House and thus on the president.[38]

If the *Congressional Quarterly* and *National Journal* pieces offered too positive a picture of DPS, Heineman and Hessler may be too harsh. There were some quite competent people on the staff including a few sound policy analysts. At the same time, tremendous pressures on Eizenstat and his staff led to a harried, hurried pace that often cut into quality. Weaknesses were magnified as the staff became increasingly overburdened and grew more powerful. The brashness of some of the younger staff or the inadequacies of weaker staff members became more observable. *The Domestic Policy Staff ended up being less than the sum of its parts.*

Eizenstat: An Assessment

Several summary statements can be made about Eizenstat as a policy generalist and head of an analytic unit. First, he had a rare objectivity. An EOP policy analyst indicated to me that Eizenstat could go into a meeting with a position worked out by his staff with which he agreed, take the position, be confronted with contrary evidence, and reject the staff position. Second, unlike any other member of the Carter inner circle, Eizenstat tried to live in both worlds of politics and policy. Third, on balance, he overemphasized politics in the policy/politics equation. Fourth, Eizenstat did not appreciate how little rigorous policy analysis his staff did or its importance in complementing his lawyer-generalist orientation. Fifth, like his boss, Eizenstat did not well-manage his staff. Sixth, much criticism of Eizenstat reflected criticism of Carter. As the ever devoted staff person, Eizenstat tried to carry out faithfully the president's bidding even though he himself did not necessarily agree with what the president wanted or how he wanted to proceed. Most of all, Eizenstat was a man in the middle. On the one hand, the highly political types in the inner circle, not surprisingly, often saw the book- ish, studious Eizenstat as being politically naive. And in the narrow sense of their perspective cast in terms of short-run electoral politics, he may have been naive at times or irrelevant in selling the president to the voters. On the other hand, as the only member of the inner circle with policy credentials, it is hardly surprising that the EOP policy analysis and budget people questioned his policy purity and capability as they viewed him from outside that inner circle.

Eizenstat had a different, and much wider, vision of politics than the other key members of the inner circle. He believed strongly that the president needed the broad Democratic Party coalition, not simply in electoral politics but in terms of the capacity of a Democratic presi- dent to govern. He thought close ties with the congressional Democrats and the key interest groups in the Democratic coalition were critical, not just in reelecting the president but also in policy development over time. Especially in the early period, the Carter inner-circle members who could have been expected to handle these relationships did poorly. As one interviewee put it, "Hell, Ham never even returned phone calls." Jordan especially, but some of the other inner circle too, appeared at times to think that politics consisted of campaigning every four years for office and taking polls. In a White House terribly weak at the very top in ongoing relationships with Congress and the key interest groups, Eizenstat had his problems. As an interviewee who served in the Carter subcabinet observed: "Stu was basically unable or unwilling to deal with Jordan. If he couldn't deal with Ham, there could be no fusion of policy and politics. To be sure the ultimate responsibility was Carter's. But Stu could have done more than he did."

Professional policy analyst interviewees—especially people from OMB—labeled Eizenstat as analytically naive and far too political. They claimed that an Eizenstat decision depended on the last public interest group he talked with. Such criticism flowed in part from the budget professional's mentality that likes to cast analysts as nonpolitical and in part from "sour grapes" because of the relative power configuration that made Eizenstat more powerful than OMB director James McIntyre after he replaced Lance. At the same time, Eizenstat did place too much emphasis on the political aspects of policy issues in his role as policy generalist. One explanation is that the failure of the political types in the inner circle to have any concern for policy except in the narrowest electoral terms forced Eizenstat and DPS to overcompensate. Or, it could have been that Eizenstat's political biases combined with his own lack of knowledge of policy analysis and that of his top aides better explain the overemphasis on politics. The EOP policy analyst, who spoke favorably of Eizenstat's objectivity, said of the other two top people in DPS: "[Bert] Carp was really good at political analysis but was almost exclusively [doing] political analysis without any policy analysis. Rubinstein was super bright but very young and inexperienced. Further, he was a lawyer with no analytic framework. So the three people at the top simply did not push for policy analysis." Neither the interviewee nor I felt that any of the three individuals were unqualified for their positions at the top of a unit concerned with issues crosscutting policy and politics. Rather the DPS analytic problem came from the lack of balance at the top. A strong policy analyst in the leadership group could have provided a policy counterweight and technical quality control in DPS. A few more policy analysts also could have demanded either better analyses or analyses more relevant to the president's needs from the policy-analyst-dominated agency staffs—a fighting-fire-with-fire argument. Eizenstat simply did not have much of an understanding of policy analysis and at times seemed to see it as mainly a technical number crunching kind of activity. It is these kinds of quite personal elements that bedevil those of us who would offer prescriptions on the structure and staffing of the EOP.

Eizenstat had management problems within DPS and in DPS' relationships with other EOP units and the agencies. Once he became the main domestic policy adviser, too much work became a continuing state of affairs that kept Eizenstat and his staff under constant pressure and mitigated against extensive staff interaction or critical analyses. In the main, DPS simply did not have much time to think and this problem flowed at least in part from Eizenstat's mismanagement. As an EOP policy analyst observed: "Eizenstat felt the president wanted to be involved in a tremendous number of issues and did not block or cut off issues to protect him. This meant that Stu's plate kept getting more and more full. . . . Eizenstat was programmed with a vengeance. It was extremely difficult to get him to spend much time on an issue. A member of Congress tried to get Eizenstat to bring in good people and talk out a problem. But Stu never would reflect deeply on an issue in this manner—he claimed he never had the time." Moreover, some of the young, often abrasive, activists on the staff brought external relationship problems that Eizenstat handled poorly. A Carter administration EOP staff member used the case of a quite intelligent young staff member who had considerable experience and expertise in the assigned specialty area gained as an outside activist but no credentials from within government or the academic community. Such a situation could easily bring conflict with older, more credentialed agency or EOP career staff. The former EOP staff member questioned whether the young staff person could have worked out these relationships alone and drew a broader conclusion: "Stu never really did understand this kind of bureaucratic dynamics and this was a real weakness that diminished the effectiveness of his staff. Stu did not appreciate either power or bureaucratic politics and that meant he did not appreciate how to use his staff, did not appreciate how threatening and abrasive some of these people from the outside seemed to be."

A number of Eizenstat's management difficulties occurred at the subpresidential level as exemplified by the relationship problem just discussed. Others came at the point of relationship between Eizenstat and the president, where Eizenstat can be faulted for not getting the president to see the harm of his handling too many issues or the need for priorities so that President Carter could concentrate his attention. Many of Eizenstat's organizational problems, however, flowed from the basic weakness in the Carter White House itself—from the vacuum at the top. Part of the enigma of the Carter presidency is that this highly analytic man who saw organization as a critical aspect of his presidency was such a poor manager of staff and had so little appreciation of how staffs needed to be organized. Most of all Carter seem to have almost no appreciation of the dynamics of policy making where bureaucratic politics and personalities loom so large. Operating under these adverse circumstances and when compared to people who occupied similar positions in past administrations, Eizenstat does not fare badly. One comes away after many interviews, including ones with Eizenstat himself, with great admiration for his intelligence, industry, and integrity. He stands out in the Carter administration and emerges as an unusually modest and likable individual for one who made it to the top so young.

Eizenstat and DPS filled some of the vacuum Carter created. Eizenstat, not only the ablest member of the inner circle but also the only one who could live comfortably in the world of politics and policy, had more and more power thrust on him. Eizenstat labored hard and with some success in serving his president. This is not to deny that he erred badly at times and mismanaged his staff. But it also is the case that (1) President Carter made Eizenstat's lot difficult through his own presidential mismanagement; (2) Eizenstat, the good soldier and too much the "respectful son," did what the president wanted even when it was wrongheaded; and (3) Eizenstat was forced to overextend himself as he tried to right matters when other inner-circle actors were failing the president.

A Different Perspective on DPS

As mentioned earlier, my final assessment of DPS is that the unit ended up being less than the sum of its parts. It should be underscored that this assessment rests on the assumption that policy analysis is a central function of the domestic policy unit. For a policy analyst looking at a policy staff, such an assumption is so basic that it is more implicit than explicit. But is it a fair assumption? A case might be made that the White House domestic policy unit should be made up primarily or perhaps even exclusively of broad generalists whose orientation is much more political than policy-dominated. History supports such a claim. Unlike the National Security Council staff, domestic policy units do not have a strong policy analyst tradition. The two most prominent heads before Eizenstat were also generalist lawyers—Joseph Califano and John Ehrlichman. Beyond history, the vacuum at the top in the Carter administration that Eizenstat tried to fill had brought grave political problems. Eizenstat and his staff were drawn more and more into political activities including some lobbying on the Hill. The imbalance that overemphasized politics relative to policy had been forced on Eizenstat and DPS by the circumstances of the Carter administration.

Why then would DPS need more policy analysts of the type that staffed agency offices or a person with such skills in the leadership group? Not only does Professor Hargrove point out that Eizenstat believed policy analysis expertise should "reside in the departments and agencies," Hargrove further argues that the Council of Economic Advisers and NSC staff functions are "based on academic disciplines" and need to be clearly distinguished from domestic policy making.[39] Needless to say, I advocate that competent policy analysts be in the agencies and departments and further that agency analytic units should do the major analyses in the executive branch. But Hargrove's differentiation between domestic policy making and economic and foreign policy making is misleading at best. If agencies need policy analysts so does the White House both to help in the interpretation of the major agency analyses and to guide the agencies toward the specific analyses needed by the president.

Even more basically, a competent policy analyst at the leadership level in a White House domestic policy unit will sharpen that unit's policy thinking, particularly if the top domestic staff are lawyers, and make it more likely that sound agency policy analysis will make it to the White House inner circle. The comment about lawyers is not meant to imply that they cannot be good domestic policy advisers but that lawyers and policy analyst economists can complement each other. Lawyers generally lack the analytic and quantitative skills to make the best use of high-powered quantitative analyses, while "hard-nosed" policy analysis types are much too biased against "soft" information not readily treated by their available techniques.[40] Although I appreciate the political pressures on Eizenstat because of the failure of other inner-circle members to do their jobs effectively, I still argue that Eizenstat and DPS did not perform as well as he and his unit might have had there been a better balance between the able DPS lawyers and technically sound, politically savvy policy analysts, particularly at the top.

OVERVIEW OF THE CARTER ADMINISTRATION
AND DOMESTIC POLICY GENERALISTS

How the heads of the four domestic-policy-oriented EOP units fared as policy generalists in the Carter administration illuminates several key aspects of the policy generalist role: the way that generalists define their scope and method of operations, how they are perceived by the president and other key White House actors, and the importance of the mix of technical and political skills possessed or perceived to be possessed by the policy generalist. Critical to the Carter experience, as discussed, is that Bert Lance immediately became the president's generalist policy peer—trusted friend and confidante, the person who knew how Carter thought, the adviser for all seasons. Hardly a surprising result, Lance had occupied a similar status in the past. In that sense, Lance stands as the "traditional" generalist peer emerging at the start of an administration in that he lacked either the substantive credentials of an acknowledged specialist, such as Henry Kissinger, or an outside track record of directly relevant experience, such as that possessed by James Baker as political strategist when he joined the Reagan administration. Lance's claim historically has been the best of all: He had the president's confidence built upon recognized past personal service to his president.

It is useful at this point to distinguish more clearly between a policy and a political orientation. The latter orientation should be read as implying either partisan or electoral politics, in this case as they impact on the president and his party. Policy is used rather broadly to include both the purely technical or substantive aspects of a policy area and the institutional factors. For example, a policy analyst scrutinizing a proposed federal manpower training innovation to be funded through grants to subnational governments might be concerned with bureaucratic politics in the Department of Labor, organizational problems at both federal and subnational levels, and local or state political issues that might impinge upon the implementation of the policy. Moreover, the policy analyst working for political people has the responsibility to tease out any partisan or electoral political issues embedded in the policy analysis and to alert the political types. But that is not the same as doing the kind of political work that political professionals perform. The point to underscore is that policy analysts at the top are involved in varying degrees with political issues. My distinctions in this section are made in terms of top EOP policy analysts, not analysts at lower government levels or those outside government. Hence, when this section labels Frank Press as being mainly a scientist, I do not have in mind the laboratory scientist but rather a policy type who emphasizes science and generally stays away from the (partisan or electoral) political implications of the issue.

After Lance left, neither his successor James McIntyre, the Council of Economic Advisers' Charles Schultze, nor the Office of Science and Technology Policy's Frank Press could be ruled out as possible inner-circle members who might at least have shared the top domestic policy advisory role with Eizenstat. Indeed, both in terms of credentials and experience, Eizenstat seemed the least likely choice to dominate domestic policy. McIntyre clearly stood as a contender because of OMB's traditional role in domestic policy making. Moreover, McIntyre, a Georgian who had been a strong budget director for Governor Carter, was hard-working, well-organized, and had served with some distinction as Lance's deputy.

Three factors worked against McIntyre. First, Carter waited several months after Lance left to appoint McIntyre as OMB director. McIntyre served as acting director with none of the key White House actors expecting that he would be appointed to the top position. During that time OMB operated in limbo. With Lance leaving under a cloud, morale declined. Also OMB's perceived power and status dropped because of McIntyre's tenuous position as acting director. The historic powerhouse of the EOP seemingly reached its lowest ebb in memory during this period and McIntyre (albeit more victim than sinner because of Carter's procrastination in appointing him OMB head) was tainted by that organizational low point. Second, and a factor also affecting Schultze and Press, Carter, an interviewee told me, had a tendency to "slot" people. McIntyre, his budget head in Georgia, became compartmentalized by Carter as his budget technician. Ironically, the "downgrading" of McIntyre to this status had been reinforced by Lance's earlier preeminence as Carter's most powerful adviser in that McIntyre's perceived role as deputy director had been to keep OMB running smoothly, that is, as a manager while his boss was the policy adviser. Finally, McIntyre appears to have been in over his head at OMB—a case of the Peter Principle exacerbated by the tenuousness of his acting director status over several months. Interviewees' opinions about McIntyre were quite varied. Some thought McIntyre extremely weak. Others believed he was much underrated. These people felt McIntyre well might have performed a number of high-level jobs in the Carter administration quite effectively but that at OMB he held a particularly demanding position. No one, however, thought McIntyre was on top of the job at OMB.

Nobody thought Charles Schultze possessed less than a first-rate intellect. He came into the Carter administration with a track record indicating that he could dominate domestic policy. Schultze had been a highly regarded director of the, then, Bureau of the Budget under Lyndon Johnson, had wide experience inside and outside of government, and was held in high regard as a policy-oriented macroeconomist. That Lance ranked above Schultze in the pecking order is hardly surprising, but why Schultze did not become a power in domestic policy making after Lance left, and even had problems in his own "turf" area of macroeconomics, remains somewhat of an enigma. Three explanations may be offered, the first of which is Carter's aforementioned tendency to compartmentalize people. Second, Carter's memorandum-oriented style did not make the best use of Schultze's effectiveness in the give-and-take of extended discussion. The point is not that Schultze was unable to write a good memorandum for the president but rather that he had a rare talent through discussion to clarify ideas and issues and to illuminate possible alternatives. Yet Carter, highly analytic and a quick learner with the ability to use Schultze's main strength to the fullest in verbal give-and-take, did not do so to any great degree, perhaps in part because of the next point.

One well-placed Carter administration interviewee offered as a third explanation that Schultze, the highly credentialed substantive specialist, *chose* to present himself to Carter in a way that did not accord with the scientific certainty with which Carter was comfortable. Schultze, in his earlier years, had been much more confident of his underlying macroeconomic base and analytic framework. Schultze made the strongest case with great certainty because he believed in his argument and had both the intellectual and presentational skills to back it up. During the Carter administration, however, the interviewee argued that Schultze went through a period where he had begun to doubt the assumptions and tenets of his underlying economic model. Although he had started to think through changes, Schultze still had serious doubts that emerged in his advice to the president. Under the circumstances, Schultze was not willing to put his argument in the most positive and unambiguous terms even though he clearly had the intellectual capacity to do it. When Schultze began to see the weakness of his "model," his integrity brought him to present matters in a way that did not satisfy a president who still thought in terms of scientific absolutes. Whether Schultze realized what was happening in his interchanges with the president is unknown to me.

Press, in contrast, saw himself and the Office of Science and Technology Policy staff mainly as neutral scientists, an image quite appealing to Carter. In his account of his OSTP experience, written at the end of the Carter administration, Press observed that "I have found it advantageous to be viewed as a professional rather than a political appointee" and stated that "OSTP has come to be viewed primarily as a source of nonpolitical, expert advice . . . [and is perceived as] a highly professional office."[41] Press packaged himself and OSTP as scientists obtaining the facts and rendering nonpartisan, science-based judgments. Press's White House peers saw him exactly as he presented himself—that is, as scientist, not politician. Based on the interviews, I should point out that Press was held in the highest regard by those who worked with him. All of the other heads of analytic units came in for criticism during my interviews, but not Press. His inside reputation clearly added to his image, yet his science base stands out as critical.

The comparison between Schultze and Press is an intriguing one. The argument is not that Press was a better bureaucratic strategist in figuring out that Carter preferred the aura of scientific certainty. Rather it is that two men of integrity were at different intellectual stages. Schultze found himself at the point at which he was abandoning the confidence that had underpinned his economics and policy analysis; Press still believed in the scientific model in its purest terms. Press's description of himself and OSTP recalls the original characterization of the policy analyst made during the late 1950s and early 1960s as super technician applying the powerful tools of science to yield hard, objective, neutral information and analysis. "Neutral competence," objective expert determining the facts—these notions were tarnished as policy analysts moved into social areas and as economists began to have difficulty with macroeconomic policies. But the image of the neutral technician still fit Press a decade later.

Frank Press was not an ivory tower scientist above the fray. He started from his science base and moved into other relevant areas such as economics and diplomacy. However, Press's efforts were a careful moving out from a science-dominated area, not a foraging into electoral politics. Take the efforts of OSTP to improve United States-China relations by using science and technology linkages. As a former OSTP staff person told me, the important point in designing the United States-China science and technology agreement was that it was initiated by OSTP because of the recognition that the scientific and technology link stood as the strongest one in the overall U.S.-China relationship, and that, as such, it could be used as a political/diplomatic tool.

In addition, Press, being a good bureaucratic politician, could protect himself and OSTP in the White House structure. Moreover, Press knew how to work with the scientific community and appropriate congressional committees and subcommittees. In this respect, he may have been a much more adroit bureaucratic politician than Eizenstat or Schultze. We do not know how Press would have operated with a broader, more ambiguous portfolio as a member of the inner circle. What we do know is that he performed well in his self-chosen, more limited role of scientific generalist. Press represents the prototypical example of the technically oriented generalist willing to synthesize across policies, given that the policies are well within his office's technical competence, but not move generally into the political arena.

Eizenstat represents the other extreme—the politically oriented policy generalist. Eizenstat could claim neither the mantle of hard science nor the analytic framework and research orientation of a policy analyst. Eizenstat is the classic lawyer/policy generalist without a specialist substantive background or the tools of modern research and policy analysis. If Eizenstat comes out low on the technical credentials scale compared to a Frank Press, he scores well on the political dimension in both orientation and experience. Eizenstat may not have been the most seasoned presidential campaign veteran or the ultimate Washington insider, but he had considerable political experience. He went "both ways" in having policy and political credentials. But as might be expected in combining policy and politics, Eizenstat did not have a preeminent reputation in either.

Such an observation in no way denigrates Eizenstat's skills or analytic ability. It recognizes what may be the most critical characteristic of the emerging policy generalist—breadth at the expense of great depth. Gaining sufficient depth to be rated strong in a policy area may involve such an investment in time and effort both in the policy area itself and in the required technical tools as to make unlikely the needed level of investment in politics. Or else, acquiring the policy substance and techniques may indicate a predisposition not to be comfortable in politics. In any case, the higher policy generalists go, the greater the breadth of demands across policies and between policy and politics and the more it becomes clear that they need help. A critical test of leadership for top policy generalists will be to understand what they do *not* know and how to compensate for lack of knowledge or skill through their staff.

There is a final leadership quality, perhaps the hardest one of all for the top policy generalists, that is well-illustrated by Eizenstat's experience in the Carter administration. At the center of Eizenstat's problems were the president himself and Hamilton Jordan. Eizenstat suffered not only because of what Carter did not understand about the interrelationships of policy and politics but also from his own diffidence toward the president (Carter & Sons). Jordan, the inner-circle's chief political specialist also ranked higher than Eizenstat in the White House pecking order. These two men, the president and Jordan, stood between Eizenstat and the needed policy/political synthesis. The ultimate test for top policy generalists is whether they can develop strong peer relationships with the president and their counterpart top political generalists.

CARTER AND CLINTON

Bill Clinton tried mightily to avoid being labeled "another Jimmy Carter," going so far as to claim in a 1992 interview that "Jimmy Carter and I are as different as daylight and dark," and four years later schemed to keep the only living former Democratic president away from the 1996 Chicago presidential convention.[42] As I indicated at the outset of the chapter, some similarities between the two former southern governors are striking: their high intelligence and analytic orientation, the mutual desire to be their own top policy analysts, and their organizational weaknesses, including their failure to perceive the importance of a strong chief of staff. But in terms of character and style, Carter and Clinton are like day and night. First, Clinton stands out as a superb politician whose empathy and charm can capture an audience and whose sharp political skills can sell a policy. Carter, as the trustee-ship president, came across as a rigid, humorless moralist who sought, usually unsuccessfully, to guide citizens and Congress away from pure politics toward the public good. Second, and relatedly, Bill Clinton had few fixed policy objectives and a deviousness that brought wide distrust; Carter, based on his presidency and the years afterward, emerges as the most honorable of recent presidents.

The third major difference involves courage. Clinton showed little of that trait as exemplified by his acceptance in 1996 of a harsh welfare bill where he gave in to Republican measures predicted to cast a million more children into poverty; in sharpest contrast, Carter, in his July 15, 1979 address to the nation on energy and national goals, took the high ground by telling the American people that they were a big part of the problem. President Carter's speech, which at times soared to the ancient prophetic level of a Jeremiah, forewarned Americans of the dangers of their behavior. The admonishment to conserve energy, then in short supply because of OPEC's withholding of oil, turned into a broader charge about the general need to sacrifice if the nation was to solve its problems. Carter's warning is worth quoting at some length:

> The threat is nearly invisible in ordinary ways. It is a crisis of confidence. It is a crisis that strikes at the very heart and soul and spirit of our national will. We can see this crisis in the growing doubt about the meaning of our own lives and in the loss of a unity of purpose for our Nation.
>
> The erosion of our confidence in the future is threatening to destroy the social and political fabric of America. . . .
>
> We are at a turning point in our history. There are two paths to choose. One is a path I've warned about tonight, the path that leads to fragmentation and self-interest. Down that road lies a mistaken idea of freedom, the right to grasp for ourselves some advantage over others. That path would be one of constant conflict between narrow interests ending in chaos and immobility. It is a certain route to failure.
>
> All the traditions of our past, all the lessons of our heritage, all the promises of our future point to another path, the path of common purpose and the restoration of American values. That path leads to true freedom for our Nation and ourselves. We can take the first steps down that path as we begin to solve our energy problem. . . .
>
> I do not promise you that this struggle for freedom will be easy. I do not promise a quick way out of our Nation's problems, when the truth is that the only way out is an all-out effort. What I do promise you is that I will lead our fight, and I will enforce fairness in our struggle, and I will ensure honesty. And above all, I will act.
>
> We can manage the short-term shortages more effectively and we will, but there are no short-term solutions to our long-range problems. There is simply no way to avoid sacrifice.[43]

The address showed Carter at his best—moral, courageous, a president calling the American people to arms, not for major military combat that would increase his political standing, but to give up greed. Amazingly, the public responded favorably at first. But then Carter performed at his worst in firing several cabinet members including Califano, making the president seem a petty tyrant. Upon reflection, the American people decided they did not like being called to task for their behavior nor sacrificing. The July 15, 1979 message later became the touchstone for Ronald Reagan to tell voters that the dead hand of government, not they, had hurt America and personal sacrifice was uncalled for. Whether readers find Carter's jeremiad to the point then and even more relevant today or the misguided ramblings of a moralistic, self-righteous prig, Carter's stand surely showed both his high courage and his lack of political leadership skills, thereby setting the stage for the upcoming chapters on Reagan and Clinton.

NOTES

1. For a superb treatment of a policy peer relationship—that between Dulles and Eisenhower—see Stephen I. Ambrose, *Eisenhower: The President*, Simon & Schuster, 1984.

2. Ben W. Heineman Jr., "Marrying Politics and Policy" in Lester M. Salamon and Michael S. Lund (eds.), *The Reagan Presidency and Governing of America*, Urban Institute Press, 1984, p. 169.

3. Ben W. Heineman Jr. and Curtis A. Hessler, *Memorandum for the President: A Strategic Approach to Domestic Affairs in the 1980s*, Random House, 1980, p. 35, emphasis in the original.

4. Erwin C. Hargrove, *Jimmy Carter as President: Leadership and the Politics of the Public Good*, Louisiana State University Press, 1988, pp. 191–193.

5. Charles O. Jones, *The Trusteeship Presidency: Jimmy Carter and the United States Congress*, Louisiana State University Press, 1988, pp. 215 and 217.

6. Burton I. Kaufman, *The Presidency of James Earl Carter, Jr.*, University Press of Kansas, 1993, p. 3.

7. Haynes Johnson, *In the Absence of Power: Governing America*, Viking, 1980, p. 39.

8. Betty Glad, *Jimmy Carter: In Search of the Great White House*, Norton, 1980, p. 476.

9. William E. Leuchtenburg, *In the Shadow of FDR: From Harry Truman to Ronald Reagan*, Cornell University Press, 1983, pp. 200–201.

10. Johnson, *In the Absence of Power*, p. 278.

11. Hargrove, *Jimmy Carter as President*, p. 28.

12. Lawrence E. Lynn Jr. and David deF. Whitman, *The President as Policymaker: Jimmy Carter and Welfare Reform*, Temple University Press, 1981, pp. 272–273.

13. Joseph A. Califano Jr., *Governing America*, Simon & Schuster, 1981, pp. 402–403.

14. Erwin C. Hargrove, "The Uses and Limits of Skill in Presidential Leadership: The Case of Jimmy Carter," International Society of Political Psychology, Toronto, Canada, June 1984, p. 10.

15. For a discussion of Carter's preference for memoranda and a comparison with President Nixon, see Dom Bonafede, "How The White House Helps Carter Make Up His Mind," *National Journal*, April 15, 1978, p. 586.

16. *Washington Post*, October 5, 1982.

17. Joel Havemann, "The Carter Band—Trying to Follow Carter's Baton," *National Journal*, July 16, 1977, p. 1109.

18. Johnson, *In the Absence of Power*, pp. 200, 206–207.

19. Jimmy Carter, *Keeping Faith: Memories of a President*, Bantam Books, 1982, p. 127, italics in the original.

20. Ibid., pp. 217–228.

21. Ibid., p. 568, italics in the original.

22. Harry McPherson, *A Political Education*, Little, Brown, 1972, p. 253.

23. Larry Light, "White House Domestic Policy Staff Plays an Important Role in Formulating Legislation," *Congressional Quarterly*, October 6, 1979, p. 2201.

24. For a good summary of specific congressional problems in Carter's first year, see Jones, *The Trusteeship Presidency*, p. 214.

25. Hargrove, *Jimmy Carter as President*, p. 182.

26. For a brief discussion of collective responsibility, see Walter Williams, *Washington, Westminstser and Whitehall*, Cambridge University Press, 1988, p. 8.

27. Peter Hennessy, *Cabinet*, Basil Blackwell, 1986, p. 4.

28. Quoted in Samuel Kernell and Samuel L. Popkin (eds.), *Chief of Staff: Twenty-Five Years of Managing the Presidency*, University of California Press, 1986, p. 169.

29. Philip G. Henderson, *Managing the Presidency: The Eisenhower Legacy—From Kennedy to Reagan*, Westview Press, 1988, p. 81.

30. Johnson, *In the Absence of Power*, p. 26.

31. Ibid., p. 25.

32. Ibid.

33. Glad, *Jimmy Carter*, p. 427.

34. Havemann, "The Carter Band," p. 1108.

35. Hargrove, *Jimmy Carter as President*, p. 46.

36. Light, "White House Domestic Policy Staff Plays an Important Role in Formulating Legislation"; and Dom Bonafede, "Stuart Eizenstat—Carter's Right-Hand Man," *National Journal*, June 9, 1979. These articles offer extended descriptions of DPS operations including sketches of individual staff members.

37. Light, "White House Domestic Policy Staff Plays an Important Role in Formulating Legislation," p. 2204.

38. Heineman and Hessler, *Memorandum for the President*, p. 208, emphasis added.

39. Hargrove, *Jimmy Carter as President*, pp. 39–41.

40. For an extended treatment of lawyers and economists, see Walter Williams, *Mismanaging America: The Rise of the Anti-Analytic Presidency*, University Press of Kansas, 1990, pp. 34–40.

41. Frank Press, "Science and Technology in the White House, 1977 to 1980: Part I," *Science*, January 9, 1981, pp. 139–141.

42. *New York Times*, August 28, 1996.

43. *Weekly Compilation of Presidential Documents*, Week Ending July 20, 1979, vol. 15, no. 29, pp. 1237–1238, 1240.

6 | The Anti-Analytic Presidency

The story of the Reagan and Bush presidencies is one of steep decline in domestic policy information development in the executive branch and in the competence and status of the EOP and agency domestic policy analysis staffs. Ronald Reagan so dominates the entire period with his ideological certainty that spurned contrary information and his organizational incompetence that the twelve years can be labeled "the Reagan Era." The surprise of this period is that President Bush did so little to undo the damage to executive branch policy information and analysis that occurred in the eight years of the Reagan administration. In sharp contrast to his predecessor, Bush's record during his years of service in government prior to his presidency showed him to be a nonideological, pragmatic problem solver. Indeed, some commentators at the start of his presidency compared him to Dwight Eisenhower with the experience to be an able managerial president. But George Bush was no Dwight Eisenhower. Although not anti-analytic, President Bush cared little about policy information and analysis in the domestic policy area and did not undertake a concerted effort to undo the Reagan damage. This chapter first surveys the decline in executive branch policy information and analysis in the twelve years of the Reagan Era and then seeks to explain the actions of the two sharply contrasting leaders.

THE REAGAN ERA

The Reagan organizational and staffing legacy so dominated President Bush's design of his domestic policy-making process that the discussion of what happened to domestic policy information and analysis in the two presidencies is combined in a single section. Juxtaposing the Reagan and Bush domestic policy processes also sheds light on the latter's unexpected organizational ineptitude. To the extent Reagan's policy information and analysis legacy provided a sound base on which to build, President Bush's changes could have been incremental. A weak policy-making process, in turn, required a major overhaul to facilitate effective policy making. Hence Bush's acceptance of the Reagan legacy as adequate to support his policy-making process itself offers strong evidence about Bush's own lack of organizational competence.

Policy Information

In his two terms, Ronald Reagan literally waged a war on policy information by cutting deeply into the quantity and quality of the data available to the federal government. A material reduction occurred in the underlying information and analytic base needed to guide the economy, to assess policy results, to manage ongoing programs prudently, and to safeguard federal assets. In particular, domestic policy funds for evaluation and R&D were cut sharply and the quality of the evaluations suffered. For example, budget authority from 1980 to 1986 for major statistical organizations such as the Bureau of the Census and the Bureau of Labor Statistics dropped by one-fifth in constant dollars, while funds for evaluations fell by over one-third in real dollars between 1980 and 1984. As to the former, the cutbacks threatened the collection and development of current economic data that support major statistical series such as those for national income that are central for government and business. The sharp decline in evaluation funding reduced the capacity of federal and subnational governments to manage federally funded programs.[1]

After the four years of the Bush presidency, the General Accounting Office (GAO), in its second *Transition Series,* reported that discussions with the agencies and OMB provided no evidence of a meaningful increase in the investment in program evaluation in the executive branch during the Bush presidency.[2] Nowhere was GAO's criticism stronger than in the area of basic financial and accounting data to support the management and operation of the legislatively mandated programs that the executive agencies are charged with administering: "Widespread financial management weaknesses are crippling the ability of our leaders to effectively run the federal government. ... Not only does the government do an abysmal job of rudimentary bookkeeping, but it is also far from having the modern financial systems one would expect of a superpower."[3] Although President Bush made some limited efforts at improving policy information, the executive branch by the end of his presidency had seriously flawed data, or in some cases none at all, for formulating domestic and economic policy choices and managing programs. The lack of domestic policy information to support prudent management ranged from evaluative data on program operating performance—deemed "largely nonexistent" by GAO—to the most basic financial management control information needed to safeguard billions of dollars in federal long-term investments (e.g., Department of Defense assets) and in federal promises (e.g., savings and loan guarantees).[4]

Organizing and Staffing the EOP

At the start of his administration, President Reagan made Edwin Meese his top domestic policy generalist, bestowing cabinet rank on him. The president also downgraded the EOP policy analysis units except OMB so that only the budget office had strong domestic policy analytic capability in the EOP. In a *National Journal* article, Ronald Brownstein and Dick Kirschten caught the flavor of the domestic policy unit: "From the time Reagan moved into the Oval Office, no one has ever bothered to turn on the lights at the White House's Office of Policy Development."[5] At the outset of the administration, relative policy competence and decision-making style played a crucial role. Meese simply lacked the domestic policy and macroeconomic tools to manage the domestic policy process in the name of the president, while OMB director David Stockman, in contrast, had been a student of the budget in his days as a congressman. While he overestimated his command of budget and macroeconomic issues, Stockman had far more knowledge than any of the major players at the top of the administration. The problem went beyond Meese's limitations as the top domestic policy generalist to Stockman's overconfidence that led him to keep his own budget professionals from scrutinizing his budget plan and providing a needed input of neutral competence. Stockman himself admitted five years later that the 1981 budget plan that set in motion the record budget deficits of the Reagan Era had been "fatally flawed" and President Reagan "had been misled by a crew of overzealous—and ultimately incompetent—advisers."[6]

The Meese-Stockman relationship is critical for understanding the Reagan policy process. After passing over Meese for chief of staff, President Reagan gave him the policy portfolio and that made him Stockman's boss. Meese, as policy czar, became part of the powerful group that also included chief of staff James Baker and deputy chief of staff Michael Deaver and that came to be called the "Triumvirate." This group stood unchallenged as Reagan's premier policy and political advisers and hence held the primary staff responsibility for the efficacy of the White House policy process. Instead of seeking wide policy input to air differences and vet policy proposals, the Triumvirate often walled off the president from other advisers. Stockman wrote that he never met with the president alone during the many months of the 1981 budget process; yet he made the critical budget decisions because, as he observed, Meese and Deaver "were illiterate when it came to the essential equation of policy."[7] Chief of staff Baker, himself no student of budgets, in addition stayed away from Meese's policy domain and concentrated on the politics of selling the budget. Thus, the making of the 1981 budget fell to Stockman.

Stockman had a deep knowledge of the federal budget process from his days as a congressman. But his actual understanding paled in terms of his belief in the extent of his knowledge. This hubris led Stockman to look to the senior OMB career staff not for high-level analysis and advice but for backup information and detailed clerical checking. Compounding the problem further, Stockman developed the 1981 budget so quickly that most of the agency political executives were not even on board. This lack of scrutiny was particularly important because Stockman lacked analytic standards and stood ready to hide or misuse information, whatever the case demanded, to sell his agenda. Stockman's ideological fervor, lack of integrity, arrogance, and secrecy robbed the budget process of neutral competence, institutional memory, and multiple advocacy.

The Reagan budget experience strikingly underscores the dangers of an inadequate presidential policy-making process, of flawed information and analysis unchecked by rigorous scrutiny, and of the incompetent policy generalist. As to the latter, President Reagan himself had little or no knowledge of budgets and no interest in budget details so that the Triumvirate generally and policy czar Meese specifically had a heavy responsibility for managing a process that thoroughly vetted information and analysis. Instead, a barely operating policy process allowed David Stockman to be a lone operator with unbelievable power in crafting the first Reagan budget. As will be discussed shortly, OMB director Richard Darman and chief of staff John Sununu in the Bush administration had even more power over domestic and economic policy and for a longer period of time than did Stockman, but the latter had more actual policy impact because of the importance of the initial Reagan budget. Here is a pristine case of raw analytic power and its dangers. As I have written: "Information and analysis in Stockman's hands were weapons to be used fairly or unfairly in the larger battle. . . . Information is a dangerous commodity in the hands of the ideologue, and particularly so in the case of an ideological policy analyst who uses complex concepts and numbers masterfully as weapons to score points."[8] But it needs to be underscored that the failed process came about because of the actions of President Reagan's top White House political appointees. In choosing his key White House aides and cabinet secretaries—no more than thirty people at the most—a president shapes how his administration operates including how policy analysis will be carried out. Pick wrong and the presidency will be mismanaged.

The second through fourth years of President Reagan's first term saw extremely tight political control at the top exerted mainly by chief of staff Baker, his deputy Richard Darman, and Stockman. The Baker/Darman approach brought virtuoso political manipulation to protect the Reagan image. The dominant operational style involved the quick fix, the frantic search for information to solve the immediate problem. A penchant for secrecy, an over-reliance on a tiny circle of like-thinking advisers, a readiness to act without sound information and analysis, and an absence of any strategic thinking characterized the Baker-Darman style. It led to Reagan's high political standing before the 1984 election but covered over a number of major policy problems including mounting budget and trade deficits and the emerging savings and loan crisis. In Reagan's second term, Donald Regan, who had been secretary of the treasury, traded jobs with Baker and built the wall of isolation around the president higher yet as he became Reagan's only policy generalist and seemingly the domestic policy deputy president. In comparison, the Baker/Darman process produced more discussion with other White House staff than did that of Regan. Bob Schieffer and Gary Gates have pointed out: "The decision making had been more free-form during the first term and as Richard Darman . . . later said, 'Seeing the interplay between us, a lot of things happened. First of all, Ronald Reagan learned much more about reality.'"[9] However, Darman's comparison is to the Regan process where President Reagan's interaction with other staff approached zero. The policy process in Reagan's first term bore almost no resemblance to well-ordered multiple advocacy. For example, Stockman, until he left in the middle of the second term, continued to practice an extreme version of top-down budgeting in OMB and the agencies. The top of the White House owned the budget process, the agencies were minor players.

George Bush, with a highly centralized and politicized White House, followed suit as the Baker and Darman style of secrecy and tight control by a small inner circle became the basic plan for the Bush White House, including the personal styles of top staff. OMB director Darman mirrored Stockman; the new chief of staff Sununu operated like Donald Regan. These two appointments are so critical because Sununu and Darman dominated domestic policy and shaped the policy-making process itself. Both Darman and Sununu were brilliant and knowledgeable about policy. Darman, like Stockman, mastered the budget and amazed people with his grasp of details. Sununu, who had been an engineering professor and governor of New Hampshire, brought state program experience and a highly analytic mind to the job. Their obvious talents, however, became liabilities in part because of other personal traits and in part because of Bush's benign neglect of domestic and economic policy.

President Bush made clear publicly that he much preferred national security policy. He created a domestic policy regency of chief of staff Sununu and OMB Director Darman who spurned information and advice, were imperious and secretive, and operated with a top-down style that cut off ideas from below. *New York Times* reporter Andrew Rosenthal wrote: "Sununu exacerbated Mr. Bush's limitations, rather than making up for them. . . . This was a White House without a long-range agenda, without a communications strategy and without first-rate thinkers in many of the top jobs. 'John Sununu and a thousand interns,' went the joke among White House officials disgusted with the lack of exchange in ideas and with Mr. Sununu's need to surround himself with people who would not challenge his authority."[10] Darman, who inherited a talented career analytic staff at OMB, too seldom drew on this reservoir. Just as Stockman did, Darman misused the talented, experienced professional staff at OMB in relying much too often on his top political aides for advice on major decisions.

Bush's benign neglect in the domestic and economic policy making, on the one hand, gave EOP subordinates more control over appointments and facilitated the building of stronger policy units than under Reagan. On the other hand, Bush's disinterest permitted power battles that resulted in Sununu and Darman dominating policy making even though the president had picked two technically competent analysts to head the key policy units. Roger Porter, who was a professor at Harvard's John F. Kennedy School of Government between serving in high positions in the Ford and Reagan administrations, headed the domestic policy unit and had been granted greater power on paper than previous heads in having responsibility for both domestic and economic advice. The respected Stanford economist Michael Boskin became chair of the Council of Economic Advisers. With Bush not being overtly anti-analytic like Reagan, Porter and Boskin were able to assemble relatively competent staffs.

Because President Bush did not choose to manage the EOP process for domestic and economic policy making himself or to designate a single manager with full authority and clear instructions for generating wide debate, individual power and personality dominated. In domestic policy, the outcome was straightforward. Despite his technical competence and his in-depth experience with a viable multiple advocacy process during the Ford presidency, Porter had neither the personality nor the raw power to make himself an equal of Sununu and Darman. Porter took the assignments handed down to him which at times could be important as in the case of the Clean Air Act. But his role was far less than might have been expected from his position so high on the organization's chart, his own experience, and his relatively competent staff.

Economic policy making involved greater complexity because secretary of the treasury Nicholas Brady had strong personal ties to the president and had been seen at the outset as the president's chief economic coordinator, a traditional role for the secretary of the treasury.

But the president never gave Brady full coordinating power. Further, as pointed out by *Washington Post* writer Bob Woodward in his detailed October 1992 account of economic policy making based on off-the-record interviews: "[Brady] is considered a weak secretary, according to sources inside and outside the administration who have regular contact with him."[11] Clear animosity characterized the relationship between Brady and Darman, who according to Woodward, "had a penchant for bad-mouthing his colleagues" and had called Brady a " 'dolt' who could not pass an introductory economics exam in any American university."[12] Brady knew of Darman's opinion and tried to control him by indicating his close ties to Bush. Relationships were also poor with Boskin who was highly competent and had a talented staff but lacked Brady's power. Woodward reported that Darman had privately pronounced Boskin "irrelevant to economic policymaking" and tried to keep him out of important economic meetings.[13] As for Sununu, Boskin became upset because of Bush's rosy accounts of the economy based on Sununu's overly optimistic assessments. Woodward wrote: "For weeks, Boskin tried to speak to Bush directly, but Sununu rebuffed him. On several occasions, Boskin and Sununu got into shouting matches at staff meetings."[14] Boskin got through to warn the president directly of his unrealistic statements on an economy clearly in trouble only after threatening Sununu that he would resign if he could not see Bush (and, we can assume, go public). It cannot be overstated how much the personal animosities undercut policy making. In the case of Darman, Sununu, and Boskin, neither brilliance nor in-depth knowledge helped make the process work. Staff behavior became destructive with its combination of Sununu and Darman's arrogance that spurned advice and a desire for power in Darman and Sununu that was extreme even in the White House.

The Bush policy-making process needs further exploration because it shows how Bush cut himself off from broader advice and failed to exert control over brilliant, but highly flawed staff members. At the top of the Bush process were two extraordinarily tight loops with the president, secretary of state James Baker, national security adviser Brent Scowcroft, and a small number of people around them handling foreign policy, and with Sununu and Darman so dominating domestic policy that they could legitimately be called "Deputy Presidents." The most striking aspect of the foreign and domestic/economic policy domains is that people with titles that should have made them central actors (e.g., Brady and Porter) and key EOP organizations such as the National Security Council staff, were outside of the loops. In the White House, the president, Scowcroft, and his deputy Robert Gates "handled literally everything."[15] They were joined by Secretary Baker who restricted the number of players around him to a bare minimum. In *Hell of a Ride*, where vicious, often tasteless humor badly marred the book, John Podhoretz did score a bull's eye when he wrote of the president's "notorious problem with 'the vision thing' and his own preference for the airless loop [whereby] George Bush, the first member of the ultraexclusive Yale secret society Skull and Bones to reach the Oval Office, turned American foreign and defense policy into a boys' club."[16]

While foreign policy, as discussed, had a clubby atmosphere with its conviviality, friendship, and loyalty, domestic and economic policy were conducted on a bloody battleground dominated by Sununu and Darman who were brilliant, egotistical, nasty, and unscrupulous. Podhoretz described senior staff meetings in which Sununu and Darman sat at opposite ends of the table and the former had the role of hatchetman. The bureaucratic terrorism came to be labeled as "being Darmanized" with Darman described by Podhoretz as "extraordinarily uncouth" and as using "terms of abuse in a remarkably personal manner."[17] The example given is Darman reading from a speech by poor Roger Porter without naming him and saying "I would like to call everyone's attention to one of the *stupidest* things I ever read."[18]

The reader may be bothered by my dwelling on this behavior and quoting Podhoretz at some length; I do so, however, because of the relevance to competent White House policy making. Both Sununu and Darman had the brains and the tools to be superb analysts but converted the policy-making process to a chamber of horrors. They were similar in capability, style, and orientation to David Stockman, hence I do not see their acts as a single aberration. Rather this kind of bureaucratic-political behavior, albeit generally in lesser degree, is as much a part of public policy analysis as techniques and methods. Particularly at higher levels, policy and politics are inseparable. Further, the presence of other technically competent analysts such as Porter and Boskin in the presidential policy process underscores the point that competence alone is not enough. Good teamwork and professional integrity are necessary components of an effective analytic process.

The Executive Agencies

President Reagan sought extremely tight presidential control of the domestic agencies both by keeping major decisions at the top of the White House, mainly in the Stockman-dominated budget process, and by subcabinet appointments whose first loyalty was to the Reagan agenda. The Reagan political executives often had contempt for career civil servants and would exclude them from agency policy meetings. What characterized so many of the Reagan political executives was their ideological commitment without strong organizational knowledge. They had neither the inclination nor the expertise to draw on the skills of the career civil servants. In addition to appointing often incompetent subcabinet political executives to manage the agencies, President Reagan reduced the technical competence and morale of agency civil servants by decimating the analytic offices, decreasing the number of nondefense civil servants, keeping pay below market rates, and continuing to attack government in general and "bureaucrats" in particular. I have argued that "by 1989 it was appropriate to speak of a hollow, incompetent federal government in the domestic policy arena."[19]

President Bush had a mixed record in organizing and staffing the agencies. In sharp contrast to Reagan's attacks, President Bush praised civil servants and obtained pay increases. By not appointing ideologues as political executives and by permitting changes such as stronger analytic offices, Bush did allow his secretaries greater organizational freedom than in the Reagan years. At the same time, as already discussed, White House control over major agency decisions under Sununu and Darman was, if anything, tighter than under Reagan. Decentralization, to the extent it occurred, meant that the agencies, after the big budget and program decisions were made at the top, could do what they wanted if the choices caused no political embarrassment. In sum, President Bush inherited a hollow, inept domestic government and made some changes but did not undertake the effort needed to raise materially the capacity of the executive agencies to manage programs effectively or efficiently after the severe damage of the Reagan years.

RONALD REAGAN AS LEADER AND MANAGER

Although numerous authors, including this writer, emphasized President Reagan's many weaknesses and have harshly criticized him and his presidency, the most telling negative portraits are by Lou Cannon in his definitive biography and by George Shultz in his massive account of his years as Reagan's secretary of state. The two gain credence in being both sharp observers and biased toward Reagan. Moreover, Shultz had been a distinguished public manager both as secretary of labor and treasury and OMB director in the Nixon-Ford years and as Reagan's secretary of state. This section first draws heavily on these two accounts, particularly that of Shultz because of its vivid and frightening account of management, analysis, and advice in the Reagan White House. Finally, the discussion turns to the conceptual distinctions between the leader and the manager roles. It considers the differences that are more vividly illustrated by President Reagan than by any other postwar president because he became both that era's most powerful political leader and its most inept manager.

"The Role of a Lifetime"

Lou Cannon titled his massive study of the Reagan years: *President Reagan: The Role of a Lifetime* to indicate that Reagan was first and foremost a professional actor who took each real-life part as a movie role and did not (and by 1981 probably could not) himself distinguish the difference.[20] Reagan's worldview formed in the Hollywood of bold heroes and dastardly villains mixed together patriotism and fantasy. Reagan never escaped that world: "[Reagan] made sense of foreign policy through his long-developed habit of devising dramatic, all-purpose stories with moralistic messages, forceful plots and well-developed heroes and villains. . . . The more Reagan repeated a story, the more he believed it and the more he resisted information that undermined its premises. . . . Ronald Reagan's subordinates often despaired of him because he seemed to inhabit a fantasy world where cinematic events competed for attention with reality."[21] The core of Reagan's unreality mixed together detachment and ignorance. Schieffer and Gates captured the former succinctly in observing, "Reagan's people came to see him more as an abstract idea than as a flesh-and-blood leader. . . . Reagan's disengaged style would come to be recognized as the most striking characteristic of his presidency."[22] For our purposes, Reagan's ignorance, using that term in its literal sense of lacking in knowledge, training, and/or information, is even more important. Although not unintelligent, Reagan seldom used his mental skills on organizational or policy issues. Thus, his passivity and lack of curiosity combined with his ignorance to produce a president who did not know and had no interest in knowing. This detachment and disinterest could at times make President Reagan's lack of information astounding. A case in point is a meeting on the budget with Senators Sam Nunn and Barry Goldwater where Reagan admitted he had been an active supporter of the Gramm-Rudman legislation but had not been told about the absolutely critical requirement of Gramm-Rudman that made budget cuts mandatory if Congress did not meet the specified budget reduction goals. Schieffer and Gates observed: "[Gramm-Rudman] had been one of the most highly publicized and fiercely debated bills in recent congressional history. Yet Reagan, who had signed the legislation into law, was unabashedly taking the position that he had not understood its purpose."[23]

President Reagan's striking difference from all the other men who have been the chief executive during the modern presidency cannot be overempha-

sized. It is not simply a matter of degree. The following combination clearly distinguishes him from any chief executive of the modern presidency that began with Franklin Roosevelt: Reagan detested government and saw himself outside of it even as president, totally ignored most information and analysis, understood almost nothing about how government operated generally and how the large-scale federal bureaucratic agencies performed specifically, comprehended little or nothing about most policy issues, and often could not separate fact from fantasy. This uniqueness merits a further comment because readers may see my claim as hyperbole or as an extreme bias against Reagan. Not so. Few admirers or detractors questioned Reagan's lack of knowledge or his detachment. His speech writer, Peggy Noonan, his most ardent admirer among the many White House staff members who have written insider books on the Reagan administration, observed: "There were times when I would see the earnest young people in the middle levels of the administration trying to get somebody to listen to their thoughts . . . and see the sunny president who did not seem to know or notice, and I would think to myself (if I was tired enough, frustrated enough) that the battle for the mind of Ronald Reagan was like the trench warfare of World War I: Never have so many fought so hard for such barren terrain."[24]

"What did the president know and when did he know it?" became the crucial, potentially incriminating question for President Nixon in Watergate and President Reagan in the Iran-contra affair. This question applies equally, however, to all policy decisions. What did President Reagan know when he made any of his administration's critical decisions or left them to others to make? The answer is almost always, quite little or nothing. Moreover, communicating with President Reagan became a more difficult task because of his hearing problems. Again, Cannon succinctly grasped the difficulty of the task: "[I]t was commonplace for Reagan's principal policy advisers to find the president inattentive, unfocused and incurious and to depart from meetings not knowing what, if anything, had been decided. . . . Communicating with Reagan was an art form in which few excelled and that no one, with the possible exception of Nancy Reagan, had totally mastered."[25]

The White House Policy-making Process

In *Turmoil and Triumph*, George Shultz gives President Reagan high marks on vision (seeing the big picture), the ability to break through entrenched thinking, decisiveness, and strength under fire. All are desirable characteristics of a persuasive leader who can point out where to go and induce people to move in that direction but in the main do not address President Reagan's managerial competence. On this dimension, Shultz's evidence showed severe shortcomings that reinforce earlier discussions of the president's unwillingness to face facts, his limited interest in and understanding of information and analysis, his limitations in picking competent policy advisers, and his lack of comprehension of the need for a sound ongoing policy process. Shultz also pointed out that Reagan's decisiveness had a bad side in that once he decided, the president often refused to change even when facts and analysis showed him to be wrong. Shultz praised President Reagan as having good judgment if provided the right information.[26] The problem, as so much of *Turmoil and Triumph* attested, was that (1) President Reagan's own National Security Council staff and the Central Intelligence Agency under William Casey were feeding Reagan bad information purposely, and (2) even when a number of the key foreign policy actors were trying to help him, they lacked the analytic competence to do so. What stands out in Shultz's extended account is that the Reagan White House combined incompetence, irresponsibility, and dishonesty in its top staff. NSC adviser William Clark offers the best example of incompetence, as he operated with almost no substantive knowledge and limited understanding of the NSC process itself. Over time some improvement in foreign policy knowledge in the NSC staff was outweighed by a shocking lack of responsibility and integrity. Shultz noted that the NSC staff lied to him and other members of the cabinet and observed: "White House and NSC staffs . . . were operating on the fringes of loyalty to the president and of common sense. . . . A responsible staff should have kept the president fully informed and should have continuously warned him of the legal and constitutional problems created by the actions taken or not taken."[27]

The executive branch is hard to manage. Granting White House staff members who are loyal only to the president more power than cabinet secretaries does make easier the president's task of political control over the entire executive branch. Although Shultz argued strongly that presidents can gain overall by not placing White House staff over cabinet members, it remains a debatable point. However, the claim that the president should pick advisers who are both competent and loyal to him is hardly controversial. Yet as Shultz made clear, President Reagan lacked the capacity to sort people out and had "a tendency to rely on his staff and friends to the point of accepting uncritically— even wishfully—advice that was sometimes amateurish and even irresponsible."[28] Lou Cannon went even further: "Reagan did not really know what a national security adviser was supposed to do. . . . [His national security advisers worked] in a monarchical presidency where the king clung merrily to his opinions, believed in happy endings and allowed his policies to make their own way."[29] Cannon added that national security adviser Robert (Bud) MacFarlane, told him " 'The president doesn't even remember my name.' "[30]

Ronald Reagan offers the extreme case of a president whose great leadership capacity combined with an unbelievable lack of knowledge about institutional structure and function. He is *sui generis*. At the same time no example makes the case of a president's impact on federal policy analysis and research so strikingly. President Reagan and his top appointees were able to undermine the practice of policy analysis in the federal government and severely limit the scope and quality of policy research. Their actions subverted the policy analysis revolution that had begun in 1961 in the Department of Defense including the efforts through rigorous evaluation and field experimentation to develop sound information on how effectively ongoing policies were working and how well new policy ideas might work.

Leaders and Managers

As discussed earlier, presidents in their power to select all of the key managers in the executive branch—be they cabinet secretaries and subcabinet members, or White House staff assigned managerial powers by the president—have the most fundamental of executive responsibilities. In any large, complex organization including the federal executive branch, chief executives cannot run the enterprise alone, so they must select the top managers to whom chief executives delegate basic responsibilities for which they must still answer. That is, delegation does not shift ultimate responsibility from chief executives but casts them as supervisors of the principal delegatees. Chief managers' monitoring of delegatees' efforts is critical to how well their organizations are managed. That the president must be the chief manager is not a normative claim that the president *ought* to do so but results from the explicit assignment of that function to him by the Constitution. His dual role of political leader and manager is fundamental and cannot be avoided— delegated away—under the present constitutional structure. How competent Ronald Reagan was in handling the basic constitutional responsibilities of leader and manager is central for understanding his presidency.

The terms "leader" and "manager" can be distinguished. The statement that an individual is only a manager implies that he or she is good at various institutional tasks needed to keep an organization going but is not capable of instilling a higher mission or fundamentally changing the organization's direction. The latter is the job of the leader. The distinction is helpful in sorting out two different tasks that likely require different sets of skills although some are common to both. For example, both the leader and the manager need persuasive skills, even though the former may need a higher order of that skill to change direction than the manager does to keep the organization successfully on a steady course. The dichotomy, however, is most misleading if it suggests one individual cannot be both leader and manager. Mintzberg, a major writer on business, used "manager" as the broader term and included "leader" as one of the manager's ten roles.[31] But however the two critical functions are combined, the overriding point is that competent chief executives—be they heads of businesses or presidents of the United States—must have persuasive competence and managerial competence. The balance between the two competences generally will differ, with a president needing more persuasive power than a corporate chief executive because of demands in the political arena. But each needs a considerable quantity of both. Reagan, however, displayed an incredible imbalance between the two competencies: he was the postwar era's most extraordinarily up-front, persuasive leader and, by far, the most incompetent manager.

Reagan paradoxically comes across as both hard working and lazy. He labored to increase his primary strength of public argument. Lou Cannon and David Hoffman noted: "Reagan works hard in his residence, according to aides. But one acknowledged that much of this work is essentially the rehearsing of a trained communicator rather than the intellectual activity of a president who is trying to master difficult subjects. The president is said to spend much of his time rewriting speeches and polishing points he wants to make rather than acquiring new information."[32] The lazy side of Reagan is captured by Bob Woodward in describing the reaction to Reagan's short work week by the workaholic CIA director William Casey: "Casey noted in amazement that [Reagan] worked from nine to five on Mondays, Tuesdays, and Thursdays, and from nine to one on Wednesdays, when he'd take the afternoon off for horseback riding or exercise; and on Fridays he left sometime between one and three for Camp David. During the working hours in the Oval Office, the President often had blocks of free time—two, even three hours . . . [when] he would call for his fan mail and sit and answer it."[33] The observations of a limited schedule and of hard work that seem in direct conflict can be reconciled by recognizing that Ronald Reagan brought a good mind and a trained, highly professional eye to his primary concern of selling his political ideas and expended considerable effort in this task, but simply chose not to think rigorously about policy nor to be involved in managing the policy process. That is why he had so much free time. A good mind or not, policy and management in any complexity were beyond him.

Most strikingly, Reagan's political team used his physical image of being in charge to package and make believable President Reagan as super leader and super manager. The image of "Manager Reagan" that vanished in the Iran-contra scandal lasted well into Reagan's second term. Historian Garry Wills caught the real Reagan as manager-leader better than anyone in casting him as a public president "[who] acts for his own administration as he did for GE [General Electric], as a symbol and spokesman."[34] It is a most telling comment. Reagan had been employed by GE to speak at its plants across the country (he visited all 135 GE facilities in eight years) and to host the GE Theatre on television.[35] Reagan did exactly what GE wanted and did it well. However, Reagan never became a part of GE management. He emerged as their public "symbol and spokesman" sent out to raise morale and the company image. That Reagan could play almost the same role as president of the United States and be acclaimed for his managerial talents is truly remarkable.

Ronald Reagan as president, in effect, abdicated his managerial role. In a true delegation within the management function, a superior grants a subordinate authority to act in his or her place but remains sufficiently involved so as to gain enough knowledge about the delegated task to monitor the subordinate's efforts to carry out that delegated responsibility. The superior, however, has the ultimate responsibility. As long as the subordinate knows what the superior wants, has the knowledge and skills to well-execute the responsibility, and seeks faithfully to do what the superior wants, the latter's failure to be active in delegation may have no serious adverse consequences. But such an arrangement is unlikely to continue for long. As former President Gerald Ford observed: " 'You cannot operate that Oval Office . . . without having yourself involved. . . . It's not an eight-hour day and it's not a five-day week. It requires lots of personal involvement.' "[36] Nowhere is the danger from Reagan's total delegation of his fundamental managerial responsibilities greater than in the area of basic decision making where he passed to his top aides full responsibility for managing the process needed to provide information and analysis in support of critical presidential decisions.

The already discussed case of the 1981 budget process showed that Reagan's ignorance became even more dangerous because of the lack of understanding of the budget by the three top aides standing between the president and Stockman whose judgment could be questioned but not his capacity for hard work or his willingness to press ahead on the 1981 tax and budget package. Much after the fact, Stockman lamented: "Designing a comprehensive plan to bring about a sweeping change in national economic governance in forty days is a preposterous, wantonly reckless notion."[37] That 1981 budget set in motion the deficit increases that averaged nearly $190 billion per year for twelve years and took the U.S. debt held by the public from $709 billion to \$3 trillion in 1992. This quadrupling of the debt in a dozen years flowed directly from Reagan's management style and policies, and indirectly from Reagan's powerful political leadership that made Americans believe that the nation was back on track despite the debt. The other dominant political leader of the modern presidency—Franklin Delano Roosevelt—in actuality masked his inability to walk on legs rendered useless by adult polio. Ronald Reagan was just as adroit symbolically. As president he might be likened to a weight lifter who over his lifetime only strengthens his right arm, and stands in such a way that only the bulging arm of political leadership is visible while the withered left arm of managerial ineptitude is hidden.

What a mighty right arm it was! No president of the modern era, except Franklin Delano Roosevelt, had the leadership skills to appear bigger than life, create a more optimistic national mood despite the underlying reality, and change the direction of political thinking. Both men, in part because of their heroic behavior after early assassination attempts (Roosevelt as president-elect) and their quick, bold actions, such as Reagan standing up to the air traffic controllers and Roosevelt saving the banking system, took on an aura of individual power and courage. For example, Reagan in effect became a "real" John Wayne character. In his first inaugural address in the depths of the Great Depression with the quite real threat of national financial collapse looming large, Roosevelt told America, "the only thing we have to fear is fear itself" and brought hope. Similarly, Ronald Reagan made people believe in 1984 that it was "morning again in America," even though soaring public and private debt fueled the booming economy. More broadly, President Reagan's optimism induced Americans to be both happier and more confident than they had been in the previous decade. Finally, Roosevelt established the liberal political thrust that drove American domestic policy until the Reagan Era when the nation shifted to a conservative view that still reigns. Indeed, in the case of Bill Clinton, his resurrection from the crushing 1994 midterm election rested in part on his rhetoric efforts proclaiming optimism, even adopting the Morning Again in America theme in 1996, and on his shift to a distinctly Reaganese political style that extended the Reagan Era.

EXPLAINING AND ASSESSING BUSH'S BEHAVIOR

George Bush saw himself as a status quo president prudently guiding the Reagan revolution. As presidential candidate, Bush campaigned on the strength of the perceived Reagan accomplishments of a booming economy and a less intrusive federal government, both claiming some credit for the success as vice president and arguing that he could skillfully further the gains through the careful, incremental steering that he saw as the foundation of his prudent governance style. As President Bush affirmed in his 1992 State of the Union address, "I pride myself that I'm a prudent man." *Time* magazine reporters Michael Duffy and Dan Goodgame in *Marching in Place: The Status Quo Presidency of George Bush* wrote: "The first duty of a president, Bush believed, was 'prudence', a quality he esteemed above all others."[38]

President Bush, it needs noting, defined prudence in the highly constrained and ahistorical terms of narrowly cautious behavior. Historically, prudence has been one of the primary public virtues, demanding both wisdom and foresight. The critical point in the broader definition is that the *current* setting facing a leader establishes the kind of response needed for prudent political behavior. That is, prudence can be cautious or bold if the demands are large. For example, the British historian G. M. Trevelyan wrote of "one of the most prudent acts of daring in history" in describing how Earl Grey, in leading the effort to enact the Great Reform Act of 1832, responded boldly in a period of great turbulence to avoid a likely British civil war.[39] If President Bush's overall presidential performance was assessed, he might be adjudged imprudent in not meeting big challenges such as huge growth in the federal debt. The claim here, however, is that Bush failed the narrow demands of prudence. That is, a sound policy information and analysis process—well-managed and well-staffed—is central to prudent presidential governance, be the definition of prudence narrow or broad. Amid the current complexity, a president needs reliable information and analysis and an ongoing institutional process for determining future problems and feasible means of treating them if he is to manage prudently. Hence, the strong expectation at the start of the Bush administration was that he would stress tight management. Such an orientation would have been consistent with an incremental presidency that had no big domestic policy objectives, much like Eisenhower who too had been a foreign policy president. Well-managing the domestic policies already in place fit perfectly with President Bush's narrow definition of prudence.

Why then did President George Bush not completely overhaul the badly organized and staffed presidency he inherited from his predecessor so as to generate a sounder information and analytic base for domestic policy formulation and prudent management efforts, or charge his top policy generalists with the task? Four interrelated personal factors are critical in explaining Bush's behavior: (1) his lack of extensive managerial experience, (2) his excessive fear of leaks, (3) his lack of policy direction and aversion to strategic policy planning, and (4) his restricted view of process and procedure. These four individual deficiencies add up to President Bush's lack of the presidential policy competence skills of strategic thinking, organizational mastery, and analytic capability. Let us keep this in mind and return to it at the end of this section.

The Four Main Individual Factors

Duffy and Goodgame observed that Bush's résumé "glossed over both his brief tenure at each post and his dearth of substantive accomplishments."[40] Once elected to Congress, where he served four years and resigned to run a losing race for senator, Bush passed quickly through a number of résumé-building jobs: 1970, ambassador to the United Nations; 1972, chairman, Republican Party; 1974, head of the U.S. Liaison Office to the People's Republic of China (before the office was upgraded to embassy status); 1976, director of the Central Intelligence Agency. The list of positions without the dates would suggest great knowledge and experience, but his actual experience—especially in large-scale organizational management—was quite thin.

The argument is not that Bush lacked reasonable foreign policy credentials but that his only direct experience in managing large-scale public organizations came from a single year as head of the CIA, hardly the most typical of agencies. The early comparisons to Eisenhower, who had spent his entire adult life mainly in staff and line managerial positions, were badly misplaced. President Bush's organizational incompetence does not represent a case of the Peter Principle, where a previously successful manager finally reaches the level of his incompetence, but that of a relatively inexperienced manager who does not grow in the job. Bush ended up as a president who did not know what he did not know. For example, the president who saw prudence as the first duty of his office did not understand that the prudent management of existing programs demanded sound performance and financial management data and careful analysis in considering incremental changes. Nor did he recognize until near the end of his presidency that the lack of an orderly EOP policy-making process caused by the explosive combination of actors in the domestic and economic areas was destroying his presidency.

President Bush had an obsession with secrecy. Georgetown University professor Colin Campbell quoted an interviewee he described as a "Republican knowledgeable about both the Reagan and Bush administrations" as follows: " 'I think you know how obsessed George Bush is about leaks. What you don't know is the fullness of the obsession. It's right up there as one of his core values. You know, service, family, religion, leaks.' "[41] The president's tendency to maximize secrecy and minimize the circle of persons with knowledge of an issue found strong reinforcement from the operating styles of Secretary of State Baker, OMB director Darman, and chief of staff Sununu. This near pathological dread of leaks pushed toward extreme centralization at the top on major policy decisions and away from multiple advocacy and drawing on the neutral competence of careerists that might have improved the base for policy making but would have increased appreciably the number of actors in the decision-making process.

Bush lacked strategic vision and had a distaste for strategic policy planning. Writing about foreign policy making and thus assessing Bush in a much more favorable case than that of domestic policy, *Washington Post* foreign editor David Ignatius still faulted Bush:

> Bush launched a war without any clear vision of the sort of Iraq he hoped to create in the aftermath. Without a plan, the administration fumbled its postwar opportunity to replace Hussein with a broadly democratic regime. A year after Desert Storm, Iraq seems almost a tar baby for Bush, rather than a feather in his cap. . . .
> Bush's difficulty with policy planning is ironic, because one of the strengths of his Establishment forebears was supposedly their ability to develop clear, long-term strategy. The George Kennans, Paul Nitzes and Allen Dulleses weren't embarrassed by this sort of intellectual exercise. But in Bush's world view, policy planning is apparently viewed as effete. Real men don't plan.[42]

In so many ways Bush, the son of Connecticut Senator Prescott Bush and a child of privileged education at Andover and Yale, seemed cut from the same cloth as Dulles, Dean Acheson, and Averell Harriman who were central figures in the strategic thinking that shaped American foreign policy in the early postwar period. Moreover, Richard Nixon, a skilled foreign policy analyst and strategist, is the postwar president whom Bush most resembled in international experience. But this heritage did not pass on. Thoughtful planning was not George Bush's style. Ignatius's real-men-don't-plan accusation rings true. Woodward, in discussing high-level Gulf War meetings attended by the president, national security adviser Brent Scowcroft, Secretary of Defense Richard Cheney, and chairman of the Joint Chiefs of Staff General Colin Powell observed: "Often they [the meetings] had no beginning, middle or end. They [the participants] would kick the ball around. Feet would be on the table, cowboy boots gleaming."[43]

Jimmy Carter lacked a strategic vision too. Although Carter, in contrast to Bush, had plenty of policy objectives, his passion for details made him too much the narrow analyst uncomfortable in thinking big. Bush, however, lacked not only vision but had few if any guiding objectives and principles. This seeming hollowness may be explained by President Bush's view of process and procedure. Mullins and Wildavsky labeled the Bush administration the "procedural presidency," and argued that for Bush "the political and economic system is expressed as process [and] . . . enhancing the process is President Bush's purpose."[44] This insight is illuminating but also can be misleading. The critically important point is that process for Bush combined both means and ends in that he thought that a good process could yield a good decision without being explicitly directed toward a desired outcome. Strategic thinking had no place in such a decision-making approach. A president with no underlying policy direction could still seek cease-lessly to reach out because he believed the process itself, without a guiding objective set out by that president, would produce a desirable result. In his "procedural presidency," it becomes clear why President Bush had no concern for the "vision thing" (except as a political liability) and appeared mystified when so much was made of it in political terms. For Bush process itself became the entire focus of the policy-making operations as it moved toward mutual accommodation as the final result. *New York Times* reporter Maureen Dowd summed up the Bush presidency as follows: "From the beginning of his administration, it was clear he had no ideas or programs he wanted to enact, that his greatest pleasure came from simply being president."[45] That statement goes too far. Bush believed he could keep the Reagan economic revolu-tion going and steer American foreign policy in a status quo presidency by exercising a high level of prudence through the incremental changes needed to stay on course. However, it clearly was the case that in contrast to Reagan who suffered because he would not allow his princi-ples and objectives to be challenged by facts, Bush so often seemed at sea because he had no inner guidance from basic principles and overriding objectives. Add to this his managerial incompetence, and we do have a presidency so lacking in purpose and so badly administered that Bush's seriousness can be called into question by as perceptive a critic as Dowd.

What is misleading about the label of "procedural presidency" is that procedure for Bush did not mean a systematic policy-planning process based on sound information and analysis and careful delibera-tion among the key actors in reaching a policy decision. In contrast to the passive Reagan, Bush always seemed in motion, calling people on the telephone, getting people's ideas. But these efforts were but the habitual actions of an outgoing, restless president to fill his day—"a president," Duffy and Goodgame argued, "who substitutes frenetic movement for lasting action."[46] Absent was the deliberation and reflec-tion needed for reasoned decision making. This is not to deny that the Bush policy-making approach could produce reasonable decisions when the new policy needed only an incremental adjustment to the old one, particularly if long-accepted principles or objectives anchored the policy direction. The weakness in Bush's concept of process arose when a critical decision demanded extended analysis based on a guiding vision and reasoned deliberation. Although not overtly anti-analytic himself, President Bush's style and orientation fueled the continuation of the anti-analytic presidency and solidified Reagan's quantum jump toward White House centralization of major decisions made without the benefit of multiple advocacy or neutral competence.

Foreign Policy Making

The case for Bush's limited policy competence—his lack of strong analytic, strategic, and organizational skills—is strong when drawn from the areas of domestic and economic policy. The claim, however, could be misleading because the critique has not considered President Bush's policy making in foreign affairs where he brought much more experience and stayed heavily involved in the process. There is little question that national security policy making was more systematic and certainly a great deal more harmonious in the hands of the active president, national security adviser Scowcroft, Secretary of State Baker, Secretary of Defense Cheney, and General Powell. But secrecy dominated the process with Baker at State keeping career staff out of policy making and the fear of leaks generally barring all but the top people. Bush's national security policy process did not involve much multiple advocacy in the broad sense used in this book and only looks good when compared to his domestic process, not to past presidencies. Bob Woodward's in-depth treatment of presidential decision making in the Gulf War showed a weak policy process: "Decisions [at NSC meetings] were made based on their likely impact on the Congress, the media and public opinion, and the focus was on managing the reaction. . . . Jim Baker seemed to think being Secretary of State was like running a big political campaign."[47] National security adviser Scowcroft, in the Gulf War period, had a difficult time managing and controlling the foreign policy process in part because of the hyperactive, unreflective president. Scowcroft seemingly could not, or would not, coordinate Gulf policy. Major meetings produced little. Woodward noted: "When the principals met, Bush liked to keep everyone around the table smiling—jokes, camaraderie, the conviviality of old friends. Positions and alternatives were not completely discussed. . . . Clear decisions rarely emerged."[48] Cheney and Powell often left such meetings unclear what, if anything, had been decided and frequently found out from Scowcroft or from television. That process generally yielded poor results. The current assessment of the Gulf War is that policy making was misguided before the war in sending the wrong signals to Saddam Hussein, disastrous after the war with no policy direction, and questionable during the war in giving Saddam no out to sue for peace and yet leaving him in power.[49] The war itself was no more than an easy military victory over a third world foe that would not fight. In retrospect, the only notable accomplishment that survives is the president's tour de force performance in building and holding together the alliance of nations that went to war against Iraq. The simple goal of winning a war brought into play the strongest skills of both Bush and Secretary Baker—keeping a negotiating process moving. As Ignatius made clear earlier, however, the Gulf War yielded no indication of strategic thinking by President Bush.

President Bush's other two major foreign policy successes—the Middle East peace efforts and the agreement to move forward on the START treaty—had similar elements. Getting the major actors together in a meaningful process in the Middle East case was the central objective. In the nuclear negotiations, the clear cold war goals that had dominated American thinking in the postwar years guided the arms talks in June 1992 between President Bush and Russian president Boris Yeltsin. In the last case, three points are critical. First, readily available information on existing arms levels for the United States and the former Soviet Union underpinned the process. Second, President Yeltsin, desperate to gain economic concessions such as most-favored-nation status that would make Russian products sent to the United States less expensive, badly needed a bargain. Third, the cold war objectives of increasing both American nuclear superiority and safety still held. Under the circumstances, President Bush negotiated a level and mix of nuclear weapons that favored the United States by eliminating Russia's most threatening first strike capability, its big land-based missiles, while retaining America's powerful nuclear submarines. The deal offered a win-win setting with both sides obtaining what they wanted—economic benefits that could help turn around a sinking Russian economic system and nuclear superiority for the United States. The Bush negotiation style fit perfectly in this case where the bargained position meshed well with America's cold war goal of nuclear superiority and safety, and the other bargainer faced a severe disadvantage in so badly needing economic help. Taking nothing away from President Bush in negotiating a sound bargain, the key point is that his lack of vision and the absence of new information and analysis were not major barriers in the nuclear arms negotiations in mid-1992 or in building the Gulf War alliance and reviving the Middle East peace process. Although not as clear cut as the domestic policy case, foreign policy making, too, supports the claim of a president with most limited policy competence skills.

President Bush inherited a poorly functioning White House policy-making process but had both ample information about its structural and staffing deficiencies and sufficient power to correct it. The chain of causality flowed from Bush's policy incompetence to the continuing existence of an inadequate structure and debilitating policy-making process. Bush was not undone by a frozen organizational structure nor a staff in place that he could not remove. Just the reverse. He had organizational freedom to create his own process with people of his own choosing. However, President Bush never grasped that good financial management data, solid performance indicators, and strong analyses indicating useful incremental changes are the basic building blocks of organizational prudence and are central to supporting a status quo president who wanted to exercise effective supervision of delegated domestic policy responsibilities with minimum effort. He failed to do so apparently because he lacked the needed organizational experience and knowledge. President Bush either did not learn from his experience prior to his presidency or did not as president learn on the job. Although not anti-analytic himself, Bush extended Reagan's anti-analytic presidency with his own analytic and managerial incompetence.

NOTES

1. For a more extended discussion of the information damage, see Walter Williams, *Mismanaging America: The Rise of the Anti-Analytic Presidency*, University Press of Kansas, 1990, pp. 69–72.

2. U.S. General Accounting Office, *Government Management Issues*, GAO/OCG–93–3TR, December 1992, p. 7.

3. U.S. General Accounting Office, *Program Evaluation Issues*, GAO/OCG–93–6TR, December 1992, pp. 4–5.

4. Ibid., p. 8.

5. Ronald Brownstein and Dick Kirschten, "Cabinet Power," *National Journal*, June 28, 1986, p. 1589.

6. David A. Stockman, *The Triumph of Politics: Why the Reagan Revolution Failed*, Harper & Row, 1986, p. 341.

7. Ibid., pp. 1 and 12.

8. Williams, *Mismanaging America*, p. 80.

9. Bob Schieffer and Gary Paul Gates, *The Acting President*, Dutton, 1989, p. 200.

10. *New York Times*, December 19, 1991.

11. Bob Woodward, "Bickering While Rome Burns: High-Level Infighting Held the Economy Hostage," *Washington Post National Weekly Edition*, October 19–25, 1992, p. 8.

12. Ibid., pp. 8–9.

13. Ibid., p. 9.

14. Ibid.

15. John Podhoretz, *Hell of a Ride: Backstage at the White House Follies 1989–1993*, Simon & Schuster, 1993, p. 56.

16. Ibid., p. 129.

17. Ibid., pp. 61–62.

18. Ibid., p. 62, italics in the original.

19. Williams, *Mismanaging America*, p. 104.

20. Lou Cannon, *President Reagan: The Role of a Lifetime*, Simon & Schuster, 1991.

21. Ibid., pp. 364 and 644.

22. Schieffer and Gates, *The Acting President*, pp. 89–90.

23. Ibid., pp. 339–340.

24. Peggy Noonan, *What I Saw at the Revolution: A Political Life in the Reagan Era*, Random House, 1990, p. 268.

25. Cannon, *President Reagan*, p. 706.

26. George Shultz, *Turmoil and Triumph: My Years as Secretary of State*, Scribner's, 1993, p. 914.

27. Ibid., pp. 726 and 815–816.

28. Ibid., p. 263.

29. Cannon, *President Reagan*, p. 341.

30. Ibid.

31. Henry Mintzberg, *The Nature of Managerial Work*, Harper & Row, 1973, pp. 92–93.

32. *Washington Post*, November 7, 1982.

33. Bob Woodward, *Veil: The Secret War of the CIA 1981–1987*, Simon & Schuster, 1987, p. 404.

34. Garry Wills, *Reagan's America: Innocents at Home*, Doubleday, 1987, p. 321.

35. Ibid., p. 283.

36. Patricia Dennis Witherspoon, *Within These Walls: A Study of Communication between Presidents and Their Senior Staffs*, Praeger, 1991, p. 187.

37. Stockman, *The Triumph of Politics*, p. 80.

38. Michael Duffy and Dan Goodgame, *Marching in Place: The Status Quo Presidency of George Bush*, Simon & Schuster, 1992, p. 70.

39. G. M. Trevelyan, *Lord Grey of the Great Reform Bill*, Longmans, Green, 1920, p. 268.

40. Duffy and Goodgame, *Marching in Place*, p. 60.

41. Colin Campbell, "The White House and the Presidency under the 'Let's Deal' President," in Colin Campbell and Bert A. Rockman (eds.), *The Bush Presidency: First Appraisal*, Chatham House, 1991, p. 208.

42. David Ignatius, "It's Lonely at the Top of the New World Order," *Washington Post National Weekly Edition*, July 6–12, 1992, p. 23.

43. Bob Woodward, *The Commanders*, Simon & Schuster, 1991, p. 41.

44. K. Mullins and Aaron Wildavsky, "The Procedural Presidency of George Bush," *Political Science Quarterly*, 1992, 107, p. 47.

45. *New York Times*, November 5, 1992.

46. Duffy and Goodgame, *Marching in Place*, p. 73.

47. Woodward, *The Commanders*, p. 81.

48. Ibid., p. 302.

49. Roger Hilsman, *George Bush vs Saddam Hussein: Military Success! Political Failure!* Lyford, 1992; and Jean E. Smith, *George Bush's War*, Henry Holt, 1992.

7 | Bill Clinton and Undisciplined Rationality

No president has entered the White House with a greater commitment to the hard scrutiny of policy or with more striking analytic skills than did William Jefferson Clinton. Nor has a president since Lyndon Johnson combined high intelligence, in-depth policy knowledge, the ability to integrate policy and politics, and the orientation and skills to play the political game adroitly. Further, Clinton's acclaimed performance in his economic summit a month before his inauguration underscored that America had found the analytic president par excellence. Yet, President Clinton created a nightmare analytic structure fueled by his overheated analytic intensity and lack of discipline. The effort to be both his own chief of staff, with his nominal designee rendered almost irrelevant, and his administration's top domestic policy analyst proved to be an institutional disaster. President Clinton loved policy analysis not wisely but too well. To unravel how the Clinton administration went so wrong in its analytic efforts, we need to recognize that Bill Clinton's striking strengths and weaknesses are, as David Broder noted, "so inextricably interwoven that it is unrealistic to suppose that you can eliminate one without sacrificing the other."[1] Part of the analytic problem is Clinton himself, yet external factors forced him to make his most important organizational and staffing choices in the transition period and to undertake a quick start at the outset of his presidency when hubris is at its highest and institutional knowledge at its lowest. My approach to Bill Clinton and policy analysis will stress the importance of his individual assets and liabilities; however, both the institutional structure and the harsh political climate loom large.

A primary purpose of this and the next chapter is to analyze the structure, staffing, and style of the Clinton policy-making process and to look toward the future as we confront the tangled strengths and weaknesses of this first president from the postwar generation. My critique of the Clinton policy analysis effort will concentrate on the first half of Clinton's initial term that featured the high political activism of a hyperactive president driven by the one-hundred-days syndrome. At issue is the place of policy analysis in today's presidency where public distrust of government is rampant and the pressures on a new president to act immediately make extended presidential policy analysis difficult, if not impossible. In the three decades since I joined the first social policy analysis office in the federal government, I have never seen so many political obstacles to the effective use of policy analysis in national governance or so great a need for its effective use as the nation starts the long path toward a basic transformation of social policy.

Nothing is more striking in the Clinton first term than the mid-course transformation from active governance to a counterpunching campaigning style that carried him from his low point after the November 1994 election, where pundits questioned Clinton's relevance, to his landslide electoral college vote victory two years later. President Clinton came to office as an activist leader ready to pursue a relatively liberal agenda, topped by his effort to push through universal health coverage. The failure of his health legislation and the epic midterm election defeat that brought in the first Republican Congress since the Eisenhower presidency ended Clinton activism. Although Clinton did not totally abandon social policy governing to adopt a poll-driven style aimed only at maximizing his highly polished campaign skill, the shift is sufficiently dramatic to label his first two years as "the activist domestic policy governing period" and the second half of that first term as "the defensive campaigning period." The greatest irony is the adoption by the most informed and analytic president of the modern era of the style and rhetoric of Ronald Reagan, the least informed, most anti-analytic one of that period.

Few presidents have been subjected to such close scrutiny so quickly as has Bill Clinton. Several books on the Clinton presidency and a biography by David Maraniss provide a detailed picture of the man and his administration with books by Elizabeth Drew, John Brummett, Bob Woodward, and Haynes Johnson and David Broder (as co-authors), all offering strikingly similar detailed accounts of the opening half of the Clinton first term—no hidden-hand presidency here.[2] Maraniss' biography, which ends with Clinton's 1991 announcement to run for president, made clear the traits that so distinguished Clinton as president were well-formed by his high school days. Drew, in her second book on the Clinton administration, treated the president's battle with Newt Gingrich and the Republican Congress, thereby providing a portrait of the big events of the last half of Clinton's first term. Broder, in a column on the Maraniss book, wrote aptly that "reading his [Clinton's] past is eerily like watching the present."[3] Colin Campbell and Bert Rockman have edited *The Clinton Presidency* that covers the first two plus years of that administration and is particularly illuminating on the structure, staffing, and style of the Clinton analytic process.[4]

Dick Morris' *Behind the Oval Office* tells the incredible tale of how the egomaniac political consultant saved the Clinton presidency.[5] Finally, I also have relied on my off-the-record interviews with then current or retired elected officials, political executives, and career civil servants; journalists; and scholars of the presidency.

Clinton's first term underscores some of the basic premises of the book. First, sound policy information and analysis are critical to government performance; but these are tools of governance—means, not ends. Second, whether data and analysis are used or misused, whether these means are employed in support of worthy or unworthy objectives, and how sound data and analysis are fit into the president's politics/policy equation, all depend in part on the individual president's personal competence, style, and predilections, and finally his integrity. Of critical importance is the individual baggage a president brings to office—brains and experience, political leadership skills, policy objectives, courage, and commitment to principles. Third, just as important is the political climate and economic environment. And nowhere is this interplay of individual and environmental forces more vivid than in Bill Clinton's first four years. In the policy analysis era that began with Kennedy, Johnson and Clinton stand out in terms of the combination of intelligence, analytic competence (much lower for Johnson), policy knowledge, and political skills. The political and economic climate, however, could hardly have been more different. Johnson became president at the cusp of national confidence and trust in government with America still in its abnormally high growth period after World War II; Clinton took office amid slower growth, deep pessimism, and almost paranoid distrust of the federal government. President Johnson pushed through a legislative program to fight poverty that rivaled the New Deal in its scope while President Clinton signed into law welfare legislation that made the first retreat from the basic commitments in Roosevelt's Social Security Act of 1935. Is the main explanation for the two presidents' behavior political climate? Reasonable persons will differ as to answers, but seldom is the issue cast so strikingly as in the case of Bill Clinton.

As to organization, this chapter and chapter 8 need to be considered together. Chapter 7 first looks at a key example of Clinton's intertangled strengths and weaknesses that reveals much about the president and policy analysis and then compares Clinton with Ronald Reagan and John Kennedy to illuminate not only problems facing Clinton but ones likely to plague future presidents. The chapter next addresses the Clinton policy process generally in his active phase of governance and concludes with a treatment of the chaotic health care debacle. Chapter 8 first asks how so brilliant a president, with his breathtaking array of policy and political skills, could have been so inept in his first two years as he tried to lead major policy changes. The chapter then analyzes the period after November 1994 when Clinton saved himself by reverting to his formidable campaigning ability that mainly utilized the president's political style and skills to counter-punch Speaker Newt Gingrich and the Contract With America and pushed the political center so far to the right that the self-styled "New Democrat" was hard to distinguish from a conservative Republican like Senator Robert Dole. Finally, I will draw on the Clinton policy and political experience (1) to highlight the problems that have so complicated presidential leadership over the last thirty years and made reasoned governance, including extended policy analysis in support of policy making, increasingly difficult, and (2) to try to put in perspective the first term of this enigmatic president.

OPEN-MINDED CHAOS

A crucial Clinton shortcoming, organizational incompetence, and a seeming virtue, a belief in hard facts combined with open-mindedness, brought disarray to the presidential policy-making process and made Clinton appear to be indecisive, lacking in core convictions, or both. As to the former, Colin Campbell, one of the editors of *The Clinton Presidency*, concluded that "Clinton is so pathologically a-institutional that no manner of reorganization of his team would have any lasting effects."[6] Campbell's co-editor Bert Rockman went even further after considering the Carter style as well as Clinton's: "There is no doubt that one of Bill Clinton's deepest weaknesses as president is his unwillingness to think about organization and staffing (or to have someone think about these matters for him). . . . Democratic presidents seem to love a system of White House organization that virtually ensures that they will be on top of nothing until deadlines force a level of intense (and often unvetted) engagement."[7] Just so.

Although there is no reason to belabor this point in that I have argued at length that organizational incompetence has been the pivotal missing link in the presidency since Dwight Eisenhower, a couple of comments are needed.[8] First, the Reagan White House succeeded in masking that president's organizational deficiencies until the Iran-contra scandal, but Clinton's ineptitude, like so much else, leaped out early on and hurt the president's image and the credibility of his decisions. Second, that Clinton's brilliance and his twelve years as governor, albeit of a small state, provided him no organizational insight is particularly discouraging. Did Clinton's unwillingness to consider organization reflect a deeper psychological factor or was it part of his lack of discipline and proclivity for quick face-to-face debate rather than the development of position papers of an orderly decision-making process?

Elizabeth Drew wrote: "The Clinton people, . . . set great store by using honest numbers."[9] Clinton believed in rigorously derived data, hardly a passion in the Reagan-Bush years. He added the admirable trait of being open-minded and ready to change his views when new facts warranted it. These characteristics are the hallmarks of sound analysis and surely ones that policy analysts see as highly desirable in a president and his top aides. But there is a potential downside too. Bert Rockman argued in comparing Presidents Clinton and Carter: "The consequence of being open-minded and subject to policy facts (as Carter often was) and sensitive to their interplay with political facts (as Carter rarely was) is indecision, uncertainty, and delay. These features of Clinton's endless process of making up his mind certainly had an impact on his executive style in managing—if that is the right word—the White House."[10]

Several comments are needed on Rockman's assertion in that it implies that openness to facts leads *pari pasu* to indecision and delay. First, Clinton's traits, which are so critical to reasoned decision making, play out in his chaotic policy process that fostered endless debate. Second, Rockman also throws in the interplay with political facts, which, when added to the brew of policy process chaos, surely can contribute to indecision and delay. Third, Drew cited a "longtime friend of Clinton's" who claimed that in the White House the president became "so overwhelmed" that he lost confidence and tested his ideas so much with his aides that he ended up with a "postponement process."[11] The Clinton experience does not lead to the conclusion that open-mindedness and adaptability in an *orderly* policy-making process will produce indecision and delay. Nor is Clinton a tough-minded decision maker who is open to facts and ideas during deliberations but understands the need for decisiveness and closure on debate if timely decisions are to be made. After all, there is always one more fact that might be found or another idea to be explored so the process can become almost endless. The competent decision maker must strike a reasonable balance between the need for more information and analysis and the need for a timely choice.

Policy analysts are justified in arguing the need for both honest numbers and for decision makers who are receptive to new facts and ready to change policy decisions when later findings warrant it, while at the same time rejecting that these desirable traits necessarily lead to excessive delay or indecision. However, we also need to recognize: (1) Rockman's well-taken point about President Clinton that "his own, mostly desirable, intellectual habits of open-mindedness . . . risks the danger of open-endedness and [of] adaptability . . . risks the danger of seeming to lack conviction"; (2) Drew's insight that "Clinton carried a lot of information in his head, something that didn't always work to his advantage. Reagan, being underinformed, could be utterly clear about simple goals; Clinton, being exceedingly informed, sometimes got lost in his facts"; and (3) Clinton's institutionally chaotic personal style and his, at times, oversensitive reaction to changing political facts added to the disarray that surrounded Clinton.[12] The three statements underscore the importance of Clinton's large and intertwined strengths and weaknesses.

TWO KEY COMPARISONS

Comparing Clinton to Reagan and Kennedy further illuminates the analytic dimensions of the Clinton presidency. In many respects, Reagan and Clinton are polar opposites. Ronald Reagan first gained political office when he won the California governorship just prior to age fifty-five after a full career as an actor. Bill Clinton, in clear contrast, is the quintessential example of the career politician. David Maraniss titled his book *First in His Class* because Clinton was the first of "the thousands of bright, ambitious people from the postwar baby boom generation . . . to reach the White House."[13] In 1978 Clinton gained 63 percent of the Arkansas vote to become America's youngest governor in four decades. His strong analytic capability and his in-depth knowledge of policy make him the archetype of the political careerists and the complete opposite of Reagan. At the same time, Clinton suffered the great fear of the professional politician who dreads defeat because it can spell the end of his political career. Clinton so often seemed to be searching for what he thought voters wanted in sharp contrast to Reagan's unchanging message. Both Reagan and Clinton needed to be restrained from off-the-wall remarks. President Reagan—so prone to make almost unreal statements if not controlled—had an actor's comfort with a carefully prepared script by his staff. Clinton refused to be reined in, or else could not be, even if he wanted to do so. Most aptly, David Broder wrote that Clinton's "sprawling, undisciplined character . . . constantly impels him to go beyond the bounds of prudence."[14] As will be discussed, such behavior changed markedly when Clinton adopted his campaigning style.

Reagan came across as credible and a strong leader who stood by what he said, where Clinton in his two governance years so often appeared untrustworthy and vacillating. In comparing the two presidents, we have such totally different behavior that it is hard to believe they are not carefully designed Weberian archetypes. Two differences show the polar extremes. The first-year budgets of both presidents produced huge changes. In 1981 public perception had President

Reagan, almost single-handedly, forcing Congress to heel. Twelve years later the public saw the Democratic Congress saving the Clinton initial-year budget so it would not crush the second Democratic president in the last quarter century as it had Jimmy Carter in his first year. The second example is the interpretation of strong economic performance in 1984 and 1994. In the former case, America had rallied and Reagan was acclaimed the hero of the booming economy. A decade later, Clinton, in his initial two years, received little or no credit for a strong economic record including a budget that drastically reduced the deficit. Are these dramatic differences mainly a matter of the public's perceptions that fit poorly with reality? In particular, the public's sharply contrasting assessments of Reagan in 1984 and of Clinton at the mid-term election in 1994 may have come from a combination of Reagan's powerful leadership style and optimism that unduly inflated the public's view of his competence. This issue of perceived image will be touched on again after the consideration of President Kennedy whom the public hailed as a highly competent leader in the early 1960s and has continued to hold in high esteem over the intervening three decades.

Richard Reeves' *President Kennedy* looks back at John Kennedy's three years as president from the perspective of thirty years to offer a portrait of another young, brilliant, highly analytic, open-minded president who was undisciplined in the policy process. The striking similarity between Kennedy and Clinton looms so large because Reeves' view of Kennedy stands in sharp distinction to Arthur Schlesinger Jr.'s and Theodore Sorenson's highly regarded 1965 books that praised the Kennedy presidency as one of significant personal growth in which greater wisdom came from several crises.[15] Reeves wrote: "The Kennedy I found certainly did not know what he was doing at the beginning, and in some ways never changed at all, particularly in a certain love for chaos, the kind that kept other men off-balance."[16] Kennedy and Clinton used almost the same techniques in their policy processes where undisciplined rationality ruled. However, after three years in office, Kennedy had the image of a strong leader on top of the situation. The big difference between the two presidents is that President Kennedy also showed steely discipline in maintaining his public image.

Reeves caught the essential Kennedy both as to governance and public leadership:

> The man at the center was a gifted professional politician reacting to events he often neither foresaw nor understood, handling some well, others badly, but always ready with plausible explanations. He was intelligent, detached, curious, candid if not always honest, and he was

careless and dangerously disorganized. He was also very impatient, addicted to excitement, living his life as if it were a race against boredom. . . .

Kennedy was decisive, though he never made a decision until he had to, and then invariably he chose the most moderate of available options. . . . He had little ideology beyond anti-Communism and faith in active, pragmatic government. And he had less emotion. What he had was an attitude, a way of taking on the world, substituting intelligence for ideas or idealism, questions for answers. What convictions he did have, on nuclear proliferation or civil rights or the use of military power, he was often willing to suspend, particularly if that avoided confrontation with Congress or the risk of being called soft.[17]

President Kennedy had no interest in organizational structure and process, except to sweep aside Dwight Eisenhower's "bent toward order" and make himself "the center of all the action."[18] Kennedy chose to be his own chief of staff and favored a spokes-of-the-wheel approach with no gatekeeper between him and several of his top White House staff. Although a few of his cabinet were important advisers, he cast aside the cabinet as an advisory group and tended to view the executive agencies as obstructionist from the secretary down through the career civil servants.

Kennedy prided himself on "cool objectivity, pure information gathering, dispassionate analysis, a decisive decision-making mechanism unswayed by sentiment. . . . [He] preferred hallways meetings . . . [and] short conversations and long hours substituted for organization."[19] Although a highly intelligent leader who lived comfortably with divergent views and the give-and-take of policy debate, he saw no value in a well-managed policy process and was too much involved in policy deliberations to stand back as an unbiased judge of alternative policies put before him. Kennedy's preference to be briefed on the run drove him and his staff to a frenetic pace. John Kennedy, the rational thinker, lacked the strategic and managerial skills and the patience required for developing and maintaining a viable ongoing process that could have yielded sound, timely information and analysis to guide policies.

The image that comes across so vividly in *President Kennedy* is not of a bold leader with a clear vision of where he wanted to take America, but of a cautious politician without much foresight who avoided even those steps he believed were right if such action threatened his reelection. While Kennedy loved to play the game of politics and did it well, there seemed seldom to be any higher goal than political standing. Father Theodore Hesburgh, then president of Notre Dame University and a member of the Civil Rights Commission, observed that he "left one meeting after another with the President thinking that

Kennedy would love to do something about the painful inequities of formal and official segregation, but that he saw personal involvement in the passions of the civil rights issues as a good way to guarantee that he would not be reelected."[20] Kennedy, who seemingly had no core and little political courage, still came across in his administration as a forceful president calling for a revitalized nation—the epitome of dynamic, youthful, visionary leadership. As with Reagan, the factors that stand out are the highly successful White House management of the presidential image that demanded strong discipline by both presidents.

Although undisciplined in his policy process, Kennedy went to the other extreme in the management of his political image. Kennedy, who had Addison's disease, an adrenal gland failure that could be fatal, misled the nation on the malady. Moreover, despite the fact that the disease often incapacitated the president, his public appearances gave the impression of youthful vigor and strength, much as Roosevelt had despite being in a wheelchair. Kennedy managed his public image with iron discipline and can be compared with Presidents Roosevelt and Reagan in looking and acting like a national leader. In sharp contrast, Elizabeth Drew in *On the Edge* rendered this insightful judgment of Bill Clinton's political leadership problems:

> The cluster of defects that could be listed under the term "character"—his "Slick Willy" aspect and all that that conveyed, his inclination to avoid responsibility for some of his acts, his lack of discipline, and his reckless streak (at least in the past)—endangered his presidency. . . .
>
> Because of the public doubts about him, and because of the "character" issues, and also because he had been undisciplined in talking about his efforts, Clinton . . . wasn't getting credit for his substantial accomplishments. His presidency was a blur.[21]

At a time when America needed a president with a broad realistic strategy and the capacity to bind people together, the nation chose a man of many strengths but whose political style produced a blur rather than an image of powerful leadership. His big flaws could overwhelm his great strengths and policy accomplishments. Unlike Kennedy and Reagan, President Clinton in his first two years had problems projecting himself as a political leader on top of the job with a vision worth fighting for. How and why President Clinton's image became so sullied in his two active governance years is treated in the next three sections.

BILL CLINTON AND POLICY MAKING

The main thrust of this section is to criticize Clinton's presidential policy-making process in his first two years and underscore his undisciplined brilliance and hubris. What is so troubling is that the harsh criticism is aimed at a man who came to the presidency with a striking array of skills. On the asset side, Clinton matches up favorably with any of the postwar presidents. One of my interviewees—a brilliant policy analyst himself—argued that Clinton is the smartest person to ever hold the modern presidency, the most knowledgeable about policy, and a first-rate social science analyst. "First in his class"—the ablest member of the baby boom generation—hits the mark. But so often a Clinton asset, such as spectacular intelligence, combined in a specific case with a debilitating flaw. One of the actors in the health care debate, John Rother, chief lobbyist for the American Association of Retired Persons, was shocked that Clinton voluntarily retreated from his commitment to 100 percent health coverage and told Johnson and Broder his thoughts at the time: " 'This is fucking unbelievable. Here's a President . . . I believe is the smartest one we've had since Thomas Jefferson, and he doesn't know beans about negotiating. Ronald Reagan could teach him how to negotiate. You come in strong, you maintain your moral position, and you cut your deal at the end. You don't give it away in public with nothing coming back.' "[22] Whether the president meant to retreat from the full commitment to a lesser one—to use Clinton's own words, " 'somewhere in the ballpark of ninety-five percent or upwards' "—is not clear.[23] The remark came after a formal speech to the National Governors Association, a group with which the former governor had been especially candid in the past, and he may only have been recognizing the practical difficulties of total coverage. But clearly the "brainy" president had raised doubts because of his tendencies to give in too soon and to talk too much.

The Clinton policy process marched into trouble immediately. Drew, who subtitled a chapter in *On the Edge* "They Hit the Ground Barely Standing," quoted a senior White House official, who saw part of the problem as "headiness, if not arrogance" and claimed: " '[The media] suggested that we were more masters of our fate than reality allows, or we were in a position to be coming off the transition. We just weren't ready—emotionally, intellectually, organizationally, or substantively."[24] Hubris emerged as a big factor at the beginning, and here President-elect Clinton's spectacular economic summit performance played a critical role. In that meeting in Little Rock on December 14 and 15, 1992, which was attended by roughly three hundred distinguished participants and was carried over the two days by CNN and C-SPAN, Bill Clinton completely dominated the summit. Elizabeth Drew, writing roughly two years later, claimed "Clinton was a smash . . . making a strong impression as an informed and serious figure."[25] Based on interviews with persons who attended the summit, I believe that Drew's opinion, if anything, understated how much Clinton's tour de force performance impressed the audience by the demonstration of his striking command of concepts and policies. Even economic Nobel Laureates sang Clinton's praises about his economic and policy thinking. For all his talents and experience, President-elect Clinton, before the summit, still suffered from the small-southern-state-governor label with the obvious comparison to Jimmy Carter who also was highly intelligent but seemed lost in the White House. The economic summit showed Clinton able to dazzle Washington insiders including a bevy of top policy economists. Clinton had leaped over the Jimmy Carter barrier and stood ready to be like his hero John Kennedy. Unfortunately, Clinton and Kennedy matched up most closely on the attribute of undisciplined rationality in their policy processes.

A disciplined presidential policy process demands sound management, orderly procedures with a well-delineated structure to support them, solid policy analysis, and a president willing to sit atop the process as a judge in considering the presentation of policy alternatives rather than as a hands-on analyst. The president's chief of staff is the critical first staff choice and must have the authority and the competence to manage the other top aides in the policy process and the president himself in maintaining the integrity of that process. A Carnegie Endowment for International Peace and Institute for International Economics 1992 memorandum to the president-elect, developed by a distinguished group of thirty people who had served presidents during the postwar era, defined the "strong" chief as "senior to the rest of the White House staff; not an all-powerful Prime Minister, but an 'honest broker' with coordinating responsibilities over the rest of the White House staff and the Cabinet."[26] All members of this Commission on Government Renewal, including former top Kennedy aide Theodore Sorensen, recommended the strong chief of staff model and rejected the "spokes-of-the-wheel" model. President Jimmy Carter's second chief of staff Jack Watson called the president as the hub of the wheel a "fatal mistake."[27] The chief of staff should be first among equals with the charge and the power to create an orderly policy process fueled by a wide range of sound policy information and analysis and to enforce discipline among the key players so they do their homework and do not make end runs to the president.

Although the Commission refrained from rating chiefs of staff, John Sununu in the Bush administration and Reagan's Donald Regan surely stand at one extreme as the dangerous, all-powerful prime minister. Clinton's first chief of staff Thomas "Mack" McLarty exemplifies the polar opposite of far too weak. Mack McLarty had been Clinton's childhood friend and had become the chief executive of a large natural gas company but lacked Washington experience. McLarty saw himself as an honest broker yet had little idea of the complexity of the task or of the political toughness needed to manage the president and the many people trying to subvert the policy process with direct runs to the Oval Office. The job demanded far more competence than McLarty could deliver and more power than the president granted. During McLarty's tenure, Clinton, like Kennedy, operated as his own chief of staff with some semblance of the spokes-of-the-wheel model that served Kennedy in the early 1960s. But by the 1990s, the president's agenda had become too overloaded for him to use such a structure effectively. To make matters worse, the Clinton process went beyond the Kennedy approach to a point where the only constant was the overactive president who kept most of the power himself as both his own chief of staff and chief policy analyst. Even his friends were unclear whether Clinton wanted the process to operate in such confusion or whether he simply did not have a clear picture of the desired process in his own mind.[28]

THE DOMESTIC POLICY PROCESS

Domestic policy making on paper was lodged principally in three entities: the Domestic Policy Council, the National Economic Council, and the President's Task Force on National Health Reform (needless to say, other actors such as OMB had an interest). The logical home was the Domestic Policy Council with Carol Rasco, its chief staff person as assistant to the president for domestic policy. But the domestic policy staff quickly turned out to be a nonstarter, a weaker institutional actor even than its counterparts in the Reagan and Bush years. Elizabeth Drew pointed out that Rasco had worked for Governor Clinton in Arkansas and was "very close to Mrs. Clinton" (the two had children the same age); however, the Domestic Policy Council and Rasco "floundered, in part because the economic team ran over her, in part because health care policy was made elsewhere, and in part because she didn't assert herself in the near chaos."[29] Also, an interviewee told me that "Rasco had no real policy expertise" and hence little personal capacity to be more than a bit player in the heated domestic policy process.

All these reasons for the failure of the domestic policy staff were important. The National Economic Council (NEC), with its chief staff person Robert Rubin, quickly emerged as a powerhouse across all economic policy, and that carried into domestic policy at times. At its formation, the health care task force under Hillary Clinton took the universal health coverage issue, the overriding domestic policy concern, away from Rasco. The "near chaos" jumbled both policy and the ill-defined domestic process together to create a terrain where individual power and competence were at a premium and Rasco, despite her title and long association with the Clintons, lacked the skill and the toughness to be much more than an observer and occasional minor player, staffing a toothless Domestic Policy Council. The remaining two main actors offer a view of Clinton policy making in his first two years at its best in the NEC and at its worst in the health task force.

The National Economic Council

In considering the NEC and Robert Rubin its director, a comparison to President Ford's Economic Policy Board and its executive director William Seidman is useful. The EPB and the NEC had much in common. Both created a powerful council made up of the key economic actors. Both established staff support with the director cast as honest broker expected to manage fairly a process that brought inputs from the principal economic advisers. Also, both entities had the secretary of the treasury as the chief spokesman for economic policy. In the Clinton administration, Secretary of the Treasury Lloyd Bentsen "had an uncommon influence on Clinton from the start."[30]

As in the case of Seidman in the Ford administration, Rubin centered the process with his "scrupulous neutrality."[31] At the same time, unlike Seidman who saw himself as only a manager, Rubin became a substantive player and had the credentials to be one. With an estimated wealth of over $100 million, Rubin, who came to the NEC position from the cochairmanship of Goldman, Sachs, knew Wall Street and the bond market and had been an economic adviser to Clinton in the campaign.[32] As to his prestige and his modesty, Rubin became one of the two people on Clinton's short list to head the treasury but told Clinton, "Bentsen would be better. . . . [because] he knew Congress and the media."[33] Johnson and Broder provide a slightly different but related description of Rubin: "Soft-spoken and conciliatory in manner, he let people figure out how much wisdom his head contained—which Clinton was quick to do."[34]

Rubin had the rare ability to be both a respected honest broker as well as a key policy adviser on occasion with his opinions being particularly sought on the reaction of the stock and bond markets to policy proposals such as a middle-class tax cut. This dual role led Colin Campbell to claim that "the atmospherics of economic policymaking in the administration seem to belie the existence of neutral brokerage."[35] But other analysts stressed Rubin's commitment to being an honest broker and if anything criticized his tendency to go too far in eliciting wide comment. In the best account of the NEC at its zenith under Rubin, the National Journal's Paul Starobin wrote: "Some critics fret that Rubin et al. have become slaves to the goal of a fair, inclusive process at the expense of rapid movement on pressing matters. It's not that issues are poorly decided, the critics say, but that opportunities for advancing the President's agenda are missed. Maybe Kissinger and Darman were devious, but at least they got things done fast."[36] In sum, Rubin joins Seidman as an outstanding honest broker.

Going on with the comparison of the NEC and the EPB, the former had a larger, stronger staff. What the NEC lacked in contrast to the EPB was a sound structure to give the process order and this defect overwhelmed the staff. Much of the problem came from the president, who unlike Ford, did not act as a magistrate or help provide discipline. Rubin had two outstanding deputies. Bowman Cutter, who had served as OMB deputy director under Carter and later as vice chairman of the Coopers & Lybrand accounting firm, ran the NEC operation on a daily basis. The other deputy, Gene Sperling, described by Starobin as "a 35-year-old whiz kid," had degrees from the Yale Law School and the Wharton Business School and had served as a key Clinton adviser in the campaign. The twenty-member professional staff mixed together economists and lawyers, a Harvard Business School professor, and several former congressional staff including a Congressional Budget Office analyst. Yet, Starobin claimed that "three-fourths of the NEC staff's time is devoted to matters needing resolution within a month" and reported a federal agency official commenting as follows on the NEC, " 'If there is any group of people overworked in the Administration, it's them.' "[37]

The NEC purposely lacked a formal structure. Sperling argued: "The NEC really is a commitment to a process rather than a structure. It's a commitment that the relevant people have a chance to contribute and that decisions go to the president in a pro/con style."[38] This failure created a goodly amount of chaos. Starobin quoted Dick Klaus, a Washington consultant and former Air Force staff member who had advised on defense policy in the campaign, as follows: " 'There's no structure. There are lots of meetings—endless meetings and graduate seminars. Meetings without decisions and decisions without implementation. There is not a coherent philosophy.' "[39] It is hardly surprising that this lack of discipline without a structure to impose an orderly flow of papers and elicit reasoned comments came to pass even in the unit that showed the Clinton administration in its best light.

Two points on the NEC need making in closing. First, the NEC had a fine staff, an exceptional leadership team, and performed well with its biggest problems being Clinton's own activist, undisciplined rationality that spilled over and swamped the NEC effort. Second, Rubin stands out as both honorable and able. In comparison to Stuart Eizenstat who had both qualities, Rubin had far more experience being several years older, more confidence in his ability, a much greater understanding of the importance of policy analysis and sound information in the policy process, and a better balanced view of the politics/

policy equation. Both had becoming modesty. Each ultimately failed to check their president's worst tendencies, perhaps an impossible task in both cases. Another comparison to Rubin is relevant, this time with the key staff person at the top of the health task force. Paul Starobin captured the differences:

> In interviews, a number of Administration sources and Washington insiders sketched a pointed contrast between Rubin and Ira C. Magaziner . . . [who] is widely seen as manipulative, secretive and arrogant. (Some in the administration called Magaziner "The Ira-tollah.")
> Rubin "doesn't assume that he will be the source of all knowledge," said an insider who has had extensive dealings with Rubin and Magaziner. "Magaziner won't listen: You can tell him he's wrong, you can show him he's wrong, you can present all the evidence in the world that he's wrong, and he still won't think he's wrong."[40]

The President's Task Force on National Health Reform

President Clinton's failed effort to enact universal health care coverage is both the dominant domestic policy and the critical policy-making process story of his first term. In what follows, no attempt will be made to look generally at health care reform or to raise questions such as whether a different approach (e.g., the Canadian single payer system) could have been enacted or whether the legislation that failed might have passed in whole or in part if the president and/or the Democratic leadership in Congress had been more adroit. In fairness to Clinton, the health care effort may have been doomed from the start. An astute interviewee who saw health care reform play out from a ringside seat in Washington told me:

> The effort was doomed to failure. Fundamental reform never could have been pulled off even by the most brilliant president with the best of staff organizations. Fundamental health reform involves either spending a great deal of money (which in the fiscal era we live in was impossible) or redistribution which wasn't going to happen. About 50 percent of the population was well served by the existing system and they are the most powerful and articulate 50 percent. In addition, the first waves of the managed care flood were lapping on middle America which was fearful that health reform would mean more of the same from the government.

Be that as it may, the concern in this subsection is not substantive policy per se but the underlying analytic effort. The focus will be on the President's Task Force on National Health Reform (hereafter the "task force"), looking specifically both at the task force structure,

staffing, and process, and at the behavior of the three main actors—
the president, the task force leader Hillary Clinton, and its day-to-day
operating chief Ira Magaziner.

Haynes Johnson's and David Broder's *The System*—an in-depth
(600-plus page) account of the Clinton attempt to enact universal health
coverage—includes a detailed discussion of the roles of the three main
actors and the operation of the task force and provides the base for
my relatively brief treatment of this immensely complicated effort. For
nearly three years, the authors "conducted repeated lengthy interviews
. . . [with] the major players in the drama from the White House and
Capitol Hill and many of the competing interest groups" and plowed
through a mass of government papers, journal articles, and books.[41]
Drawing heavily on this treasure trove, my bare-bones critique will
set out a number of summary points, some being direct quotes from
the book, about the task force and briefly discuss them:

1. Even before President Clinton had been inaugurated, health
    policy experts reported to him that "the costs of universal care
    would be felt long before significant savings could be achieved
    from reforms," but he rejected the argument, believing instead
    Ira Magaziner's claim that " 'universal coverage can be fi-
    nanced from savings from cost controls in four years.' "[42]
2. Hillary Clinton and Ira Magaziner " 'had long evinced an ex-
    traordinary self-confidence (coupled with a tendency to be
    dismissive of others) and a conviction that no social problem,
    however complex and seemingly intractable, could resist his
    or her applied power to solve it.' "[43]
3. Both Clintons and Magaziner showed a striking knowledge of
    the facts and figures of the health care issue; however, none
    of the three had either the deep understanding derived from
    immersion in the health area over an extended period of time
    or an appreciation of the value of this deep understanding by
    experienced health policy experts.
4. "The biggest mistake of all may have been the President's
    decision that the way to handle the [health reform] issue was
    with a White House task force headed by his wife and his
    Oxford classmate [Magaziner]."[44]
5. Magaziner was able "to preserve the final key decisions" for
    the Clintons and himself.[45]
6. "The Clintons seemed to be in thrall to Magaziner" and rejected
    "the gravest reservations" about the task force's direction from
    top White House staff such as OMB director Leon Panetta and
    key cabinet members, such as Bentsen and Health and Human
    Services Secretary Donna Shalala.[46]

7. The huge, secretive task force was poorly structured, ill-managed, and lacked " 'most of the big-time players in the health game.' "[47]
8. The task force effort " 'wasn't a disciplined policy-development process that would result in a piece of legislation that was fully vetted by experts and political people.' "[48]

To sum up these eight points: The Clinton health reform story tells how an exceptionally bright, policy-knowledgeable, analytic president; his extremely able, policy-oriented wife; and a brilliant, experienced consultant—all three both deeply committed to meaningful reform and willing to exert great effort to bring it about—produced a presidential domestic policy-making process debacle of epic proportions. The structural, staffing, and process errors were sufficiently great to rank with those of the Reagan 1981 budget policy-making process. It is not a charge made lightly and rests both on the policy importance of the two efforts and on the number of major policy process mistakes. The Reagan 1981 budget policy, in succeeding, started the nation on a twelve-year path of massive yearly deficits. The failed Clinton effort well may have missed the widest policy window for important health insurance reform since the mid-1960's enactment of Medicare and Medicaid, even if national health insurance was not in the cards. Of central importance is the fact that both policy processes were driven by brilliant, secretive, arrogant, and closed-minded staff persons—David Stockman and Ira Magaziner and, I would add, Hillary Clinton, who had a *direct* staff role much like that of McLarty or Rubin, however she and the president might have perceived it. Most discouragingly, the second massive policy process failure came on the watch of an analytic superstar president.

The health policy-making process took a critical wrong turn during President Clinton's transition period, and that misstep foreshadowed all that was to come. Judy Feder, a longtime health policy analyst, had the health care portfolio during that period. Her team produced a report on January 10, 1993 that showed much higher health care costs than Clinton expected. Before presenting the report to the Clinton insiders in Little Rock, Feder talked to her former boss, West Virginia Senator Jay Rockefeller about whether to show the high cost estimates to President-elect Clinton. The senator advised honesty and later told Johnson and Broder, " 'I was wrong. She got crushed. They [the Clinton insiders] were furious at her. Clinton personally was furious at her, because he couldn't do what he wanted.' "[49]

Congressional Budget Office director Robert Reischauer, both a superb policy analyst and a sophisticated Washington political insider, concluded that the "pre-inaugural Little Rock meeting where Judy Feder was sent to the salt mines for telling the Clintons about the slim possibilities of cost control . . . was a signal the Clintons weren't going to face the real-world problems of the economic and political costs of reform."[50] In an interview a top health policy analyst told me how appalled he had been when the Clintons and Magaziner completely rejected the early warnings from Feder and other health policy professionals and continued to hold that huge savings could be wrung quickly from the health care system to pay for the additional cost of universal coverage. At this point we are not looking at an organizational mistake, although the error had major organizational implications, but a fundamental policy misstep in substituting a pie-in-the-sky scenario for a calculation based on available information realistically interpreted. Here President Clinton looks much like President Reagan in 1981 when he bought the supply-side thesis that large income tax rate reductions would stimulate sufficient additional economic activity and accompanying new tax revenues to offset the cost of the tax rate reduction. Clinton too was opting for the magic bullet of painless change. The president accepted what Johnson and Broder called Magaziner's "mantra"—universal coverage is possible without a tax increase because huge savings can be wrung out of the existing system.[51] Here is the lack of reality and hubris that so often marks the start of a new presidency. The task force that would spring up had to bear this burden.

The Clintons and Magaziner had limited understanding of structural dynamics and organizational behavior. First, giving the top spot to Mrs. Clinton both stifled debate and locked the president in. One of Clinton's staunchest Democratic critics Washington (state) Representative James McDermott—a health care specialist who had been a practicing physician and who was pushing a single-payer structure—made clear to Johnson and Broder the former factor:

> Jim McDermott, noting the deference paid the First Lady by congressional colleagues whom he knew believed her to be wrong, remembered thinking, "It shows you the way politics really is, that no one's going to tell the president's wife: 'Ma'am, you don't have any clothes on.' Nobody's going to say that."[52]

Even worse, President Clinton could not act as if somehow he had no ownership of a staff-generated proposal he had in fact approved, place all blame on staff for deficiencies, and dramatically shift direction. With Hillary Clinton at the point position, the president left himself no leeway for this often-used tactical adjustment that saves a president's reputation by leaving a staff person out on a limb. No matter how able the First Lady, the president committed a fatal organizational error in giving her the up-front leadership role on the administration's biggest domestic policy initiative.

Of all the organizational mistakes, the structure and operation of the task force stands out as the most bizarre. Johnson and Broder reported: "What emerged was a process that Magaziner himself jokingly called 'managed chaos'. . . . Eventually more than six hundred thirty people, broken down into eight 'cluster teams' and thirty-four 'working groups' were slaving away."[53] Magaziner's joking judgment gave himself too much credit, it was "mismanaged chaos." With a cast of hundreds, Magaziner tried to keep the workings of the task force secret, drove it night and day, and, as noted, wanted to reserve all the big decisions for himself and the Clintons. As a young congressional staff person on the task force, Roger Berry, observed: " '[Y]ou felt like you were delivering a ton of words to a black hole and somehow, in the end, they [the Clintons and Magaziner] were going to decide what they were going to do anyway. So there was a lot of frustration. It was just too big, too crazy, too diffuse.' "[54]

Magaziner seemingly never slept and thought nothing of meetings night after night that went to midnight or later. Magaziner combined brilliance, imagination, and command of the health care facts and figures with confidence, an unbelievable commitment to hard work, and loyalty to the Clintons. What he lacked was organization competence and a deep understanding of health care. Also, he did not have on the huge staff the heavy hitters like Henry Aaron of the Brookings Institution to provide wisdom beyond mere knowledge. In this regard Magaziner, David Stockman and several others are disturbingly similar, a key point returned to shortly. But let us not put all the blame on Ira Magaziner for this mother of organizational monstrosities. Bill and Hillary Clinton too deserve star billing as Ira's bosses.

NOTES

1. *Seattle Times*, February 5, 1995.

2. Bob Woodward, *The Agenda: Inside the Clinton White House*, Simon & Schuster, 1994; Elizabeth Drew, *On the Edge: The Clinton Presidency*, Simon & Schuster, 1994; John Brummett, *High Wire: The Education of Bill Clinton*, Hyperion, 1994; Haynes Johnson and David S. Broder, *The System: The American Way of Politics at the Breaking Point*, Little, Brown, 1996; David Maraniss, *First in His Class: A Biography of Bill Clinton*, Simon & Schuster, 1995; and Elizabeth Drew, *Showdown: The Struggle Between the Gingrich Congress and the Clinton White House*, Simon & Schuster, 1996.

3. *Seattle Times*, February 15, 1995.

4. Colin Campbell and Bert A. Rockman (eds.), *The Clinton Presidency: First Appraisal,* Chatham House, 1996.

5. Dick Morris, *Behind the Oval Office: Winning the Presidency in the Nineties,* Random House, 1997.

6. Colin Campbell and Bert A. Rockman, "Introduction," in Campbell and Rockman (eds.), *The Clinton Presidency,* p. 5.

7. Bert A. Rockman, "Leadership Style and the Clinton Presidency," in ibid., p. 352.

8. Walter Williams, *Mismanaging America: The Rise of the Anti-Analytic Presidency,* University Press of Kansas, 1990.

9. Drew, *On the Edge,* p. 79.

10. Rockman, "Leadership Style and the Clinton on Presidency," p. 349.

11. Drew, *On the Edge,* p. 232.

12. Rockman, "Leadership Style and the Clinton Presidency," p. 354; Drew, *On the Edge,* p. 79.

13. Maraniss, *First in His Class,* p. 9.

14. *Seattle Times,* February 15, 1995.

15. Arthur M. Schlesinger Jr., *A Thousand Days: John F. Kennedy in the White House,* Houghton Mifflin, 1965; Theodore C. Sorenson, *Kennedy,* Harper & Row, 1965; and Richard Reeves, *President Kennedy: Profile of Power,* Simon & Schuster, 1993.

16. Reeves, *President Kennedy,* p. 18.

17. Ibid., p. 19.

18. Ibid., p. 23.

19. Ibid., pp. 52–53, 467.

20. Ibid., pp. 467–468.

21. Drew, *On the Edge,* pp. 418–419.

22. Quoted in Johnson and Broder, *The System,* p. 457.

23. The quote is from ibid., p. 456.

24. Drew, *On the Edge,* pp. 36–37.

25. Ibid., p. 27.

26. Carnegie Endowment for International Peace and Institute for International Economics, *Memorandum to the President-Elect: Harnessing Process to Purpose,* 1992, p. 10.

27. Ibid., p. 9.

28. Drew, *On the Edge,* pp. 348–349.

29. Ibid., pp. 22 and 348.

30. Ibid., p. 63.

31. Woodward, *The Agenda,* p. 156.

32. Drew, *On the Edge,* pp. 26 and 73.

33. Woodward, *The Agenda,* p. 62.

34. Johnson and Broder, *The System,* p. 134.

35. Colin Campbell, "Management in a Sandbox: Why the Clinton White House Failed to Cope with Gridlock," in Campbell and Rockman (eds.), *The Clinton Presidency,* p. 77.

36. Paul Starobin, "The Broker," *National Journal,* May 16, 1994, pp. 878–883 (the quote is at pp. 882–883).

37. Ibid., p. 883.

38. Quoted in *Washington Post*, June 13, 1993.

39. Quoted in Starobin, "The Broker," p. 879.

40. Ibid.

41. Johnson and Broder, *The System*, p. xiii.

42. Ibid., pp. 85 and 110.

43. Ibid., p. 108.

44. Ibid., p. 112.

45. Ibid., p. 113.

46. Ibid., pp. 161–162.

47. Ibid., p. 116.

48. Ibid., p. 115.

49. Ibid., p. 109.

50. Ibid., p. 118.

51. Ibid., p. 85.

52. Ibid., p. 176.

53. Ibid., p. 113.

54. Ibid., pp. 130–131.

8 | Governing and Campaigning

How do Clinton's general policy-making problems and the health debacle in particular—admittedly a worst-case example—accord with the earlier claims of the president's brilliance and deep knowledge of policy? Actually, quite well. First, it is hardly surprising that a dominant governor entering the White House from a small state would never have seen a first-rate policy process, would be overconfident about his ability to make sound policy on the run, and would appoint a Rhodes scholar friend as the top health policy aide to join him and Hillary Clinton, even though none of the three had extended experience in the health policy arena. Jimmy Carter too had governed a small state and earned a reputation as highly intelligent and analytic. In their small southern state governments, the two men could dominate state policy without rigorous policy processes. Neither came to the White House familiar with a managed process that can yield well-thought-through policy options and be structured to facilitate orderly deliberations. Elizabeth Drew quoted a Clinton administration official commenting on a meeting on health care during Clinton's first week in office attended by the Clintons, Robert Rubin, Leon Panetta and Alice Rivlin (the top two OMB officials), Council of Economic Advisers chairwoman Laura Tyson, and others to discuss a Magaziner draft paper: " 'Everyone thought Ira's process paper was a joke because nobody's ever seen anything like it in their whole career, and *everyone suddenly realized that Clinton had never seen a first-rate policy process.' "*[1]* President Clinton, despite his own analytic capabilities and many years of engaging in policy debates, had never experienced a well-functioning policy process built on a structure underpinned by orderly procedures where background papers were produced and vetted by competent policy analysts to establish a sound base for deliberations by the top policy makers.

THE DOWNSIDE OF BRILLIANCE

The Clinton health care problem went beyond process to substance, or more particularly to the kind of knowledge in a policy area that seldom can be acquired quickly however bright and hard working the learner. The mastering of facts and figures that can be done both quickly and in great quantity—indeed, a dazzling display to those of us neither super bright nor indefatigable—is not the same thing as gaining deep understanding. The distinction is a subtle one that even Johnson and Broder appear to have missed:

> The charge made by Jim McDermott and others on Capitol Hill that it [the task force process] was all an elaborate facade for educating Magaziner and the First Lady is . . . false. By the end of 1992, Magaziner had invested a huge amount of time in attempting to master health care. One can argue that his conclusions were wrong, or that he was too rigid in adhering to them. But he cannot be called a policy innocent. Hillary Clinton had done less on health care and needed more time to get up to speed, but Sheila Burke's [Senate minority leader Robert Dole's top aide] comment about Hillary being "a worthy opponent and a worthy proponent"—coming from a prominent Republican staffer capable of high partisanship—indicates how well the First Lady had mastered her brief.[2]

Indeed, Ira Magaziner and Hillary Clinton were not health policy innocents but that is not the same as them being experienced, sophisticated health policy analysts.

This fundamental distinction between acquiring facts and figures and gaining deep understanding is shown vividly in the case of Magaziner and Stockman. In early 1981, when Stockman stood astride the federal budget with a command of the numbers that seemed to bespeak of him as a super budgeteer, I interviewed a "real" super budgeteer who had had a spectacular career in the federal government before going into the private sector and had been an early consultant to Stockman. The experienced budget heavyweight told me that Stockman did not fully appreciate the subtle interactions between the federal budget and the economy. Now Stockman may have been even brighter than the interviewee, but Stockman did not have the experience on the firing line that the interviewee had. Although I am not sure Johnson and Broder themselves perceived the critical distinction, they did capture an important aspect of it when they noted that Magaziner's consulting career had been marked by his boldness and original ideas, but then cited a caveat by Mitt Romney, a Republican businessman who had worked in a consulting firm with Magaziner and thought highly of him: " 'You have to understand what consultants do. They analyze an operation and come up with dozens of ways to change it. Then the management has to judge what the ideas are worth. . . . Ira generated lots of ideas. But he had no sense of which were usable and which were not.' "[3] This inability to distinguish bad ideas from good ones is not restricted to consultants. At OEO in the 1960s, I once had on my staff an exceptionally creative and articulate policy analyst who could lay out a superb idea and a few poor ones and then defend each one fervently. The defense was not contrived because the analyst could not separate the winner, which I certainly did not have the creativity to craft, from weak ideas that well might include one or more that made little sense. My job was to single out the brilliant idea and certainly to cast out the poor ones no matter how strongly the creative analyst argued for any (or all) of them. Magaziner, as a consultant or analyst in a subordinate role is one thing, being the person with these flaws at the top is another.

Magaziner in a key position, with his arrogance, secretiveness, and belief he knew more than anyone else, looked frighteningly like Stockman. But there was a big difference: Two knowledgeable people— the brilliant Clintons, not Reagan and Meese—were in the game too. The relationship of the president, the First Lady as leader of the health task force, and the task force's operations chief can be labeled "Triumvirate II" à la the Reagan administration. This relationship reveals a presidential policy advice trinity of questions: How much does the president know about a policy issue? What does he not know? Whom will he trust for advice on that policy issue? The cases of the 1981 Reagan budget and the Clinton health care initiative in juxtaposing the polar extremes of presidential ignorance and knowledge offer an ideal base for exploring the policy advice trinity.

In the 1981 case, the answers to the three questions were that Ronald Reagan knew almost nothing about the details of the supply-side revolution that drove his budget, his Triumvirate knew little more, and OMB director David Stockman was trusted despite the fact that he was not close to the president or any of the three top advisers. This five-person relationship led me to argue in 1990 that Stockman can legitimately claim to be "the master of the tax and budget revolution in the policy formulation period. . . . [I]n the post-World War II era no presidential aide has operated so independently of the president . . . [and] no policy analyst in the domestic policy arena has exercised so much White House power."[4] Six years later, as the Bush chapter made clear, the argument might be made that Richard Darman and John Sununu could challenge Stockman on independence from the president and on the amount of domestic policy power, but certainly not on the level of policy impact. However, their roles as deputy presidents in no way diminish Stockman's role, but rather reinforce the danger of too-powerful, unchecked presidential staff members.

In the Clinton health care case, the answers carry to the other extreme of knowledge where, in the case of the first question, the president appeared as well-informed on a major domestic policy issue as any postwar president. The other two answers to the policy advice trinity—that the president did not know as much as he thought he knew and that he blindly trusted Magaziner—drove the health care policy process. The 1981 budget and the 1993 health care cases move from near zero presidential knowledge to an impressively high level; the movement also carries from ignorance to hubris. On the what-does-the-president-not-know question in 1993, Triumvirate II all thought they knew enough to ignore the experts. Within the administration itself, there were a most impressive array of trusted experts—Lloyd Bentsen, Leon Panetta, Alice Rivlin, Robert Rubin, and Laura Tyson—on any economic issues. Also ignored were what CBO director Robert Reischauer, as noted earlier, called " 'the big-time players in the health care game,' " most of whom were not in the administration.[5]

Why did the president side with Magaziner against the other key advisers such as Rubin whom he also trusted? One possibility is that in effect the future decision had been made in the transition period when the president-elect picked his former Oxford colleague. As Johnson and Broder wrote: "Clinton gave him [Magaziner] assurances he would be in charge of coordinating all health matters, including those involving the President, the vice president, and the First Lady. . . . The pledge was given unstintingly because Clinton had developed great confidence in his fellow Rhodes scholar."[6] The authors go on to quote President Clinton directly from their own interview with him as to why he trusted Magaziner so much: (1) " 'few people . . . understood the health care system' " as well as he did, (2) his friend from the campaign " 'understood what I thought had to be done,' " and (3) Magaziner had made " 'several million dollars advising corporations about what kinds of changes they ought to make to meet the demands of the global economy. So I thought there was some evidence that he had pretty good judgment.' "[7] In short, here was a person who had proved himself to Clinton over the years as friend and as campaign trail adviser, something other advisers to whom Clinton might have turned such as Rubin and Rivlin could not claim.

Another explanation rests on the unprecedented case of the First Lady running the president's top domestic policy initiative. In this case, President Clinton's arguments made to Johnson and Broder for trusting Magaziner may mainly have been rationalizations skirting the president being trapped in having to go with Magaziner or repudiate his wife. Thus, the brilliant president might have been doomed in a modern day Greek tragedy where the false steps of committing to his friend, choosing his wife as leader of his task force, or perhaps both intertwined, foreordained the policy process debacle. But the unchangeable path of the classic Greek play seems too neat for the analytic president who figuratively gobbled up information and analytic arguments. Moreover, as the health care policy process developed over time, President Clinton himself, in acquiring great amounts of information and engaging in endless deliberations, became as knowledgeable as we might expect any president to be about a major issue that he had not been involved in first hand, such as Eisenhower and Nixon had in foreign and defense policy.

A further explanation for why the best and the brightest can go so wrong in the process of governance is found embedded in the very nature of Clinton's and Kennedy's brilliance. Crafting policy alternatives draws on the analyst's adroitness and mental quickness, whilst management, and the even duller label for it "administration," appears pedestrian with images of sterile organization charts, solemn formal meetings, and tedious personnel problems. This preference for big policy thinking can arise because of the lengthy experience generally required to gain the kind of deep organizational understanding that had been so badly lacking in the crafting of the Clinton health care effort. The move to such understanding so often involves institutional issues that concern program implementation and management. For example, just as Magaziner thought, American health care did suffer from waste, fraud, and abuse as do most public and private operations. Magaziner's mantra about big savings in health care did not rest as much on his overestimate of the magnitude of waste, fraud, and abuse (although such estimates tend to be far too high), as on his lack of organizational realism about how long it would take to overcome the entrenched institutional blockages that stymied the potential savings.

The wondrous quick thinking and penetrating logic of the super policy wonks such as the president and Magaziner work much better for spectacular policy ideas than for organizational insights. Moreover, the super policy types generally overvalue the contribution of thinking through the policy issues as compared to working through the implementation issues. Perhaps worst of all, spectacularly brilliant analysts, such as the president and his former Oxford classmate, well may brush aside organizational blockages, grossly underestimate how difficult institutional barriers will be, have no facility for organizational thinking, exhibit impatience with those who want to focus on organizational difficulties, or some combination of these.

President Clinton's organizational incompetence led to a destructive combination of actions at the outset of his presidency. First, he promised both generally, and most specifically in the high visibility case of health care reform, to emulate Franklin Roosevelt's one-hundred-day achievement of quick, dramatic legislative changes that might have made sense in the Great Depression to save the banking system but were unrealistic in the sour politics of the 1990s. Second, candidate Clinton, to prove his claim of being a tight-fisted New Democrat, pledged to pare back government including a 25-percent cut in White House staff. It was a surefire combination for disaster—a mixture of intellectual hubris and organizational blindness. Johnson and Broder quoted the president directly: " 'I had cut back the staff of the White House as I said I would, and we'd roughly doubled the workload of the White House because I was taking on all these major initiatives, one right after the other. We didn't have the resources to do it, and we should have.' "[8] Organizational blindness became the Achilles' heel of yet another spectacularly bright policy analyst.

We need to explore further why President Clinton, with a dozen years of gubernatorial experience, made such egregious organizational blunders. Two possible explanations are reasonable. Considering each in its extreme form facilitates the discussion. The first is that Clinton totally disconnected campaigning and governing, in effect saying: "Make the arguments needed to win however much they may complicate governance." Candidate Clinton might have understood the organizational downside of promising a fast start and lean staffing but figured the upbeat promises, especially downsizing government, would help in the tight race. Moreover, Clinton might have been fully aware that the campaign promises needed to be kept, but believed it to be better to govern with a weight tied to his leg than not to govern at all. If the most Machiavellian position is taken, the Clinton statement to Johnson and Broder may have been highly self-serving in substituting the claim of an honest organizational error instead of admitting that he realized the promises hamstrung him but that he made them to win. The president's "Slick Willie" reputation hardly rules out such a campaign ploy. The second explanation is more straightforward. Clinton's organizational inexperience before his election as "boy" governor did not hurt him in Arkansas as already discussed briefly. However, the deficiency blindsided him—as well as the First Lady and Magaziner—in his critical domestic policy battle to enact universal health care protection. Given my belief that "organizational mastery has been the pivotal missing ingredient in the presidencies since Eisenhower," I opt for organizational ineptitude over Machiavellian campaign trickery if a clear choice must be made between the competing explanations.[9] The most sensible answer, however, blends both. That is, the demands of campaigning led to organizationally unrealistic promises by then candidate Clinton who did not fully appreciate the dangers because he lacked the managerial sophistication to see the consequences of the promises.

History, alas, does not necessarily yield clear answers or offer unambiguous guides for the future. Going from near zero knowledge in the Reagan case to striking knowledge in the Clinton example does not guarantee presidential wisdom or that increasing amounts of policy information and analysis *pari passu* improve presidential choices. The English biologist and author Thomas Henry Huxley, writing twelve decades ago in the Victorian era, captured the Clinton problem succinctly: "If a little knowledge is dangerous, where is the man who has so much as to be out of danger?" Today the notion of a president with sufficient knowledge to be out of danger in any major policy area seems preposterous; and Bill Clinton, who well may be the brightest president since Jefferson, underscores this point dramatically.

THE GOVERNANCE DILEMMA

The critique of the Clinton policy-making efforts rested on the administration's first two years during which Mack McLarty served most of the time as an extremely weak chief of staff, and the undisciplined policy-making process was in fullest flower. To stem the growing chaos, the president turned to OMB director Leon Panetta as chief of staff. Panetta, who previously had served many years in Congress and chaired the House Budget Committee, had watched the Clinton process from the outset as OMB director. He looked like a perfect choice. Moreover, Panetta had pressed the president for controls so that he could be a strong chief of staff. With pledges of support not only from the president but Hillary Clinton and Vice President Al Gore, Panetta thought he had complete authority to manage the White House policy-making process. However, the results were mixed. The policy process did become more orderly as Panetta slowed the host of White House staff rushing into the Oval Office and brought in staff with more organizational skills and power. *National Journal* reporter Burt Solomon who covers the White House described Erskine B. Bowles, the deputy chief of staff for operations, as "something of a lord of discipline . . . a skilled manager . . . [whose] main duty has been . . . to keep the process on track, to ensure that decisions get made and implemented."[10] At the same time, Elizabeth Drew, who also stressed Bowles' role in improving White House policy making, found that President Clinton's lack of discipline continued: "Despite pledges to Panetta by the President, the Vice President, and the First Lady when he was offered the job of Chief of Staff, Panetta was never really empowered to run the White House. . . . [Clinton] still lacked discipline, jumping from subject to subject and theme to theme. (This was also a failure on the part of his staff.)"[11]

No structure and process, however sound it appeared on the organization chart, could check the policy-activist president who still wanted to be his own top analyst engaged as an advocate in policy deliberations. In his column on Maraniss' biography of Clinton *First in His Class*, David Broder caught the organizational dilemma: "After reading this book, I certainly see how fatuous it was, for example, to think that a change of chiefs of staff would fundamentally alter the operations of a White House that so perfectly reflects the intense contradictions within the man at the center."[12] The fundamental point is that a chief of staff, however great his or her skills, could not have brought strong policy-making discipline to the Clinton White House during the active policy governance effort in the administration's first two years. No matter how smart or how much he knew about policy, Clinton simply could not or would not force himself to operate in a disciplined manner in that period. However, the lack of policy-making discipline became much less important after the surprising November 1994 elections brought a Republican majority in both houses of Congress. The seeming repudiation of the president in the November election resulted in a critical shift from offense to defense where Clinton moved to a campaigning style and harried Newt Gingrich in his sometimes frantic attempt to enact the Contract with America.

Offense versus Defense

Clinton's first term is divided for discussion purposes between the active governing phase running no longer than the 1994 midterm election and the defensive campaigning in the rest of the first term. Making this division does not ignore either the general claim that a president is always campaigning or the specific one that Bill Clinton has been especially prone to a continuous campaign style sensitive to the latest poll. At the same time, the two periods are strikingly different. President Clinton vigorously pursued a policy agenda until the Democrats lost the Congress in November 1994. Then, the new Republican Congress claimed its Contract with America gave it, and particularly the new Speaker of the House Newt Gingrich, the mandate to govern. Pundits speculated as to whether or not President Clinton had become irrelevant, in effect "unelected" by the voters, even though the Constitution kept him in office. President Clinton responded by reinventing himself politically as a tough right-of-center New Democrat—distinctly different from Gingrich and certainly his block of hard-right freshmen but not from Senate Majority Leader Robert Dole. It stood as the central component of his politics strategy.

On the single dimension of political standing, what happened in the two distinct periods is most discouraging for those hoping for (1) the use of honest numbers and sound policy analysis at the highest levels of the federal government, (2) policy making that realistically addresses the nation's most serious domestic policy problems, and (3) courageous political leadership. Paul Quirk and Joseph Hinchliffe's assessment of Clinton's first two years in "Domestic Policy: The Trials of a Centerist Democrat" highlighted the distinction between a policy-making effort and the ensuing political standing:

> In an old joke, a doctor reports that "the operation was a success, but the patient died." In the first two years of his presidency, Clinton's New Democrat strategy for domestic policy was a partial success. But President Clinton, at midterm, was a clear-cut political failure. . . .
>
> The New Democratic agenda enabled Clinton to achieve a considerable amount of significant policy change. For one thing, the centerist general stance did not interfere with his successful promotion of several liberal measures that had widespread public support: The family- and medical-leave bill, the motor voter bill, the National Service program, and the Brady bill. More directly reflecting New Democrat themes, Clinton was able to push through an economic program with a significant deficit-reduction package, which balanced spending cuts with tax increases on upper-income groups. He secured a major crime bill and related measures that incorporated both liberal and conservative methods of fighting crime. And although Clinton fell far short of obtaining a health-care reform bill and did not get much beyond conversation about welfare reform, he arguably made some progress toward identifying feasible options in both areas. One suspects that if, at the beginning of his term, Clinton had been offered a guarantee of this much midterm accomplishment, he would have been tempted to take it.[13]

Readers might quarrel with the liberal, conservative, and New Democrat designations; see the failure to push health care through the open policy window and to move further on welfare reform as blighting the effort; and doubt if Clinton would have settled for not winning some form of national health insurance or to "ending welfare as we know it." However, this much can be said: (1) Clinton did try hard to govern in mounting an activist agenda and in seriously seeking sound data and analysis to undergird his policy making, (2) he did push parts of his agenda through Congress and the yearly deficit had started to decline significantly, and (3) the Clinton governing effort brought a devastating political defeat for the president and the Democratic Congress. The result led one of the foremost students of the presidency, Bert Rockman, to this conclusion in his midterm assessment of Clinton:

> [P]residents given to thinking in serious ways about public policy are doomed to fail. Why? Serious thinking about policy means relating pieces of the puzzle, how costs connect to benefits, what the incentives are for various actors to produce different sorts of goods, and so forth. Comprehensive thinking about public policy leads to frustration in the American system because the system inevitably fragments and often isolates policy choices. Presidents with commitments to serious policy

thinking inevitably will be ridiculed as technocrats when their grand schemes come crashing down to earth. The key to success is simplicity, not intellectual consistency or congruency. Some of this is politics wherever it takes place. A big part of it is the character of the American political system. Another part of it is what we expect presidents to do, which is to think big, despite knowing that big thoughts are likely to be pulverized in the political system. Somehow, but I don't know how, we need to realign expectations about presidential leadership with the realities of the American political system and the uncertainty endemic to it of creating and sustaining majorities. Or, less likely, we need to think about realigning the system to accord with the expectations that most often accompany changes in presidential leadership. In the meantime, the system will continue to chew up presidents and spit them out with considerable regularity. It is time to ask: if Clinton cannot succeed, who could?[14]

Clinton in essence answered Rockman's question in political, not policy, terms: (1) be lucky enough to have a Speaker of the House Newt Gingrich as a policy-driven congressional foe who seemingly irritated the American people more than Clinton; (2) pound him to pieces with brilliant rhetoric; (3) move much closer to the opposition's positions that remain popular as in the case of ending welfare as we know it; and (4) hire Dick Morris and let all policy choices be determined by Morris' polls.

The Republican Congress led by Speaker Gingrich and Senate Majority Leader Dole in a secondary role appeared to be in full command as it began the effort to enact the Contract with America that sought fundamental policy changes. The Republicans' active governance effort had the same fate as Clinton's. First, much of the Contract with America did not pass, and Speaker Gingrich almost vanished as Democrats made him the big Republican villain, the public "rewarded" him with an unprecedented level of rejection for a congressional leader, and even House of Representatives Republican colleagues shunned him in their 1996 reelection campaigns. Second, President Clinton went into a campaign strategy where he brilliantly outmaneuvered the congressional Republicans, recast himself as a far more conservative New Democrat (indeed, the Republicans claimed Clinton stole their agenda), and pulled back from proposing anything but low-cost, high-vote-appeal programs. The latter led the *New York Times'* caustic columnist Maureen Dowd to lament: "Given the new Clinton fondness for microscopic policies—following up on his listing in the platform of his toll-free hot line (1-800-799-SAFE) for women in trouble, Hillary Rodham Clinton urged 48-hour hospital stays for new moms—I began to long for important, passionate ideas. The era of big government might be over, but does the era of trompe l'oeil government have to begin?"[15]

In fairness to President Clinton, at the start of the Gingrich Congress, he did face what critics saw as a daunting, nearly impossible, task if he was to save his presidency. Moreover, Clinton's campaigning and governing overlapped as he fought against radical elements of the Contract with America such as a balanced budget amendment to the Constitution. Governing and campaigning merged as Clinton's defense followed the Republican agenda while his offense followed the polls. The combination of the Republican Congress' highly active governance and Clinton's adroit campaign effort over the second half of his first term, and no doubt a strong economy, resurrected the president.

President Clinton's shift to the right is reflected in his efforts on welfare reform in the first term. One of the president's 1992 campaign promises claimed he would "end welfare as we know it." He cobbled together a piece of legislation blending liberal features such as child care, better health coverage, and increased education and job opportunities and conservative ones including a two-year welfare limit. His proposal initially would have brought increased outlays through expanded services over time aimed at helping welfare recipients to escape poverty through work. Although, as Quirk and Hinchliffe noted, Senator Moynihan "accused Clinton of using welfare reform as " 'boob bait for Bubbas,' " Clinton did stress added services to help people off the rolls.[16] As noted, Clinton made no progress with his welfare reform proposals.

A tougher version of welfare reform had a central place in the Republican policy agenda so both parties had promised to end welfare as we know it. And this promise drove both Clinton and the Republicans to negotiate endlessly for an acceptable change. The Republican measure, unlike Clinton's first-term proposal, cut deeply into the welfare budget. President Clinton did turn back some of the most punitive aspects of the Republican proposal. However, the new version still had much harsher measures than Clinton had proposed and Draconian cost reductions, not just in welfare, but in food stamps. The president tried to hide, without success, his acceptance of these measures. As Drew pointed out: "While the Senate was debating the welfare bill, the administration was sitting on a report by the Department of Health and Human Services estimating that the Senate bill would throw about a million children off welfare. The White House released it under pressure from Moynihan, who made scathing remarks on the Senate floor about the President's role in the welfare debate."[17] Once what was to be the final welfare bill made it through Congress, Clinton's advisers fought a highly charged battle over whether he should sign it. The struggle involved policy-oriented advisers such as then OMB director Alice Rivlin arguing for a veto and political advisers led by Dick Morris who wrote that he told the president "flatly that a welfare bill would cost him the election."[18] The president signed the legislation. The politicians had won over the policy types. Campaigning triumphed over governing.

Welfare reform was but one aspect of the remaking of Bill Clinton into a conservative New Democrat well to the right of the traditional Democratic Party. The president lamented that he had raised taxes too much in 1993 and called the conservative Democrat Ben Wattenberg to tell him "that his own 1994 welfare proposal hadn't been tough enough, and criticized himself for excessive liberalism."[19] Realistic programs addressing major domestic issues and courageous and strong political leadership had been abandoned. Bill Clinton had discovered that standing for nothing either controversial or expensive offered the optimum campaign strategy for winning. Courageous, strong political leadership had been abandoned. The Clinton reinvention tells much about political leadership in America as the nation moves toward the millennium. The president's shift from being a New Democrat with some liberal/leanings to a New Democrat incorporating much of the conservative Republican agenda was part of his move from being a policy-oriented leader willing to fight for his policy objectives to the nation's premier cheerleader seeking to reflect faithfully what the polls said voters wanted. But whatever one's judgment about the Clinton transformation, there is no question that Clinton's campaigning and counterpunching the Republicans' active governance effort worked far better in terms of political popularity than his own active governance.

Clinton as Reagan

President Clinton saved himself politically by being like Kennedy and Reagan. As to the former, Clinton's political discipline improved and he submerged whatever principles he had to winning reelection. Recall Reeves' penetrating assessment of Kennedy that "what convictions he did have, on nuclear proliferation or civil rights or the use of military power, he was often willing to suspend, particularly if that avoided confrontation with Congress or the risk of being called soft," and Reeves' quoting of Father Hesburgh on Kennedy's unwillingness to be involved in the civil rights fight.[20] Emulating Kennedy, Clinton's words often substituted for deeds and submerged principles while indicating youth (an obvious asset against the seventy-three-year-old presidential challenger Bob Dole), strength, and decisiveness. The dominant role model for Clinton, however, turned out to be Ronald Reagan as several observers pointed out. On election day, then *New York Times* Washington bureau chief R.W. Apple Jr. wrote: "In a partisan inversion that was no accident, Mr. Clinton cast himself as Ronald Reagan, peddling the politics of good humor. In debates and on the stump, he has asked, like President Reagan in 1984, whether voters considered themselves better off than four years ago. And on the final weekend of the campaign, he brazenly borrowed the Reagan slogan, 'It's morning in America.' "[21] Apple's colleague Maureen Dowd argued that "Clinton refashioned himself as a virtual Reagan, complete with a more stately gait, salutes and tributes to 'morning in America.' "[22] As to the latter, it needs noting that the 1996 economy—featuring low inflation and unemployment, a markedly smaller deficit, low interest rates, and solid growth without borrowing from the future as Reagan did with his massive deficits—surely justified Clinton's Reaganesque claim of morning again in America more than Reagan's 1984 economy. Even if it was not morning in America in either 1984 or 1996 because of the problems pushed below the surface, such as the widening income gap, high levels of poverty, and tens of millions of people uninsured, Clinton was not stretching in pronouncing the 1996 economy strikingly strong with many Americans doing better than in 1992.

Haley Barbour, the Republican national chairman, observed that "Bill Clinton went out and there were days that sounded like Ronald Reagan had taken over his body" and praised Clinton as "the most outstanding political performer of my lifetime."[23] Clinton's optimism, his empathy, his claims of wondrous American economic performance, and even his physical demeanor, all were pure Reagan. Nor was it an act, Clinton playing Reagan; just as it was not Reagan playing John Wayne. Barbour is right that Clinton is the political performer of our era, more so than Reagan as the latter was much more of a one-dimensional figure caught by the notion of letting Reagan be Reagan. Clinton brought a larger repertoire—unbelievable empathy, sunny optimism, boyish charm—and more guile in fine-tuning his performance. It was not that the individual behaviors were false but that they were packaged by the president's own calculating, subtle mind with Slick Willie below the surface. And here is the most critical difference between the two leaders. Reagan, the former Hollywood actor, to be sure, was scripted by his handlers; yet the scripting had to do with presentation, not principles. No one doubted Reagan's most basic principles seemed carved in stone so solid that facts could not intrude. Clinton in contrast did his own scripting in calling on his wide array of political skills—often with quick, dazzling shifts to create the right mood.

One of the most intriguing aspects of the Reaganization of Clinton is that he beat Speaker of the House Newt Gingrich as the rightful heir. Style became as important as substance. During the early months after the November 1994 midterm election, similarities between Clinton and Gingrich were stressed. Both were super policy wonks who dominated meetings and were fascinated by the intricacies of policy that apparently drove other participants to distraction. There were differences. The Contract with America was mean Reaganism, overtly harsh and punitive. Moreover, in the hubris flowing from the Republican midterm congressional victory, Gingrich found himself being pulled rightward by two powerful Texas congressional Republicans, Majority Leader Richard Armey and Majority Whip Tom DeLay, and an outspoken band of seventy-three new Republican representatives, many of whom were true believers in the harshest form of Reaganism in both style and substance. The Democrats brilliantly made Speaker Gingrich the symbol of a Republican thrust going too far to the right and Gingrich's often arrogant, combative behavior made clear he was not the sunny, tall-striding, soft-spoken Reagan. Clinton was.

Clinton's Reaganization went beyond copying Reagan to embracing Reaganism. As the Republican Congress in its Contract with America moved to the right, President Clinton followed. The already discussed 1996 welfare legislation symbolized the shift from the relatively liberal universal health coverage effort to a vindictive attitude toward welfare recipients and a general turning away from the poor. A *Washington Post* editorial contrasted the fact that the Social Security Administration on October 16, 1996 automatically raised benefits for the upcoming year by 2.9 percent so as to have Social Security income keep up with inflation with the lack of such an adjustment for food stamp recipients:

> [T]his enlightened social policy turns out to apply only to some Americans. A principal part of the so-called welfare reform bill Congress passed earlier this year—and the President, in a betrayal of his supposed principles, signed—was a sharp cut in the projected future cost of the food stamp program. Most of this was achieved by ending for food stamps precisely the kind of annual, "automatic" cost-of-living adjustments just announced for Social Security.[24]

The election of Bill Clinton in 1992, his successful income tax increase that fell mainly on the wealthy, and his effort to pass universal health coverage seemed to end the twelve years of the Reagan Era. But by 1996, the initial two years of the Clinton first term appeared to be a hiccup as the Reagan Era continued through its sixteenth year led by the now sunny, tall-striding, reelected president.

At his core, however, Clinton differed from Reagan in that the latter had tenaciously held objectives. In sharp contrast, Clinton, during the second half of his first term, seemed to have few, if any, worth fighting for against strong political winds. The key point is not that President Clinton's empathy, which could succor the loved ones of victims, be they killed in the Oklahoma City bombing or a major airline crash, and his boyish charm and optimism were faked, but wanting to be comforting or to be liked is neither a firm guide for policy choices nor for deciding that here is the spot to draw a line in the sand. As a successful politician, Ronald Reagan was no zealot, as were some of his hardcore followers, and brilliantly created the myth that he always held his ground. For example, Reagan somehow justified a number of badly needed tax increases in such a way that retained his "no new taxes" image. But firm objectives underlay Reagan's behavior while Clinton's actions are far more convoluted. An extremely perceptive interviewee told me: "Clinton does have bedrock principles and they are constant and consistent. The problem is that he leads his life as a master tactician (not a strategist) and he's into maximizing over the short run, never the long run. He is the classic politician with a two year time horizon." The master tactician, however, can carry pragmatism to the point that crushes a firm foundation. Given his early political experience—winning and then losing the governorship—this is not surprising especially because he had no life he liked outside of politics. Survival is the first rule for someone like that. But whatever his principles, the lack of courage and the overriding need to survive overwhelmed them so often that it is hard to cast him as a principled politician ready to dig in and fight even if his stand threatens his re-election.

THE ULTIMATE ENIGMA

The chapter earlier discussed Clinton's problem of having wondrous assets and huge liabilities so inextricably intertwined that the tangle carried with it the danger that his skills, when pushed too far, could bring highly flawed behavior. Clinton's brilliance and his wide-ranging mind, when coupled with his overwhelming need for approval, could lead him astray in governing as means and ends merged together. When he engaged in campaigning where winning an election provided a shining beacon, Clinton emerged as the master strategist able both to choose the best means and well-implement the effort. Governing required a beacon too, and here brains, as well as policy analysis, could fail him, in the latter case because policy analysis itself is but a means.

For me, Bill Clinton, of all the postwar presidents, is the most difficult to treat because he is both so intellectually challenging in his complexity and inconsistency and so infuriating. As to the latter, how can this president—literally the policy analyst's image of a decision maker with his brilliant, probing intellect, his appreciation of information and analysis, his astounding knowledge and grasp of policy substance, and his deep understanding of the subtleties of political and policy factors—end up being so similar to the premier anti-analytic president who had neither curiosity nor much policy knowledge? The answer is a painful one, taking us back to the central point that the development *and* use of honest numbers and solid analysis depend on a particular president's personal traits that go beyond his competence and appreciation of policy analysis to intangible qualities such as courage and commitment to principles. At the same time, Clinton's first term can be labeled a moderate success based on the booming economy (albeit Alan Greenspan may be the biggest hero), the accomplishments of the first two years cited by Quirk and Hinchliffe, and Clinton's brilliant defensive moves that undercut the worst parts of the Contract with America, except the misguided welfare legislation. Indeed, looking only at domestic policy, Clinton had a stronger record than his two Republican predecessors and Carter. The comparisons, however, are relative ones set against poor to terrible domestic policy performances by Clinton's three predecessors. I still question Clinton on a tougher standard that takes account of his striking potential for being a noteworthy president.

In this case of the ultimate policy wonk president, his lack of courage and commitment appeared to have undermined enlightened governance. President Clinton surely perceived the large, festering domestic policy problems facing the nation in 1996 whereas Ronald Reagan in 1984 had little or no perception of them. The latter really thought America to be back; Clinton simply chose to claim it to be morning again in America even though he knew the hard reality that the forty million persons without health coverage, for example, had only been pushed below the surface in the presidential campaign. Moreover, even if Bill Clinton had had an Eisenhower-like perception of organizational factors to complete his kit of wondrous analytic tools, his courage still would have failed him in the 1996 election campaign. Are these harsh judgments about Bill Clinton fair? The real culprit may not be the enigmatic president but the current economic and political environment that has been too much for even this extraordinarily talented president. I believed at the time President Clinton signed the 1996 welfare legislation that he could have vetoed it and made a successful case. Dick Morris, whatever else he may be, is a master of politics and thought the veto would have cost the president the election. In the current climate, courageous presidential leadership may be impossible. President Clinton in telling the hard truth that many of the people to be thrown off welfare cannot obtain anything but poor-paying jobs and their children are at severe risk could well have been— to quote from *Macbeth*—like taking "the ingredients of our poison'd chalice to our [his] lips." Thus, Walter Mondale by pointing out to Americans in 1984 that income taxes needed to be raised contributed to President Reagan's landslide victory. The evidence is hardly overwhelming to support a belief that courageous presidential leadership is possible and honest numbers and honest analyses can help make the case. If not, the prospects in the executive branch for honest analysts doing sound policy work is not good.

NOTES

1. Elizabeth Drew, *On the Edge: The Clinton Presidency*, Simon & Schuster, 1994, p. 192, italics added.

2. Haynes Johnson and David S. Broder, *The System: The American Way of Politics at the Breaking Point*, Little, Brown, 1996, p. 173.

3. Ibid., p. 106.

4. Walter Williams, *Mismanaging America: The Rise of the Anti-Analytic Presidency*, University Press of Kansas, 1990, pp. 76–77.

5. Johnson and Broder, *The System*, p. 116.

6. Ibid., p. 104.

7. Ibid.

8. Ibid., p. 232.

9. Williams, *Mismanaging America*, p. 119.

10. Burt Solomon, "Losing a Lord of Discipline in a Place that Surely Needs One," *National Journal*, September 16, 1995, p. 2300.

11. Elizabeth Drew, *Showdown: The Struggle between the Gingrich Congress and the Clinton White House*, Simon & Schuster, 1996, p. 190.

12. *Seattle Times*, February 5, 1995.

13. Paul J. Quirk and Joseph Hinchliffe, "Domestic Policy: The Trials of a Centerist Democrat," in Colin Campbell and Bert A. Rockman (eds.), *The Clinton Presidency: First Appraisal*, Chatham House, 1996, p. 283.

14. Bert A. Rockman, "Leadership Style and the Clinton Presidency," in ibid., p. 358.

15. *New York Times*, August 29, 1996.

16. Quirk and Hinchliffe, "Domestic Policy: The Trials of a Centerist Democrat," p. 280.

17. Drew, *Showdown*, p. 315.

18. Dick Morris, *Behind the Oval Office: Winning the Presidency in the Nineties*, Random House, 1997, p. 300.

19. Drew, *Showdown*, p. 309.

20. Richard Reeves, *President Kennedy: Profile of Power*, Simon & Schuster, 1993, pp. 19 and 467–468.

21. *New York Times*, November 5, 1996.

22. *New York Times*, November 7, 1996.

23. Ibid.

24. *Washington Post National Weekly Edition*, October 28–November 3, 1996.

9 | Congress and Policy Analysis

Congress embraced policy analysis long after the executive branch with the big push coming from the 1970 Amendments to the Legislative Reorganization Act of 1946 and the Congressional Budget and Impoundment Control Act signed into law 12 July 1974 by President Richard Nixon. The shift of power toward Congress took on even greater importance when President Nixon, under whom executive branch policy analysis had flourished, resigned less than a month later on August 9. Congress in the 1970s increased its analytic capacity both in its standing committees and in the congressional support agency structure consisting of the General Accounting Office (GAO), the Congressional Research Service (CRS) that is part of the Library of Congress, the Office of Technology Assessment (OTA), and the Congressional Budget Office (CBO). How striking the change is reflected by the fact that during my service at the Office of Economic Opportunity ending in 1969, GAO's main activity was auditing carried out by accountants, not policy analysts, and the Legislative Reference Service, the predecessor of the CRS, engaged in little analysis or research before the 1970 amendments with which, to quote former CRS deputy director William Robinson, Congress declared "analytical independence from the executive branch."[1] OTA arrived on the scene in 1972.

Congress now has analytic capacity widely dispersed throughout its committee structure, and some of these staffs have a tradition of analytic activity. But in this brief treatment, the nature of congressional analytic effort can be captured by looking at the congressional support agencies that serve all of Congress. These agencies have quite different missions and modes of operation. The CRS, which can trace its statutory start to 1914, is charged with (1) advising and assisting Congress in the assessment of legislative proposals and of recommendations by the president submitted to Congress, and (2) developing alternative proposals and assessing their impacts. CRS's highest priority is service to congressional committees, and it provides to these committees and also to members a wide variety of services—answering single questions, producing issue briefs that educate members and staff about the hundreds of issues facing Congress, and participating in in-depth consultations with individual members. What makes these many services offered by a staff of around eight hundred persons distinctive is that they involve a confidential client-consultant relationship so that, unlike the other support agencies, CRS's publications are not routinely made available to the executive branch or the public. GAO is Congress' investigative arm with a staff of several thousand persons. It responds to congressional requests to assess programs and makes recommendations for improving them. The only support agency that makes recommendations, all GAO studies not classified for national security purposes are available to the public. OTA (now abolished) was established "to provide congressional committees with objective analyses of the emerging, difficult, and often technical issues of today."[2] CBO's underlying purpose is to give Congress its own capacity to perform budgetary and economic projections. Congress' reliance on CBO budget, economic, and scorekeeping estimates and projections has made that office highly visible and contributed greatly to its power. Both OTA and CBO, which have had staffs on the order of two hundred persons, have published their studies.

The four agencies have all fared differently. In 1995 the Republican-led Congress killed OTA. At the same time, the GAO lost status, had its staff reduced from about five thousand to thirty-five hundred, and suffered wide criticism. The main charges cast the organization as a big, overstaffed bureaucracy that did not perform efficiently and characterized its comptroller general Charles Bowsher as "going beyond the numbers"—a transgression feared by all the agencies as we will see shortly. CBO had become the most powerful new analytic office in two decades as shown most strikingly by its critical role in challenging President Clinton and the Democratic majority on health care and Speaker of the House Newt Gingrich and the Republican majority on the Contract with America. CBO has been a bastion of competence, clout, integrity, and courage, often generating strong criticism from both Democratic and Republican congressional members and staffs. CRS, however, stands as by far the most popular support agency and also has a sterling reputation. Interviewees generally felt the assessments of the four agencies well-deserved. One saw Congress doing the "right thing" with OTA in eliminating a nonessential agency, and others believed the agency never got off the ground. Although none of the interviewees doubted GAO could benefit from some judicious downsizing, estimates varied as to how big a cut was needed. Further, a policy analyst, who had served on EOP and congressional analytic staffs, worried that a likely meat ax approach could do great harm, a most reasonable fear.

How the four agencies saw their roles and functions, why they garnered praise or criticism, and what happened to them offer critical evidence about how to proceed in the future. This chapter first turns to the question of credibility and status that has been central to all four support agencies and then focuses on CBO and CRS, which have been the outstanding analytic office successes of the last two decades. The look at CBO and CRS sharpens several issues critical to the future direction of federal policy analysis. First are the potential implications for the executive branch of the strong performance of the two congressional units: (1) what institutional elements in the CBO and CRS experiences can be used to improve executive branch analytic units? and (2) why did the strong analytic performance in Congress not stimulate better analysis in the executive branch, in that we expect growing analytic strength to force rivals to respond in kind? Second, the CBO case, where the agency torpedoed the Clinton health plan on its institutional unworkability, illuminates the implementation difficulties that are mainly ignored in the analysis of complex policy proposals. Why, after roughly a quarter century of implementation research that shows again and again how difficult it is to put a new policy in place, does extensive implementation analysis only occur in exceptional cases such as when the Clinton administration sought fundamental institutional changes in the vast, complex health care system? Third, the CRS experience highlights the value of a confidential analyst-client relationship where trust can be built over time as the analyst demonstrates his or her competence and dependability. The irony is that the Congress mandates this confidentiality with CRS and yet challenges such protection in the executive branch with the claim of the public's need to know. Fourth, the acknowledged superiority of the CBO budget and economic numbers to those of OMB and the Council of Economic Advisers illuminates the central place of policy analysis staffs; the intense pressures for state-of-the-art methodologies, high competence, and nonpartisanship, at least in highly visible controversies between the White House and Congress; the severe limits of the available policy tools; and the concomitant danger that the numbers in the heat of the battle become sanctified and drive out critical policy issues.

CREDIBILITY AND STATUS

[It should be noted at the outset of this section that the present tense of verbs will be used for presentational purposes even though OTA is no more.—Author] Although the four congressional support agencies vary significantly in the kinds of analysis and research they undertake, each professes "objectivity"—the favorite term of the agencies so I will use it—as its most basic value. That is hardly surprising since the units must answer to 535 masters and service committee staffs that have partisan majority and minority analysts. The support agencies would be committing bureaucratic suicide in trying to push their own agenda. But objectivity in and of itself does not bring power. Also needed are both institutional clout and the technical capacity to produce numbers and analyses that can stand outside scrutiny. This search for objectivity by the congressional agencies, however, starts with the striving to be "purer than the purest." It flows not only from bureaucratic necessity but from the dictates of the analytic profession about acceptable uses of evidence. Competent nonpartisanship—neutral competence—is "the holy grail" driving the operation of these institutions.

Organization for Policy Analysis, edited by Carol Weiss, provides chapters on institutional structure and practice by a then current member of each of the four congressional support agencies in which all of the authors painstakingly stress their units' fairness, accuracy, and objectivity. CRS's then deputy director William Robinson stated: "Great effort is made to ensure balance and accuracy in all products and services. . . . CRS places objectivity and nonpartisanship at the top of its value hierarchy."[3] Harry Havens, then a GAO assistant comptroller general, observed: "GAO's reliance on hard data and its insistence on establishing the reliability of data before using them are visible indicators of the institution's concern for credibility. That credibility is built on GAO's values of independence, objectivity, and accuracy."[4] James Blum, then assistant director for budget analysis and now CBO deputy director, pointed out that the unit did not take a position on any policy issues and then wrote: "The nonpartisan stance has been instrumental in preserving CBO's reputation for professionalism and has enhanced the credibility of its budget estimates and analyses. . . . [The] willingness to publish the methods underlying its cost estimates and other analyses adds to the general acceptance of CBO's work as objective and impartial."[5] Finally, Nancy Carson, then program manager for science, education and transportation at the Office of Technology Assessment, joined the chorus: "OTA's credibility rests on its objectivity, its comprehensiveness, and its rigor. . . . OTA is . . . open, and works by extensive internal and external review."[6]

Despite the fact that the statements in the last paragraph by the four members of the congressional support agencies may sound like standard boilerplate wording and appear interchangeable, they hold up in practice. Much like the strong nongovernmental think tanks, the four congressional support agencies (except CRS) widely distribute their work and are subjected to hard scrutiny both by other policy analysts and researchers and partisans striving to undercut an unfavorable analysis. CRS too seeks peer review and requires internal reviews at several levels. The four staffs adhere strongly to the scientific values of their professions and further know that their power in the federal government rests on their external credibility in a way that well may not be the case in the executive branch where personal factors often dominate (e.g., long service to a president or cabinet member). Executive branch policy analysis offices also publish the results of some of their work so they too face validity checks by outsiders. The fact remains, however, the top policy specialists are political executives directly serving presidents and agency heads or their designees. Partisanship is a valued commodity and nowhere is that more the case than in the White House. This is to say no more or no less than that executive branch political executives and congressional support agency heads respond to quite different signals from their masters—the former, to come out with answers their political bosses want; the latter, to be as accurate as they can so neither Republicans nor Democrats can charge bias. As Stuart Eizenstat, President Jimmy Carter's top domestic policy adviser, observed about CBO being consistently more accurate on economic forecasts and deficit projections than the executive branch: "What does that mean? It means that the president says, 'Look I think we're in a four-and-one-half-percent growth year and therefore that leaves room for more spending' or 'that enables us to cut the budget'. . . . And CBO says, 'No, we think that growth is going to be three percent.' And therefore you've just lost something on the order of $20 billion [in tax revenues for the budget]."[7] Two points need making. First, CBO's greater accuracy does not flow from higher technical competence—no doubt a rather obvious assertion but a crucial one in understanding the interplay of politics and policy. Second, I do not want to characterize the CBO as more pure than they are. They too try to stay out of harm's way, if possible. In the Eizenstat example, CBO might think growth will be lower than 3 percent and feel it needs to be a bit closer to the president, especially if his party is in power in Congress. But whatever the qualifications, CBO has generally been more accurate than the White House.

The quest for independence and accuracy does not protect the congressional support agencies either from technical error or from harsh political criticism. The former claim simply reasserts the fallibility of the available techniques so that "the numbers" can legitimately be challenged on technical grounds. The latter can come either from one political party or frequently from both at the same time, such as if an economic projection or a budget estimate does not accord fully with the political needs of either party (e.g., too low for one, not low enough for the other). Any perceived deviation from objectivity can bring down the wrath of Congress. GAO's policy of recommendations offers a case in point in that such recommendations well may appear to have strong value judgments embedded in them. While GAO no doubt believes that the agency is only speaking truth to power so that recommendations do not breach objectivity, there is an appearance they do so and this well may help explain the major cuts in Congress' largest support agency. The CBO in the Republican-led Congress (the first time since the Eisenhower presidency) offers a striking example of how the office can infuriate members of the party in power. As Eric Pianin of the *Washington Post* noted in September 1995:

> House Republicans once thought June E. O'Neill would be the answer to their budget problems. Now they are worried that the new director of the Congressional Budget Office may be their biggest problem.
>
> When House Budget Committee Chairman John R. Kasich of Ohio picked O'Neill to head the CBO last February, he described the New York University economics professor as "fabulous" and "highly qualified." Kasich boasted that she was sympathetic to the new Republican majority's efforts to get the tradition-bound CBO to adopt more "dynamic" methods of calculating the effects of GOP policies and tax cuts in reducing the deficit and boosting the economy.
>
> Two months later, Kasich changed his tune: "O'Neill and her staff had a "very stupid way of doing things," he complained. "They're being very unrealistic."
>
> Kasich's startling turnabout followed a CBO warning that a Republican proposal for moving millions of Medicare recipients from a fee-for-service system to managed health care was not likely to save nearly as much money as the GOP had been counting on. . . .
>
> Traditionally the person heading the agency has displayed stubborn independence, much to the annoyance of Democrats and Republicans. Last year, then CBO director Robert D. Reischauer, a Democratic appointee, dealt a crippling blow to President Clinton's health care reform plan by concluding that it would produce far smaller savings than the administration had claimed.[8]

Three points need making about the falling out of Kasich and O'Neill. First, when the Republicans captured Congress, they wanted their person in the top CBO spot and chose a little-known economist whom Kasich thought would dish up a more palatable offering than her predecessor who had stood up against volleys from Democrats and Republicans. Second, the Republicans faced restrictions flowing from the norm of nonpartisan competence in the congressional support agencies that limited their choice to a person with appropriate technical credentials and status. For example, the Republicans wanted to teach the CBO and the Democrats a lesson and pushed former Reagan administration OMB director James Miller as the new head of CBO. Miller had been known during his OMB tenure for his strong partisanship and his limited competence, being nicknamed "Miller Lite" in this last regard. But the congressional Republicans backed off as the White House had not done with Miller nearly a decade earlier in appointing him David Stockman's successor at OMB. Nor, it need be noted, would a president or cabinet member necessarily feel bound by the norm of nonpartisan competence in appointing the director of an EOP policy staff or an agency assistant secretary heading a policy analysis unit. Moreover, O'Neill herself would be restricted by the internal analytic standards of the CBO staff and potential external criticism from Democratic members of Congress, the network of organizations representing the aged, and health experts in think tanks and academia. CBO's twenty-year record of accuracy and objectivity severely limited any new director. Any effort to go against this analytic standard would not only elicit sharp inside criticism but would leak out, certainly to ex-CBO staff who could blow the whistle on any effort to do the numbers to fit the demands of the new Republican congressional majority. Third, credible numbers can bring great power, but it needs to be recognized that the power in this case, as noted earlier, flowed in good part, at least initially, from the 1974 budget act that led to congressional reliance on the CBO cost estimates as the official budget numbers.

CBO: HIGH VISIBILITY AND POWER

At the high point of executive branch domestic policy analysis capabilities in the first half of the 1970s, when agency central analytic units still flourished and EOP domestic policy analysis had grown much stronger, Congress sought analytic parity. As we have seen, executive branch domestic policy analytic strength thereafter leveled off and then declined precipitously during the Reagan-Bush years. In sharp contrast, despite serious setbacks including the demise of OTA, policy analysis in the congressional support agencies has thrived, and the striking successes of the Congressional Budget Office and the Congressional Research Service are critical for considering what can be done to improve analytic performance in the executive branch. I need to note at this point that the General Accounting Office too has had an impressive record; however, it will not be considered in any detail because it is a much larger scale organization than "traditional" analytic offices and continues to be as much an audit operation as an analytic one. One reason CBO and CRS provide so illustrative a base is their stark difference with the former being highly visible and the latter operating as an insider with confidential advice. In this and the next major section on CRS, we need to explore how each analytic office won its deserved reputation for analytic competence and credibility.

CBO's First Year

Unlike the Greek goddess Athena who sprang fully armed from her father Zeus' head, CBO had to fight hard for power. Nowhere is the bureaucratic struggle more clear than in CBO's initial year where the encounter occurred on congressional turf and showed both the interrelationship of technical analytic competence and institutional status in the power equation, and the importance of competition among analytic staffs in producing sound, credible information and analysis for policy makers. For this account of CBO's initial year, I draw on two of my studies, one written in mid-1974 before CBO had been organized and staffed and the other in February 1976 after a trial run of the new budget process. On the issues of capability and status, I argued: "[I]t is absolutely necessary [for Congress] to have an analytic staff that matches in competence the best of the executive branch analytic staffs. CBO is pivotal. And I am convinced that CBO must not only be highly skilled but powerful, influential, and large if the Budget Act is to work."[9]

Congress haggled for six months over the CBO directorship with the Senate pushing for the new breed policy analyst and the House putting forth a highly distinguished, but traditional budget specialist. The Senate finally won and picked Alice Rivlin, who had been assistant secretary for planning and evaluation at the Department of Health, Education, and Welfare (now Health and Human Services). She in turn chose as deputy director, Robert Levine, who had headed the Office of Research, Plans, Programs and Evaluation at the Office of Economic Opportunity. Rivlin and Levine, drawing on their experiences in heading the premier domestic policy analysis units in the Johnson presidency, zeroed in on analytic competence as the necessary hiring requirement. At the same time, CBO had a rocky start partly because the six-months delay in choosing the director meant the office had little impact on the FY1976 budget trial run.

The Congressional Budget Act, besides creating CBO, established two new budget committees. The staffs of these committees, which had been in business six months longer than CBO, and CBO had a tense, often acrimonious relationship as the three new staffs sought bureaucratic power. The budget act clearly gave CBO higher status than the two budget staffs. However, the battle for standing became complicated because the budget staffs served the new budget committees that were themselves trying to establish their status vis à vis the powerful committees, such as the appropriations committees, the House Ways and Means Committee, and the Senate Finance Committee, that had control of the budget before the 1974 act. Whatever an organization's or an individual's ascribed status, its actual status must be won through current or past performance. In the case of an executive branch analytic unit head, high status can flow from a personal relationship (e.g., an agency head chooses a trusted subordinate with limited analytic skills to head the analytic office), but that avenue was not open to CBO with its many masters. Competence offered CBO its only route to power. As I wrote in 1976 when high achieved status was far from certain:

> In technical terms . . . the CBO staff appears to be as competent as any of the analytic staffs in Washington. The putting together of this staff is the CBO's biggest accomplishment thus far. If the budget process ultimately works well, my guess is that we will come to see the rapid development of this staff as one of the really crucial factors. . . .
>
> We should not minimize the problems created for the CBO in comparison to all executive branch analytic offices in having both to serve many decisionmakers and to remain nonpartisan. But even with these difficulties, *I think the CBO has a reasonable chance of making policy analysis an important part of the congressional budget process.*[10]

Neither I nor, I suspect, the CBO leaders had any idea of how prominent the office would be a decade later.

Competence proved to be a central aspect of CBO's astoundingly high achieved status in the congressional budget process. In a 1995 interview, a former CBO staff member told me not to praise the early staff too much as there were some hired who did not work out. A point well-taken, but it is one almost certainly true for any new analytic office. However, the nucleus of a superior staff was on board including the three people I believe most responsible for CBO success—Alice Rivlin; her then special assistant Robert Reischauer who became an outstanding director; and now deputy director James Blum who built the Budget Analysis Division that won CBO its greatest early credibility and who has served continuously to date including as acting director.

These three highly competent analysts and others have made the Congressional Budget Office the high-visibility cutting edge in Congress' effort to regain power from the executive branch. Hedrick Smith in *The Power Game* caught the importance of the new office that engaged in an independent analysis of the budget where previously Congress had to depend on executive branch estimates:

> That single change—an independent Congressional Budget Office—was crucial, and symptomatic. Such congressional power was unthinkable in the era of John Kennedy and Lyndon Johnson. . . .
>
> [CBO] technically has no power; it passes no legislation. Unlike committee staffs, it cannot actually supervise the promoting, revising, or funding of programs. Its power derives purely from the intangible elements of information and credibility. Yet the CBO represents the most

important institutional shift of power on domestic issues between the executive branch and Congress in several decades.[11]

On 21 June 1974 Senator Samuel Ervin, one of the principal architects of the Congressional Budget Act, had the foresight to label the act "the most important piece of legislation that I have worked on during the 20 years I have served in the Senate."[12] At the moment of extreme presidential weakness, Congress brought forth a policy analysis unit to challenge the executive branch over the federal budget.

Nearly a quarter of a century later, the Congressional Budget Office is the success story of federal policy analysis units, having won credit both for high competence with the "best numbers in town" and for dogged integrity and courageous leadership in facing down President Clinton and Speaker Newt Gingrich. But the assumption should not be made that there is some surefire formula for creating analytic competence and power. A congressional insider interviewee told me in discussing CBO's success: "That CBO hung in there and built its power is not only a tribute to Alice Rivlin and her great staff, but nothing short of a damn miracle."

My 1974 paper also argued that the development of strong analytic capacity in the new budget process would be beneficial to the entire federal system by driving both Congress in using its other staffs and the executive branch toward more and more credible analysis to support the policy process. I claimed: *"[N]othing holds back the development and use of analysis in the federal government as much as lack of strong analytic capability in the Congress."*[13] The argument made several years before the start of the Reagan administration did not anticipate the rise of the anti-analytic presidency during which, beginning in 1981, politics crushed mere numbers. That critical year saw President Reagan and his budget director David Stockman sell to Congress a highly flawed budget. As the latter confessed in *The Triumph of Politics* published in 1986, an inadvertent error by Stockman on proposed defense spending put the defense budget out-of-control and his purposeful invention of "$15 billion per year of utterly phony cuts" masked that the Reagan administration's first deficit would exceed $100 billion.[14] Thereafter, Reagan administration budgets came "dead-on-arrival" in part because of partisan politics. But the administration's economic projections and budget estimates, which year after year simply were not believable as compared to those of CBO, became key factors too. Matters had deteriorated so much in the Reagan and Bush presidencies that President Clinton began his first year by promising that his budget would use CBO economic projections rather than those made by his administration. That's real power flowing from competence and credibility. It also is striking evidence of the fall in the EOP's perceived integrity.

The Dimensions of Credibility and Competence

"CBO must have the best numbers in town or it loses effectiveness." That statement by a former CBO staff person goes a long way toward explaining CBO's credibility and vulnerability. "Get it right or else" could well be emblazoned on CBO's letterhead. Its high visibility and its capacity to embarrass and even destroy top priority legislation of the president and the Congress means that CBO generally lacks assured continuing protection. As we will see shortly, the inside role of CRS allows for long-time patrons in a way not open to the exposed CBO. The point is not that CBO never has friends. A veteran newspaper reporter told me that the new director, June O'Neill, did not "get pushed to the wall" when she was picked because the House and Senate Budget Committee chairmen, John Kasich and Pete Domenici, recognized that sound numbers matter. But, as we saw, Kasich's support turned to anger when CBO estimates did not substantiate Republican claims about Medicare savings.

High visibility means the incentives push CBO toward hiring a competent staff, following sound analytic practices, and producing the best numbers in town even when the estimates and projections can anger presidents and congressional leaders. This is because "fixing" the numbers to fit what a Democratic- or Republican-led Congress wants will bring loss of credibility. Better damned for being right than for being wrong. Another element of credibility is showing no favorites over time. CBO worked with Republicans before the Democrats lost power in 1994 and that paid off. As a CBO staff member pointed out, "an established base of trust over time," built through CBO's credible service to the Republicans when out of power, helps explain why the House and Senate Budget Committees, after they shifted from Democratic to Republican leadership, did not add a lot of new staff to check up on CBO. Such trust represented a signal institutional victory for CBO that came about both because of the budget committees' belief in CBO's credibility and competence over time and because of the prudent bureaucratic behavior in CBO's continuing good service to the party out of power.

There is an obverse, darker side to CBO's high achieved credibility: too much credence may be placed in estimates that still should be viewed skeptically even if they are the best ones in town. A congressional staff person suggested to me that the average member or staffer has no idea what the numbers mean and how fallible the "best" estimates and projections may be. Take CBO cost estimates where "the Congressional Budget Act requires that each bill reported by an authorizing committee be accompanied by a CBO estimate of the five-year costs of the legislation."[15] These costs can take on a life of their own in being seen as highly accurate rather than as good ballpark estimates.

A CBO staff member pointed out that members and staff seldom are interested in the limitations of the numbers. Harvard's Theda Skocpol observed in *Boomerang* where she tried to exonerate the Clintons and Magaziner from blame in the health care effort and shift that blame to other actors including the CBO: "Today's drafters of legislation live in fear that the CBO will, ultimately, reject their proposals as not 'costed out.' "[16] In the health care case, I see the CBO staff and Reischauer as the heroes, not the villains. But more generally CBO well may be too powerful. The fault, however, lies mainly with CBO's congressional masters who need to have a basic understanding of the strengths and limitations of data and analyses if these are to be well-used in the policy process.

Leadership

In considering CBO leadership, it needs underscoring that the director-ship is billed as a nonpartisan position; however, each director has been a Democratic or Republican "choice" expected by their political masters to be responsive to the party that picked them. Alice Rivlin (1975–1983) started the process as the choice of the Democrats; Rudolph Penner (1983–1987) was selected by the Republicans since it was their turn; Robert Reischauer (1989–1995) became his Democratic successor after a couple of years of acting directors; and the Republicans picked June O'Neill in 1995. CBO in its first two decades has had two excep-tional leaders—Rivlin and Reischauer. The former, an ex-CBO staff member told me, had "tremendous integrity and lots of courage." As indicated earlier, Rivlin came in under siege by the two budget commit-tee staffs and had to battle for CBO's bureaucratic position. The fact that the budget act in mandating the use of CBO estimates and projections provided a powerful weapon for winning institutional clout must not be overlooked, but neither should Rivlin's toughness. Moreover, as the same former CBO staff person noted, Rivlin's brightness mixed well with her "willingness to say I'm wrong." A CBO staffer observed that Rivlin had a "knack for hiring competent people and giving them lots of room to do their thing." The comment affirms my earlier quoted two-decades-old statement that "we will come to see the rapid develop-ment of that staff as one of the really crucial factors . . . if the budget process ultimately works well"—a point I cannot resist making given the low batting averages of this and other crystal ball gazers.

Rivlin did back off in one case that needs noting. As Professor Roy Meyers, a former CBO staff member, wrote in a forthcoming piece: "[I]n 1981, CBO departed somewhat from its consensus economic model to move closer to the [Reagan] administration's 'supply-side' forecast. At the time, CBO leaders felt that not doing so would make CBO vulnerable to substantial retributions from the Republican-controlled Senate."[17] The decision proved to be an embarrassment to CBO, but as Shakespeare wrote in *King Henry IV* : "The better part of valor is discretion." It well may have been if we hark back to the unbelievable pressure to accept the supply-side thesis in the face of the Reagan-Stockman juggernaut that year. Looking back over the nearly fifteen years, CBO did not suffer great harm to its credibility and an unyielding Rivlin stand likely would have been foolhardy. Moreover, as a CBO staff person told me in 1996: "The 1981 forecasting episode does not represent current practice, nor practice since that time. I would think the current administration is much more influenced by CBO forecasts than the reverse." Rivlin's courage and integrity over her eight-year tenure still stand out.

Rivlin's later experiences at OMB are instructive in comparing the different worlds of a congressional support agency head and a high EOP official. Both President Clinton in 1993, with Rivlin as OMB deputy director, and the Congress in 1995, after Rivlin had replaced Panetta, accepted the CBO economic projections. The previously quoted CBO staff member made this ironic observation: "Poor Alice had to sit through several showings last year of the video tape of President Clinton's 1993 State of the Union address during which he defended his use of CBO economic assumptions before jeering House Republicans when she appeared before the JEC [Joint Economic Committee] and House Budget Committee to present the administration's more optimistic numbers." As discussed earlier, the administration's economic assumptions were not pie-in-the-sky fabrications and fit well with outside economic assumptions as did those of CBO; however, Rivlin's reputation as the virtuous policy analyst suffered. For example, Alan Greenspan was confirmed 91 to 7 for his third term as Federal Reserve Board chairman and the Senate voted 98 to 0 in approving the nomination of Lawrence Meyer, while Rivlin had 41 votes cast against her appointment as vice chairwoman of the Federal Reserve Board.

It should be underscored that Rivlin's discomfort can be seen as only fair. In the Carter administration, the CBO macroeconomic projections brought her great praise because these forecasts were deemed as more accurate (realistic) than those of the administration. The irony here is that Rivlin's high reputation as an economist had been won by work not concerned with economic forecasting. In contrast, the Council of Economic Adviser chairman Charles Schultze, who had been a key actor in crafting the much castigated administration projections, had previously been Rivlin's colleague at Brookings and that organization's top economic forecaster. I need to note that (1) I have known Rivlin since the mid-1960s, when I served on the OEO analytic staff and she at HEW, and Schultze for several years longer starting when I was a Ph.D. student of his and then a faculty colleague, and

(2) I consider both to be outstanding policy analysts as well as individuals with the highest professional standards and great integrity. That is the key point: Even the most able and honest policy analysts cannot survive without playing the institutional game.

Like Rivlin, Robert Reischauer brought to the job great competence, open-mindedness, a broad overview, probity, and courage. Reischauer possessed good internal management skills and the ability to charm people. All of these traits combined with his workaholism. As one interviewee indicated, Reischauer "can't stand not being busy." Unlike Rivlin who had limited capacity for small talk, Reischauer was comfortable chatting with Democrats and Republicans, and members from both political parties would call on Reischauer for advice. Also a CBO staff member said that Reischauer made himself available to the media on a background basis to help educate them and spent lots of time on this activity.

On the key dimension of courage, Reischauer's test came when he withstood intense pressure on President Clinton's health plan from the Democrats who told Reischauer that if he did not "get in line" to forget his reappointment as director in 1995. A former CBO staff person told me a Republican member of Congress indicated to Reischauer that he would stand by Reischauer after he supported the president because the member knew Reischauer had to cave in. Another former CBO staffer, Roy Meyers, in his discussion of the controversy over Clinton's health care plan, indicated that one critical battle turned on a technical issue that Reischauer could have used as cover for supporting the president:

> [The] health care plan . . . proposed employer mandates to provide health care insurance and health care alliances to administer the plans. Opponents of the plan claimed that the mandates were equivalent to a tax and that the alliances were equivalent to government agencies, and therefore all health expenditures should be placed on-budget. After months of speculation and after political pressure from both sides of the argument, CBO agreed with . . . [the opponents'] argument, though in its report CBO stated that this decision was merely a recommendation and that Congress and the president should decide the question as a policy issue. The episode stimulated the Clinton administration to complain that CBO had too much power for a group of electorally-unaccountable bureaucrats.[18]

Two comments on the quote are needed. First, the CBO recommendation was just that in the sense that this Congress, which had Democratic majorities in both Houses, could have rejected the recommendations. Second, President Clinton's views on unelected staff members surely became more benign when the Republican-appointed director June O'Neill did similar damage to the Republican health plan. I am not bothered by an unelected "bureaucrat" speaking truth to the powers that be—certainly not in public, as in this case, or in private to an elected official(s) who can still reject the advice. Reischauer showed exemplary courage in executing his legislated duties; his "masters" did not. The marvelous story is that when the furious Democratic leadership asked Reischauer what he thought he was doing in supporting the Republican argument, Reischauer replied "my job."

Reischauer was a hard to act for June O'Neill to follow. Although a competent technician, O'Neill lacked both Reischauer's managerial and interpersonal capabilities and his strategic overview. However, O'Neill had worked at CBO in the late 1970s and, to quote an interviewee, "learned first hand how to be successful in working with the Congress in a highly charged political atmosphere [so] it should not be a surprise that she has followed the nonpartisan CBO style." This interviewee recognized that O'Neill was "not in Bob's league," but argued that she is a competent analyst and has good instincts. Much like Rudolph Penner, the earlier Republican director who served after Rivlin, O'Neill will have done well, as the just quoted CBO staff member said, "if she can hold the fort." She did in her first big test. Her accomplishment was no small task in the face of the Republican Congress that picked O'Neill because the leadership expected her to go along with their agenda. Although she surprised and vexed the Republican leadership with her position on health care, as discussed earlier, O'Neill's principled and courageous stand still did not insulate her from equally strong attacks by Democrats. Reporter Robert Pear wrote in the December 11, 1995 edition of the *New York Times*:

> [OMB director Alice] Rivlin has repeatedly challenged the forecasts and estimates of the Congressional agency she once headed.
> Democrats in Congress have been even more critical. . . . [Senate Democratic leader Tom Daschle] said, "Today, I think, it's a Republican-orchestrated, Republican-run, Republican-dominated organization that can't be relied upon as a bipartisan resource any longer."
> But Mark G. Desautels, a spokesman for The Congressional Budget Office said that June E. O'Neill . . . believed that she had "conducted herself in a thoroughly nonpartisan manner" since taking office.[19]

A high-visibility policy analyst pursuing nonpartisanship is not a job for the thin-skinned.

Implementation Analysis

A quarter century ago, after having served on the Office of Economic Opportunity analytic staff, I wrote that "implementation was the

Achilles heel of the Johnson Administration's social policy."[20] Today implementation problems loom as large or larger as underscored by Reischauer's challenging President Clinton's massive health care plan on implementation grounds. Reischauer's efforts have already been discussed as an example of his courage and CBO's institutional clout. Now we need to consider the CBO stand in terms of competence and commitment to analytic standards in order both to elaborate on these two factors and to discuss the implementation issue.

The Clinton health care plan with its employer mandates and health care alliances portended dramatic institutional changes including a massive new bureaucratic structure that had embedded in it mind-boggling implementation difficulties. In such a case, proponents like to blithely ignore the implementation issues, if they can possibly avoid them. Moreover, such concerns are usually pushed below the surface by policy analysts or given cursory treatment. CBO makes cost estimates on numerous legislative proposals and the final figures, if favorable, at least implicitly suggest that the program will work well without huge implementation difficulties and costs. That is, implementation is not analyzed so as to estimate the potential costs either of implementation failure or of straightening out major problems in the field even if the program does finally get put in place successfully. This is not surprising in the light of the technical difficulties in making such cost estimates, the near zero demand from policy entrepreneurs and politicians who do not want to face up to messy structural and staff problems, and policy analysts' general lack of experience, and likely capability, in executing in-depth implementation analyses. But the identity of the main culprit—the potential user (demand)—is clear. As a former CBO staff member told me: "The main constraint has been the preferences of executives (or perhaps the incentives they face). But Reischauer deserves as much credit as you can give him." Although we shortly turn to Reischauer and CBO's critical, high-visibility place in the health care battle, the point should not be lost that the demand side of the policy analysis equation—that is, what the political masters want—remains a central driving force in determining what staff policy analysts serve up.

The president and the Democratic leaders, based on CBO's past history in costing out legislation without focusing on the implementation difficulties, did not expect Clinton's health plan would become the big exception. But the proposal brought a different response from CBO because the proposed changes could bring institutional turmoil that would severely harm the current health system. Reischauer chose to bring up these "other considerations" (that is, the usually ignored implementation questions) beyond the usual cost estimates for two main reasons. First, massive systemic changes like the health care proposal are rare events and the potential damages from implementation to critical institutions are hard to overlook entirely except, of course, by advocates. Second, CBO had highly competent analysts working on health care issues and was in a strong position technically to raise the implementation issue. A brief word is needed about CBO's organizational structure to explore this last point. The Budget Analysis Division with roughly one-third of the CBO staff does the costing and scorekeeping on the budget. The typical budget analyst's time is consumed by number crunching and far removed from issues of program implementation. CBO also has four program divisions that house the staff doing policy analysis including in-depth work on key ongoing issues such as health. The two economics divisions that do forecasts and tax analysis can be ignored for this discussion.

With CBO's highly competent staff of health experts and its store of knowledge, Reischauer did not need to go beyond the underlying numbers—a sin the bureaucratically adroit director would not have cared to chance. Reischauer's argument boiled down to the question of workability. Only a carefully planned effort over time that took into account a host of institutional difficulties, ranging from bureaucratic battles to the lack of needed infrastructure, had a reasonable chance of successful implementation. Further, the probability of working would decline rapidly if efforts were made to mount the massive changes quickly. It is hardly surprising that policy advocates hate implementation questions being brought up because they usually caution proceeding slowly. Most basically, implementation concerns about complex, large-scale policy changes make clear how much the proposed changes are a leap of faith. The analysts' efforts to cost them out should not be allowed to obscure that the dollars shown need to be used with extreme care and a healthy skepticism as to accuracy. And where could this be more true than in the effort to alter fundamentally the vast American health care systems?

In this particular case, we see the analyst at his best. Reischauer did not claim President Clinton's health care proposal was inherently unsound or that it would not be successful over time. He did not offer an alternative, warned of the grave limitations of his own estimates, and underscored how little was known about the impact of this massive institutional change. Reischauer could make his case and stand by it because he and his organization had such a strong reputation for high-quality, nonpartisan analysis; and, in the health care area, CBO's competence and capacity stood out. Reischauer had the troops to back up his battle with both the White House and the then Democratic Congress. He owned the best numbers in town and stayed within them. Reischauer needed all his skills and a strong base to stand up to an onslaught by the president and the Democratic congressional leadership that threatened both his job and his organization.

The Policy Analyst as Hero

No one has told the story of the pressures CBO faced in the health care analysis as well as Haynes Johnson and David Broder in *The System*. I want to summarize their account; but before doing so, a couple of comments are needed on why their book is so important. First, the two authors rank at the top of the serious journalists who write about American politics. Their unstinting praise of Reischauer and the CBO analysts who "risked jobs and careers to remain true to the highest standards of public service" can hardly be attacked by critics of hard-nosed policy analysis as either politically naive or self-serving.[21] Second, Johnson and Broder had the kind of access to the major participants, including President Clinton, in the midst of the health care battle that goes only to major journalists, certainly not to academics. The two journalists talked at length with CBO's critics so their assessment of CBO's role comes after hearing both sides. This does not necessarily make them objective or wise or fair but their judgment was based on an extremely wide range of information from the key players, a listing of which required three pages.[22]

CBO had two main analytic tasks in assessing the Clinton health plan for Congress. As is the case in legislative proposals, CBO had to "score" the Clinton plan to determine costs. As already discussed, scoring is CBO's bread-and-butter task. The second task carried into new territory because the Clinton health plan proposed a massive structural change that would create state-sponsored regional health alliances. These new institutions would take over the choosing of health insurance, previously done by individual companies for their employees. The main goal for the alliances was to raise the quality of health coverage available to employees. The critical question concerned whether the alliances should be treated as government agencies levying taxes that would appear on the federal budget or as private entities and hence off budget. Were the alliances "big government," as the Republicans claimed, or nongovernmental agencies?

Johnson and Broder's account of the alliance issue emphasized the tremendous pressure put on Reischauer to rule the alliances off budget:

> Some . . . accused him of trying to destroy a President. Others angrily warned him that if health reform died because of an unfavorable CBO verdict, children would suffer and some would die. . . . "You have the shittiest job in America," [Washington State Representative Jim] Mc-Dermott said one afternoon. . . .
>
> [Senator Ted] Kennedy assailed Reischauer, bellowing his outrage: Reischauer was going to bring down the Clinton administration. Here was a President with a once-in-a-lifetime opportunity to do something as historic as health reform, and you, a minor staff official, are taking it upon yourself to thwart the will of the American people. . . .

Kennedy's reaction was not some spur-of-the-moment eruption. He and his top aides were sincerely convinced that Reischauer was about to exceed his authority—"flat-out dishonesty and flat-out lawlessness," one of them raged—and, furthermore, was flat-out wrong.

As time for the decision neared, Reischauer summoned his executives to a meeting at seven o'clock at night in his office. Panic had set in at the White House. There were suggestions that CBO put off its report. Either that, or analyze the Republican alternatives as well as the Clinton plan.[23]

The anguish is like that faced by the OEO policy analysts and the negative income tax researchers in deciding to provide preliminary information to the House of Representatives. But in the bitter politics of the 1990s, the potential costs to the analysts are far higher and so, I think, is the level of anguish engendered, a point underscored vividly by the CBO ruling that threatened to derail the best chance for universal health coverage in the postwar era.

The yet unpublished CBO report had a chapter on the alliances classifying them as government agencies. Reischauer called together his top staff because he feared the decision could bring the elimination of CBO. The group discussed the Hamlet-like choice for an hour and a half. Reischauer wanted the executive group to vote yes or no on whether to keep the controversial chapter in the report. Each person received a piece of paper and all voted yes. Johnson and Broder are worth quoting at some length again:

> This triumph of principle over politics was never reported; their deliberations, and their vote, remained private. But theirs was an example, almost completely misunderstood amid all the assaults on government and its employees, of one part of The System—the largely anonymous and detached policy analysts—performing in the interests of the other part, the political side. Reischauer and his professional staff understood that their mission was not to advance any particular policy but to provide the policy makers with the most reliable data that would enable them to perform their jobs. It was a signal example of how The System should work in the best public interest by not allowing itself to be politicized by narrow or ideological interests.[24]

I want to step back from the heated battle for a final point. The fear that CBO would be eliminated or severely cut back well may have been unrealistic. Nor, if it had, would Reischauer, in particular, nor many of the other analysts have had their careers ruined. Lots of doors would have been open. The critical choice involved making a truly important decision that did have the potential to harm or help millions of people. The ultimate choice boiled down to analytic integrity. As

Reischauer said to Johnson and Broder, "'We're going to tell it the way it is no matter what happens. Lightning strikes and thunder rumbles.'"[25] Make no mistake, the choice has an element of hubris when the professional policy analysts decided to go with their analysis knowing it almost certainly undercut a Democratic president and a Democratic Congress, the duly elected officials. The issue is beyond telling the boss the truth behind closed doors. Reischauer made the call in the bright light of open public controversy. We need to look at Congress' policy analysts behind closed doors before coming back to the role of highly visible policy analysts.

CRS: THE LOW-PROFILE LIFE OF THE INSIDER

A CBO staffer lamented that CRS has a fantastic reputation with Congress, far higher than that of CBO. The difference is not in terms of CRS's competence or nonpartisanship, but its operation as a consummate insider organization. Former CRS deputy director William Robinson has written of the agency's confidential client-consultant relationship: "As a result of that role as personal consultant, along with stringent statutory constraints on publishing its reports or studies for noncongressional use, CRS has operated with a very low profile in the public community."[26] Several points need to be made about Robinson's statement. First, CBO and CRS are diametrically opposite in terms of exposure because Congress mandates one of them to be on the front line and the other to consider its work as internal congressional documents. Second, CRS is not a clandestine organization telling members of Congress what they want to hear or cooking up arguments and analyses to be used as weapons by congressional advocates. Not only would such stealth destroy CRS credibility over time, it is anathema to the professional policy analysts who staff the unit. Third, what CRS does is not widely known in the policy community even though more and more of its in-depth analyses are being published as congressional committee reprints. While CBO no doubt wishes its products were not subjected so often to harsh investigation, CRS probably would like to make its best work publicly available more often. Fourth, CRS seeks to be, as Robert Browning wrote, "purer than the purest." Robinson observed: "Great effort is made to ensure balance and accuracy in all products and services. . . . [CRS] encourages peer review and requires review of all new written products at the section and division levels and a final review in the agency Office of Policy."[27]

The CRS has two main tasks—assessing legislative proposals and evaluating possible alternatives. It is worthwhile to spell out the legislative language of the 1970 amendments to the Legislative Reorganization Act of 1946 that mandated these two functions and in so doing mandated policy analysis within the Library of Congress as the Legislative Reference Service became CRS:

> (d) It shall be the duty of the Congressional Research Service, without partisan bias—
> (1) upon request, to advise and assist any committee of the Senate or House of Representatives and any joint committee of Congress in the analysis, appraisal, and evaluation of legislative proposals within that committee's jurisdiction, or of recommendations submitted to Congress, by the President or any executive agency, so as to assist the committee in—
> (A) determining the advisability of enacting such proposals;
> (B) estimating the probable results of such proposals and alternatives thereto; and
> (C) evaluating alternative methods for accomplishing those results; and, by providing such other research and analytical services as the committee considers appropriate for these purposes, otherwise to assist in furnishing a basis for the proper evaluation and determination of legislative proposals and recommendations generally; and in the performance of this duty the Service shall have authority, when so authorized by a committee and acting as the agent of that committee, to request of any department or agency of the United States the production of such books, records, correspondence, memoranda, papers, and documents as the Service considers necessary, and such department or agency of the United States shall comply with such request; and, further, in the performance of this and any other relevant duty, the Service shall maintain continuous liaison with all committees. . . . (Section 203[d][1] of 2 USC 166).[28]

These two tasks are to be carried out without partisan bias and without transparency. As a CRS interviewee observed: "CRS will not share information even subtly with other congressional users—even to the point of not admitting to working on an issue for a client (to know that we were involved would trigger interest at a point that might be premature for its release and maximum tactical advantage). We will only share when we have explicit permission from the original requester."

Congress's shielding of CRS is well-known in today's world where the press and others including Congress itself in the case of the executive branch seek out such information through various means such as the Freedom of Information Act. What is so remarkable is its degree of institutionalization where CRS freely admits to invisible analysis for unnamed congressional clients while refusing to disclose the identity of the party served except with explicit consent. In the 1960s when I was at the Office of Economic Opportunity, executive privilege absolutely protected—and hence institutionalized—invisible analysis. Much like CRS, the Bureau of the Budget made much of being able to provide protected analysis to the president without partisan spin. Today a president still can have "invisible analysis" as one well-placed policy analyst pointed out: "The president has some very good invisible analysis done for him by a small group of people whom he can trust—the CEA, OMB, etc. This is the analysis that there is a high degree of certainty will never become public. It is unbiased (if the president demands it to be) and of high quality. This analysis is much like that done by CRS for its clients." But only Congress still can get away with such overt institutionalization (a point returned to shortly).

CRS is so valuable to Congress because it provides a broad array of services including (1) preparation of background papers and briefings; (2) assistance in hearings including designing the hearings and gathering information, providing questions for members to ask committee witnesses, and testifying before committees; (3) development of issue briefs on 350 to 450 issues facing Congress each year; and (4) identification of twenty or so "hot" issues in the next year that are likely to arrive at the legislative stage.[29] CRS policy analysts can serve as good substitutes for committee staffs and provide uniformity which makes for an effective use of resources. Former deputy director Robinson underscored the consultant role in more general terms:

> By the end of the decade [the 1980s], one of the key roles played by CRS became that of policy consultant, with close attachment to the legislative process. The increased experience of the analytical staff enhanced their capacity to function effectively as policy consultants both by deepening their subject expertise and enriching their institutional memory—knowing firsthand what ideas had been tried by the committee before, the reactions of interested parties, procedural tactics tried, committee jurisdictions threatened, legislative outcomes and their impacts, and some notions about what options might be pursued usefully at the present stage of debate.[30]

This consultant-client relationship needs exploring because it can provide one of, if not the, most valuable of analytic activities. The service being supplied involves a continuing effort not restricted to written documents and usually includes a one-on-one verbal interaction and informal written communications. The main product likely will not be a formal document with explicit institutional vetting, although ultimately such a document with all the technical trimming may emerge long after the most important aspects of interaction have occurred.

In conceptualizing the consultant-client relationship, consider three related, but separable, elements of policy analysis and advice—the *available information*, both that used and that not used either because it was explicitly rejected or because its existence was not known by the analyst; the *analysis* that may be in verbal or written form or both; and the *analyst* delivering the product. The starting place is to recognize that any analysis suffers from unavoidably flawed information and hence the analysis and the analyst can always be challenged. But having accepted this basic problem, the question remains as to how the analyst uses the information and performs the analysis and what the process is for considering the information itself, the analysis, and the implications of it. Personal competence, perception, and interaction are central factors. Individuals who possess the capacity to cope with the information and analysis, to trust each other, and to interact in a confidential setting may offer the best environment for reasoned understanding over time. The CRS confidential consultant-client setting has these dimensions. The CRS analyst can bring the technical competence and the substantive and organizational knowledge including institutional memory to the interaction and, if needed, educate the client. The latter can explicate the problems at issue, provide information that the analyst lacks, and interact with the CRS consultant over time to give further dimension to the issues under consideration.

That Congress has created such an atmosphere with CRS and values it highly indicates that establishing such a relationship is still possible. But, as discussed briefly, Congress itself, as well as the media, has made such institutional shielding more and more difficult in the executive branch. This confidentiality problem is exemplified by one element of the Whitewater controversy between President Clinton and Congress concerning whether the former could claim the lawyer-client privilege. The issue is complicated because it involved two sets of lawyers. One group contained the president's personal lawyers in private practice; the other, his White House staff lawyers. In the case at hand, William Kennedy 3rd, an associate White House counsel, had taken notes at a Whitewater meeting that included both the president's private and government lawyers. At basic issue stood the public's right to know as Senator Alfonse D'Amato, Republican chairman of the Senate Whitewater committee observed: " 'The American people are entitled to the notes.' "[31] The question of the president's privileged communications with his lawyers was not settled. After the Senate voted to hold Kennedy in contempt for not disclosing the notes, the White House turned them over and the Senate agreed that the president's claim to a privileged relationship had not been waived.

This case in which the Senate searched for a smoking gun in the Whitewater notes shows the controversy in its starkest terms where the Senate's need to know in the public interest clashes with the historic claim of privileged communication between lawyer and client or more broadly between an adviser and an executive. New York University law professor Stephen Gillers has pointed out that this "privilege dates back to Elizabeth I [queen from 1558 to 1603] and was part of American law at independence" and observed that "Bill Clinton may be the only C.E.O. in America who can't talk with his lawyer in private."[32] If so or even if the president can still speak confidentially with his private— that is personal, not government lawyers—Whitewater still threatens the president's privileged communications with White House lawyers and concomitantly the consultant-client relationship in the executive branch. Will an agency head and a policy analyst be able to speak in candor without fear of being forced by Congress or a court to reveal the discussion? Will any documents such as an internal memorandum or notes from a meeting be shielded? The CRS experience indicates that such confidentiality can be desirable and the issue will be further considered in a later chapter.

One other aspect of the CRS relationship with Congress needs considering. CRS's low profile should not be construed as the quiet life. The policy analysts may be part of the Library of Congress but as an interviewee told me, the atmosphere is far from "the hushed tones of a library, a place frequented by slow, deliberate, . . . reclusive monk-like creatures [but rather has] a firehouse atmosphere of fighter-pilot analysts who are busy conducting quick-response fire-fights while tending the analytic needs of forty plus committees." This description may be overstated (too macho). Still, the harried, hurried atmosphere accords with my own experience in an agency analytic office. Despite this, the strong staffs fight for time to strive for accuracy and for some reflection to look for subtle meaning. It is the mark of the strong staff that defines itself by high professional standards in a setting that demands relatively rapid response with necessary tradeoffs between soundness and timeliness.

FINAL COMMENTS

The Clinton-congressional budget battle in 1995–1996 makes clear both the importance of the expert estimates and forecasts and the press for the best numbers that can be developed. The *New York Times* economic editor Peter Passell in his December 21, 1995 column wrote: "When the bean counters at the Congressional Budget Office disagree with their counterparts on the President's Council of Economic Advisers, whom do you trust? The question has emerged as the issue of the hour in the political duel over deficit reduction."[33] Stripped to its essence, the question of trust—in this case of analysts making sophisticated economic forecasts—stood out. The trust issue included both a technical, professional competence element as to the methodological excellence of the economic forecasts and one of professional integrity as to the potential bias that might have slanted the estimates to fit a policy or political position. Both competence and nonpartisanship were being evaluated.

Passell went on to point out that both CBO and CEA have done respectable forecasting jobs in the past; CBO has performed somewhat better, and this particular year was a toss up as to the best estimates with slightly different, defendable assumptions about unknown factors. But then Passell makes the key point:

> If there is one grand moral to this tale, it's that budget negotiators' time horizon is too long. The one thing forecasters ought to agree about, says Robert D. Reischauer ... is that "what you predict won't come to pass."
>
> No one knows whether the economy will grow at 2 percent, 2.5 percent, or even 3 percent over the next seven years. ...
>
> There is probably no way for the negotiators to acknowledge this reality and to redefine the terms of the budget battle. But that should not stop the rest of us from focusing on the real economic issue of how well the new budget reflects national priorities.[34]

The nation needs sound numbers and analyses as a basis for making decisions. At the same time, state-of-the-art information, analyses, and forecasts still should to be marked "handle with care." Even the best job that can be done with the available tools can obscure the underlying issues. Either the fundamental, unremitting distrust of the number crunchers to do their level best and be nonpartisan or the belief that the numbers not only are developed with the best available methods but accurately forecast the future is dangerous. Is there a sensible middle ground between either paranoia about or blind trust in the information experts? Can politicians and the public well-use data and analyses and neither distort them nor carry the implications too far?

The histories of CRS and CBO deliver the critical messages of the successful development of honest numbers by policy analysts of high technical skills and integrity, even in the current hostile political environment. Moreover, a basic premise of this book is that such sound numbers and competent policy analysts with a high commitment to professional standards are necessary conditions for more enlightened policy making. But to set out these necessary conditions still leaves the most vexing of questions: How much will meeting these conditions help in fostering more enlightened policy making? One of my most astute interviewees who has served as a policy analyst in both the EOP and a congressional support agency put the question most sharply:

> With respect to CBO, I agree with your characterization of competence and integrity. My only comment takes the form of a question, one to which I do not have the answer. Why has the building of such formidable

analytic capacity not been accompanied by better decisionmaking? The empirical results (i.e., the budgetary outcomes, with respect to both the fiscal aggregates and ... the composition of spending) over the past twenty years are hardly a tribute to the social value of strong analytic units serving the decisionmakers. Do you really think those outcomes would have been worse in the absence of CBO? It is hard for me to believe so.

The interviewee may be too harsh in the assessment; however, as an observer of the last two decades, I cannot reject the pessimism of the quote out-of-hand.

NOTES

1. William H. Robinson, "The Congressional Research Service: Policy Consultant, Think Tank, and Information Factory," in Carol H. Weiss (ed.), *Organizations for Policy Analysis: Helping Government Think*, Sage, 1992, p. 184.
2. Nancy Carson, "Process, Prescience, and Pragmatism: The Office of Technology Assessment," in ibid., p. 236.
3. Robinson, "The Congressional Research Service: Policy Consultant, Think Tank, and Information Factory," pp. 182 and 188.
4. Harry S. Havens, "The Evolution of the General Accounting Office: From Voucher Audits to Program Evaluations," in Weiss (ed.), *Organizations for Policy Analysis*, p. 212.
5. James L. Blum, The Congressional Budget Office: On the One Hand, On the Other," in Weiss (ed.), *Organizations for Policy Analysis*, pp. 225–226
6. Carson, "Process, Prescience, and Pragmatism," pp. 243–244.
7. Hedrick Smith, *The Power Game: How Washington Works*, Random House, 1988, p. 23.
8. *Washington Post National Weekly Edition,* September 11–17, 1995, p. 32.
9. Walter Williams, "The Congressional Budget Office: A Critical Link in Budget Reform," Institute of Governmental Research (University of Washington), July 1974, p. 4.
10. Walter Williams, "Congress, Budgetmaking and Policy Analysis: A Critique after the Fiscal Year 1976 Trial Run," Institute of Governmental Research (University of Washington), February 1976, pp. 54–55 and 75, italics in the original.
11. Smith, *The Power Game*, pp. 23 and 290.
12. *Congressional Record–Senate*, June 21, 1974, S11221.
13. Williams, "The Congressional Budget Office," p. 20, italics in the original.
14. David A. Stockman, *The Triumph of Politics: Why the Reagan Revolution Failed*, Harper & Row, 1986, p. 353.
15. Roy T. Meyers, "Congressional Budget Office: The Fiscal Support Agency for the United States Congress," forthcoming, in Jay Shafritz (ed.) *International Encyclopedia of Public Policy and Administration*, Holt, 1997.

16. Theda Skocpol, *Boomerang: Clinton's Health Security Effort and the Turn against Government*, Norton, 1996, p. 67.

17. Meyers, "Congressional Budget Office."

18. Ibid.

19. *New York Times*, December 11, 1995.

20. Walter Williams, *Social Policy Research and Analysis: The Experience in the Federal Social Agencies*, Elsevier, 1971, p. 11.

21. Haynes Johnson and David S. Broder, *The System: The American Way of Politics at the Breaking Point*, Little, Brown, 1996, p. 636.

22. Ibid., pp. xv–xvii.

23. Ibid., p. 284–285.

24. Ibid., p. 286.

25. Ibid.

26. Robinson, "The Congressional Research Service: Policy Consultant, Think Tank, and Information Factory," p. 182.

27. Ibid., pp. 182, 191.

28. Quoted in ibid., p. 184.

29. Ibid., pp. 188, 196.

30. Ibid., p. 194.

31. Quoted in *New York Times*, December 22, 1995.

32. *New York Times*, December 21, 1995.

33. *New York Times*, December 21, 1995.

34. Ibid.

10 | The Big Picture and Policy Analysis

In thinking about the future of federal policy analysis, we need to consider the larger information environment that now impinges so heavily on efforts by the national government and nongovernment policy analysis and research organizations to develop sound, credible policy data. The overriding issues of the growing distrust of the federal government generally and the concomitant collapse of citizen confidence in "establishment" policy data and analyses come to the fore. A key aspect of rising distrust and falling public confidence is the fast eroding base of widely agreed upon policy information that can support reasoned policy debate. The numbers developed by the major government and private and nonprofit institutions that historically have supplied policy information and analysis to the public and the media are being challenged by new sources such as the Internet and partisan organizations that often produce bogus and/or highly slanted data and analyses that take on a life of their own whatever the efforts to indicate the lack of validity. The need today is not just for honest numbers, but for honest and credible ones.

Citizens' loss of trust in the federal government has arisen in part because the American people have lost confidence not only in a president and members of Congress and in a particular administration, but also in the presidency and the Congress and even more broadly in the government created by the Constitution. This loss of trust in the federal institutions of governance threatens American democracy. The constitutional institutions must have a permanency, an enduring legitimacy. Individual presidents are temporary occupants of the Oval Office; the presidency continues. Voters may err and choose an incompetent president or member of Congress, but the democratic process, as spelled out in the Constitution, allows them to remove that person or persons in the next election. However, to function effectively over time, the institutions must remain unsullied so as to provide the newly elected persons a high level of trust or legitimacy—an adequate platform for competent performance. If not, if a nation's basic

237

institutions themselves become debased, the political foundations of the country are at risk. That is the case today as the long-established federal government developers and interpreters of national statistics are caught up in the larger crisis of distrust fueled by political leaders, the media, the Internet, and a citizenry both ignorant about basic social and economic statistics and increasingly ready to believe that the "establishment" information institutions are fabricating the numbers for political purposes.

As to organization, this chapter first focuses on the media generally and television specifically as the main sources of the public's policy information. In *Breaking the News: How the Media Undermines American Democracy*, James Fallows, editor of *U.S. News and World Report*, charged that the media have failed in their most basic role of informing the public on key policy issues and instead have been a major factor in fostering distrust:

> Deep forces in America's political, social, and economic structures account for most of the frustration of today's politics, but the media's attitudes have played a surprisingly important and destructive role. Issues that affect the collective interests of Americans—crime, health care, education, economic growth—are presented mainly as arenas in which politicians can fight. The press is often referred to as the Fourth Branch of Government, which means that it should provide the information we need so as to make sense of public problems. But far from making it easier to cope with public challenges, the media often make it harder. By choosing to present public life as a contest among scheming political leaders, all of whom the public should view with suspicion, the news media help bring about that very result.[1]

One of the victims has been the government and nongovernment information institutions including the federal analytic offices.

The next section looks at how these institutions' credibility has been further damaged by direct actions both by the president and Congress and by policy research organizations themselves. Part of the problem is that the nation's leaders have used information and analysis as political weapons. In the previously discussed 1995 budget battle, Congress had sought to discredit the Clinton administration budget and economic estimates as politically manipulated even though both CBO and administration numbers were in fact sound. Why should the public think any federal government data credible when one branch of that government loudly accuses another branch of "jimmying" the numbers? Less dramatic but extremely damaging in the long term is the federal government's disinvestment in information development capacity and its unwillingness to undertake needed evaluations and experiments. Policy research organizations inside and outside of the government too have undercut their own credibility in misusing information and analysis to support highly partisan positions. The fiercest battles and some of the worst cases of distorted information and analyses have occurred within the nongovernmental policy research industry. Too much of this outpouring warrants media and public distrust.

The chapter turns next to the American public, which the Constitution casts in such a difficult role, and to the emerging electronic revolution exemplified by the Internet with its capacity for instantaneous, interactive communications and far wider public policy discourse. Pity the poor American voter. Martin Wattenberg has argued that electoral politics is much more difficult and time-consuming for the average person in the United States than for citizens in almost any other democracy.[2] James MacGregor Burns went further to claim that "no polity on earth [has] put such civic demands on its citizens as [does] the American. . . . It is above all the decline of party in the United States that has made the citizen's task so overpowering."[3] Yet, just as two-hundred years ago, the Constitution demands citizen vigilance in the political process however complex the issues and however vast the available information. James Madison's warning, written over three decades after he helped shape the Constitution, still rings true: "[T]he people who mean to be their own Governors, must arm themselves with the power knowledge gives."[4] However, survey after survey over the years show high levels of public ignorance about American public policy issues and often strikingly inaccurate knowledge about the basic economic and social statistics. A July 22-August 2, 1996 *Washington Post*/Kaiser Family Foundation/Harvard University survey found that only 16 percent of the interviewees said correctly that inflation had declined in the previous five years, and that 70 percent believed the federal budget deficit had risen in the previous five years while only 12 percent said correctly that the deficit had declined. Nor were people in the ballpark in their specific knowledge of economic statistics as interviewees on the average thought that the unemployment rate of a little over 5 percent stood at over 20 percent (more than a quarter said it was above 30 percent) and that the inflation rate of 2.9 percent was nearly five times as high at 13.5 percent.[5] Joining with the public ignorance is the citizens' belief that the published government statistics are wrong. An Excel Omnibus Study from September 20 to September 24, 1996, which was taken in conjunction with the larger survey just discussed, found that 46 percent of the interviewees who had "heard or read about government statistics reporting that the unemployment rate is lower than in recent years" believed these reports to be inaccurate.[6] Citizen ignorance and distrust of basic policy information can be key factors in whether political leaders make sound policies or continue bad ones. *Washington Post* reporters Richard Morin and John Berry, writing about the *Washington Post*/Kaiser Foundation/Harvard University survey, argued that when citizens are wrong on the basic economic data, politicians are afraid to make sound policy decisions.[7] Citizens' ignorance about basic federal government policy information and/or their belief that it is inaccurate undermine the federal policy-making process, and concomitantly the efforts of federal policy analysts and information specialists.

The electronic revolution is now thrown into this maelstrom of citizens' striking ignorance about basic economic and social statistics and the disbelief in their accuracy. That revolution is a mixed blessing—a means that can be used either to foster or to thwart democracy. As to the former, it offers the promise of greater and faster provision of policy information and analysis and of the technical capacity to support citizens and policymakers interacting instantaneously. The electronics age on its dark side threatens mindboggling information overload and the wide transmission of distorted and fabricated information that is difficult to refute. No one can predict whether the electronic revolution will revivify American democracy by bringing citizens and policymakers together in a well-functioning marketplace of policy ideas that facilitates reasoned political debate or will further damage the political process by flooding it with flawed and false information. But two related points can be made. First, the Internet is the freest of markets with almost no barriers to the sending and receiving of information and with limited capacity to validate accuracy or to refute widely disseminated false information. As already noted, the Internet is the latest powerful information means to be used or misused. Second, how the larger information environment plays out will dominate how policy analysis and research are practiced in the federal government and subnational governments and in the policy research industry. These broad factors, not issues concerning theory or methodology, will dominate the shape of the policy analysis profession.

This chapter will establish the broad base for the final one that considers the likely direction of the analytic profession itself. The most discouraging realization is that the profession depends so heavily on factors beyond its control. In particular, political leaders through their behavior can further erode trust in government and in so doing undermine media and public believability in the data and in the analyses of policy analysts and researchers. My fear is that policy analysts will be driven in two different directions. One is to abandon any efforts at neutral competence and be hired guns serving the partisan demands of political masters. The second is to flee to the academy and do policy work that appeals to their university peers but offers little for government policy makers. Both carry the seeds of destruction for the analytic profession as we know it.

THE MEDIA AND PUBLIC POLICY INFORMATION

Unique aspects of the American political system deeply affect the link between the public and elected officials and are critical in the policy information equation. Nowhere is that more clear than in the case of the media, and particularly television, which is now the most powerful medium disseminating political and policy information to the public. As to the uniqueness of the American political system, the political scientist Austin Ranney has pointed out: "Since the early 1900s, the United States has been the only country in the world to choose most of its candidates by the direct primary system, in which anyone can enter the contest for a party's nomination and the selection is made, not, as in most other democracies, by small groups of party leaders, but by ordinary voters who have designated themselves as party members."[8] But even though political parties in this country have never been strong like their Western European counterparts, it is only in the past three decades that parties ceased to have the critical function of choosing their presidential candidates. The media have replaced political parties as the main link between presidential candidates and the voters and between the president and the public. And television with its powerful images has become more and more dominating. In *Channels of Power,* published in 1983, Ranney argued: "Many observers, including myself, believe that the advent of television is the most important change since World War II in just about every aspect of American life, and certainly in the environment in which government functions. . . . [T]he advent of television as the principal source of political reality for most Americans has altered the political game profoundly, perhaps more profoundly than all the parties' rules changes and new state and federal laws put together."[9] Television and the television personalities who dominate the news programs have taken center stage away from print journalism and its pundits.

The profundity of the changes cannot be overstated. First came the shift in the institutions aiding the public in choosing presidential candidates from political parties to the media. The former had as primary functions sorting out and picking candidates and mounting the campaigns to elect them. The media in contrast have a main task of developing and presenting news and entertainment for profit. As Harvard University political scientist Thomas Patterson has pointed out: "[T]he press is not a substitute for political institutions. A press-based electoral system is not a suitable basis for that most pivotal of all decisions, the choice of a president."[10] Second, print journalism lost out to television as the primary supplier of information on political candidates and elected officials. Before the coming of the half-hour news program on television in 1963, a presidential candidate's aides sought, as the best means of selling their man, a favorable column or a front page article in the *Washington Post* or the *New York Times*. The coming of major network primetime, thirty-minute television news programs shifted the goal to a good video of the candidate on the six o'clock news.[11]

The change from the word to the image transformed electoral politics in the Reagan Era as presidential success and high approval ratings came to depend less on presidential policy performance and more on presidential image. Robert Denton argued in *The Primetime Presidency of Ronald Reagan* that what is critical to maintain presidential popularity is "controlling the videos in the evening news" so that television has become "the primary tool of and battleground for governing the nation."[12] Such a statement goes too far in part because Ronald Reagan's powerful political style made him so compelling on television that his TV image and the Reagan persona became one. Other presidential images, as the Bush years made clear, are not as powerful so that policy performance still can count heavily. An example of the shift from word to image will help at this point. In discussing President Reagan, Professor Denton portrayed how Lesley Stahl, CBS News White House correspondent, tried unsuccessfully to show that the president's deeds contradicted his words:

> [Stahl's] video showed Reagan with handicapped Olympians, at a senior citizen housing project, at home riding horses and cutting wood, in visions from Normandy, with the Vietnam Unknown Soldier, and comforting families of dead marines. While the verbal report was critical and negative, the visual was positive and reinforced the values espoused by Reagan for years. A member of Reagan's staff was actually pleased with the piece. "We're in the middle of a campaign and you give us four-and-a-half minutes of great pictures of Ronald Reagan . . . and that's all the American people see." The point is that the pictures tell the story more than the verbiage. Television, as "cool," requires the viewer to participate in the generally positive "Americana" experiences. In effect, the viewers were sharing them (and in some cases sharing them for a second or third time) with Reagan.[13]

A memorable Bill Moyers PBS television program on November 22, 1989 showed Stahl years later still perplexed by the failure of her words, with a bewildered look on her face as she discussed her earlier television program with Moyers. In contrast, Michael Deaver, one of the driving forces behind the presentation of the Reagan image, talked smugly on

Moyers' program about how that positive image overwhelmed Stahl's harsh comments that bespoke of policy failures. Too much must not be made of this example because the comparison really is between an image composed of a charismatic president participating in highly positive activities and a political commentator making derogatory comments. As communications specialist Professor Kathleen Hall Jamieson has pointed out: "The discussion of whether pictures dominate words or words pictures is confused by its assumption that one invariably dominates the other, that music plays no role in cueing recall, and that the impact of each remains the same with repeated exposure."[14] At the same time, Deaver made a telling point in underscoring how Reagan's television image dominated Stahl's television words that pointed out the dishonesty behind that image. Even more profoundly, television images have overwhelmed competing word-driven media such as newspapers and magazines in imparting political and policy information and in interpreting the meaning.

Nowhere is the media role in misshaping American politics and undercutting the key institutions of the political system nearly so visible as in its obsession with scandal. Over the last decade the criticism of the media has risen to new heights. In 1991 University of Virginia political scientist Larry Sabato titled his highly critical book *Feeding Frenzy: How Attack Journalism Has Transformed American Politics*; Suzanne Garment, American Enterprise Institute scholar and former Washington columnist for the *Wall Street Journal*, chose as her title in her caustic criticism of the media, *Scandal: The Crisis of Mistrust in American Politics*.[15] The charge is that the media have degenerated to "pack" or "junkyard" journalism with a self-righteous bent to find any flaw in less-than-perfect candidates and to "go after a wounded politician like sharks in a feeding frenzy."[16] A respected member of the media, Richard Clurman, former chief of correspondents for the Time-Life News Service, wrote: "By the mid-80s, the media had made themselves the cop on every beat, the umpire and unofficial scorer of the biggest game going—the affairs of the world. Too often journalists played the game, as one of them said, as if it were 'all pitch and no catch.' "[17] This often irresponsible scandalmongering, where the media focus far more on gossip than governance, has helped create a crisis of mistrust and a flight from the substance of policy making, including policy data, to personal character.

At the same time the media is destroying its own credibility. A routine ploy by presidential candidates is to try to lessen the damage of a negative media story by claiming, too often with justification, media bias. *Los Angeles Times* reporter Tom Rosenstiel caught the problem in discussing the top print reporters, especially those in Washington: "Some made their biggest reputation by being TV pontificators—staking out provocative positions and doling out advice on TV talk shows. Others did it by writing essay-like features, more personal than even straight analysis stories, which were now being played on page one."[18] In my research on this and other books, I have often used off-the-record interviews with print journalists, trust them, and find their knowledge and insights invaluable. At the same time, I am amazed at how much personal opinion has become the common currency of straight news stories. Newspapers no longer are the place where readers can find a scrupulous effort to report "just the facts" in news coverage. It is a shift in another institution that has been caught up in a rapidly changing environment where it is partly culpable but also a victim of powerful forces beyond its control. Be that as it may, the result is to further complicate the public's choosing competent elected officials and sorting out what is sound information and analysis.

Distrust permeates and misshapes presidential and congressional campaigns. Recent national elections underscore how much the public distrusts the establishment media people who in turn have come to distrust the candidates. Increasingly, members of the establishment media see the presidential campaign in particular as a horse race where candidates are constantly trying to manipulate the public to gain advantage, and so focus the spotlight on the candidates' flawed character rather than analyzing policy statements. In *Out of Order*, Thomas Patterson's penetrating critique of the press, he highlighted the media's "unrelenting negativism" and its impact:

> [Candidates] have to communicate with an electorate that is continuously warned by the press to mistrust them. A wall of suspicion is thus created, and disbelief sets in. . . .
>
> It is this climate of suspicion that allows a candidacy like Ross Perot's to surface and thrive. The press is not the chief cause of this political malaise, but it bears primary responsibility for creating the campaign environment that encourages the malaise. . . .
>
> A well-functioning [electoral] system should strengthen presidential leadership, give force to voters' opinions, and set the stage for effective governance. The present system does none of these things. Its weaknesses are substantial and painfully apparent: self-selected candidates, overloaded voters, a miscast press.[19]

Patterson offers a most disturbing bill of indictment where distrust reigns in the process by which America chooses presidents and *pari passu* makes it unlikely that candidates will have a real chance to address the systemic problems that demand such a high level of competence. This state of affairs reverberates through the federal policy information and analysis process.

FEDERAL POLICY STAFFS, THINK TANKS, AND THE POLITICS OF CREDIBILITY

Federal policy analysis and research offices and nongovernment policy research organizations have befouled their own nests, thereby diminishing their credibility with the media and the public. Some of the cases have been inadvertent where experts legitimately disagreed and the public interpreted the give-and-take as meaning both were wrong or were trying to mislead citizens. But too many cases involve acts by members of policy research organizations in which professional staff should have recognized the threats to credibility. One clear example is when one policy organization accuses another one of lying, distorting facts and arguments, or acting in some other highly unprofessional manner. In the case of the federal government, however, the most serious assaults on credibility generally come from overt acts by presidents, top agency political executives, and Congress. The credibility of federal analytic offices and data development organizations (e.g., the Bureau of Labor Statistics and Bureau of the Census) are compromised by acts of the policy analysts' and researchers' political masters who are focusing on more politically pressing problems than the sanctity of the numbers and well may have little or no appreciation of or concern for how their actions can diminish the credibility of government data.

Credibility Starts at the Top

The basic point about political leaders being far more important than federal government policy analysts and information developers in the latter's credibility keeps recurring. Readers may feel that the author, to quote from *Hamlet*, "doth protest too much, me-thinks" in absolving the policy professionals of primary blame. My purpose, however, is not to praise the purity of the professionals but to specify clearly their limited role in the politics of credibility, even in the case of the numbers themselves. Examples abound. Two recent ones particularly stress the credibility issue. Voters in Arizona and California approved ballot initiatives allowing doctors to prescribe marijuana to reduce pain. The Clinton administration announced that the two state initiatives would be overridden by federal marijuana policy and maintained that no evidence supported the use of marijuana for pain reduction. Anthony Lewis, the distinguished *New York Times* columnist, pointed out the falsity of the federal government's argument about available evidence and the reason for it:

> The medical claims and counterclaims are just that: claims. They have never been resolved by approved scientific methods. And the ad-

ministration response effectively blocked what could have been a highly useful test of the claims in Arizona and California. . . .

The Clinton Administration was not alone in its reaction to the state referendums. Conservatives who usually talk about states' rights cheered the Clinton decision to override state law.

The reason is no secret. Drugs arouse paranoia in politicians. That is why, for many decades, drug policy has been immune to examination in the light of reason and experience.[20]

The second example arises from the long-running controversy over whether American troops had been exposed to Iraqi chemical weapons during or immediately after the Gulf War. *New York Times* reporter Philip Shenon in a special report entitled "Chronicle of Denial," which drew on his extended coverage of the chemical arms exposure controversy, zeroed in on the government's credibility:

After years of denials, the Pentagon now acknowledges that more than 20,000 troops may have been exposed when a battalion of American combat engineers blew up the Kamisiyah ammunition depot in the southern Iraqi desert in March 1991. . . .

While the relationship between . . . episodes [of exposure] and the veterans' health problems remains unclear, the resulting credibility crisis from so many years of denial has only added to the misery of gulf war veterans whose health has faltered since the war.

Many of them are now left with the suspicion that military commanders cared more about the perception of the war as a military triumph than about getting to the bottom of the health problems reported by those who were sent to fight. Many ailing gulf war veterans are unwilling at this point to accept any explanation from the Pentagon. . . .

A review of thousands of Government documents and hundreds of interviews with government officials, scientists, doctors and veterans' advocates undermines the Pentagon's claims since the war that it had aggressively investigated the causes of the illnesses reported by gulf war veterans.

The Pentagon has insisted that its earlier errors in public pronouncements were the result of incomplete, inadequate information. Secretary [William J.] Perry said in December that any perception that the Defense Department had tried to withhold information on the issue was "dead wrong."[21]

The potential cover-up of chemical weapons in the Gulf War has involved current and now retired top military officers including General Norman Schwarzkopf, commander of American troops in the war; then chairman of the Joint Chiefs of Staff, Colin Powell; the Pentagon; and possibly President Bush. The issue is whether the federal government lied, or at least purposely misled, a half million-plus troops in order to protect military and civilian reputations and prevent claims that could run in the tens of billions of dollars if veterans have been harmed by the exposure to Iraqi chemical weapons.

The Gulf War case could come to rank with the other information abuses of epic proportions: Vietnam, Watergate, Iran-contra, and the savings and loan scandal. Writing in 1976 on Watergate, Elliot Richardson, one of the most honorable of public servants, drew from an earlier case that threatened government credibility, the 1958 shooting down of American pilot Gary Powers' U-2 reconnaissance plane over the Soviet Union and the subsequent denial by President Dwight Eisenhower, to observe:

> When looking back over this [U-2] experience, I came across James Madison's statement: "A popular Government, without popular information, or the means of acquiring it, is but a Prologue to a Farce or a Tragedy; or, perhaps both." I was struck by its relevance to Watergate. Here, with a vengeance, was a government responsible to the people which had deprived them both of information and of the means of acquiring it. The consequence, which had at first seemed only the prologue to a farce, soon became the prologue to a tragedy and, for Watergate actors, tragedy itself. But for the impetus it gave to the adoption of reforms and the restoration of openness, Watergate might have been a tragedy for popular government also.
>
> In a sense, all the abuses of Watergate had been abuses of information: its theft, distortion, fabrication, misuse, misrepresentation, concealment, and suppression.[22]

In the two decades since Richardson wrote, his characterization of Watergate as a massive abuse of information now applies to a host of later cases; however, the reforms and restoration of openness have been inadequate barriers to the kinds of information abuses Richardson catalogued. And the question leaps forth: *Why should the public and the media trust the federal government when presidents, Congress members, and the federal agencies have stolen, distorted, fabricated, misused, misrepresented, concealed, and suppressed information in a frightening number of cases?*

Information credibility often has been undermined through acts of omission or commission by the top political officials whom the federal policy analysts and information development specialists serve, the federal analytic and information staffs themselves, and the nonprofit or private policy research organizations. A number of examples have already been considered, including the well-publicized 1995 honest numbers dispute when Congress loudly, but wrongly, accused the president and his top policy people including OMB director Alice Rivlin of cooking the economic projections and budget estimates. Think tanks on the ideological left and right have publicly attacked each others' information as distorted or worse. Even when the disputes over information and interpretation are conducted in a professional manner without wild accusations, the efforts can undercut credibility. In a prescient statement made in 1978 concerning impeccably credentialed experts who analyze the same body of data but arrive at opposite interpretations and policy prescriptions, Henry Aaron lamented: "What is an ordinary member of the tribe to do when the witch doctors disagree?"[23] Political scientist Hugh Heclo made a statement even more relevant today than when he argued in 1979 that "experts [make] more sophisticated claims and counterclaims to the point that the nonspecialist becomes inclined to concede everything and believe nothing he hears."[24] Heclo in effect answered the Aaron question—"believe nothing."

An Insidious Danger

A far less visible threat to credibility—the federal government's discontinuation of relevant databases and underinvestment or actual disinvestment in information development capacity—may be the most dangerous of all in rendering the basic government data unsound. The charge is that the federal government, which has been the main developer of economic and social statistics dating back to the first census in 1790, through shortsightedness and penny-wise, pound-foolish actions is risking a deteriorated database so unsound it cannot support reasoned policy deliberations. The serious cutbacks in information capacity began in the Reagan presidency and led the General Accounting Office in 1988 to claim that the administration had "gravely eroded" information development capacity in the executive branch and in so doing had failed to execute the "responsibility of [the federal] government to the people of this country."[25] New York Times reporter Jonathan Fuerbringer highlighted the dangers for policy makers when he wrote that "statisticians and economists, both in and out of government, say that a combination of budget cuts and deregulation—much of it a legacy of the Reagan Era—is eroding important [statistical] yardsticks and undermining policymakers striving to guide the economy."[26] The Reagan Era was marked by sharp reductions in federal information development staffs and in the collection of data, by the failure to improve information sampling techniques, and by the deregulation of industries such as the airlines that reduced company information reporting. These changes together severely decreased the variety and amount of collected data. In my review of the damage wrought by the Reagan administration changes, I pointed out:

> [T]he quality of the basic economic data that support the decisions
> made by government at all levels . . . can affect billions of dollars and
> millions of lives. Such data are the primary fuel that runs the decision
> process. If these numbers are inaccurate, not timely, or not relevant for
> key policy decisions by governments and businesses, the policymaking
> process can collapse. Loss of confidence in them can paralyze the process.
> On the other hand, misplaced confidence in faulty statistics—not know-
> ing how bad the numbers are—portends bad policies. Although policy-
> makers and the public need to understand that available methods
> technically cannot yield faultless numbers, it is reasonable to expect that
> every effort within reason is being made to obtain sound data.[27]

The effort is not being made. There have been some attempts at improvement since 1988, but by and large the federal government information effort continues to deteriorate. *USA Today* reporter Beth Belton
pointed out that the *Economist* magazine over the years has ranked the
United States sixth or lower on the quality of their government reports
and observed: "Canada and Great Britain spend five times more per
dollar of GDP than the US spends to collect and analyze economic
data."[28] *Washington Post* columnist Robert Samuelson blamed Congress
for "slowly crippling" the federal information development effort "by
starving it for money" and underscored the shortsightedness:

> Between fiscal 1990 and 1997, the Bureau of Economic Analysis
> (which prepares the GDP) requested $36.7 million for statistical improve-
> ments. Of the request, Congress approved only $6.5 million. In five of
> the seven years, no money at all was approved. The BEA's experience
> is typical; most statistical agencies are being squeezed. . . .
> The irony is that the budget savings are puny. In 1995, the 11
> most important statistical agencies spent about $1.2 billion, reports Janet
> Norwood, the former commissioner of the Bureau of Labor Statistics. This
> was less than one-tenth of 1 percent of federal spending of $1.5 trillion.[29]

Needed data not collected may not be retrievable at a later date. Unsound or marginally sound data often cannot be upgraded to soundness.

The federal government underinvestment, disinvestment, and
discontinuation of needed data collection can blight future policy making. The danger to the underlying federal data system—and it is critical
to underscore this point—is a future one. The capacity still exists to
produce sound numbers. But that capacity relative to the task is being
eroded; and, unless the damage ceases, the data can become unsound,
not because of partisan bias, but because of inadequacies in staff competence and data development capacity. It is not that BLS or Census will

cease to strive for soundness but that cutbacks in staff, research and development funds, and needed external databases will finally undermine the government data system. The point has been stressed that the biggest threat to honest numbers is political, not theoretical and methodological. Yet, ultimately the political decisions to starve the federal statistical units can lead to debilitating technical weaknesses so that the federal government will no longer have the capacity to produce sound numbers.

CIVIC VIRTUE

The preceding subsection focused on the future danger of undermining the soundness of the data while this section centers on the most immediate threat to credibility of the numbers—the American public that is the wild card in the policy analysis and information equation. The notion of citizens' obligations to the nation is critical for understanding the present turbulence in the American political system. The founders of the republic did not envision each citizen eligible to vote as a paragon of virtue endlessly reading political pamphlets. They were too realistic for that, but the founders did understand that rights and obligations needed to be linked and balanced for the political system to work. The problem is that the postwar era brought a shift toward rights and away from obligations. Citizens expect more and more from government and yet see themselves as less and less responsible for how government performs. The consequence has been the declining legitimacy of government. Trust in government evolves best when active citizens choose elected officials carefully and watch them closely enough to see that these officials merit reelection. Trust in government is a central element of democracy going beyond structure. It is the fundamental intangible factor that, if lost, can reduce government effectiveness, no matter what that government does, until trust is restored. Once lost, restoration of trust in government ought to be an overriding political task of federal elected leaders because the absence of trust can breed a political divisiveness that makes effective governance exceedingly difficult.

   The place to start in our look at the role of the citizen in American democracy is *The Federalist* written mainly by Alexander Hamilton and James Madison. (John Jay, the third author, fell ill and wrote only a few of the eighty-five essays.) The noted historian Clinton Rossiter called *The Federalist* "the most important [American] work in political science . . . [and] the one product of the American mind that is rightly counted among the classics of political theory."[30] What is so amazing is that *The Federalist*, authored under the pseudonym "Publius," is a collection of essays to the public "written with a haste that often bordered on the frantic, printed and published [in New York City newspapers] as if they were the most perishable kind of daily news," to quote Rossiter again.[31] These brilliant pieces on the meaning of the Constitution, finally collected in *The Federalist*, were not a learned tome aimed at august scholars, but newspaper articles to inform voters. Publius did not feel the need to coddle, nor would the authors let citizens off the hook today.

What would the two great constitutionalists think if they suddenly sprang to life in this age of instant, interactive information? Madison, who lived until he was eighty-five, never swayed from his fundamental belief that a well-informed, diligent citizenry stood as the final and most important bulwark protecting the American political system. In discussing civic virtue, Madison pointed out that mere structure (for example, the Constitution's now venerated checks and balances that Madison helped craft) would not be sufficient to keep elected officials working for the public good and warned: "To suppose that any form of government will secure liberty or happiness without any virtue in the people is a chimerical idea. If there be sufficient virtue and intelligence in the community, it will be exercised in the selection of these men [public officials]; so that we do not depend on their virtue, or put confidence in our rulers, but in the people who are to choose them."[32] Madison would be appalled on reading today that survey after survey testifies to the extent that the public is uninformed about the most basic aspects of the American political system. On whatever dimension we look, citizens show scant knowledge about government and governance. Madison today would not find the healthy informed skepticism by citizens that he saw as central to viable democratic governance but rather an ignorant cynicism. In the absence of citizen virtue and intelligence, Madison could only conclude that the worst enemy of the Constitution is not the politicians but the often ill-informed public.

Alexander Hamilton, who served as President George Washington's secretary of the treasury, stands out as the nation's first, and likely greatest, policy wonk because he both understood the numbers and had a compelling vision of a future America. Hamilton became the key actor building the governmental foundation needed in order for the United States to become a great nation, leading the historian Forrest McDonald to label Hamilton as Washington's "prime minister" in the first president's second term.[33] Paul Van Riper called Hamilton the "guiding genius" who kept the new government afloat and acclaimed him the "founder of the American administrative state"; Jerry McCaffery argued that "Hamilton's role in debt management, securing the currency, and providing and defending a stable revenue base mark him as a Founding Father of the American budget system."[34] Returned to earth, Hamilton of all his eighteenth-century peers, even his brilliant antagonist Thomas Jefferson, would have seen the promise of the electronic revolution for developing sound policy information for government policy makers and the public. He would recognize immediately the tremendous potential of the new technology to enlighten citizens and help arm them with sufficient virtue and intelligence to exert an open-minded skepticism of government, rather than today's apathetic distrust. At the same time, Hamilton and Madison both would be struck by the nation's policy complexity and the difficulty of becoming the well-informed, politically engaged citizen Publius called for in *The Federalist* and that the Constitution continues to demand. In particular, Hamilton, the great number cruncher, would see the perils of information overload for sound governance and the tremendous burden on citizens if they are to understand the policy problems facing the United States. Whether the fantastic new electronic technologies will fulfill their promise or put American democracy further in peril is unclear. No technological fix, no Bill Gatesian wizardry, will overcome citizen indifference and ignorance. Like it or not, just as the nation's founders foresaw, the problem and the solution remain the American public.

Joining citizens' ignorance is their belief that the basic government economic data are inaccurate. The previously discussed Excel Omnibus Study carried out September 20–24, 1996 for the *Washington Post* found that 45 percent thought a "big reason" for the inaccuracy was because "the federal government makes too many mistakes," and 48 percent believed a big reason to be that "the federal government deliberately manipulates the numbers to mislead the public about how the economy is really doing."[35] Citizen ignorance and distrust of federal government policy information can be critical in whether or not politicians are willing to make sound policies or discontinue bad ones. *Washington Post* reporters Richard Morin and John Berry in discussing the results of the *Washington Post*/Kaiser Foundation/Harvard survey quoted University of Nebraska economist William Walstad, a specialist on the study of the relationship of people's actual knowledge about the economy: "[A]cross the board, economic knowledge has the most consistent influence on people's views of the economy, creating the basis on which good public policy can be made and ill-conceived policy can be countered."[36] Then, they observed: "Walstad and other analysts note the flip side: When the public is wrong about so many basic facts about the economy, it's very difficult for politicians to make good policy decisions."[37] As examples, consider Social Security and federal income rates. Current retirees overwhelmingly believe that their contributions have fully paid for their Social Security benefits while most have contributed but a small part. Yet, cutting benefits or even correcting the inflation rate used to adjust benefits are attacked as robbing retirees. Although the United States has low federal income tax rates compared to other highly industrialized nations, many Americans believe they pay the highest rates in the world and see all income tax increases as unwarranted or worse. Under the circumstances, sensible policies would put politicians at grave risk.

Citizens' ignorance about basic policy information and/or their belief that it is dishonestly manipulated by the government strikes at the core of American democracy. This brings us to the disturbing dichotomy between whether sound, relevant, timely policy information can be developed (a question of the producers' resources and competence) and whether such data will be considered credible by the public (a question of the recipients' interpretation). The former depends primarily on what goes into it—the quality of the available information, which rests in part on the level of available resources, and the policy analysts' and researchers' capability and integrity. Credibility depends mainly on the receiver of the information. To illustrate this distinction, consider the overall unemployment rate developed each month by the Bureau of Labor Statistics. This statistic would appear to be a pristine case of an honest number developed by federal government staffs that have high-level technicians who use acceptable statistical methods for gathering and processing the underlying data and who are almost militantly scrupulous about both their objectivity and their independence from political manipulation. Beyond BLS capability and integrity is another factor: the dynamics of the political and policy environment. A president would find it almost impossible to pressure BLS successfully to produce a more favorable unemployment number to help him politically because BLS professionals, even if they did not go public, would "leak" word of any White House effort to do so. That is, the honesty of the data is reinforced by the political dangers of pressuring BLS by a president or his political executives.

To argue that widely published government statistics are honest in the sense of being nonpartisan numbers developed by competent professionals using acceptable methods is not to claim the data derived cannot be challenged on legitimate grounds. For example, there is no single agreed on definition of unemployment. Critics have claimed that the current statistic counts people with a minimum of paid employment in the period or fails to include discouraged workers who want work but do not seek jobs because they have given up hope of finding them. These definitional arguments will go on. So will ones about field techniques used. Finally, analysts can disagree strongly on what a number means. If unemployment jumps from 5.1 percent to 5.5 percent during a Democratic presidency, Republicans could interpret it as the sign of a serious economic decline while the Democrats could claim the increase is but a blip on a healthy economic path. Economists with no ax to grind—Henry Aaron's "witch doctors"—too can arrive at opposite opinions about the meaning of the change. All of the kinds of disagreements discussed in this paragraph are legitimate among honest, reasonable people. What is not warranted is the growing citizen belief that the federal government fabricates its basic economic data.

The new dimension is that the government statistics are being challenged, not as in the past because of the definition used or the methodology or staff competence, but because those data are believed to be knowingly manipulated to mislead or actually lie to the public. Such a claim is one of the most serious charges that can be made against the government and its professional policy analysts and researchers. It could be that the public does not appreciate the distinction being made or else does not see the allegations as anything more than reflecting its overall distrust of the federal government carried to doubting that government's numbers. The government data that information professionals believe to be safe from fabrication and hence inviolable, citizens perceive as simply another place where the federal government can twist the truth to its advantage. A fundamental problem between the public and the policy information specialists is that the latter see the Pentagon being less than honest on Iraqi chemical weapons or HHS dissembling on the tested efficacy of marijuana to reduce pain as completely different from BLS publishing a politically manipulated unemployment statistic. Moreover, the specialists recognize that disagreements over the definition of unemployment, the appropriate sample frame, or the interpretation of a change in the monthly unemployment rate do not in any way indicate that BLS fixed the unemployment statistic because of presidential or congressional pressures. This basic difference between the public and the professionals helps explain the collapsing public credibility of the underlying federal data system that historically has supplied honest, credible numbers.

A clear danger is that alternative information will be believed by the public in part because it fits their predilections and in part because those data are seen as coming from a source outside the federal government. This supposed legitimacy will become increasingly important if the Internet reaches a far larger number of people. Consider the case of Pierre Salinger, the respected reporter who relied on false information on the Internet and went public to claim "friendly fire" downed TWA Flight 800. His gullibility adds another dimension to the problem of valid information—the fantastic growth of false information spewed out by electronic devices and the increasing tendency for professionals and the public not to be able to tell truth from falsehood. We might smile when a veteran reporter and former Kennedy White House aide falls for a bogus story on the Internet or pity his embarrassment at age seventy-one, but the problem goes far beyond the individual case. *Chicago Tribune* reporter James Coates, in his article on the Salinger incident, claimed: "America is awash in a growing and often disruptive avalanche of false information that takes on a life of its own in the electronic ether on the Internet, talk radio and voice mail until it becomes impervious to denial and debunking."[38] Bad information may drive out good as people take as true what they want to believe and refuse to accept hard evidence refuting that information no matter how outlandish. Internet information and interpretation can be unchallengeable for true believers, blocking out refutations from other sources including the think tanks and the established media.

Northwestern University sociologist Bernard Beck argued that the Salinger case captures a growing trend: " 'There is a very strong strain of media populism because of the Internet in today's society, and people grasp for these false stories because they think the Internet can be trusted more than can major institutions of America.' "[39] *San Francisco Chronicle* reporter Edward Lempinen in another piece looking at the Internet after the Salinger fiasco went to the heart of the information validity problem in discussing a computer consultant Ed Mead: "With thousands of other info junkies, Mead stands at a new frontier in electronic culture where the distinction between verified news, popular speculation and wild conspiracy theory is increasingly blurred. . . . [S]ome critics worry that the Net's lack of standards for accuracy will cause confusion and further erode the trust in public institutions."[40] That the Internet is becoming more believable to persons than the major public and private institutions historically responsible for developing and disseminating data and analysis is truly a striking development. It is also an extremely dangerous one as my colleague and Internet authority Andrew Gordon has made clear:

> No matter how scrupulously maintained the initial starting point, the cybernaut may be linked to sites containing information which is hopelessly out of date, half-baked, insensitively written or just plain wrong. Many popular sites are maintained by volunteers, transient graduate students, people lacking the resources or initiative to bring information up to date, or individuals who are strongly biased on important issues. Easy access to a wealth of information promotes a flowering of democratic ideals, but users are often hopelessly confused about which information has been subject to cross-checking and scrutiny.[41]

The electronic revolution is upon us, both citizens and policy analysts alike. Given the spectacular pace of technical breakthroughs, increasingly sophisticated means of interactive communications will set the tone of policy information development, interpretation, and use. Should a modern day Ned Ludd try to stop it, not as in nineteenth-century England to save jobs, but to protect the nation? In considering the promise and peril of the electronic revolution for policy making, for citizen involvement, and ultimately for American democracy, the former should not be ignored but the potential harms loom largest. The apt metaphor is the tank that Denzel Washington commanded in the movie *Courage Under Fire,* where using this high technology weapon, he destroyed an American tank and killed its crew in the confusion of a night battle in Desert Storm. The investigators ruled the action justified because every effort was made to determine if the tank was an Iraqi vehicle that had penetrated the U.S. tank columns in the chaos of the darkness, smoke, and sand. The inadvertent killing of American troops by their comrades represents a case of what is called "friendly fire." The sophisticated machinery being used with state-of-the-art skills for the desired objective of destroying the enemy tank not only failed to achieve the goal but inadvertently hit an American tank. This high-tech super tank provides the vivid image of a powerful electronic device that can be used either for good or evil and, even when employed for good goals, can be inadvertently destructive.

NOTES

1. James Fallows, *Breaking the News: How the Media Undermines American Democracy,* Pantheon, 1996, p. 7.
2. Martin P. Wattenberg, *The Decline of American Political Parties,* Harvard University Press, 1984, p. 13.
3. James MacGregor Burns, *The Power to Lead,* Simon & Schuster, 1984, pp. 160–161.
4. Gaillard Hunt (ed.), *The Writings of James Madison,* Putnam, 1910, vol. 9, p. 103.
5. All data in this and the previous sentence are from the *Washington Post*/Kaiser Family Foundation/Harvard University Survey Project, *Survey of Americans and Economists on the Economy,* October 1996, pp. 2–4.
6. Unpublished survey results supplied by the *Washington Post.*
7. *Washington Post,* October 13, 1996.
8. Austin Ranney, *Channels of Power,* Basic Books, 1983, pp. 93.
9. Ibid., pp. 89 and 123.
10. Thomas E. Patterson, *Out of Order,* Knopf, 1993, p. 52.
11. David Halberstam, *The Powers That Be,* Dell, 1979, pp. 569–570.
12. Robert E. Denton Jr., *The Primetime Presidency of Ronald Reagan: The Era of the Television Presidency,* Praeger, 1988, pp. 71 and 91.
13. Ibid., p. 70.
14. Kathleen Hall Jamieson, *Dirty Politics: Deception, Distraction, and Democracy,* Oxford University Press, 1992, p. 127.
15. Larry J. Sabato, *Feeding Frenzy: How Attack Journalism Has Transformed American Politics,* Free Press, 1991, and Suzanne Garment, *Scandal: The Crisis of Mistrust in American Politics,* Time Books, 1991.

16. Sabato, *Feeding Frenzy*, p. 1.

17. Richard M. Clurman, *Beyond Malice: The Media's Years of Reckoning*, Transaction Books, 1988, p. 27.

18. Tom Rosenstiel, *Strange Bedfellows: How Television and the Presidential Candidates Changed American Politics, 1992*, Hyperion, 1993, p. 50.

19. Patterson, *Out of Order*, pp. 172–173, 242.

20. *New York Times*, January 6, 1997.

21. *New York Times*, January 2, 1997.

22. Elliot Richardson, *The Creative Balance: Government, Politics, and the Individual in America's Third Century*, Holt, Rinehart & Winston, 1976, p. 105.

23. Henry J. Aaron, *Politics and Professors*, Brookings, 1978, p. 159.

24. Hugh Heclo, "Issue Networks and the Executive Establishment," in Anthony King (ed.), *The New American Political System*, Yale University Press, 1979, pp. 12–13.

25. U.S. General Accounting Office, "Program Evaluation Issues," *Transition Series*, GAO/OCG–89–8-TR, November 1988, pages 1 and 7.

26. *New York Times*, October 30, 1989.

27. Walter Williams, *Mismanaging America: The Rise of the Anti-Analytic Presidency*, University Press of Kansas, 1990, p. 70. The review of Reagan information policy is at pp. 69–72.

28. *USA Today*, December 3, 1996.

29. *Washington Post National Weekly Edition*, December 9–15, 1996.

30. Clinton Rossiter, "Introduction," in Alexander Hamilton, James Madison and John Jay, *The Federalist Papers*, New American Library, 1961, p. vii.

31. Ibid., p. viii.

32. Quoted in Herbert J. Storing, *What the Anti-Federalists Were For: The Political Thought of the Opponents of the Constitution*, University of Chicago Press, 1981, p. 72.

33. Forrest McDonald, *Alexander Hamilton: A Biography*, Norton, 1979, pp. 285–305.

34. Paul P. Van Riper, "The American Administrative State: Wilson and the Founders," in Ralph C. Chandler (ed.), *A Centennial History of the American Administrative State*, Free Press, 1987, p. 12; Jerry L. McCaffery, "The Development of Public Budgeting in the United States," in ibid., p. 356.

35. Unpublished survey results furnished by the *Washington Post*. This survey was carried out to supplement the *Washington Post*/Kaiser Family Foundation/Harvard University survey previously discussed.

36. *Washington Post*, October 13, 1996.

37. Ibid.

38. *Seattle Times*, November 11, 1996.

39. Quoted in ibid.

40. *San Francisco Chronicle*, November 20, 1996.

41. Andrew C. Gordon, "Journalism and the Internet," *Media Studies Journal*, vol. 9, no. 3, Summer 1995, p.174.

11 | Whither Federal Policy Analysis?

The last chapter considered how the current hostile political environment and the electronics era with its information overload affect the development and use of policy research and analysis. This chapter addresses three interrelated questions: What should be the main objective(s) of public policy analysis and which standards should guide policy analysts generally and specifically in government? What should be the role and functions of federal policy analysis staffs in this time of both high skepticism about the national government and its ability to ameliorate social problems and a rapidly increasing movement toward devolving federal responsibilities and funds to state and local governments? What can be done to develop and/or support strong social policy analytic and research efforts in the federal government? The first two questions are fundamental ones focusing on the federal policy analyst's raison d'être. The beginning inquiry looks specifically at what policy analysts in government should try to accomplish and what kind of professional standards should govern their efforts. The second is its organizational embodiment seeking to determine a suitable institutional place for federal policy analysis units in a time markedly different from the halcyon period of American overconfidence three decades earlier.

The final question of the future direction of the federal policy analysis and research effort must take account of larger forces. First, the future path of social policy analysis depends heavily on how the newest phase of American federalism evolves. At question are the appropriate goals and functions of the federal executive branch itself in administering grants-in-aid to states and localities and the specific mission of the social agencies in today's rapidly changing federalism. Second, as the last chapter discussed, the direction of policy analysis is bound up in the striking technological changes in the electronic era, the public's ignorance of the major policy-making data, and its rising belief that the federal government fabricates basic statistics (e.g., unemployment and inflation) for political purposes. The information and misinformation that pour forth today so often are weapons in ideological battles and the attacks are so fierce that the nation is eroding the base of agreed upon sound numbers that can support reasoned deliberations. The information developed by the major government and private and nonprofit institutions that historically supplied a solid database for well-informed debate appears to be losing credibility and this leads to the book's final point: First and foremost, the restoration of credible numbers to underpin policy making demands strong, sustained political leadership, but policy analysts too have an important role.

GOALS AND STANDARDS

In making the case for the traditional role of the policy analyst seeking to produce a better basis for policy making, employing tools and techniques generally consistent with the concept of neutral competence, the main alternative needs to be set out and critiqued. To do so, I will draw heavily on a penetrating review essay by University of Chicago professor Edward Lawlor. He considered three books which set out and argue for a new direction in policy analysis that can be labeled "the argumentative school or perspective" and noted: "If there is any movement in the conceptualization and practice of policy analysis, it is the emergence of the rhetorical, argumentative, interpretative, narrative and advocacy perspectives on planning and policy analysis."[1] Lawlor's review focused most of its attention on *The Argumentative Turn in Policy Analysis and Planning* edited by Frank Fischer and John Forester (see Note 1). What immediately stands out about the volume is how different the several authors and their perspectives are from traditional policy analysis and from former or current federal policy analysts such as Alice Rivlin, Robert Reischauer, Robert Levine, William Morrill, and Lawrence Lynn. The first thing to note about the new direction is the strong planning focus. Although the two most successful social policy analysis units had "plans" or "planning" in their titles, the terms in no way implied an urban planning approach. Rightly or wrongly, the early policy analysts in fact either ignored or explicitly rejected that long-established orientation. Second, if any of the authors in the Fischer and Forester volume are economists, their brief résumés do not note it. Third, and most revealing, none of the authors appear to have had extensive service in federal policy analysis offices. The argumentative school proponents in the Fischer and Forester book range across a number of academic areas including political science, sociology, urban and regional planning, and public policy and administration and for the most part have no significant government experience—or, perhaps more importantly, do not see it as important enough to include in their résumés. As the British say, "different as chalk and cheese" in backgrounds from the traditional policy analyst economists who both have held high positions in the federal analytic offices and readily highlight this past service.

Although the argumentative perspective offers a wide range of ideas and worldviews, clear themes about analytic goals and operational styles can be discerned. Bruce Jennings, the executive director of the Hastings Center, has cast the ends of policy analysis in its most moralistic wrapping:

> It is my contention that policy analysis ought to be held to a higher normative standard, one that attempts to capture a civic conception of participatory governance and policy debate leading to the emergence of a guiding consensus on the fundamental and common ends of public life. . . . It aims to inform public policy . . . with standards and ideals that ask the community to be better than it has in the past. . . . Policy analysis as counsel strives . . . to fashion an interpretation of what the common good and justice require that can survive a collective process of rational assessment and deliberation.[2]

The thrust of Jennings' argument is clear: The policy analyst is a moralist seeking a higher order, a better world. It is not clear, however, whether an individual analyst could hold such tenets and still work in hierarchical institutions and serve elected officials and their appointees. In his Fischer and Forester volume piece, political scientist John Dryzek claims without qualification that the argumentative approach must involve "consensus formation [that] might well be distorted by the influence of hierarchies based on prestige, professional status, or argumentative ability" and that the analyst's main task is to defeat this distortion:

> A vindication of the argumentative turn in policy and planning therefore requires a radicalization in the form of relentless efforts on the part of the analyst to counter these agents of distortion. . . . [Analysts] can choose to side with authoritarian technocracy or with liberal democracy. My own position is that defensible policy analysis must side with open communication and unrestrictive participation; in other words, with participatory and discursive democracy.[3]

The policy analyst is thus cast as a radicalized moralist with a true believer vision of liberal democracy, which guiding code appears to rule out policy analysts serving a duly elected government unless its political officials and their appointees fully accept the moralistic vision.

The operational theme of the argumentative school is exemplified by James Throgmorton, a professor in the University of Iowa's Graduate Program in Urban and Regional Planning: "I want to suggest that all planning and analysis is rhetorical, and that tools such as survey research, computer modeling, and forecasting can be thought of as rhetorical tropes; that is, as figures of speech and argument that give persuasive power to larger narratives of what they are a part."[4] Lawlor interpreted Throgmorton's statement as leading to "analysis as mere marketing, adding quantitative or analytic justification to political positions that are preordained. . . . [and] practicing analysts merely as 'hired guns' for a given political agenda."[5] Although from a different perspective than that of the argumentative school, an even more blatant version of the hired-gun mentality is found in political scientist Terry Moe's already discussed notion of "responsive competence" that he holds should replace neutral competence.[6] As I indicated in my 1990 critique of the concept as it applies to serving a president: "Responsive competence, however, can degenerate into just plain responsiveness driven by personal loyalty to the 'man,' without much competence."[7]

Lawlor's final paragraph in his review captured the fundamental flaws in the proposed new direction for policy analysis:

> To disconnect policy analysts from their disciplinary roots and charge them with the general communicative functions espoused by the new argumentative school would not only remove "tools" as a defining feature of the field, it would further undermine the already shaky intellectual identity of the field. Postpositivism and so-called postmodernism in policy analysis is a swamp of ambiguity, relativism, and self-doubt. The new argumentation, framed as an integral part of the policy process, and with an unapologetic normative agenda, creates more problems for the policy analysis business than it solves. To paraphrase a famous Texas politician, "The new argumentation dog can't hunt."[8]

Lawlor's main concern is with policy analysis as a profession—how the activity is defined, which standards of credentialing apply, and how policy analysts differ from other professionals such as lawyers and journalists. He, like I, see policy analysts adhering to the research standards of the university as the guide to behavior and seeking to produce analysis without a political spin. Rejected are approaches that either (1) start with a preconceived argument and selectively present only the evidence that supports the case, or (2) try to figure out what answers the political masters want and provide them, however shaky the evidence.

The question must be put, however, as to whether the notion of neutral competence as a standard is realistic either for government policy analysts or for researchers in independent public policy research organizations. At best, the answer is of the "yes, but" variety. Recall poor Judy Feder who told President-elect Clinton the "truth" as advised by Senator Jay Rockefeller who lamented that "she got crushed" with Clinton and his aides furious because Clinton "couldn't do what he wanted"; or the pounding Robert Reischauer and June O'Neill took as CBO directors when they stood up respectively to highly partisan Democratic and Republican majorities who too were furious about not getting the "right" answers. In today's political environment, principled policy analysts who take strong stands either on the appropriate use of the numbers or on the worth of a policy and lose the argument well may suffer a decline in status and influence or feel they must leave the government. The decisions to resign over the 1996 welfare bill of three Department of Health and Human Services officials—assistant secretary for children and families, Mary Jo Bane; acting assistant secretary for planning and evaluation, Peter Edelman; and deputy assistant secretary for planning and evaluation, Wendell Primus—well illustrate the problem with each case providing a different slant on principled protest and professional competence.

Although Bane headed a program staff not an analytic unit, she had been a highly regarded academic policy researcher before joining HHS and one of the main architects of the earlier Clinton welfare plan. In the latter case, she had been strongly criticized by fellow liberals for putting strict work requirements in the Clinton plan. Bane stood her ground and defended the Clinton plan by stressing "that welfare reform emphasizing work was necessary and desirable, but that putting welfare recipients to work would cost money."[9] However, she could not accommodate to Clinton's decision to accept a Republican welfare bill that cut federal funds by an estimated $50 billion and allowed states to make additional cuts of perhaps $40 billion over six years. So Bane resigned. Peter Edelman and his wife Marion Wright Edelman, who had founded the Children's Defense Fund, were long-time friends of the Clintons. As *New York Times* reporter Neil Lewis pointed out: "[Mrs. Edelman] provided invaluable help to the Clintons' political careers, nurturing Mrs. Clinton's identity as an advocate of children's causes and rushing to help Mr. Clinton's presidential campaign during rough moments in 1992."[10] Edelman himself not only had problems with President Clinton's rightward shift but personally had suffered from the president's unwillingness to risk a confirmation fight over a judgeship he had promised Edelman. Still, Edelman stayed. However, President Clinton's embracing of the Republican bill went too far. Edelman wrote his ASPE staff: "I have devoted the last 30-plus years to doing whatever I could to help in reducing poverty in America. I believe the recently enacted welfare bill goes in the opposite direction."[11] It is worth noting that "Mrs. Edelman denounced him [Clinton] for what she called a 'moment of shame' and making 'a mockery of his pledge not to hurt children'" because the Republican bill was estimated to increase the number of poor kids by over a million.[12] After the White House tried to hide these estimates only to be embarrassed when New York Democratic Senator Patrick Moynihan forced the release, Primus resigned indicating that *"to remain would be to disown all the analysis my office has produced regarding the impact of the bill."*[13] Primus' resignation offers a pristine case in the executive branch of standing up for and going down for honest numbers instead of being responsive.

Some final comments on the three resignations are needed. The first thing to observe is that at the time they left, none exited with a strong voice of protest, for example, writing op-ed pieces or appearing on television talk shows. Bane and Edelman resigned on September 11, 1996, a month after Clinton signed the legislation while Primus left without fanfare the previous month. My own view is that in resigning the appropriate behavior generally should be exit with strong voice calling the culprits to task. Both Bane and Edelman wrote articles in the *American Prospect* and in the *Atlantic Monthly*, respectively, that were highly critical of the welfare legislation and the president, but neither appeared until early 1997.[14] In the current political climate, however, a strong exit may lessen any impact by appearing to be self-promotion on the path to celebrity status. *Washington Post* columnist E. J. Dionne Jr. made a strikingly apt comment: "Three members of the Clinton administration have resigned—not because of scandals, nor to get a big book contract, but for reasons of (I hope you're sitting down) *principle.*"[15] The three analysts were not only defending the integrity of the numbers or the soundness of the analysis per se, but protesting a policy choice by their political masters. Values and objectives were at question and this principled stand over policy leads back to the argumentative school's moralistic stance. As already touched on, the approach seems so deeply committed to unrestricted open communication and full public participation that it rules out policy analysts serving in the current federal structure where hierarchy and a degree of secrecy have a place. The approach may be suitable for academic policy analysts but not for government staffs and many think tank policy analysts who work on government-funded policy research projects.

The argumentative school also jumbles together means and ends, not keeping separate a policy analyst's own goals, the objectives for policy analysis itself, and the means appropriate for each objective. Take as example the objective that brought the three HHS resignations—reducing poverty. In pursuit of this objective and associated ones such as increasing opportunity for disadvantaged persons, a policy analyst might seek them in a number of ways such as working in a think tank, a nonprofit charitable organization, or a federal policy analysis office. Mary Jo Bane and Peter Edelman might have rejected serving in HHS during the Reagan or Bush administration (not that they would have been offered a high position) but have found such a role at the start of the Clinton administration a suitable institutional means for trying to reduce poverty. The two policy analysts no doubt believed that HHS under Secretary Donna Shalala, who had strong liberal credentials, and President Clinton would pursue forcefully the objective of reducing poverty and left when he accepted higher poverty in an act of clear political expediency. Both Bane and Edelman came to the Clinton administration as liberals committed to fight poverty and left bloodied but with their principles still more or less intact.

Determining the objectives of policy analysis within a federal agency raises another issue that has vexed analysts since the 1960s. Although a federal domestic agency may have a goal of reducing poverty or of lessening pollution, its policy analysis office will be several stages removed from direct pursuit of such objectives. The staff unit is responsible for neither final decision making nor field implementation. Hence, even though the analyst personally may have an outcome objective (e.g., reducing poverty), the realistic organizational goal still can be improving the information and analytic base for decision making. The improved base—label it an "intermediate objective"—is expected in this case to move policy toward the larger outcome goal. Once the intermediate objective is accepted, then producing honest numbers and solid analysis can be seen as the means and employing high professional standards can be viewed as the necessary requirement for developing the needed data and analysis. Two related points need making. First, the intermediate objective of the improved information and analytic decision-making base and the means of neutral competence can easily fit with much of the political spectrum from liberal to conservative. Second, some policy analysts will choose to be federal career civil servants ready to serve any duly elected government of whatever political coloration and try to provide a strong base for decision making to further the government in power's objectives. Over the years, I have told my policy analysis students that I admire individuals with a long-term commitment to government service, have worked with exceptionally able people who were federal career civil servants, and believe such a commitment is badly needed. However, I could not do so myself, being too much the liberal partisan. Careerist policy analysts also can seek to improve the base of decision making and adhere to high professional standards, and in addition be prepared to work with in-and-outers who are unwilling to be in a government that does not pursue their specific policy objectives or their particular political philosophy.

These comments may strike readers as overstating the obvious, but the obvious can become obscured and lost as we proceed in the density of a philosophical and ideological jumble of ideas. The basic point is that the relatively modest objective of improving the information and analytic base through neutral competence is still reasonable for the practicing policy analysts in government and policy think tanks. This formulation rejects the roles of analyst as hired gun or as the moralist interpreter of the common good and an unswerving battler for participating in discursive democracy. In the latter case, these notions are not being rejected as unworthy but rather as incompatible with service as a government policy analyst in the real world of hierarchy and institutional secrecy. Instead, the main problem comes from the opposite direction because of the strong appeal of the analyst adviser as hired gun using whatever means are needed to meet the demands of and/or support the predilections of political leaders. The critical issue is whether or not neutral competence can actually be practiced successfully in the federal government generally and in the executive branch specifically.

SOCIAL POLICY ANALYSIS IN THE FEDERAL GOVERNMENT—THEN AND NOW

Social policy analysis came to the federal government at the apex of confidence in America, the national government, and the capacity of science to solve basic societal problems. The high hopes that the nation, which had won World War II on foreign fields, could conquer social ills at home faded quickly. As I observed in 1971: "From the years of the Johnson administration's War on Poverty, far more has been learned about the problems of mounting programs and utilizing policy analysis in a social agency to reduce poverty and the barriers to equal opportunity than about solutions. . . .[T]he confidence that marked the beginning of the War on Poverty has faded in the face of this experience, to be replaced by a deep skepticism that the competence and the commitment to solve some of our more difficult social problems exist."[16] Whether the United States has the competence and the commitment to treat successfully the deep social problems that still exist looms as large today as it did then. So does the question of what policy analysis can contribute to the solution of these problems. To elaborate on the question of the potential of social policy analysis, it is useful to pinpoint what has changed and what has remained the same in the quarter century since I wrote the quoted paragraph.

Social Policy Research and Analysis, which was published in 1971, underscored the shortage of social policy analysts and researchers. Over the years, the changes have been dramatic with striking increases in the number of competent analysts and capable public policy research organizations. Also, much more is known about organizing and staffing policy analysis offices in the federal government. Today we have an adequate number of social policy analysts, sufficient capacity in the public policy research industry, and enough knowledge about the staffing and structuring of analytic units to create strong analytic organizations in the presidential, executive agency, and legislative branches of the federal government. Supply in these terms is more than ample and need not be considered again. What has blocked the greater development of competent analytic offices is the lack of demand by political leaders. The harsh political climate and the politicization and centralization of the presidential branch help explain deficient demand; however, two more basic problems have plagued social policy analysis for a quarter of a century and still do. First, no telling evidence shows social policy analysis leads to better decisions or more effective policies. Second, social policy research has not produced workable policies likely to bring benefits that have a reasonable likelihood of *dramatically* improving the lot of poor and near poor individuals and families at acceptable cost levels.

After arguing that the analytic offices established in the Office of Economic Opportunity and the (then) Department of Health, Education and Welfare achieved the objective of producing a better base for decision making, I lamented: "To claim that the central analytical offices in OEO and HEW produced a better basis for decisionmaking is not to demonstrate that better decisions were made, or that the decisions (even if better) were implemented in a way to bring about more effective programs."[17] In starkest terms, those of us who advocate the expansion of policy analysis in the federal government cannot argue, based on hard evidence, that a strong policy analysis office with adequate research funds serving a highly competent, analytically oriented political leader—the ideal organizational setting—will materially increase the likelihood of effective social policies.

Three obvious points of qualification leap to mind. First, the analyst's input is early in the policy-making process and is but one part of the base for decision making. If that base can be improved, that is a realistic contribution. Second, although the policy analysts' masters—the president and congressional leaders—are far more powerful than the analysts, these leaders must try to govern facing both severe structural and political limits on their institutional powers and outside (exogenous) forces that can crush their best efforts. Moreover, when the results are in, and this may be many years later, it is generally impossible to isolate the leaders' own contributions. Third, the logic of the argument that sound policy information and analysis are more useful than bad or no information or shoddy analysis surely makes sense. But even here, it should be stressed that sound data and analyses are limited by the available technical capacity. In the earlier discussed fiscal year 1996 budget battle, CBO's honest numbers—"the best information in town"—were treated wrongly as highly accurate macroeconomic projections, even though they were ballpark figures at best because of economists' limited capacity to predict accurately over a seven-year period. At the same time, if policy analysts make clear that the best information that can be produced still may be shaky, subject to challenge, and hence needing to be handled carefully, the logic of honest, even if flawed, data being better than no information or distorted numbers still holds.

All these caveats would be far less important if the fruits of the best social policy research including evaluations and field experiments had yielded "workable policy options," which I define as feasible choices having high probabilities both of being well-implemented at reasonable costs and of achieving dramatic improvements. Those of us who joined the War on Poverty at its inception did take on faith that workable policy options could be found and politicians, many of whom also believed in the potential of big policy payoffs in those heady days, made the unrealistic promises that have haunted Johnson's War on Poverty ever since. In some cases the gains have been important if not striking, but the overwhelming fact is that most of the relatively modest, short-term service delivery programs in such critical areas as manpower training and education remain largely ineffective. Moreover, no strong empirical evidence shows that high-cost, extended programs will have dramatic payoffs. At the same time, there is no good evidence that the anti-poverty efforts have done untold damage as so many now claim. Wipe out the Great Society programs and America will be saved may be good political propaganda, but it is hardly supported by the available information. Reality is much more gray. We must accept that for many of the most pressing social problems, there simply may be no dramatic service delivery fixes in the foreseeable future. That is hardly a sensible reason, however, not to use policy analysis and research to seek better social policy approaches.

SOCIAL POLICY ANALYSIS IN THE DEVOLUTION REVOLUTION

The key questions about the future direction of social policy analysis concern the appropriate staff mission in federal social service delivery programs during this period of increasing devolution to state and local governments. For purposes of discussion, these questions will take the devolution of federally funded income and service delivery programs as a given and further assume that most of the 1996 changes for female-headed families will stay in place. The main focus will be on social service delivery grants-in-aid where devolution could make the responsible federal agency no more than a pass-through for federal funds. The argument will be made that (1) the social agencies, which have actively managed social service delivery program grants-in-aid in the past, ought to continue to have important roles as long as federal grants-in-aid funds are involved, and (2) the agencies' analytic units should have a critical place, particularly in helping develop sound information for guiding state and local projects funded in whole or in part by the national government. Carrying out these responsibilities, however, demands basic changes in agency capacity and orientation. To spell out this argument, it is necessary to consider briefly the overall relationship of the social agencies and subnational governments in the past.

Shared governance where federal grants-in-aid have created major overlapping federal and subnational government roles has been a troubled arena since the federal government in the mid-1960s became heavily involved in areas either historically the sole responsibility of states and localities such as K-12 education or previously outside the scope of all governments such as community action and development. In the early period, limited capacity to mount War on Poverty programs existed at all levels of government, and state and local governments were particularly weak. Moreover, beyond capacity, state and local governments were seen as culprits holding back the progress of programs for the poor and disadvantaged. The Community Action Program, the largest Office of Economic Opportunity program by far, encouraged potential local grantees to become nonprofit organizations and completely bypass local governments.

After states and localities gained greater capacity and accepted major responsibilities for poor and disadvantaged persons, the federal role was increasingly called into question and steps were taken to allow subnational governments greater freedom in administering federal grants-in-aid. In the Nixon-Ford years, the federal government enacted block grants that permitted grantees far more responsibility but did retain a significant federal agency managerial role. After studying the two key pieces of New Federalism block grant legislation in the Nixon-Ford years—the Comprehensive Employment and Training Act and the Community Development Block Grant program—I argued in 1980:

> [T]he management strategies of social agencies charged with the governance of social service delivery programs should have as a central objective increasing. . . . the capacity of local service deliverers. This central objective . . . would demand a basic reorientation and restructuring of a social agency if it is to be well implemented. . . .
>
> A failure to improve field governance raises basic questions about the social agencies' ability to make work the uneasy partnership that has emerged in the grants-in-aid era. At basic issue is whether or not the heavy reliance on federal management makes sense. Let us be clear; this translates into a test of whether or not the social agencies make sense other than as check writers in the social service delivery programs.[18]

By the mid-1990s, driven partly by a states rights ideology and partly by budget-cutting efforts that fell disproportionately on social service delivery programs, the federal government had completely shut off funding in some cases and pulled back to the lightest of hands in others as it devolved responsibility for social services to the states.

This shift flowed from three basic premises holding that states and localities (1) are more responsive to their citizens' needs and serve them better than Washington bureaucracies, (2) provide natural experiments for different program options and hence are better laboratories for finding more effective policies than the federal government, and (3) can produce major savings by delivering services more effectively. If these premises are valid, the argument can be made that social agencies in the service delivery areas should be no more than checkwriting conduits for continuing federal funds so that agency staffs would no longer be involved in substantive program monitoring and evaluation or in the development of policy information including through the support of policy research. Most of the discussion that follows concerns the validity of the premises, but a prior issue involves the question of feasibility. As to the latter, however high the current fervor for the devolution of programmatic responsibilities, neither the agencies nor Congress, the latter in particular, have been comfortable for long with no more than financial controls to insure funds are spent legally. For example, at the height of President Nixon's New Federalism, the State and Local Fiscal Act of 1972 (popularly labeled "general revenue sharing") sent funds with no strings attached save for financial accountability to subnational governments. Almost immediately, Congress members disliked the loss of control and in a few years did away with the first attempt at a pass-through policy.

One point appears irrefutable: As long as federal funds are involved, both Congress and the federal agencies will either want to keep some control or will fear they cannot escape criticism if allegations are made that federal funds have been misused. As to the latter, *Seattle Times* reporters Eric Nalder, Deborah Nelson, and Alex Tizon spent six months, and won a Pulitzer Prize, investigating an extreme example in the case of a deregulated Department of Housing and Urban Development low-income housing assistance program serving Native Americans. HUD had distributed almost $3 billion to tribal-housing authorities over five years. The reporters found that the program, first under HUD secretary Jack Kemp in the Bush administration and then under Henry Cisneros in the Clinton administration, "drastically cut its monitoring of how that money has been distributed and spent," and observed that deregulation "has turned HUD into a cash machine . . . [with] so little monitoring, in fact, that it's impossible to determine how much has been inappropriately spent."[19] HUD's hands-off policy reached such an unbelievable level that a top Washington HUD official reprimanded a regional office subordinate for looking into flagrant violations writing: "We don't 'allow' Tribes, anymore than they 'allow' HUD . . . WE ARE PARTNERS!"[20] Such excessive deregulation with little or no monitoring makes no sense for the federal agency or, as the *Seattle Times* reporters made clear, for poor Native Americans because funds got channeled to wealthier tribal leaders. Moreover, there is no escape for federal officials—the scandal cannot be pushed away by the federal government in claiming no responsibility because it had let a lesser government make all the decisions in the spirit of devolution (more on this shortly).

Of the three basic premises, the one that holds the states are laboratories for reform goes most directly to the issue of a continuing function for agency policy analysis offices in federally funded social service delivery programs. Welfare waivers best illuminate the states-as-laboratories issue. States were granted such waivers by the Department of Health and Human Services to undertake on an experimental basis initiatives in conflict with the existing law. As Professors Donald Norris and Lyke Thompson point out in their edited volume treating six state welfare reform efforts, the passage in 1988 of the Family Support Act (FSA) "that made workfare a part of federal policy . . . became the jumping-off point for a broader, continuing movement of welfare reform [changes] . . . 'beyond those required under federal . . . law.' "[21] When HHS granted waivers to states to try out these new initiatives, states-as-laboratories had a critical test. The Norris and Thompson volume's in-depth case studies of major state welfare reform efforts in Wisconsin, California, Michigan, New Jersey, Maryland, and Ohio render highly questionable any assumption that states can serve effectively as laboratories that develop and rigorously assess field experiments involving new policy initiatives. In their final chapter that drew lessons from the six-state experience, Norris and Thompson observed: "Welfare reform was not an exercise in a rational policy-making process; did not involve the use of prospective policy analysis; and did not involve consideration of the needs of policy implementation. . . . The politics of welfare reform was primarily about politics, not about poverty or welfare, and had distinctly ideological and symbolic overtones. At best, the problems and needs of the poor received secondary attention."[22] As discussed in Chapter 1, University of Wisconsin at Madison economist Michael Wiseman, in his review of the Norris and Thompson volume, argued that the six case studies indicated the failure of the states to be viable laboratories for experiments because the efforts were ill-designed and uncoordinated and rightly placed much of the blame on HHS because it did little monitoring and put no pressure on the states to design sound experiments.

In a later article on welfare reform in Wisconsin, Wiseman elaborated on HHS's lack of monitoring and performance standards and made a compelling case for a major federal agency role, even in the face of continuing devolution:

> Performance indicators are not unwarranted federal intrusions into state business; at least half of the money spent will continue to come from Washington. Unfortunately, the reform legislation passed by Congress in 1995 and cutbacks in funding for federal agencies responsible for public assistance administration virtually eliminate performance data collection. . . .
> Much remains unknown about welfare policy. Operating alone, states have little incentive to evaluate or to face results . . . "honestly." Even under a block grant system, responsible welfare administration that is mindful of wise use of tax dollars and concerned about poverty must play an active role in monitoring and assuring public awareness of what states do and in encouraging, coordinating, and assessing state innovation.[23]

Given the continuation of federal funding, there is no justification for failing to mount a strong monitoring effort and demanding realistic performance indicators. These are not federal general revenue-sharing funds but dollars aimed at welfare reform experiments in which the national government has a basic interest in ensuring federal monies are well-spent and that the experiments are designed to develop detailed information that can be used to compare different new policy options and provide design and implementation guides for the more effective ones.

In the Reagan administration, the social policy agencies significantly reduced monitoring, evaluation, and the development of policy information and research to aid in the agencies' management of federally funded social service delivery programs.[24] The decline in part flowed from the underlying ideological belief that the federal government is inferior to subnational governments and must be restrained. However, the cutbacks also stemmed from a fundamental lack of understanding of the organizational demands placed on the federal agencies if they are to manage deregulation successfully. At issue is the form of control structure needed. As I observed in discussing both command-and-control systems, which utilize detailed regulations, and deregulated management approaches: "Both forms of control require monitoring, but deregulation generally requires even greater monitoring. . . . [B]oth greater regulation and less regulation . . . demand an *adequate cadre of competent monitors.*"[25] Effective agency management also needs relevant, sound, timely programmatic information for service delivery projects funded through federal grants-in-aid. Finally, effective agency management of federally funded programs administered and operated by subnational governments requires the former to ensure that the latter develop and use sound information in implementing, managing, and operating the federally funded projects.

Federally funded, state-operated social service delivery experiments need to be well-designed and carefully implemented and should produce an adequate flow of data to support both needed implementation changes over time and the evaluation of project outcomes. President Clinton, in his postinaugural address to the National Governors' Association (NGA), told his former peers that he would continue to support waivers for further state welfare reform experiments, but, as Wiseman noted, the president had "a proviso": " '[If] we're going to have more waivers and you're going to be able to experiment in projects that use federal dollars, let's measure the experiment, let's be honest about it. And if it works, let's tell everybody it works so we can all do it, and if it doesn't, lets have the courage to quit and admit it didn't.' "[26] When states receive federal funds for experimentation, their responsibility should be both to assess the projects honestly, which can be translated as crafting and executing well-designed experiments, and to have the courage to report honestly on the results including admitting failure. What also needs to be noted is that the funding agencies in turn should have the responsibility for insisting on such honesty, determining over time that it continues, and requiring appropriate corrective action if needed. This federal role too demands courage.

Both state and federal efforts also must have strong leadership. State University of New York at Albany professor Irene Lurie put the leadership dimension in perspective in her paper subtitled "Reforming Welfare Must Be Both Dazzling and Dull" that drew on her ten-state study of the implementation of the Job Opportunities and Basic Skills (JOBS) Training program administered by HHS: "One overarching lesson emerges: Successful reform requires not only a promising policy design and leaders who can explain it with compelling [dazzling] vision, but also leaders who will pay attention to the unglamorous [dull] management details of implementing it."[27] Proffering the "dazzling"— especially in selling an appealing vision—fits politicians' needs far more than pushing for the "dull" details that are central to better performance. It is not that politicians are unable to score points by demanding good management and sound monitoring. Rather, such efforts, however dazzling the call to arms, also demand dull follow-through.

Federal dollars for social service delivery programs may be further reduced, and deregulation seems certain to remain the order of the day, but it is most unlikely that presidents and Congress will ignore the pressures from states and localities and interest groups for continued funding or that Congress will be comfortable with mere checkwriting that attaches no strings except fiscal responsibility. The devolution revolution, however, does offer the opportunity both to reduce the federal output of detailed regulations and to improve state and local capability to delivery social services. As to the former, command-and-control systems that stress government-made rules as the primary regulatory control mechanism usually are labor intensive in requiring large cadres of people to do the time-consuming tasks of developing highly specific regulations and guidelines and of monitoring for precise compliance with the detailed federal rules. Moreover, this approach tends to stultify state and local initiatives and misuse federal staff. The opposite danger is that the agencies, fearful that any management will be construed as violating the spirit of deregulation, will try to avoid it lest they be condemned as unduly reducing state and/or local autonomy. The *Seattle Times'* five articles on the HUD low-income housing program for Native Americans appeared on Monday through Friday (December 2–6, 1996); the December 8 Sunday lead front page story bore the headline "Gorton Promises Hearing on What HUD Funds Bought," and a subheading, "Congressional Auditors Asked to Launch Probe."[28] Eric Nolder and Deborah Nelson in the Sunday article indicated that (1) Senator Slade Gorton (R–Wash.), chair of a subcommittee overseeing the Bureau of Indian Affairs and Native American education and housing spending, would hold hearings "to draft new rules to better ensure that money for Native American housing goes to 'the most needy' and not to 'tribes that don't need it'"; (2) Representative Jerry Lewis (R–Calif.), chair of a committee that controls HUD spending, asked GAO to investigate the allegations; and (3) departing HUD secretary Henry Cisneros, having learned about the *Seattle Times* findings, had called in the HUD inspector general to begin investigations.[29]

The HUD case underscores how much competent federal monitoring is needed. Some of the Native American housing authorities were clearly violating the legislative mandate to provide housing to low-income persons, instead using funds targeted for the needy to build large houses for wealthier tribal members. Moreover, the violations could be uncovered with reasonable effort. In the most striking case, there stood the telltale evidence in the form of a 5,296-square-foot house built for wealthier tribe members with funds from the program aimed at low-income Native Americans. Further, some of the tribal housing authority staffs lacked the competence and professional commitment to manage the programs and badly needed HUD technical assistance. Whether HUD itself had the capacity to do this task well is another question.

In the current environment of distrust and devolution, my 1980 call for increasing the capacity of state and local social service delivery organizations as a basic agency objective remains relevant and likely more feasible. As to the latter, this devolution thrust provides the social agencies an opportunity both to cut deeply into generating detailed rules and regulations that now so burden subnational governments and to focus far more on performance capability in the field. The first big hurdle is changing the agencies. Not only would the agencies need to strengthen their own capacity to provide technical assistance, there must be a basic reorientation toward the field. Such a shift is critical both in reordering the agency structure and focus and in establishing a new direction for information development. As to the former, I observed: "The regional offices are the barometer of whether the agency is serious about implementing a field-oriented strategy. It is in the regional offices that we are most likely to determine whether or not headquarters has accepted the primacy of the field in the performance game by shifting better qualified staff . . . and by stressing advice and capacity over control and compliance."[30] Such a shift also requires a strengthening and reorientation of agency analytic offices toward information development that aids in capacity-building. But there is no way to avoid the problem that the information needed for capacity-building and overall program improvement can also show mismanagement including violations of legislative intent or agency regulations even if no hands are in the till. Making building greater capacity in service delivery organizations a central federal agency objective does not negate the potential of the needed information to adversely affect both individuals involved in managing and operating programs at all levels of government and their organizations.

If this capacity building objective is adopted and seriously pursued, sound field information that addresses state and local organizational behavior is the basic fuel required for competent agency management. In particular, agency analysts should have a central role both in developing the data and the appropriate procedures for collecting them, and in interpreting the implications for increasing capacity in the field. In elaborating on the role of the analytic offices, the federal agency capacity-building function can to be divided into its three component parts. The first is the more general agency effort to raise staff competence and improve the organizational structure and procedures of service delivery organizations so that these institutions have greater capacity to manage and operate various social delivery projects in the field. The second function is to help service delivery organizations implement new and improved managerial approaches and/or policies for specific projects. These two functions differ only in that the first involves the building of general organizational capacity while the second focuses on the design, implementation, and operation of specific policies such as training welfare recipients or providing low-income housing services. Program, not analytic, staffs should have responsibility for carrying out these functions in the field.

The third capacity-building function involves seeking and developing the information required to support the other two functions and should rest with agency analytic staffs. Here is the traditional analytic office role of information development, but there may be a key difference. The analytic units well may be located within specific program units and focus far more than in the past on information to be used in the field not only by agency program staff but by managers and operators in social service delivery organizations. Although this information would also be useful to agency central analytic offices and EOP units such as OMB in making overall policy decisions, the driving force should be to develop information needed to enhance agency capacity-building efforts that focus downward toward service delivery.

The analytic staffs should be particularly concerned with large-scale evaluations and experimental projects to develop information in support of the overall agency capacity-building effort. These offices also could play the key federal role in helping states and localities become viable laboratories honestly measuring state experiments as President Clinton called for in his earlier quoted NGA speech. If experiments are to yield useful data, the need is for careful design and implementation and the rigorous measurement of the results. Such an effort will benefit from comparable experimental project sites in several states and that requires a well-coordinated multistate effort conducted by an experimental team responsible for the overall design and management of that endeavor. Even if the states themselves establish the needed entity through an umbrella organization, the federal analytic offices should be involved in determining that the experiments are well-designed, that the data effort is well-managed, and that the results are obtained in a timely manner and widely disseminated. I believe that the federal analytic offices may be in a better position than the states to carry out this overall effort to develop multistate experiments if the federal agencies can refocus toward the field. Much depends on leadership at all levels of government, the issue addressed in the next section.

Before turning to the leadership question, our three original premises need a final mention. As already discussed, little hard evidence exists to support or refute them. At the same time, it is clear that the stakes are high. The HUD low-income housing case showed gross violations of the intent of the law and striking mismanagement. The question of criminal corruption will be left to others, but there is no question that shoddy performances by HUD and the tribes visibly harmed poor Native Americans and left them living in inferior housing while tribal leaders and their friends and relatives benefited despite their often relatively high incomes. The new welfare legislation, given the failure of job training and placement programs in the past, threatens large numbers of children as well as their parents if the latter are cut from the welfare rolls. Senator Daniel Patrick Moynihan's 1995 comment, quoted earlier, that "we do not know what we are doing" in the welfare area underscores the urgency of developing honest numbers and of being honest about their meaning.[31] Whether, as I argue, the federal social agencies and particularly their analytic offices should have the central role in the quest for sound, timely, relevant data can be debated, but the need for honest numbers that politicians and the public believe credible cannot. If honest numbers are to be had, strong political leadership is required.

HONEST NUMBERS AND THE POLITICAL LEADERSHIP

In considering the issue of whether or not the national government will develop a solid empirical base to guide policy making, the starting point is that honest numbers can be produced in sufficient quantity to support social policy making. The mature public policy research industry appears to have enough competent, experienced policy analysts to adequately staff federal and subnational government analytic offices and sufficient technical and organizational capacity to carry out well-designed and well-executed policy studies including major field experiments. As must be clear from the three decades of experience in the presidency, the executive agencies, and the congressional support agencies, we find both responsive competence that gives political leaders answers dominated by partisan needs and neutral competence that employs requisite methodologies without political spin. Now it is true that the incentives drive toward neutral competence in the congressional support agencies and responsive competence in the executive branch. Such behavior, however, only indicates that presidents now want information and advice that fit their predilections, not that they are unable to demand and obtain honest numbers. *New York Times* reporter Louis Uchitelle, writing from the 1996 American Economics Association annual meeting, underscored this point in a piece on President Clinton's nomination of Janet Yellen as chairwoman of the Council of Economic Advisers by quoting Roger Porter who held high positions in the Reagan and Bush administrations and two former CEA chairs:

> "Given the profusion of economists in government in recent years," Mr. Porter said, "is the Council of Economic Advisers as important or necessary as it once was? From the viewpoint of the President, it is. The C.E.A. is in the best position to give unbiased analysis and advice, while other economists argue from the special interests of the agencies or departments they represent."

That requires "face time" with the President, as Murray Weiden-
baum of Washington University, President Reagan's first council chairman, put it. . . . "You cannot draw these things on a blackboard," said
Herbert Stein, who was council chairman in the Nixon Administration
and for a time under Gerald Ford. "So much depends on personal relations."[32]

The point could not be more clear: Even in the case of the president's
economist, where there is the long tradition of telling the president
how things really are, he must choose to hear the CEA chair.

The lack of honest numbers today is not at base a question of
methodology, analytic competence, or organizational structure. The
development and use of honest numbers boils down mainly to the
question of politicians' competence, commitment, courage, and leadership ability. The policy analyst per se is best seen as part of the supply,
not the demand side of the policy-making equation. First, policy analysts do not decide how high they will be located in the organizational
structure or whether their information, analyses, and advice will be
sought by the top decision makers. Recall that even in the golden
years of domestic policy analysis, Department of Health, Education
and Welfare assistant secretary for planning and evaluation Alice Rivlin
with all her analytic skills was essentially ignored by Secretary Wilbur
Cohen; yet, her successor Lewis Butler, despite limited analytic experience and knowledge, had great influence with Cohen's successor Robert
Finch because this secretary had strong political ties to his policy analyst. Second, chief policy analysts determine neither the size of their
staffs nor the funds available to support policy research including
major evaluations and experiments. These facts of life have long been
recognized. Based on the Johnson administration experience in the
1960s, I wrote: "A central analyst is likely to have a significant effect
on agency policy only if the agency head (a) recognizes the importance
of analysis . . . (b) gives the analyst high status in the agency, including
a direct tie to the decisionmaking and implementation process; and (c)
provides the analyst with sufficient personnel positions so that he can
develop a viable analytical staff."[33] The statement holds today and now
applies to the EOP too.

A final point about the subordinate role of top policy analysts
needs making: When their political bosses are not interested in honest
numbers or not willing to use such data as policy analysts believe they
should be used, the analysts' options are limited. A top analyst can
try persuasion, but may not have direct access to the final decision
maker. The alternatives in effect may be arguing strongly with the risk
of losing clout or being fired; threatening to resign in protest as CEA
chairman Michael Boskin did to force chief of staff John Sununu to let

him see President Bush; actually resigning; or keeping quiet. Although a persuasive policy analyst may be able to educate a political leader over time on the value of sound information and analysis and gain more influence, the overriding reality is that the rank of the analysts in the policy advising pecking order, their actual influence, and the available analytic and research resources (slots and funds) are determined primarily by the analysts' political masters. The main exception underscores the argument. CBO directors serving four-year fixed appointments and 535 masters stand out as the rare case of up-front heroics where the analysts survived.

THE FUTURE OF POLICY ANALYSIS

This historical critique of social policy analysis has underscored that the trend over the years is toward less willingness in the federal government generally, and certainly in the executive branch, (1) to demand sound, timely, relevant policy information and analyses and highly competent, principled policy analysts; (2) to fund the development of sound data through major evaluations and field experiments; and (3) to employ honest numbers and analyses as major elements in policy making. Most discouraging of all, the disbelief in the credibility of federal government data and analyses grows while the faith in highly partisan numbers slanted to fit hard-core ideological beliefs increases. Relatedly, the emerging world of the electronic revolution with its accurate and inaccurate data now threatens to inundate policy makers and the public and make validation increasingly difficult. The honest numbers issue in its broadest dimensions raises the question of whether policy information and analyses will be viewed by politicians and/or the public as more than partisan weapons with which to engage in ideological battles. Are we moving beyond the point in the current political environment where honest *and* credible numbers—that is, data not only sound but also believed to be sound—can underpin reasoned public policy debate? If so, policy analysts will find the main route to high status and influence in the federal government to be as hired guns responding to partisan political masters who demand information and analyses crafted to fit the political claim of the day.

The basic threat is to the analytic profession as we have known it. The profession could go in two polar directions. At one extreme will be the retreat into academe more and more focusing on the hard university currency of promotion, prestige, and pay. At the other extreme stands pure political responsiveness. Looking back over a quarter of a century to my 1971 book, *Social Policy Research and Analysis*, the basic concerns then and now are similar. Then I saw the ball in social science's court, recognized that that community's sins were mainly sins of omission, and asked, in the final sentence of the book's final paragraph, "whether the social science research community has the wisdom and the will to develop the needed research and to work for its use in the policy process to overcome poverty and the barriers to equal opportunity."[34] After a productive period of policy research by universities and think tanks that did provide sound policy information, my first concern now is a retreat by policy analysts and researchers into the protective shell of academic work done for their peers, not for government policy makers and analysts. That is, accomplished policy researchers will move from relevant policy work to more and more sterile policy studies which produce peer-reviewed journal articles interesting mainly to those peers.

The second great danger—a concern in 1971 but not as overriding as now—is policy analyst activists who see dishonest numbers and slanted analyses as legitimate means of serving their political bosses. The threat, it needs underscoring, is not to the jobs or the pay or even necessarily the prestige of policy analysts and researchers, but to the integrity and relevance of the profession. Numbers will still be produced at all levels of government; analytic advocates for hire will continue to be paid well; university professors can develop and do battle over policy studies that may not actually be of much value in the real world but will still fuel promotion; tenured professors can bemoan current developments as I do, or rationalize them as do individuals calling for political responsiveness.

It is as experts committed to nonpartisan analysis and ultimately as citizens that we should be most concerned by the current movement away from the government funding of large-scale policy research to support policy making and the flight from neutral competence lest honest numbers be driven out and replaced with ones crafted to fit any policy claim, however wrongheaded. Information experts need to make their case. As noted in Chapter 1, Brookings' senior economist Charles Schultze, writing in 1968 just after he had left as director of the Bureau of the Budget, charged policy analysts to be " 'partisan efficiency advocates'—the champions of analysis and efficiency."[35] Schultze's call came nearly three decades ago in a vastly different era. Today those arguing for a restoration of neutral competence are being put down as hopelessly naive by "politically sophisticated" academics. But Haynes Johnson and David Broder, hardly naive politically with their Pulitzer Prizes for their political commentaries and their highly regarded books on American politics to prove it, made CBO director Robert Reischauer one of the few heroes in *The System*. They maintain that Reischauer's efforts and those of his staff offer a signal example of how "The System should work in the best public interest by not allowing itself to be politicized by narrow or ideological interests."[36]

Johnson and Broder's central argument is not to take partisan politics out of policy making but to provide honest numbers and non-partisan analyses as a base for reasoned political debate. Neither Johnson and Broder nor I maintain that the numbers ought to dominate political debate. However, a politics that ignores sound data and analysis—and ignoring includes either paying no attention to available honest numbers or not seeking them out—undermines policy making and democracy. In making the case for honest numbers, we can move to higher authority yet by going back to Madison and Hamilton. The former, at age seventy-one, wrote in 1822 a letter to W. T. Barry these words that have already been quoted in this volume and ring true even more today than then: "A popular Government, without popular information, or the means of acquiring it, is but a Prologue to a Farce or a Tragedy; or, perhaps both. Knowledge will forever govern ignorance. And the people who mean to be their own Governors, must arm themselves with power which knowledge gives."[37] Perhaps, the call should be to the barricades à la Patrick Henry, "Give me honest numbers or give me death!" Probably not. Still, if the American people do not appreciate Hamilton's great insight that a sound fiscal and administrative system is essential to the creation and maintenance of a great nation and do not heed Madison's admonition about popular information and civic virtue, the American political system and democracy as we know are in dire trouble.[38]

Mine is the Cassandra cry of deepest pessimism as one who believes in honest numbers and honest analysis as central to the future of the analytic profession and to democratic policy deliberations. As a veteran of Johnson's War on Poverty, I have confessed that policy analysts including me were naively overconfident during that period, both about what analysts could do with their kit of tools to improve policy making and about what service delivery programs could accomplish for the poor and the disadvantaged. But it is also the case that the policy analysts, who served in the analytic offices at the Office of Economic Opportunity and the Department of Health, Education and Welfare (and its successor departments) starting in the 1960s, did take the lead in developing the large-scale experiments and evaluations and other policy-relevant research needed for future policy making. The resulting data from numerous sound studies over the years have made uncomfortably clear that relatively low-cost service delivery programs did not bring material improvement in the lives of poor persons.

What the available information also shows plainly is that the War on Poverty remains unwon with America experiencing the highest rate of poverty among the advanced industrialized nations. The earlier social policy studies do not support massive new service delivery programs. But neither does this experience with these programs justify the current grossly inadequate funding of policy-relevant research including experiments and evaluations aimed at producing sound information for new program design and implementation. This is the inexcusable failure of political leadership that the policy analysis profession should cry out against.

To do so, however, these policy analysts must reaffirm the profession's own commitment to honest numbers and honest analysis. As was the case in 1971, the ball again is in the court of social policy analysts and researchers. I hold that they should practice neutral competence and undertake sound policy studies. My charge also is that the analytic profession must make the argument for sound policy studies and for the failure of political leadership in this undertaking. At the same time, a clear message of this history is the need for humility by policy analysts and researchers in recognition of the weaknesses of the available tools and methods. But being more humble does not lessen the call for the recommitment to neutral competence and for spelling out the dangers of unsound policy data and interpretations nor does it abrogate the scandal of political leaders who fail to stand up for honest numbers and honest analysis.

NOTES

1. Edward F. Lawlor, book review, *Journal of Policy Analysis and Management*, Winter 1996, p. 112. The books reviewed are: Frank Fischer and John Forester (eds.), *The Argumentative Turn in Policy Analysis and Planning*, Duke University Press, 1993; Emery Roe, *Narrative Policy Analysis: Theory and Practice*, Duke University Press, 1994; and Paul Sabatier and Hank C. Jenkins-Smith (eds.), *Policy Change and Learning*, Westview Press, 1993.

2. Bruce Jennings, "Counsel and Consensus: Norms of Argument in Health Policy," in Fischer and Forester (eds.), *The Argumentative Turn in Policy Analysis and Planning*, pp. 102–104.

3. John S. Dryzek, "Policy Analysis and Planning: From Science to Argument," in ibid., p. 227–229.

4. James A. Throgmorton, "Survey Research as Rhetorical Trope: Electric Power Planning Arguments in Chicago," in ibid., p. 117.

5. Lawlor, book review, p. 114.

6. Terry M. Moe, "The Political Presidency," in John E. Chubb and Paul E. Peterson (eds.), *The New Direction in American Politics*, Brookings, 1985, p. 239.

7. Walter Williams, *Mismanaging America: The Rise of the Anti-Analytic Presidency*, University Press of Kansas, 1990, p. 12. See pp. 98–100 for my discussion.

8. Lawlor, book review, p. 120.

9. *Washington Post National Weekly Edition*, September 23–29, 1996.

10. *New York Times*, September 13, 1996.

11. *New York Times*, September 12, 1996.

12. *New York Times*, September 13, 1996.

13. *New York Times*, September 12, 1996, italics added.

14. Mary Jo Bane, "Welfare as We Might Know It," *American Prospect*, January–February 1997, pp. 47–53; Pete Edelman, "The Worst Thing Bill Clinton Has Done," *Atlantic Monthly*, March 1997, pp. 43–58.

15. *Washington Post National Weekly Edition*, September 23–29, 1996, italics in the original.

16. Walter Williams, *Social Policy Research and Analysis: The Experience in the Federal Social Agencies*, Elsevier, 1971, p. 189.

17. Ibid., p. 191.

18. Walter Williams, *Government by Agency: Lessons from the Social Program Grants-in-Aid Experience*, Academic Press, 1980, pp. 261 and 272.

19. *Seattle Times*, December 1, 1996.

20. Quoted in ibid., capital letters in the original.

21. Donald F. Norris and Lyke Thompson (eds.), *The Politics of Welfare Reform*, Sage, 1995, pp. 1–2.

22. Ibid., pp. 229 and 231.

23. Michael E. Wiseman, "State Strategies for Welfare Reform: The Wisconsin Story," *Journal of Policy Analysis and Management*, Fall 1996, p. 543.

24. Walter Williams, *Mismanaging America*, pp. 69–72.

25. Ibid., p. 102, italics in the original.

26. Wiseman, "State Strategies for Welfare Reform," p. 543. Wiseman's quote from the president's talk is taken from a transcript provided by the National Governors' Association.

27. Irene Lurie, "A Lesson from the JOBS Program: Reforming Welfare Must Be Both Dazzling and Dull," *Journal of Policy Analysis and Management*, Fall 1996, p. 573.

28. *Seattle Times*, December 8, 1996.

29. Ibid.

30. Williams, *Government by Agency*, p. 249.

31. Quoted in the *Washington Post National Weekly Edition*, August 7–13, 1995.

32. *New York Times*, January 7, 1997.

33. Williams, *Social Policy Research and Analysis*, pp. 14–15.

34. Ibid., p. 193.

35. Charles L. Schultze, *The Politics of Economics and Public Spending*, Brookings, 1968, p. 96.

36. Haynes Johnson and David S. Broder, *The System: The American Way of Politics at the Breaking Point*, Little, Brown, 1996, p. 286.

37. Gaillard Hunt (ed.), *The Writings of James Madison*, G. P. Putnam's Sons, 1910, vol. 9, p. 103.

38. The description of Hamilton's insight draws on Forest McDonald, *Alexander Hamilton: A Biography*, Norton, 1979, p. 96.

Index

DATE DUE

1/2/99			
GAYLORD			PRINTED IN U.S.A.